Explorations
of Maturity

THE CENTURY PSYCHOLOGY SERIES

Richard M. Elliott, Gardner Lindzey,
and Kenneth MacCorquodale,

Editors

Explorations
of Maturity

Studies of Mature
and Immature
College Men

DOUGLAS H. HEATH

HAVERFORD COLLEGE

WITH THE ASSISTANCE OF
HARRIET E. HEATH

New York
APPLETON-CENTURY-CROFTS
DIVISION OF MEREDITH PUBLISHING COMPANY

ACKNOWLEDGMENTS

Page 21: From: "The Concept of Development from a Comparative and Organismic Point of View" by Heinz Werner in THE CONCEPT OF DEVELOPMENT: AN ISSUE IN THE STUDY OF HUMAN BEHAVIOR, Dale B. Harris, editor. The University of Minnesota Press, Minneapolis. Copyright 1957 by the University of Minnesota. Pp. 126–127.

Pages 12, 17, and 36: From: "Creativity in Perspective" by H. H. Anderson and from "The Creativeness of Life" by E. W. Sinnot in CREATIVITY AND ITS CULTIVATION, H. H. Anderson, editor. New York, Harper & Row, Publishers, Incorporated, 1959. Pp. 238, 16–17, 15.

Page 331: NEW INTRODUCTORY LECTURES ON PSYCHO-ANALYSIS by Sigmund Freud. Translated by W. J. H. Sprott. Copyright, 1933, by Sigmund Freud. Copyright Renewed © 1961 by W. J. H. Sprott. W. W. Norton & Company, Inc., New York, N.Y. P. 107. Published in England by The Hogarth Press Ltd., London.

Page 317: THE PSYCHOANALYTIC STUDY OF THE CHILD, Vol. 10, H. Hartmann; A. Freud, *et al.,* editors. New York, International Universities Press, 1955. Pp. 11–12.

Page 27: THE PSYCHOLOGY OF INTELLIGENCE (1947), by Jean Piaget. New York, Harcourt, Brace & World, Inc., 1950. P. 9. By permission of Routledge & Kegan Paul Ltd., London.

Pages 39 & 40: REMEMBERING. A STUDY IN EXPERIMENTAL AND SOCIAL PSYCHOLOGY by F. C. Bartlett. Cambridge, England, Cambridge University Press, 1932. Pp. 201, 221, 223.

Page 224: A STUDY OF THINKING by J. S. Bruner, J. J. Goodnow, & G. A. Austin. New York, John Wiley & Sons, 1956. P. 111.

Page 337: TOWARD A PSYCHOLOGY OF BEING by A. H. Maslow. Princeton, D. Van Nostrand Co., 1962. P. 172.

*To the young men whose lives
this book describes*

Preface

It is remarkable and ironic that despite widespread public and professional preoccupation and speculation about mental health, maturity, and personal effectiveness, most generalizations and reflections are based on clinical observations of emotionally unhealthy and immature rather than on disciplined studies of psychologically healthy and mature persons. Only a handful of investigators have studied mentally healthy, mature, or effective persons. A number of factors contribute to this paradox, including theoretical confusion, disagreements about research strategies, and lack of tests and measures known to yield appropriate information about mature and effective persons. My conviction was that these inhibiting factors could not be removed by more words. Only by more data from wide-ranging, but reflective, studies could the difficulties be surmounted.

"Who is a mature person?" This question, which initiated the pilot studies of the research in 1954 and the more formal studies since 1957, is the theme of this book. The book has four parts. Part I examines the theoretical complexities that have made research on maturity and mental health historically so unrewarding. To make a fresh start toward resolving—or, hopefully, at least, clarifying—these issues, Chapter 1 inductively identifies from biological, developmental, and personality observation in addition to theory, five developmental trends—for example, increased stability, integration, allocentricism, autonomy, and availability of experience to awareness—provisionally hypothesized to describe a *maturing* person. But what structures conceptually define a maturing *person?* Chapter 2 suggests a person can be understood conceptually in terms of schemata (including the self-image schema) skills, and valuators. The hypothesis that ties the book together is that the schemata, skills, and valuators of a mature person are more stable, integrated, allocentric, autonomous, and available to awareness than the comparable structures of an immature person.

Part II introduces the first of two different ways of investigating differences between mature and immature persons: a search for measures that differentiate between mature and immature persons on the hypothesized developmental dimensions. Before discussing such measures, Chapter 3 describes the research population, the methodological problems involved in using judge-selected groups, and the samples used in the study. To describe the maturity of the schemata, skill, and valuator organization of the mature and immature person, I used a new and incompletely validated method of analyzing Rorschach responses. Chapter 4 describes that scoring system as well as its validity linkages to more conventional measures of personality such as the Minnesota Multiphasic Personality Inventory (MMPI). Chapter 5 explores in detail the structure of the self-image schema and demonstrates how the provisional developmental trends suggest some formal dimensions of the self-image (e.g., the self-image varies in stability, integration, autonomy) as well as hypotheses about the relation of the dimensions of the self-image to other measures of maturity. Like Chapter 4, this chapter concentrates on presenting new measures of such self-image dimensions, their interrelationships, and their validity linkages to other measures of personality organization such as the Rorschach and the MMPI. Chapter 6 concludes Part II by drawing together not only the results of these new scoring systems and tests but also much other information about how mature and immature men differ.

Part III focuses on the second principal method used to investigate maturity: the development of an inter-related set of measures to determine if the skills (conceptual, analytic-synthetic, and judgmental) of the more mature person are more *stable* (re-

sistant to disorganizing influences) than those of the less mature
person. In contrast to the chapters of Part II, Chapters 7 through
12 intensively investigate in considerable detail how the criterion
groups differ on only *one* of the provisional developmental trends.
These chapters approach most closely the concerns of the ego psychologist interested in methods for assessing the way in which a
person processes disturbing information, and in the personality
characteristics associated with efficient and inefficient ego functioning. Chapter 7 explains why so much care was devoted to the
developmental trend toward stability; Chapter 8 reports a measure that validly identifies how disturbing different types of information are to a person; Chapters 9 through 11 describe the skill
measures (whose content is the disturbing information just measured in Chapter 8) and their personality correlates; and Chapter
12 summarily evaluates the hypothesis that mature persons are
more stably organized (they process disturbing information more
skillfully and recover from skill disorganization more readily)
than are immature persons.

Part IV returns to some of the issues discussed earlier in
Part I. Chapter 13 compares the predictive efficacy of consensual
judgments with the most promising psychological methods for
identifying mature and immature persons, and attempts to determine if the underlying factor structure of the principal measures used in the study approximates the provisional developmental map used to order the research on maturity. Chapter 14
concludes the book by reexamining many of the earlier unsettled
theoretical issues and by reassessing the adequacy of the tentative
developmental conception of maturity used to guide the studies.
The chapter concludes by reexamining the question "Who is a
mature person?"

The book was written primarily for those persons interested in the problems of mental health, maturity, and developmental, as well as personality theory who possess some sophistica-
tion about psychological methods and theory. Although portions
of the book have been used as supplementary reading in under-
graduate courses in personality theory, developmental, and abnormal psychology, the book will more likely find its home in
selected graduate courses and on the bookshelves of professional

persons in the field. To help less sophisticated or too busy readers who need to extract the core of the book in a hurry, I have included summaries at the end of each chapter. A reasonable understanding of the research can be secured by reading the first two chapters, browsing through the summaries of Chapters 3 and 4, skimming Chapter 5, reading Chapters 6, 7, the first few pages and summaries of Chapters 8 through 11, Chapter 12, the summary of Chapter 13, and Chapter 14.

How is it possible to express gratitude to the hundreds of persons who contributed to this research? Of those who must remain nameless, my greatest debt is to the young men of Haverford College whose personal lives the book too coldly numbers, sums, averages, and generalizes. To them I dedicate this work. Many members of the administration, faculty, and student body of the College participated as judges. To their sound and wise judgments the results amply testify. Finally, I thank the many unknown persons and the agencies they represented which supported the research financially. A major phase of the research was planned at the University of Michigan while I was on post-doctoral NSF Science Faculty and Social Science Research Council Fellowships. The actual research was supported by NIMH grants M–2460(A), M–3777(A), and M–4145, by a Danforth Foundation summer study grant, and by the Haverford College Faculty Research fund which also provided some funds for preparing this manuscript for publication.

Of the many who need not be nameless, I am most grateful to Roy Schafer and Lester Alston for evaluating the Rorschach data, George Mandler, Robert Davidon, Carl Rogers and Jack Atkinson for their advice, Peter Platinius, Philip Gerdine, and William Levy for their assistance, and Henry Murray who has influenced this book in more ways than he himself is aware.

I spent many summers and nine months of a sabbatic leave completing the major data analyses with a desk calculator before I had the opportunity to learn the advantages of a computer. Needless to say I am indebted to the Provident Mutual Life Insurance Company for making its computer available to a Haverford group led by Paul Hare and to the Managers of Haverford and Bryn Mawr Colleges for subsequently establishing a joint Computer Center made possible by a grant from the National Science Foundation. Such facilities permitted cross-checking and extending the analyses as well as the exploratory factor analysis reported in Chapter 14.

Many have read the early drafts of the book. I have profited from the stringent comments of my students, many of whom took full advantage of the opportunity to apply to this book most of the criticisms I had made of their own papers earlier in their college careers. Some of the psychologists who had been at the College as part of a College-sponsored visitors program read those portions of the early drafts related to their interests. For their perceptive and helpful comments about how to and how not to write a book, I am grateful to Robert Holt, Lowell Kelly, David McClelland, Joseph McV. Hunt, Nevitt Sanford, and M. Brewster Smith. Their encouraging and sympathetic attitudes reassured me at some very crucial moments when, in despair of ever completing the research, I wondered if the years of work had been worth the effort. Robert Birney, Donald Brown, and George Heise have also read parts of the book. I owe a special debt to Sidney Perloe whose very trenchant but supportive comments of Parts I and II forced me to make many major changes in their structure and content and to Gardner Lindzey whose perceptive judgments and close textual reading saved me from some embarrassment and the reader from considerable redundancy. Of the many faculty who reviewed drafts analyzing the College and its effects on the maturing of its students, I am most grateful to William Ambler and William Cadbury. Some of these men will be most vigorous critics of the positions taken in the book. The book's deficiencies are mine, not theirs.

I would like to acknowledge the debt of gratitude I owe to my wife for her willing assistance in developing the many new procedures, in accurately tabulating and cross-checking all the major results, and in organizing the research. Her contribution is most clearly recognizable in Part III.

Finally, I am deeply indebted to Mildred Hargreaves. Patiently and diplomatically, and with great efficiency she supervised the typing and preparation of the book for publication.

Contents

Explorations
of Maturity

PART I

The Definition of Maturity: The Language and Structure of the Research

CHAPTER 1

The Mature Person

Who is a mature person? What problems does such a question raise? These two questions lend shape to this chapter. I do not try to answer the questions by citing the many different and not so different views and biases that define who a mature person is. This has already been done (Jahoda, 1958; King, 1952). I seek an answer by asking three questions instead: first, is there, in fact, consensual agreement about the traits that phenomenally define the mature person? Why is there such agreement or disagreement? Second, what are the formal properties of the maturity construct? This analysis leads to the third and central question: What standard allows us to say this youth is a mature person, but this one is not? The chapter inductively summarizes some invariant developmental trends that describe the maturing person—any maturing person—and ends by briefly comparing a developmental definition of a mature person with the results of empirical studies of such persons.

DEFINITIONS OF THE MATURE PERSON

The word *mature* must be distinguished from other terms with which it is often confused. A mature person is not necessarily a normal person. Most writers now agree that the word

3

normal should be restricted to behavior that typifies most people in a particular situation. Among the inmates of a mental hospital, it is normal to show psychotic behavior—if you are the one without a key. In this book, I do not use the word *normal.* A mature person is also not necessarily an adjusted person. The term *adjusted* assumes the psychological worth of the sociocultural milieu to which the individual adjusts and ignores the legitimate internal demands and structure of the person himself. But what about the term *psychological (mental) health?* Some theorists like Sanford distinguish between psychological health as the "potential for dealing with strain" (1962, p. 620) and maturity as the "predominance of the efficient, the discriminating, the differentiated and realistic over the primitive, the impulsive, the passionate" (1962, p. 622). Such a distinction is not unambiguous, for as I shall demonstrate later, "potential for dealing with strain" refers to the efficient use of differentiated adaptive controls and skills for mastering the impulsive and conflictual in maintaining the stability of one's self-organization. Because many of the issues that plague both terms and their referents intersect, theorists and researchers in practice tend to use them synonymously, particularly when talking about or investigating adults. To simplify terminology, I use *maturity* and *psychological health* as synonyms. To be a mature *adult* is to be psychologically healthy; to be a psychologically healthy adult is to be mature—though in both cases, such a person is not necessarily normal or perfectly adjusted to his society. Since the term *maturity,* unlike *psychological health,* can be located within a body of theory and empirical data, I prefer to use it throughout the book, although much of the book focuses on psychological health as Sanford defines it. By *mature* I refer to psychological and not physical development and to an approachable ideal type but not an achievable end state. The subtitle of the book, *Studies of mature and immature college men,* means that of the maturing youths studied, some were identified to be more mature than others, not that some had achieved some end state of psychological development. To be more precise, instead of asking "Who is a mature person?" we should ask "What are the dimensions that define the maturing person?" How far along the developmental dimensions a person must be to be identified as no longer *immature* but now *mature* is irrelevant to the purpose of this book which is to identify and then establish measures of such developmental dimensions, and determine if in fact more mature persons are further developed on such dimensions than less mature persons.

Is there general agreement about the traits that define the word *mature?* Jahoda (1958), who has diligently collected definitions of maturity from many psychologists, claims that most experts seem to agree rather well among themselves about the traits of a mature person. To substantiate and extend the generality of her hunch further, I conducted the following imprecise but suggestive study. Definitions of maturity from the writings of thirty-five expert psychologists were collected. These definitions were based on rich and intimate experiences with a wide range of persons or on the results of diffuse and general empirical observations.[1] Forty-three non-expert college male youths were asked to select the most mature person they knew and, in five to ten minutes, describe his most central characteristics. To illustrate the perceptiveness of some of the student definitions, glance at the following:

first of all he is happy . . . despite his penetrating awareness of reality. Socially he can evaluate others . . . and most important, he can fit in without too much anxiety. . . . He is realistic and acts with uncanny certainty. Although not a fantastic intellectual or dreamer, he is both academically sound and imaginative. He never seems to try to be annoying. He seems to sense people's moods and act accordingly. He is . . . deeply religious, though far from what tradition considers "orthodox" in his religion. His social fluidity and easiness are an ever-increasing source of amazement to me.

[1] Abraham, 1925; Allport, 1961; Anderson, 1959a; Angyal, 1941, 1956; Erikson, 1959; Farnsworth, 1957; Foote and Cottrell, 1955; Freud, reported by Reik, 1948; Fromm, 1947; Goldstein, 1940; Hacker, 1945; Hanfmann, 1950; Hartmann, 1960; Horney, 1945; Jahoda, 1950; E. Jones, 1942; Jung, 1939; King, 1952; M. Klein, 1960; Kubie, 1954; McQuitty, 1954; Maslow, 1954; Meyer, 1932; Montagu, 1950; Mowrer, 1948; Murray, 1953; Reich, 1949; Rogers, 1959a; Saul, 1960; Schachtel, 1959; Shoben, 1957; M. B. Smith, 1950; Sullivan, 1953; White, 1952; Wishner, 1955. Specific results of more focused empirical studies such as Barron's (1954, 1963) were not included. These studies are reported later.

TABLE 1–1: SUMMARY OF EXPERT AND NON-EXPERT
DEFINITIONS OF MATURITY

TRAIT	35 EXPERTS		43 NON-EXPERTS	
	#	RANK ORDER	#	RANK ORDER
Realistic judgment—judicious; objective; faces reality	13	1	14	4
Social feeling—warmth; compassion for others; kindness; friendly	9	2.5	19	1
Capable of personal love— deep friendships; tenderness; personal involvement	9	2.5	4	
Adaptable—flexible; can postpone own needs to adjust; harmonizes others' needs and own	8	5	10	7
Integrated—balanced; harmonious; unity; consistency	8	5	2	
Self-reliant—self-sufficient; sense of autonomy; independent	8	5	3	
Self-control—does not get upset easily; tolerates frustration; can control emotion	7	7.5	14	4
Self-acceptance—self-respect; self-trust	7	7.5	5	
Respects, values others and their opinions—tolerant; considerate of others' rights; accepts others' limitations	6	9	15	2
Strong values—meaning or direction to life; stands up for convictions; philosophy of life	5	11.5	14	4
Integrity—sincerity; holds to word; honest; acts out of own being	5	11.5	8	10.5
Creative—productive generativity	5	11.5	1	
Openness to new experience —receptive to ideas; new growth	5	11.5	7	12.5

TRAITS INCLUDED BY NON-EXPERTS AND NOT BY EXPERTS

TRAIT	#	RANK ORDER
Wide interests—self-extended into many activities	10	7
Altruistic, generous—gives to and serves others and their welfare	10	7
Sensitive—aware of others and to experience	9	9
Happy marriage—happy family life; close family; loving parent	8	10.5
Empathic—intuitive; insightful into others' lives; understanding of others	7	12.5

A preliminary content analysis of some of the expert and non-expert definitions revealed that most of the traits mentioned could be assigned to one of thirty-seven trait categories, each defined by a number of adjectives. The traits mentioned by all of the experts and non-experts were next categorized. Table 1–1 gives the rank orders of the thirteen most frequently mentioned categories for the experts and for the non-experts.

Without any pretension of having exhausted available expert definitions or of having used the most rigorous of empirical procedures, the most striking result is the essential similarity of the traits selected both by non-experts, in five to ten minutes of reflection, and by experts, after years of reflection. Both groups of judges agreed on eight of the thirteen trait categories. In either case, the mature person emerges as a judiciously realistic individual with a reflective sense of values and an underlying meaning to his life which he maintains with integrity. However, he is not closed to new experience, but is open to continued growth. Such a person can adapt to others, can tolerate and control most of the tensions of living. He has a basic human warmth or compassion and respect for his fellow man. The experts add that he is integrated, basically accepting of himself, self-reliant, capable of tender, loving relationships, and creative. The non-experts say the mature person has wide interests, is happily married, has close family ties, is generous, empathic and sensitive to others.

Why was there reasonably good agreement between the two sets of judges? In exploring some possible reasons, I hope to illuminate some of the shadowy problems that have hindered research on maturity and mental health.

Terminological Imprecision

A critic might say the judges agreed among themselves because of the vagueness and generality of the trait names used. Unfortunately, few of the most frequently cited trait labels have been carefully defined and investigated. One has only to consider the dismal state of *empathy* research to realize the shortcomings of defining *maturity* by referring to such terms. Defining the vague term *maturity* by the use of other equally vague terms may produce agreement but little scientific enlightenment. Maturity research still pauses at the terminological threshold and for a long time progress will depend upon the preliminary but necessary work of developing specific measures of the agreed-upon terms.

Reductionist Categories

The critic might still persist. Agreement of judges is also a methodological artifact of my attempt to order and communicate a large amount of data, or, he less charitably claims, of an unconscious attempt to insure agreement. Agreement may be due to the set of rubrics or categories used to order the complex responses of the judges. Enforced similarity is thus arbitrarily produced. For example, what instances define the category *realistically faces reality?* Is the student's phrase "penetrating awareness of reality" identical with the World Federation of Mental Health Commission's (1949) phrase "to possess sufficient insight into motivations, capacities, and shortcomings to construct life goals in keeping with internal and external reality"?

Social Stereotypes

Agreement may have occurred because the judges defined a social stereotype they implicitly shared in common. For example, without intending to, students could have relied on their culturally formed stereotype of a mature person and selected the adult who most closely matched this preconception. True, it is preferable to ask students to describe the traits of a real person than to ask them to describe their concept of *maturity,* but, in any case, they may have merely rediscovered their own imposed stereotype. Given the subtle influences that language has on behavior (non-experts as well as experts read what experts write), it is possible each judge was reading the social experience of every other.

Shared Values

Perhaps the principal reason for the consensual agreement of the judges was that they, as members of Western cultures, share similar values of what is "the good life" and their definitions of the mature person were only projected personal but commonly shared prescriptive value preferences. Just how do value preferences affect the definition of maturity? Certainly to reward or prize a mentally healthy instead of a creative, a religious, a selfish, a sociopathic person is to make a value decision about who is more worthy. Or to select one type of person or way of life to be like or to follow may involve a value decision. But what is the role of value preferences in *identifying* who is the mentally healthy or mature person? Long ago, Kingsley Davis (1938) gave his answer: mental health definitions were only tinkling cymbals signifying nothing (to juxtapose St. Paul and Shakespeare) but middle-class values derived from the Protestant ethic. More recently, M. B. Smith has persuasively argued that "mental health is inherently an *evaluative* concept. . . . Mental health is personality evaluated, measured against certain criteria that either have the status of values or are derivatives of implicit values" (1959, p. 673). Most existing definitions of mental health and maturity do *seem* to be only prescriptive, masquerading and rationalized as factual statements. Even apparent empirical studies such as Maslow's (1950) investigation of self-actualized or Barron's (1954, 1963) study of personally "sound" persons were, M. B. Smith (1959) claims, based on the value preferences of Maslow or of selecting judges. Smith says to study such identified persons is not fruitless as long as one recognizes the limitations the selection criterion places upon the generalizability of the findings. Even though value preferences may creep into the selection criterion, it is still an empirical problem to discern which objectively discoverable psychological traits, if any, consistently differentiate between the identified mature and immature person. In other words, consensual agreement, even though based in part on shared value preferences, may describe a pattern of psychological traits that consistently covary in "reality." The core assumption of Smith is that there are no criteria by which to identify the mentally healthy person which are not ultimately derivable from some value propositions. It is this assumption that requires further analysis for it has not yet been demonstrated with certainty.

PROPERTIES OF THE
MATURITY CONSTRUCT

What attitude does our excursion to date indicate should be taken toward the properties of the maturity construct *qua* construct?

The experts and non-experts seem to say, "To understand the mature person, understand holistically." They describe personal traits and dispositions—not specific segmental behavioral acts. Few assert a mature act univocally implies a mature person or an immature act necessarily implies an immature person. An act of kindness in a difficult moment may appear mature but actually be a reaction formation against inadequately repressed sadistic wishes. "Hallucinatory" dreamlike states may appear immature but actually be the regressive consequence of a sensorially deprived situation (Solomon, *et al.*, 1961). It is the person-situation-culture context or pattern that defines the meaning of the act in question.

Although the judges did seem to agree about the maturity concept, they also disagreed not only about some trait categories but also about their centrality. Is it also not likely that adding judges selected from, for example, an Asian culture, would stretch the area of disagreement even further? One way to resolve the judicial disagreements is to say, "To define the mature person, define theoretically not phenomenally." Perhaps the failure of our judges to show even better agreement is due to their phenomenal and atheoretical preoccupation. I don't know. My hunch (hope?) is that the phenotypic (and evaluational) variability that currently characterizes definitions of the mature person can be replaced by a genotypic order the dimensions of which will be consistent with a general personality theory. Later I suggest how the beginnings of such a genotypic order may possibly be identified.

The judges' disagreements eloquently speak to the question, "What is the dimensional order of the theoretical map we hope to uncover?" The judges did not agree about the number of cardinal trait categories that are necessary and sufficient to define the mature person. Recall Allport's (1961) most recent list of such traits: extension of sense of self; warm relating of self to others; emotional security (self-acceptance); realistic perception, skills and assignments; self-objectification (insight and humor); and unifying philosophy of life. As humanely wise as such a list is, why end with six cardinal traits as Allport himself asks? Why not begin and end with one (self-actualization), three, or twelve? Are they each of equal importance? It is doubtful that any one unidimensional construct can encompass the complexity and diversity the judges find in the phenomenal world of the mature person. Even the psychoanalysts are abandoning reductionistic constructs such as *ego strength* to talk instead of *ego-strengths* (Hartmann, 1950). To challenge the unidimensionally inclined reader further, try teasing out one constructional principle or dimension from the following traits alleged by a group of experts to define *creativity*—one of the traits sometimes used to define a mature person:

desire to grow, capacity to be puzzled, awareness, spontaneity, spontaneous flexibility, adaptive flexibility, originality, divergent thinking, learning, openness to new experience, no boundaries, permeability of boundaries, yielding, readiness to yield, abandoning, letting go, being born every day, discarding the irrelevant, ability to toy with elements, change of activity, persistence, hard work, composition, decomposition, recomposition, differentiation, integration, . . . peace with the world, harmony, honesty, humility, enthusiasm, integrity, inner maturity, self-actualizing, skepticism, boldness, faith, courage, willingness to be alone, I see, I feel, I think, lust for temporary chaos, security, uncertainty, tolerance of ambiguity (Anderson, 1959b, p. 238) to which I would now add, "Amen!"

Our holistic orientation shapes our attitude toward another issue: can we talk of a mature person or must we talk of a person who is mature in some ways and immature in others? Are the dimensions that define the maturity construct intercorrelated or independent of each other? (Shades of the unresolved issues about the structure of intelligence hover close by, Tuddenham, 1962.) The prevailing view, certainly not authoritative in the absence of any empirical evidence, is that maturity is a multi-faceted concept whose dimensions are positively intercorrelated (Jahoda, 1958). I assume there is some general level of organismic maturity, although not all of the defining dimensions are necessarily equally correlated with that level of functioning.

Implied in this holistic stance is a conjunctive not a compensatory or disjunctive model (Coombs, 1957). A compensatory model is inadequate because a person does not become more mature by overcompensating for his failure to develop in another area. Emotional insensitivity to new experience cannot be compensated for by excessive cognitive awareness to such experiences without producing a caricature of a mature person. The disjunctive model is also not appropriate. I assume each person possesses each dimensional attribute and that a more mature person is more developed on each of the interrelated dimensions than is the less mature person.

L

DEFINITIONAL CRITERIA OF THE MATURE PERSON

The third question of the chapter asks, "What criterion allows us to say this youth is more mature than this youth?" I briefly review and evaluate some criteria that have been used to define maturity (mental health) and then consider in some detail bio-psychological developmental theories in order to identify invariant growth trends that define organismic maturing processes. Such a naturalistically based criterion will demonstrate that it is premature to accede to the contention that any definition of maturity is derivable from non-empirical, prescriptive, and evaluational preferences.

Authoritative Wisdom

Several criteria can be quickly dismissed, not because they lack historical interest, but because contemporary portrayals of their inadequacies are now plentiful (Jahoda, 1958; W. A. Scott, 1958; M. B. Smith, 1959). Short shrift can be made of the appeals to experienced authority. What standard defines an "experienced authority"? And when the experienced authorities disagree, who defines who is more "experienced" or more "authoritative"?

Humanistic Tradition

A disguised variant of the authoritative wisdom standard is the appeal to the common humanistic tradition of all great literate civilized cultures. All men endure similar existential problems in relating to their Umwelt, Mitwelt, and Eigenwelt; the spokesmen of all great cultures have used a similar language when describing the more mature person's relationships to such worlds (Fromm, 1955; Jung, 1934). Any content analysis of the words of such cultural spokesmen encounters the same prob-

lems we met in collating the words of our psychological experts
(terminological vagueness, linguistic and translation reduction-
ism, and arbitrary categorization). While not dismissing the authoritative but imprecise wisdom of the past, those of scientific
and more rebellious temperament must feel uncertainty and
doubt about the validity of the humanistic tradition as a standard.

Public Opinion

If there is no agreement about the one authority who
fulfills Jung's "old wise man" archetype or the precise message
of the humanistic tradition, cannot the measurable opinions of
representative samples of different populations serve as a standard? Surely, some truth must emerge from the collective wisdom
of living peoples? The Joint Commission on Mental Illness and
Health almost resorted to such a criterion in its survey of the
verbal habits of Americans about their health (Gurin, Veroff,
& Feld, 1960). While the authors did not explicitly define *mental
health* on the basis of sample self-reports, they did use such
self-report data to indict several favorite definitions of mental
health and maturity (self-actualizing definitions). But public
opinion is heavily molded by common language training, prevalent social values and stereotypes. In pluralistic societies, the
modal public opinion is a thin and shifting foundation upon
which to develop a firm understanding of the mature person.

Social Adjustment

An appealing variant of the public opinion standard is
the social adjustment criterion. Maturity is an achieved state of
harmony between the individual and his social group(s). What
does *harmony* mean? Is it conformity to the modal public opinion? What is a man's social group? Is it his bowling group, business partner, or family? If harmony means to fulfill the role
expectations of each of the social groups to which one belongs, is
man's essential identity only that of being a marketable com-

modity adjustable to fit each conflicting expectation? By this definition, the more mature person is likely to be found only in a homogeneous primitive society—not in the pluralistic societies of civilized man.

Psychopathological Continuum

A psychiatrically favored approach is to infer the traits of the mentally healthy person from studies of the mentally ill person. The assumption is there is some dimensional continuity between the normal and abnormal. Such an assumption permits the claim that psychoanalytic theory, induced from studies of neurotic persons, is a general theory of psychology (Hartmann, 1939a; Rapaport, 1960); it permits Leon Saul (1947) to title a book *Emotional Maturity,* describe his idea of maturity in twenty-four pages, various abnormal syndromes in one hundred and forty-seven pages, but at no time in the first and a subsequent revision (1960) to report the results of studies of mature persons. The validity of the continuum assumption is at least questionable and has on occasion been subjected to searching criticism (Allport, 1953; Eysenck, 1947). For example, Eysenck (1961) from factorial studies of traits of psychotic and neurotic persons finds that they are qualitatively and not just quantitatively different. Furthermore, some emergent phenomena may define a mentally healthy person that are not inferable from the traits of the mentally ill person. As Jahoda says, "absence of disease may constitute a necessary, but not a sufficient, criterion for mental health" (1958, p. 15). Even if the continuity assumption were valid, we are only beginning to approach a comprehensive and reliable set of dimensions describing a mental health continuum which has been validated on individuals who occupy different positions along that continuum (Lichtenberg, 1955; Lichtenberg, Cassetta, & Scanlon, 1960; 1961). Finally, phenotypically defined categories inevitably become embroiled in the cultural relativistic argument (e.g., neurotic-like acts are only culturally defined social customs; how is one to decide which cultural custom is more healthy? Benedict, 1934). In the absence of good evidence, one cannot deny that such a standard potentially may be useful. Is it possible to recast the issue in a slightly different form to see if our understanding can be advanced on another front?

Organismic Maturing Trends

One reason for the disappointing progress in developing a psychopathological standard by which to define mentally healthy persons may be the concept *mental health* itself. M. B. Smith (1961) has argued that the term has no place in any theory's nomological network of terms and implications. If so, then there are no fundamental principles by which to establish the limits or properties of the term. But no one has yet argued that the term *maturity*, which describes a region of a developmental continuum, cannot be located within a general personality theory. And, in fact, many personality theories do contain implicit and explicit statements about the properties of such a term. Could there not be invariant growth trends, such as progressive integration of the self, that describe the development of any person in any culture, even though cultures may differ in providing the necessary conditions for the optimal development of such trends? Is there a sprig of hope that theories of personality development —theories based on close naturalistic observation, clinical reconstructions, and empirical studies—may offer clues to such invariant growth trends as define the mature person? In examining the spectrum of bio-psychological developmental theories, my purpose is not to present such theories fully nor to examine their supporting data, but to highlight the key principles and concepts that may help to identify some defining growth trends.

Biological Developmental Principles

Most developmental theories concern themselves with an "(1) organism conceived as a living system; (2) time; (3) movement over time toward complexity of organization; (4) 'hierarchization,' . . . of parts or part-systems into larger units or 'wholes'; and (5) an end state of organization which is maintained with some stability or self-regulation" (Harris, 1957, p. 3). It is this end state with which I am preoccupied. Sinnott's (1959) summary of a biological view of organismic developmental principles keynotes the central conceptions to which this and succeeding chapters frequently return. He writes that

a living thing is constantly *developing*. . . . Development is not an aimless affair; each stage follows precisely its predecessor. . . . Nevertheless, through all this alteration it maintains its own particular identity, its own organized unity. Each organism has its particular series of norms, its special cycle of progressive and creative development. Continual change is the keynote of this cycle; not unguided change but change that moves toward a very definite end—the mature individual and the completion of the cycle. . . . The normal course of development toward a particular end can be blocked and altered in various ways, as by removing certain parts of the growing system, placing it under abnormal situations, or even disorganizing it completely. Under these conditions the organism shows a persistent tendency to restore lost parts, reorganizing itself, and achieve the end it would have reached unimpeded. . . . Increasing differentiation results in gradual loss of regenerative potency, especially in animals. . . . This capacity is so widespread, however, that it seems clear that something representing the whole organism, specific in its character, is present in every cell of the body and ready, should occasion require and favorable conditions occur, to proceed in its own cycle of creative change and form a new, organized whole again. This tendency in every living system to integrate its material and processes in conformity with a norm which it persistently seeks to reach emphasizes the essentially teleological character of development and function. The unity of the organism seems to inhere in the end toward which it is moving rather than in any fixed course for reaching that end, for the end may be gained not in any single linear progression but in a variety of ways, pp. 16–17.

Sinnott is saying that a maturing organism progressively integrates experience into a changing but reasonably stable structure that maintains its stability or identity even in the face of radical internal and external environmental changes. His progressive development is not capricious but is guided by a stable, inherent, individual organization. While each person's developmental movement proceeds toward its own pattern of ends, toward "a norm which it persistently seeks to reach," each person differs in the behavioral means used to fulfill this norm. Organismic structure imparts direction to development, or, in the words of another biologist, "development proceeds within the framework of the whole" (Hamburger, 1957). The theory of evolution postulates "the continual emergence of new kinds of organisms" of increased complexity and organization. Integration and organization become crucially more central, but, paradoxically, less decipherable. Recovery from disintegrating and disorganizing external and internal onslaughts becomes less genetically assured thus increasing the importance of adaptive processes for the more complex organizations. To determine those distinctive differences which define man's organizational principles, his series of norms, his "special cycle[s] of progressive and creative development" (Sinnott, 1959, p. 16), he must be compared to other evolutionary forms.

Phylogenetic Comparisons

Comparative psychologists have tried to order different species and phyla by the psychological level of their behavioral development, but the only reasonable ordering criterion found is behavioral plasticity. Schneirla asserts "that higher levels are characterized by plasticity [which] means that capacities and organizations appear which admit the possibility of systematic variations appropriate to new environmental conditions" (1957, p. 82). This plasticity or lack of reflexive-instinctive adaptive mechanisms is in man most enhanced by his capacity to symbolically represent his environment. Symbolization permits, though it does not guarantee, conscious self-control because the anticipation of consequences (alleged to be possible only through symbolic representation of future events) acts as a conditioning cue to inhibition (Shoben, 1957). Symbolization also permits man to become responsible for the consequences of his acts, as the existentialists have emphasized (May, 1961). Phylogenetic theory suggests that a maturing man may be described by a developmental trend toward increased awareness of his experience mediated through his increasing symbolic development.

Bio-psychological Development Trends

Man's plasticity early shifts the governing weight from biological to environmental factors although research on biological readiness (e.g., critical age periods, J. P. Scott, 1957, 1962) serves to remind us of the continuing interactive effect of both factors. No startling discontinuities in developmental principles mark this growing shift. Psychoanalytic psychosexual theory, too well known to require specific restatement, recognizes this continuing interaction in its description of an orderly developmental progression of libidinal (biological), ego, and object-relationships. (Cathetic development passes through auto-erotic, narcissistic, ambivalent, and genital stages.) The order of the developmental stages is allegedly fixed though some individuals may not progress as far as others. No developmental stage is ever permanently mastered, for under stress regression may occur (Abraham, 1925). Even mature individuals may show immature behavior. Classical psychoanalytic theory does not provide a detailed explanation of the mature personality. In his still authoritative presentation of psychoanalytic theory, Fenichel (1945) devotes one small paragraph to the mature or genital personality, relying for the most part on Abraham's description given in 1925. The genital personality, according to Abraham, synthesizes all of the socially positive traits characteristic of the earlier psychosexual characterological states, mastering the "remaining traces of the more primitive stages of development" (1925, p. 408). The genital personality type is not just a residual conglomeration of socially favorable traits (a definition that inevitably shades into and rests on the adjustive criterion rejected earlier) but is the consequence of a more fundamental developmental process; namely, the subjugation of the pleasure principle by the reality principle at the time the Oedipus Complex is mastered. I return to the development of the reality principle later.

Erikson (1950a, 1950b, 1959) redefines and extends psychoanalytic theory to the entire life cycle, but he does not repudiate its biological emphasis, as Fromm (1947) did when he formulated his social-psychological character types—exploitative (oral), hoarding (anal), and productive (genital). Healthy, and presumably mature, development is the successful mastery of the problems associated with each of the epigenetic stages—trust (oral), autonomy (anal), initiative (phallic), industry, identity, intimacy, generativity, and integrity (manifestations of genitality). Genitality is "mutuality of orgasm with a loved partner of the other sex with whom one is able and willing to share a mutual trust and with whom one is able and willing to regulate the cycles of work, procreation, and recreation so as to secure to the offspring, too, a satisfactory development" (1950a, pp. 230–231). Each of the above stages has its precursive conditions that facilitate and hinder the mastery of that stage. Like Freudian theory, the developmental problems are assumed to be universal and ordered in the sequence listed. This developmental map of the substantive traits that define maturity orders a number of traits our experts and non-experts agreed upon. While the *identity* concept is exciting considerable research, there seems to have been little research generated by other aspects of this model. The thrust of these bio-psychological theories is to suggest that there is a universal developmental trend toward accurately internalizing the external world and accommodating one's self to its demands. This allocentric development (as I call it later) is manifested in the reciprocal accommodations one makes in one's love relationships with another person.

Psycho-social Developmental Trends

While certainly not ignoring biological maturational trends, other theorists use more psychologically oriented models of development. Interestingly, there is uncommon agreement about psychological developmental trends among such theorists which is somewhat remarkable given the widely differing sources of empirical data (clinical reconstructions, psychotherapy trends, child observation) from which such developmental trends have been inferred.

Werner's (1957) formulation of such trends, supported by extensive experimental studies of perceptual differentiation in psychopathological groups and children, is one of the most succinct summaries available. His orthogenetic principle states,

that wherever development occurs it proceeds from a state of relative globality and lack of differentiation to a state of increasing differentiation, articulation, and hierarchic integration (1957, p. 126).

His elaboration of this abstract principle parallels that of Goldstein's and Scheerer's (1941) description of concrete-abstract behavior inferred from observations of brain-injured patients. For Werner,

the organism becomes increasingly less dominated by the immediate concrete situation; the person is less stimulus-bound and less impelled by his own affective states. A consequence of this freedom is the clearer understanding of goals, the possibility of employing substitutive means and alternative ends. There is hence a greater capacity for delay and planned action. The person is better able to exercise choice and willfully rearrange a situation. In short, he can manipulate his environment rather than passively respond to the environment. This freedom from the domination of the immediate situation also permits a more accurate assessment of others. . . . At developmentally higher levels, therefore, there is less a tendency for the world to be interpreted solely in terms of one's own needs and an increasing appreciation of the needs of others and of group goals (1957, p. 127).

Another developmental trend that defines a maturing person appears to be that he becomes more autonomous of external stimulus control.

Schachtel (1959), ranging widely in clinical and philosophic sources, pinpoints the following specific trends that define the maturing person. Development proceeds away from need-satisfaction, drive-dominated cognition, and self-seeking pleasurable relations with others toward an active, exploratory, playful openness toward the world in which the maintenance of tension (or relatedness with a loved person or object of interest) is the embracing motivational support. Affectively, development proceeds from embeddedness (passive "helpless distress") to activity ("activity coping with a drive tension or . . . active relating to the environment," p. 29). The mature person is described by a "strong development of activity-affect" manifested by zestful energy, strong feelings and the desire to maintain rather than seek tension release (p. 32). Cognitively, development proceeds from autocentric ("a fusion between sensory quality and pleasure or unpleasure feelings," p. 83) to allocentric cognitive modes (in which objectification results from responding to real sensory qualities independently of aroused pleasure-unpleasure feelings). He also implicitly assumes a developmental trend, if not motive, to focus cognitions, to exclude irrelevancies in the perceptual and cognitive field. Such focal cognition (attention in his words) is a major ego control. By excluding other field stimuli in the process of attending, responses or motives associated with the excluded stimuli are not evoked. Focal attention is not a passive but an actively controlled process which permits the knowing of reality. Maturity is defined by activity-affect, allocentric objectified cognition, controlled focal attention, and exploratory, playful cognitive motives which are autonomous of the more primitive biological drives seeking tension release.

The existentialist thread that runs through Schachtel's analysis leads naturally to Rogers' (1955, 1959a, 1961) view of the fully functioning person. His fundamental, allegedly empirically based, assumption is that man has a tendency to actualize himself, to become his potentialities. "By this I mean the directional trend which is evident in all organic and human life—the urge to expand, extend, develop, mature—the tendency to express and activate all the capacities of the organism, to the extent that such activation enhances the organism of the self" (1959b, p. 72), or, as Sinnott says, to progressively integrate one's own experience. Given this assumption Rogers, with the verifying assent of his many empirical studies, analyzes the directional trends found in client-centered therapy and projects a "hypothetical end point" which characterizes the fully functioning individual. He makes a second assumption, consistently implemented in his therapeutic procedures, that under appropriate (client-centered) therapeutic conditions these potentials will be released, their natural development will resume, and the individual will be free "to be that which [he] truly is" (1961). What are the therapeutic developmental growth trends?: "toward being process" manifested by responsiveness to be and to change, "toward being complexity" which is accepting and living all of oneself at any moment, "toward openness to experience," "toward acceptance of others," "toward trust of self." Rogers calls these valuational choices, but his implication, explicitly stated elsewhere (1955) is that these are the directional trends *any* individual will move toward "when there is psychological freedom to move in *any* direction." Although therapists of other persuasions also use personality change in therapy as a basis for projecting to the end point of mature development, the consistently non-interventionist, non-directive type of therapy used by Rogers may provide more reliable conditions for observing such trends in therapy. For Rogers, man is basically social, constructive, and trustworthy, and if society only suspended its frustrating limits and expectations, man would naturally develop to maturity. It is as if individual fulfillment produces social identity, for surely there is the underlying assumption of a potential coordinate harmony between each man and every other man. Like Fromm, he ignores the crucial determining constructive and educative influence the social environment plays in shaping potential, providing the means for its expression, and ensuring the coordination of the individual with his environment which is not necessarily guaranteed by man's inherent potentials.

These psycho-social theorists emphasize that man's growing autonomy, allocentricism, and identity fulfillment are functions of his progressive *becoming*.

Cognitive Developmental Trends

A theme that weaves through most developmental theories is the centrality of man's maturing cognitive processes in assisting his adaptation. Philosophers also have long identified man's distinctive peculiarity as his capacity for consciousness, symbolization, and rational thought—a point now being re-emphasized within psychology by such existentialist psychologists as May (1961). The two most important and comprehensive developmental theories, psychoanalytic ego psychology and Piaget's theory of intelligence and adaptation, are essentially cognitive models of the development of internal structure and organization. In their own terminologies, these theories identify similar types of developmental trends to define a maturing person. Although recent brilliant and clarifying analyses of both theories (Flavell, 1963; Hunt, 1961; Rapaport, 1960) and their relationships to each other (Wolff, 1960) are now available and eliminate the necessity for reviewing their more technical features, I sketch the main outline of each theory since the rest of the book is largely guided by some of the terminology and theoretical orientation of these two approaches.

The task of psychoanalytic ego psychology is to explain how internal organization or structures (inhibitory, selective, and regulatory ego defenses, controls and derivative drives) develop and how they interact with internal (id) and external (partly internalized in the superego) demands to ensure the adaptation of the organism. What trends describe this development according to Freud and the ego psychologists?

Development proceeds from a state described by relatively little structure (primitive drive discharge thresholds) to one of complexly interacting, highly differentiated, hierarchically organized and stable structures. The consequence of this increasingly stabilized internal organization is inhibition and control of more primitive and less differentiated motivational and cognitive systems. Freud assumes "that to every transition from one system to that immediately above it (that is, every advance to a higher stage of mental organization) there corresponds a new censorship" (1915, p. 124). Such progressive advances to more differentiated levels of ego organization are due, almost exclusively, for Freud (1900), to environmental restraints on drive reduction and to the loss of cathected environmental objects which are then reinstituted in the ego by identification ("the character of the ego is a precipitate of abandoned object-cathexes and . . . it contains a record of past object-choices" 1923, p. 36). Contemporary ego psychologists now recognize that increasing organization reflects both inherent biological maturational as well as environmental effects (Hartmann, 1939a). In any case, the developing personality structure (types of defenses, controls, interests, and superego values) of the person is primarily modeled on forms given by the person's social environment. There is, thus, the developing internalization of the external environment which has a progressively inhibiting effect on the more undifferentiated motivational wishes of the organism. The pleasure principle becomes subordinated to the reality principle.

This developmental trend is nowhere more clearly manifested than in the cognitive shift from primary (memories and their connections organized around wishes) to secondary process thinking (memories and their connections organized around reality and logical forms) (Freud, 1900). Primary process (or autocentric) coordinations are not adapted out or abandoned; they are only suppressed by the waking conscious and secondary thought (or allocentric) processes to emerge later in dreams or under other conditions. Thus, even a mature person will demonstrate, if not usefully exploit (regress in the service of the ego, Kris, 1952) primary process coordinations under certain conditions. While it is a matter of dispute about how discontinuous this developmental shift is (Freud, 1900; Gill, 1963; Hartmann, 1955), Freud, Bartlett (1932) and other theorists agree that the thought processes of the young child are organized and coordinated primarily by his own primitive motives and needs and not by any of the logical concepts, forms, and relationships found in the social environment.

Another developmental trend in psychoanalytic ego psychology is the progressive binding of drive cathexes and the resulting increased autonomy of cognitive structures from their originating sources. Freud hypothesized that each successive counter-cathectic structure not only raises the discharge threshold of the drive being defended against (increasing inhibition) but also results in a slight diminution of the intensity of that drive (the source of energy for the counter-cathexes is in some unfathomable way secured from the drive or derivative drive being repressed). With increasing structural differentiation, the derivative or counter-cathectic structures become increasingly more remote or distant from the historically earlier energy source (secondary autonomy), the intensity of which is already considerably diluted as a result of this progressive derivative process. The arousal of the drive does not automatically activate the derivative structures nor can the presence of the primitive drive be inferred from the appearance of the derivative drive. Hartmann's (1939a) notion of primary autonomy recognizes that not all structures develop in this way, that is, out of conflict. Some structures may be ontologically or genetically given as part of the inherited and constitutional structure of the individual.

The developmental trends that define a mature person for the ego psychologist can be briefly summarized: the mature person is a highly differentiated and (ego) organized person whose thought processes are coordinated by reality-given principles and whose behavior is predominantly reality-oriented. However, under appropriate conditions he may show primary process thinking though the differentiated quality of his ego organization assures him fundamental control over that regression. His cognitive structures, including attitudes and interests, are relatively autonomous of more primitive drives and needs.

Piaget (1936, 1947), too, is centrally concerned with the problem of developing structure (primarily cognitive organizations) and adaptation. "It is by adapting to things that thought organizes itself and it is by organizing itself that it structures things" (1947, p. 8). A person is an organized structure that maintains itself by simultaneously incorporating information from the environment and modifying itself to adapt to that information. Assimilation is the modification of information to fit the existing schemata structure of the individual. Accommodation is the modification and extension of the existing schemata to approximate more closely the structural requirements and demands of the incoming information. A person has an intrinsic need to stabilize and progressively integrate his own organization, that is, to achieve an equilibrium between assimilation and accommodation. In progressively assimilating, internalizing, the "whole universe of perception" (1936, p. 413), the developmental shift is away from "egocentric incorporation" (using information only to maintain one's own stability) to increased objectivity in which schemata are accurately (allocentrically) accommodated to the form of the external environment. This "progressive extraversion" implies a qualitative change in the nature of the assimilatory process, not a shift from assimilative to accommodative dominance. Operational thought (Freud's secondary thought process) is the model toward which this assimilatory-accommodatory-equilibrium progresses. In this process, distortion of both the incoming information and the existing schemata structure is minimized.

Whereas the ego psychologists have emphasized the progressive autonomy of cognitive structures from primitive drives, Piaget (like Werner) emphasizes the progressive autonomy or decentering of cognitive structures from the temporal-spatial limitations characteristic of hereditary reflexes, percepts, and sensorimotor schemata coordinations. He shows that the roots of adaptive processes describing mature cognitive activity can be genetically traced to the earlier sensorimotor assimilations and accommodations of the young infant. With biological maturation comes an increasing capacity for symbolic representation which, in combination with socially cooperative relationships, permits the person to develop from a stage in which schemata are organized around concrete sensorimotor experiences, through other stages, to one in which schemata are coordinated or organized formally in logical groupings independent of the real world. A mature person is able to operate formally on problems irrespective of the empirical, affective, or personal relevance of the content of the problem he confronts in the real world. It is this aspect of operational thought that I examine later in the research reported in Part III. The operations that define formal thought are associativity, combinativity, reversibility, identity, and tautology. Development proceeds toward various types of groupings of these operations which facilitate the conceptualization, classification, analysis and synthesis, and judging of incoming information.

"Only intelligence [operational thought], capable of all its detours and reversals by action and by thought, tends towards an all-embracing equilibrium by aiming at the assimilation of the whole of reality and the accommodation to it of action, which it thereby frees from its dependence on the initial *hic* and *nunc*" (1947, p. 9).

Both the ego psychologists and Piaget find that cognitive structures facilitating adaption are not necessarily inherent (e.g., a person is neither born with a fixed amount of ego strength nor with a constant level of intellectual ability).

Given a biological-constitutional basis (primary autonomous

structures such as hereditary sensorimotor reflexes), highly complex hierarchical cognitive structures develop out of the interaction of the organism with the environment. Piaget's detailed
descriptive analysis of how the interactive process produces
increasingly autonomous mental structures, when combined with
the ego psychologist's detailed descriptions of adaptation to
conflict situations, also assists in sketching a number of developmental trends by which to define a mature person.

INVARIANT DEVELOPMENTAL TRENDS

Recall that the purpose of this chapter is to find a
theoretical criterion by which to define a mature person. Enough
agreement exists among different judges about the phenomenal
properties of such a person to posit that there may be, in fact,
some theoretical meaning to the concept maturity (or mental
health). But the judges' disagreement about the centrality and
number of phenotypic traits suggested we seek a more genotypic
universalistic set of defining dimensions. Can the developmental
process itself suggest some constructional principles by which to
define the mature person theoretically? Are there invariant
developmental trends that account for most of the phenomena to
which the diverse theories and observations point? I believe there
are. The exact phenotypic form they take varies from social
group to social group. Many culturally selective determinants
block, fail to exploit, or stimulate the fulfillment of the potentials
inherent in each trend (Soddy, 1961).

At least five genotypic developmental dimensions that define a
maturing person can be identified from existing empirical and
theoretical work.

1. Toward Increased Stability of Organization

A maturing person becomes more stably organized,
capable of resisting and recovering from the disorganizing effects
induced by either internal or external sources of information.
He maintains his identity over time. The individual not only has

given biological homeostatic mechanisms (Cannon, 1932) but also learned schemata or structures, combined and integrated into larger structural groupings that modulate, delay, or inhibit the activation of subordinate components. Behavior becomes less impulsive and drive-determined and comes under the control of more cognitive type of structures. Empirical evidence about the differential stability of different cognitive structures (Bloom, 1964), motivational interests and values is still relatively scarce (Kelly, 1955; Strong, 1951).

2. Toward a Progressive Integration of New Information

A maturing person is open to and seeks new information which is then progressively integrated or made congruent with his self-organization. The person is an open system constantly receiving, if not seeking, new stimulation. A very wise psychologist has said ". . . yet is it not true that all animal organisms need activity and thus change? One begins (say I) to understand life when he perceives that man strives always for adaptive adjustment and then welcomes disadjustment that he may strive again, since health is activity" (Boring, 1962, p. 174). And each successive temporary equilibrium is more differentiated and integrated than the former one. Growth is accumulative integration and probably not too reversible (Bloom, 1964).

What keeps this progressive integrative process going? Theorists postulate different reasons: the given (teleological) properties of any living organism (Sinnott, 1959), the operation of an Eros instinct defined as an instinctive trend toward increasing unity and relational synthesis (Freud, 1920), an innate drive toward self-actualization (Maslow, 1950, 1954; Rogers, 1959a), the inherent tendency of a schema in response to new environmental information to seek an equilibrium (Piaget, 1936), an innately given curiosity or exploratory motive persistently pushing man to seek new sources of stimulation (Berlyne, 1960), a need for self-consistency (Lecky, 1945), or a neurophysiological need to seek varying stimuli to prevent disorganization. Preoccupation with creative needs and acts (Anderson, 1959a,b), "efforts after meaning," hypothesized adolescent thrusts after independence

(Josselyn, 1954, 1959), concepts of self-individuation (Jung, 1928), existentialist views of man's expanding self-consciousness and freedom in one way or another, reflect a belief that man's developmental tendency is not to be content with one level of integration. These theories propose that man is ever restlessly pushing on to a new organization of experience—if not to avoid disorganization, at least to avoid boredom.

3. Toward Increased Allocentricism

The maturing person becomes progressively organized around internalized reality-given (allocentric) instead of personal need-dominated (autocentric) forms. Internalization of reality, particularly social reality, increases man's adaptive potential for he develops representational structures that approximate those he bumps into while walking through his phenomenal world. Such structures include the needs and values, the patterns of thought and communication, and the responses of other persons to the individual. However, each person is not just a mirror of his environment as some self-theorists seem to suggest (Mead, 1934; Sullivan, 1953). His own constitutional, temperamental, and motivational structures and thresholds, blended by his own idiosyncratic learning experiences, modify the reality that is internalized. The first two invariant developmental trends limit the extent to which allocentric needs dominate the maturing person, who must learn to find accommodations between the demands of others and his own more autocentric demands.

4. Toward Increasing Symbolic Representations of Experience

The maturing person becomes a potentially more aware person for he can symbolically represent and mentally coordinate more and more of his external and internal worlds. Coordinate with his increasing allocentricism, the maturing person develops more accurate imaginal representations of his experience. The emerging imaginal and symbolizing property has profound consequences for man's adaptation. He becomes aware of himself and of the determinants of his acts; he can anticipate and plan; he can remember and retrospectively learn from past events or from his culture's history; he can imaginally reconstruct a variety of adaptive solutions and mentally explore their consequences without irreversible effects. With increasing capacity for imaginal representation comes a vast increase in the speed with which mental representations or schemata can be experimentally combined and uncombined. Such rapid or simultaneous mental operations permit a person to maintain an "abstract attitude," to deduce consequences within the guiding framework of a hierarchial set of assumptions and principles (Goldstein, *et al.,* 1941).

5. *Toward Increasing Autonomy*

The maturing person becomes more autonomous, for his decisions and actions become increasingly centered in, to use Rogers' terms, an "organismic valuing process" (1959a). He is not as immediately controlled or determined by his immediate environment or his motivational state or by his earlier childhood history. Autonomy has two related meanings. In Allport's (1937, 1961) and in Hartmann's (1939a, 1960) sense, contemporary decisions and actions are not necessarily expressions of some historically lingering childhood conflict or of some more primitive motivational state. In a second sense, autonomy means a maturing person is less and less under the persuasive control of both contemporary situational and motivational forces. In Angyal's words, increasing autonomy "expresses the person's striving from a state of lesser self-determination (and greater situational influence) to a state of greater self-determination (and lesser situational influence)" (1941, p. 45). Rogers and other theorists would complement Angyal's definition by saying autonomy also means increasing freedom from irrational disassociated or unconscious motivational influences. There is an expansion of the area of rational conscious choice. Man becomes less reactive and more self-active; behavior control shifts from external sensations and internal sources of pain to man's ongoing "intrinsically and spontaneously active" (Pribram, 1960, p. 32) central nervous system (e.g., his thought processes and derived motives). Development proceeds from a Lockean to a Leibnitzean view of man—to plagiarize Allport's (1955) well-known distinction.

The autonomy growth trend does not mask a non-deterministic assumption about a maturing man (that he is a free-willed organism); it only shifts the locus of the determining influences of man's choices to man's own contemporary self-structure. Action is the joint product of his phenomenal world and his self-organization.

EMPIRICAL STUDIES OF HEALTHY AND MATURE PERSONS

Who is a mature person? We have seen he can be theoretically described as a stably organized individual who seeks out and is open to new experiences but who also has the capacity to resist and/or recover from the disorganizing influences of the disturbing information he encounters. His thought processes, interpersonal relationships, and self are allocentrically organized but he does not repress persisting autocentric trends that are useful for adaptive purposes. His internal and external worlds are accurately represented and available to awareness. Finally, the mature person's decisions are relatively autonomous of the coercive effects of both his immediate environment and egocentric motives.

Does this genotypic developmental description of the mature person fit with the results of empirical studies specifically designed to describe effective, mentally healthy, sound, and mature persons? Unfortunately, of the handful of such studies completed,[2] few are immune to theoretical and serious methodological criticism. Perhaps because of the novelty, complexity, and refractoriness of the problems involved in investigating mature persons, most studies are atheoretical and diffuse explorations,

[2] Barron, 1954, 1955, 1963; Bond, 1950, 1952; Brown, 1960; Cox, 1956; Funkenstein, King, & Drolette, 1957; Getzels & Jackson, 1962; C. W. Heath, 1945; S. R. Heath, 1964; Hooten, 1945; Sanford, 1956; Terman, 1954; Warren & Heist, 1960. Other studies such as Kelly & Fiske, 1951 are more peripherally related and are not included.

rather than theoretically derived, limited, searching forays. Little explicit theoretical rationale guided what to look for or what methods to use. No two studies shared the same purpose or the same selection procedures. With the possible exception of the Vassar (Sanford, 1956) and Barron (1954, 1963) studies, few have contributed suggestions about either improving old methods or developing new ones. Firm knowledge about mature persons is limited because the studies have failed to suggest new lines of approach to subsequent investigators. Each succeeding study gives the impression that it starts its quest for the mature person anew. Few studies have been cross-validated.

The lack of comparable selection and assessment measures, the questionable reliability of some judgment procedures (particularly psychiatric interviews), and the lack of cross-validation studies suggest a detailed comparative analysis of these researches to have dubious value. Instead, the most consistent and reasonably valid findings of the studies are summarized in the following tentative generalizations:

1. Psychological health or maturity does not imply the absence of conflict or of severe problems of adjustment. Rather, it is the style of life, or the controls used to master problems, which differentiate between mature and immature persons (Barron, 1954, 1963; Bond, 1950, 1952).

2. Mature individuals are not immune to disorganizing influences; rather, it is the quality of long-term adaptive reactions to stress which differentiate more consistently between mature and immature persons (Funkenstein, et al., 1957).

3. The mature person has achieved an organization or organismic integrity that persists over long periods of time. A sound person today is likely to be judged sound several years later (C. W. Heath, 1945). He possesses adaptive controls which permit continued growth while maintaining internal organization (Brown, 1960).

4. Mature individuals have strongly persistent directing motives that assist in organizing goal-directed behavior over long periods of time (Barron, 1954, 1963; C. W. Heath, 1945; Terman, 1954).

5. Mature persons are described as self-confident (Barron, 1954, 1963; Brown, 1960; C. W. Heath, 1945; Terman, 1954; Warren &

Heist, 1960), reality-oriented (Barron, 1954, 1963; Brown, 1960; C. W. Heath, 1945; Warren & Heist, 1960), and socially adaptable (Barron, 1954, 1963; Cox, 1956; C. W. Heath, 1945; S. R. Heath, 1964). Developmental theory and empirical studies agree rather well in describing the mature person as showing considerable stability over time. This stability is derived, in part, from strong persisting motives that consistently organize experience and by adaptive controls that enable eventual recovery from disorganization. Some evidence confirms the suggestion that the mature person is more allocentric in his orientation to reality and in his social adaptability. Developmental theory does not recognize as explicitly as it should that mature persons may be very conflicted individuals. The empirical studies have only begun to measure the facets suggested by developmental theory and have not yet explicitly explored other allocentric-autocentric manifestations, the extent and accuracy of imaginal representations, or the autonomy of the mature person.

SUMMARY

There is moderate agreement about the properties of a mature person, but it is not known how much of that agreement is due to terminological, artifactual, socio-cultural and valuational factors and how much is due to some trait patterns that empirically describe mature persons. An analysis of the formal properties of the maturity construct suggested that it is a holistic concept, probably defined by several genotypic and intercorrelated dimensions. The chapter sought to find some empirically grounded but theoretically relevant criterion to identify such underlying theoretical dimensions. Reliance on authoritative wisdom, the humanistic tradition, public opinion, social adjustment, and psychopathological criteria did not advance our search to any great extent. Instead, biopsychological developmental theories offered greater promise. Our search suggested the maturity concept could be located within a broadly conceived developmental theory about the major dimensions describing the maturing process. The maturing person becomes more stably organized, integrated, allocentric, autonomous, and more of his internal and external experiences become symbolized and available to awareness. This set of invariant developmental trends was not violated by what little empirical data were available about the more phenomenal traits of mature persons.

How does such a theoretical conception match with the actual characteristics of selected mature and immature youths? To this question the rest of the book is dedicated. The next chapter gives an overview of the specific theoretical orientation of the research and of the research strategy used to answer the question.

CHAPTER 2

The Structures and
Activities of the Person

. . . life does not reside . . . in any particular substance or combination of substances, or in any specific trait such as growth or reproduction or irritability. It is to be seen, instead, in the regulatory and organizing quality all living things display which results in their essentially purposive character, both in development and behavior. Living things are *organisms*. An organism is, first of all, an organized system of structures and activities. It is not a sprawling mass of semi-independent parts and processes but is held together under a coordinating control. This system is far more significant than the materials of which it is composed (Sinnott, 1959, p. 15).

Who is this person that matures? Just as Chapter 1 identified—albeit imprecisely—the meaning of *mature*, so must this chapter present those structures and activities that define who the *person* is that matures. But I hasten to limit the grandiosity implied in that statement of intent, for I do not intend to describe a comprehensive and systematic theory of personality. Instead, I seek to stake out a point-of-view and some terms by which to talk about the person, and to identify the structures and activities of the maturing person about which the hypotheses of the research were formed.

Who is the *person* that matures? As Sinnott's quotation asserts, the "organism is, first of all, an organized system of structures and activities," that, as I suggest, tends toward increasing stability, integration, autonomy, allocentricism, and symbolic representation. The term *person* or individual refers to the visible organism with all its observed behavioral constancies and inconstancies, consistencies and inconsistencies. The term *self*, coordinate with the term person and used as a more genotypic construct, is defined as an "organized system of structures and activities." Persons differ in their degree of "unity," "identity," or behavioral consistency and can be so ordered by psychological tests or social judgments. For example, judges can be asked to identify persons who differ in degree of consistency and organization or degree of maturity. Such procedures were used in the research to infer the degree of the organization of the self. From the theoretical notions about maturing self-organization predictions were made to more specific behavioral adaptive traits of the person.

Self-organization and adaptation are reciprocal terms, for inferences about a person's degree of self-organization are based on the quality of his adaptive behavior. Adaptive processes are processes of organization made visible when considered from the viewpoint of the self (Piaget, 1936; Waelder, 1936). The organization of the self guides adaptation by determining what is perceived, how it is assimilated, and what actions are available for accommodating to the information. Adaptation produces changes in the organization of the self by opening it to a different range of environmental information. "It is by adapting to things that thought organizes itself and it is by organizing itself that it structures things" (Piaget, 1936, p. 8).

What does "to adapt" mean? To adapt is to so regulate behavior as to optimize simultaneously both the stability of the self-structures and their accommodation to environmental requirements. For Piaget, it is to seek an equilibrium between assimilation and accommodation. This synthesis of organismic and environmental requirements may or may not result in adjustment (maximal fit to others' expectancies) as suggested in Chapter 1. The mature or well organized person is not necessarily the most adjusted person, particularly if such adjustment violates his own needs and self-structure. Too great discrepancy between the self-organization of a person and the environmental information he must assimilate is a necessary condition for producing maladaptation (disorganization and defensive behavior).

SELF-STRUCTURES AND ACTIVITIES

What "structures and activities" define self-organization? What is their relation to the trends that describe the person's developing self-organization?

The principal conceptual structures and activities that define the self are schemata (e.g., memory representations), skills (e.g., "intellectual" abilities), and valuators (e.g., motives). I do use other terms such as drive, affect, and impulse, but I do not discuss them explicitly since the research focuses primarily on the organization of self-structures.

Schemata refer to those quasi-permanent representations and classifications of information that have been assimilated into the self from external and internal sources. Schemata are constructed in the process of accommodating to such information. They help to preserve the stability of the person because, for example, they limit the range and amount of disturbing information that can be assimilated. The term *information* is used when the focus of the discussion is on the adaptation of the person; *schema* is used when the focus is on the organization of the self. Skills and valuators, on the other hand, refer to those stabilized activities (primarily imaginal) that organize, coordinate, process, and transform schemata. Although when pushed near its limit the distinction (as all of these distinctions) is arbitrary, skills refer to more cognitive whereas valuators connote more motivational types of organizers of schemata. Schemata are the contemporary records of a person's past adaptations; skills and valuators are the contemporary tools available to the organizational process.

Schemata

A variety of constructs have been proposed by which to describe the person (traits, attitudes, defenses, habits, thresholds), but only one construct most adequately connotes for us the properties of Sinnott's "organized system." The *schema* connotes a structure of interrelated or organized elements, a definite pattern of relationships. Several contemporary theorists have also used the *schema* construct to emphasize the organized aspect of personality (Church, 1961; Gardner, Holzman, Klein, Linton, & Spence, 1959; Gardner, Jackson, & Messick, 1960; Harvey, Hunt, & Schroder, 1961; McClelland, 1951). The schema construct, in contrast to the *concept* (Harvey, *et al.,* 1961), is not restricted as severely by "cognitive" connotations. The schema construct has a wider reference than *cognitive map, belief matrices,* or *category* for it also connotes such affectively organized and unstable constructs as *complexes* or more stable constructs as *sentiments.* I use the term schema in an attempt to avoid separating behavior into cognitive and affective processes both of which are but different facets of any adaptive act (Piaget, 1947). However, this is not to deny that man's more cognitively organized schemata are not decisively central to his developing self-organization. Bartlett, who introduced the schema to psychologists, illustrates the diversity among schemata. Schema

refers to an active organization of past reactions, or of past experiences, which must always be supposed to be operating in any well-adapted organic response. . . . All incoming impulses of a certain kind, or mode, go together to build up an active, organizing setting: visual, auditory, various types of cutaneous impulses and the like, at a relatively low level; all the experiences connected by a common interest; in sport, in literature, history, art, science, philosophy and so on, on a higher level. There is not the slightest reason, however, to suppose that each set of incoming impulses, each new group of experiences persists as an isolated member of some passive patchwork. They have to be regarded as constituents of living, momentary settings belonging to the organism, or to whatever parts of the organism are concerned in making a

response to a given kind, and not as a number of individual events
somehow strung together and stored within the organism (1932, p.
201).

The development of schemata follows the principles discussed
in Chapter 1. They become more stabilized, integrated, autonomous, allocentrically organized, and symbolized. However, schemata can also, under certain conditions, be reorganized following
more autocentric principles. In unusual agreement with Freud's
notions about primary process organization, Bartlett describes
autocentric forms of schemata organization as

remarkably ill-assorted and incoherent. No reference to principles of
similarity, contiguity, or succession will adequately describe such forms
of individual association. Still less can these forms be satisfactorily
placed into logical categories or relations of subordination, super-
ordination, coordination and the like. . . . It is not merely the juxta-
position of events in space or time that brings them together in vivid
imaginal form, but the fact that, however near or remote, however
dissimilar or alike they may be, they are overspread by common emotions or common interests (1932, pp. 221–223).

For Bartlett (and Freud as well), the development of social
means of communication results in a relational, abstract type of
schemata coordination. "Thinking [becomes] . . . biologically
subsequent to the image-forming process. . . . But though it is a
later and a higher development, it does not supersede the method
of images" (1932, p. 225). Both image (primary process or autocentric) and thought-word (secondary process or allocentric) methods
are necessary for adaptation. The method of images is appropriate for creating and individualizing and the thought-word method
for rationalizing and generalizing coordinations. While coordinations of schemata developmentally become more allocentric, autocentric coordinations of schemata are always recoverable in
regression for other adaptive requirements. The schemata of well
organized persons should be more allocentrically organized than
those of poorly organized persons. To measure allocentric and
autocentric types of coordinations of schemata, I relied on a new
method of classifying the images or constellations of schemata
that a person projects into the Rorschach ink blots when he is

asked, in effect, to organize the blot into a meaningful unit. An example of an autocentric image is one that unrealistically combines properties from two different unrelated percepts into a new image (an elephant with antlers). Chapter 4 defines how a score for the amount of autocentric schemata given to the Rorschach can be obtained.

What are some other examples of schemata and their coordination? Visual-motor patterns represent one type of schemata coordination. Consider the ball-catching schema. The coordination of eye movements, of perception of depth, bodily posture with the anticipated trajectory of a ball is a most complex problem usually beyond the mastery of a five-year-old—unless it is a very big ball and the distances aren't too great. But soon, with practice, component habits (motor schemata) become stabilized and coordinated, may generalize into a "catching-schema" and become readily and reversibly coordinated with other motor schema such as running, fielding, and throwing to produce a hierarchically organized but smoothly coordinated adaptive response. Schemata may also be organized around space (such as "cognitive maps" of the immediate neighborhood), time (vacation dates), numbers (daily stock market reports). Church (1961), drawing very heavily on Piaget, illustrates many other types of schemata.

Of primary concern to this study are those schemata organized around persons—other persons and one's self. Such schemata can become incredibly complex and intertwined with many conflicting drives and affects. This sector of schemata organization is usually the last to become stabilized (if it ever does) and autonomous from other sub-systems such as drives and earlier conflicts. A schema organized, for example, around "mother" may be so diffusely and complexly organized in a neurotic that many years of investigation are necessary to unravel the component patterns and threads that bind the more general schema together in order to symbolize it accurately. (Chapter 8 indicates how the amount of anxiety, defined as the anxiety threshold of the schema, a person has about interpersonal types of information was measured. Chapters 9 through 12 report the personality traits of those persons who are unable to coordinate such interpersonally organized schemata appropriately.)

Schemata organized around relationships with other persons may stabilize at different points in the developmental process. The developmental sequence of schemata stabilization used in the study was the following: desertion anxieties organized around mother and father (oral period); aggression anxieties centered around mother and father (oedipal period); affectional-sexual anxieties focused toward other males (homosexual period) and toward females (heterosexual period). I expected more mature persons would show greater schema stability to information about developmentally earlier types of schemata than would less mature persons.

Considerable effort was spent in trying to identify objectively what schemata were more stable than other schemata. Although the stability of a schema can only be measured indirectly (for reasons I postpone discussing until Chapter 7), it was possible to find both a reliable and valid way to determine which schemata were more stably organized than others. Chapter 8 describes the Phrase Association Test which measures how much associative disorganization and defensive behavior a person has for information composed of different interpersonal themes. For example, a person may show more disorganization when associating to phrases containing themes about maternal rejection than to phrases describing aggressive behavior toward fathers. It was assumed that the ability and inability to accommodate adaptively to different types of information (such as themes about maternal rejection or aggression toward fathers) meant that some schemata were less drive-involved, more stabilized, than other schemata.

Schemata also become organized around a person's self and form his self-image. The self-image gives the person a sense of personal continuity, identity, and the subjective experience of uniqueness. The "me" is more than just reflected appraisals of others (Sullivan, 1953) or organized social attitudes of the generalized other (Mead, 1934). Any sector of reality can be experienced as part of "me": one's body and bodily organs, objects identified as "mine," beliefs, groups, and for some mystics, even the universe. The self-image also includes reactions to one's own skills and valuators. What defines the boundary of the "me" schema? I know of no better criterion than that used by James (1890). The self-image includes all that the person identifies as "his" and which gives "him the same emotions" (p. 291) . . . "A warmth and intimacy about them . . . [a] consciousness of personal sameness" (p. 331). The self-image is then defined by me-constancies about which a person has feelings of possession, of warmth, and of closeness about which he may, in part, be able to verbalize.

Various self-theorists have asserted that the self-image has a decisive and determining influence on the adaptation of the person (Rogers, 1959a; Snygg & Combs, 1949). Considerable research has been done within the past decade on some aspects of the self-image such as self-esteem and self-insight that are presumed to be related to adaptation (Wylie, 1961). The centrality of the self-image in mediating adaptation stems, in part, from the fact that it is a superordinate schema that may serve to integrate a large number of other schemata. As a schema, it has the function of either not assimilating (denying or repressing) information incongruent with it; severely distorting or otherwise defending itself against such information, or accommodating (changing the self-image) to contradictory information. The self-image of a person also restricts and determines the types of accommodative possibilties available to him (e.g., "I am not a good student; therefore I won't apply to college").

Because of the importance of the self-image in affecting how a person adapts to certain types of information, the differences in the self-image of well and poorly organized persons were examined in detail. The developing self-image was expected to become more stable, integrated, autonomous, allocentric, and symbolized in awareness. Well organized persons were expected to have a more mature self-image than poorly organized persons. A Self-Image Questionnaire was developed which, when administered under different instructional and experimental conditions, provided measures of these various properties that theoretically define a mature self-image. (Chapter 5 reports the studies on these properties of the self-image in various criterion groups.)

Skills

The self has been defined, in the words of Sinnott, as an "organized system of structures and activities . . . held together under a coordinating control." Schemata are the "materials of which . . . [the self] . . . is composed." They are *coordinated* by skills and valuators in accommodating to the requirements of the adaptive task. Different adaptive tasks require different types of skillful coordinations. Many types of skills (abilities, cognitive controls, ego functions) necessary for different adaptive tasks have been identified. But this is not the place to pursue psychology's long and diligent quest for the factors or structures or abilities appropriate for different adaptive tasks (mechanical, clerical, intellectual). Instead, my aim is to identify those most central skills of the maturing person that aid his adaptation to the tasks he encounters in his personal development—tasks involving separation from and aggression toward parents, affectional and sexual relations with men and women. This is but another way of asking what skills are most central to good ego strength or, more narrowly, to Freud's construct of secondary process. If we could tentatively identify some of the more important coordinating skills, we could then determine whether well organized persons do more skillfully and adaptively coordinate schemata organized around interpersonal relationships than do poorly organized persons.

Clearly, the most pressing question is how to identify the skills that facilitate adaptation? My solution was to rely on Piaget's (1947) developmental studies and theory which suggested that conceptual, analytic-synthetic, and judgmental skills were the principal methods of the mature person in coordinating schemata. (I postpone further discussion of the numerous theoretical issues involved in this solution until Part III when I present the systematic research on how mature persons maintain their stability when confronted by disturbing information.) Presumably, when faced by information that is potentially disorganizing, a more mature person's coordinating skills are more resistant to impairment than are those skills of the less mature person. That is, a mature person's conceptual, analytic, and judgmental coordinations are relatively stable and autonomous of persuasive information not directly relevant to the solution process itself; they remain allocentrically focused and resistant to regressive encroachments by conceptual condensations and autistically determined judgments. These coordinations are adaptively related with each other (a person can judgmentally evaluate which conceptual solution is correct), and are available to awareness and conscious manipulation. In Part III, I describe the tests developed to measure conceptual, analytic, and judgmental coordinations of disturbing information and the procedures used to determine how stable or resistant such skills are to the disturbing effects of threatening information.

Valuators

Valuators in concert with environmental requirements guide the coordinations of schemata to optimize self-organization and adaptation. A valuator is a dispositional type construct that includes interests, dynamic attitudes, beliefs, values, and motives. But since internal bodily demands and impulses developmentally become increasingly associated with imaginal schemata and are usually represented in awareness as images (instinct-derivatives), valuators may assume some structural properties of schemata. Why is a motive (a more "pure" motivational construct) included as a valuator? A motive is defined as a drive that has become stably coordinated with specific classes of goals or reinforcers. These goals are represented imaginally. Furthermore, in development, drives tend toward "taming" by cognizing. That is, they become associated with complex schemata patterns of anticipations, concepts, instrumental means all organized around imaginal representations which elicit approach and avoidant responses. This type of schemata grouping I call a motive. Valuators such as interests, convictions, and motives serve to organize many different types of schemata for adaptive purposes. Smith, Bruner, and White (1956) have described in some detail the integrating function of valuators (dynamic attitudes) and their complex relation to other types of schemata. From the developmental trends given in Chapter 1, I expected that the valuators of the maturing person become more stable (persist over time), integrated (minimal internal conflict between valuators), allocentric (motives centered more around others than self), autonomous (independent of childish motives), and cognitively represented (awareness of major regnant motives). The research did not explicitly focus on these possible developmental properties of valuators. No new tests were developed to measure these theoretically induced differences between the well and poorly organized youths, nor were explicit hypotheses formulated to predict specific valuator differences between extreme criterion groups. However, some standard tests of valuators were used (Strong Vocational Interest Blank, Allport's Study of Values test, and the California F scale of authoritarianism), and while these tests did not directly define the properties of maturing valuators, they did offer some hints about whether well and poorly organized men do differ on the suggested properties of maturing valuators. Chapter 6 summarizes the little evidence available about mature valuators.

SUMMARY

The chapter sketches the theoretical language used to describe the person, or, in more abstract terms, his self-organization. The structures that define self-organization are schemata, skills, and valuators. Such self-structures develop according to the developmental principles described in Chapter 1. The schemata, skills, and valuators of the more mature person were hypothesized to be more stable, integrated, allocentrically organized, autonomous, and symbolized than the self-structures of the less mature person. In pursuing this hypothesis, the research describes in Part II the measures that define the developmental maturity of a person's schemata and self-image and identifies personal, social, and life history differences between mature and immature college males. The research strategy shifts in Part III to investigate one developmental dimension in depth by discovering if well organized men are indeed, as developmental theory suggests, more stably organized persons. Do such persons skill-fully master personally disturbing information more adaptively than do poorly organized persons? What are the personality traits of persons who conceptually, analytically, and judgmentally adapt to disturbing information without regression and disor-ganization?

PART **II**

Empirical Studies of
Measures of Maturity and of
the Characteristics of Mature
and Immature College Men

CHAPTER 3

Consensual Judgments of Maturity: The Research Samples and Procedures

Consensual judgments were used to identify the most and least mature men within a small college community. While we expected more mature persons would be more stable, integrated, and allocentric than less mature persons, regardless of the social setting within which they were being studied, we did not expect the degree of their maturity or immaturity on each developmental dimension to be unaffected by the prevailing informal expectations and values of the college. A college's rewards and punishments may encourage maturing on some developmental dimensions and retard growth on others. Every empathic teacher knows some students whose growth has been stymied or even reversed by various educational forms. Greenwich Village, the army, the Junior year abroad, or a different type of college have been the salvation or, unfortunately, the progressive undoing of many a youngster in search of a temporary environment that, speaking to his condition, releases and guides his suppressed growth trends. It took only twenty-four hours for Salinger's fugitive, Holden Caulfield, to catch a glimpse of his identity in New York City. An institution's idiosyncratic expectations and values

may have even more direct and immediate effects on research
that uses consensual judgments as its selection strategy. Judges
may identify the (immaturely) adjusted rather than the (maturely)
adapted person as mature. Some very mature persons may refuse
to accommodate themselves to immature and unusual institutional forms, and from within the phenomenal world of the
judges of that institution such persons may appear to be mal-
contents and unseemly renegades. Because no objective methods
and little actual data are available by which to compare the
maturing effect of one institution to that of another (Brown,
1961; E. L. Hunt, 1963; Jacob, 1957; Sanford, 1956, 1964; Stern,
1962), I can only mention the College's more atypical forms and
values and then intuitively assess their effect on the maturing
of its students. The assessment is based on extensive freshman
psychological test data, wide-ranging searching interviews, and
many varieties of student self-reports, papers, and publications.
Hopefully, such impressions may provide clues about the limits
of maturity and immaturity our samples will represent. Following these impressions, the chapter turns to other issues involved
in using consensual judgments, describes the samples of mature
and immature youths used in the research, returns to examine
consensual judgments, and then briefly overviews the research
procedures used with the criterion groups.

THE MATURING EFFECT
OF THE COLLEGE

No institution remakes any adolescent into its own image, whatever that may be, and Haverford College is certainly
no exception. Observers of the College such as Jacob (1957) as
well as its students claim the College does transform its students' lives. Such an alleged transformation is not simply a
product of the institution's values; rather, the change is the
product of the *interaction* of the students' values and personality
structure with the values and expectations of the institution.
What then is the typical Haverford student like and how ma-

turely developed is he on the dimensions that define a mature person.

The Haverford College Underclassman

Haverford College is a small residential liberal arts men's college, whose entering freshman class numbered only one hundred and twenty-five at the time of the research. Close up, each student seems very different from every other. From far away, perhaps there is a typical Haverford student, who, from an even greater distance, may not differ noticeably from the typical bright eighteen year old males now emerging out of affluent American suburbs. What may he be like? The typical freshman comes from a moderately wealthy home and his father is likely to be a doctor, lawyer, educational administrator, or, more likely, a business executive. He comes from the upper fifth of his high school class and has scholastic aptitudes that place him above most students in the country (median verbal and quantitative CEEB scores above the 95%). When asked to describe himself on adjective check lists, he says he is mentally quick, alert, sharp-witted, critical, and highly verbal. He prefers theory, abstraction, and broad generalization to fact, rote learning, and the discipline of detail. In contrast to other college freshmen, the Haverford student is much more reflectively, if not philosophically and idealistically inclined. He values the world of thought much more than the world of action. It is by pursuing self-knowledge rather than by acting that he seeks his identity. Pragmatic compromises, economic values, manipulative power and political machinations and complexities scarcely appeal to the Haverford youth. Intellectualism and a cultivated coolness enable the typical freshman to feel both power and security in his relations with others. He is not afraid to complain, to be sharply critical of anyone and everyone (even of himself), and to argue with the most high (even with the alumni)! The Haverford student has a marvelous way of using humor and sarcasm to carry an attack. His letters to the college newspaper and his frequently epigrammatic comments during compulsory Quaker Meeting reveal a penetrating wisdom, a sharpness of insight, that is unexpected in most young men. He is studiously irreverent, calculatedly cynical, fearful of sentimentality, inhibited and restrained.

The typical Haverford freshman is not a highly assertive male marked by dash and adventurousness. He wears his beard almost shyly! He is more sensitive and perhaps more passive and may be in more conflict about his needs for others than many other college freshmen. He is not an earthy, socially initiating, self- or status seeking male of strong passions and authoritative dominating stature. Nor is he the anonymous organization man or the bureaucrat "on the way up." Conscious of himself, if not centered in himself, perhaps awkward around others, he does sense a distinctive identity, though he may not know what it is. He is thoughtful, intense, sincere, honest, but too critical and doubtful of himself. These doubts, not unusual in entering freshmen, become magnified in his early college years as he finds he never does quite well enough. What often appears as insufferable intellectual vanity is only an unconscious defense against a deepening and, for some, devastating lack of self-confidence. By identifying with the imagined reputation of the College, he justifies himself publicly, although he continues to blame and deprecate himself privately for not fulfilling his, or the College's, expectations.

The Haverford freshman (as most young American college males) does not feel comfortable in close intimate emotional relationships. Love of a woman is not with carefree abandon but with a stylized tentativeness. The typical freshman dates only infrequently; he feels his energies absorbed by heavy academic and extracurricular duties. To experience intimacy not only with one's own thoughts and more precious feelings but also with those of another does not seem to be as highly valued. He finds it safer to play it cool, rather than to allow himself to become entwined within the life of another or within the grips of a belief. He remains primarily an observer, not quite willing to commit himself. Paradoxically, the Haverford man's reluctance to allow himself to be drawn into dependent relations with either his friends or his faculty only screens a deeper and less conscious wish to be so involved, to be given affection and respect, continued reassurance and guidance. A student's most bitter source of dissatisfaction with the College is that it is not motherly enough! He thinks (unrealistically so) its administration willfully does not understand him, its faculty is indifferent to him, and its cooks don't feed him properly.

A Haverford student consciously values his freedom and autonomy. He prizes the lack of group and social pressure to make him into that which he isn't. He values personal integrity and individuality and the opportunity to express what he is, although he may not know what he is. He knows that he does not have to appear what he isn't—except to appear, if he can, as an individualist knowing what he is. But once he lets you know him, he turns out to be a delightfully shy and warm person not quite sure what to do with his more sensitive and affectionate feelings.

How developmentally mature is the modal Haverford freshman? Given his past record of high achievement (not only in academic work), the very selective screening out of youths too immature in the admissions process, and objective personality test data secured from him in his first week in College, my hunch is that he is a reasonably mature youth for his age. The *cognitive internalization* of his world is the leading edge of his personal development. He is undoubtedly far advanced in his awareness of both his personal and social worlds, in his capacity to maintain an abstract attitude, and in his intellectual assimilation and mastery of his culture. His heavy reliance on intellectual skills probably insures considerable *stability*—at least to disturbing types of intellectual information. However, his excessive cognitive development may retard the *integration* of his emotional, impulsive, aesthetic, intuitive, and social experiences into his dominating intellectualism. Jacob (1957) feels the Haverford freshman is more *allocentrically* centered than his privativistic peers in his interests and beliefs, but my data do not speak clearly on this point. He may be very cognitively realistic and logical but he may be alienated from his *autocentric* needs and find life does not have the zest, warmth, and meaning that it otherwise could have for him if he allowed himself to get closer to others and to his own impulses. There is some reason to suggest that his heavy conscious emphasis on the theoretical and intellectual and his inhibition in expressing his emotionally dependent needs indicate some lack of *autonomy* from his parents (not unique to Haverford men). The Haverford freshman seems to have as his major developmental task the incorporation into his refined cognitive organization the worlds of feeling, passion, and devotion which will then produce more than just intellectual commitment.

The College's Expectations and Values

The typical freshman, if there be such, probably does not differ from other male students of other comparable colleges that attract bright youngsters from the upper social and economic classes of contemporary America. And the College itself is probably no different from most other colleges in most respects. But both the faculty and the students say there is a distinctive Haverford atmosphere, a unique pattern of expectations and values, that makes the College idiosyncratic but effective in educating its developing students. That atmosphere, that "peculiar potency" in the words of Jacob (1957), is largely the product of the College's small size, intellectual and Quaker traditions.

The College's small student body (four hundred and sixty men) and proportionately large faculty (sixty full-time) mean that classes are small, that tutorial and individual project work are possible, and that the faculty and students are widely, and, in some cases, quite closely, known to each other. Despite such favorable opportunities for close faculty-student relations, the students mystify the faculty by failing to take advantage of such opportunities and then by complaining that the faculty is disinterested in them. The faculty expect relationships to be on an intellectual basis; the students on some more personal but vaguely indefinable basis. Some evidence suggests the youths are in conflict about strong needs to be dependent and passive. They react by overasserting their independence and autonomy. They want to know they have unlimited intellectual and other opportunities but they shy away from participating with the young and verbally aggressive faculty in optimizing those opportunities.

The College's small size facilitates communication among students, most of whom know most of the student body; it encourages the working out of common ethical codes and their quiet internalization as felt self-imposed controls. The small size also maximizes the possibility that the faculty may influence student personal and value development, particularly as there is no viable student peer culture that opposes and so competes with the values of the faculty.

The intellectual tradition of the College is sternly demanding. The faculty is a young (median age is less than forty) professionally and research-oriented group of men and women who have high expectations and persistent drives to achieve. It expects the same concentrated and devoted effort from its students. In contrast to most other college groups, the typical student accepts and defends the College's intellectual demands. He doesn't respect "gut" courses or the "gentleman C" grade. The faculty and student body do agree about what is important at Haverford. The consequence is that social partying, heavy dating, drinking, athletics and other patterns of living, of fulfilling youthful needs, are not "institutionalized" as group values. Other consequences are that the students do accept many faculty as intellectual models but they too seldom develop the level of competence both they and the faculty hold them to. To achieve and maintain his fragile self-regard, a student may turn his great ambition and his suppressed capacities for action and self-determination to other areas of concern, particularly extracurricular activities like the College publications, Glee Club, or class night variety shows, but without ever abandoning or devaluing his basic value of the importance of academic achievement. By the time a student is a senior, he plans to become a medical specialist, a laboratory researcher, or a scholarly professor but not a commanding figure in industry, a driving junior executive that leads United Fund campaigns, or a charismatic politician. The interaction between high quality students and a demanding academic environment produces distinguished records of achievement. For example, the College has had more Woodrow Wilson scholars proportional to its size than any other educational institution in the country and it ranks high on most measures of alumni scholarly productivity and eminence.

The College's Quaker tradition embodying the ideals that

value independent inquiry, self-determination, responsibility, integrity, equality, and consistently liberal, if not radical, social concerns is closely congruent with the prevailing orientation of academic intellectuals. Although the Quaker values may not have a decisive effect on the students independent of the effect of a similarly oriented faculty, the Quaker heritage silently guarantees both to the faculty and the student body freedom from autocratic and authoritarian impositions and serves as an unspoken moral framework within which more specific ethical judgments are more consciously formed. The Quaker values find expression in many forms: the absence of competition for social status, the respect for dissenting views, the stimulation of honest criticism, the absence of social cliques such as fraternities, the refusal to accept Defense Department research grants, the encouragement of student responsibility. As one example of the latter, the Student Council is one of the most powerful in the country. In addition to budgetary control over all campus organizations, it has control over the students' Honor System which regulates and enforces student academic and sexual codes. The Council has a full range of sanctions, including expulsion from College, at its disposal.

The Honor System, the codes of which are defined and exclusively enforced by the students themselves, is accepted and internalized by most students. Violations, particularly by any group of students, are perceived as threats to the trust the students place in each other, to the "fragile camaraderie of our interpersonal relationships," in the words of one Yearbook editor (Record, 1957). The effects of the Honor System are to provide some student-supported and commonly shared ethical bases for behavior, to free many students from the sharply troublesome decisions young males are sometimes forced to make when their own values conflict with those of a more typical masculine group, to reduce social pressures on the men to "make out" with their dates, to induce considerable guilt and anxiety in some youths unable to resist either the temptation to cheat on examinations and papers or to have sexual relations on the campus. The Honor System's sexual codes (no sexual relations on the campus) combined with the permissive allowance to entertain girls in one's rooms until early in the morning may produce considerable conflict and tension. Many students escape such tension by not dating frequently.

One of the most distinctive and controversial ways the College's religious tradition is implemented is compulsory Quaker Meeting in which the students and members of the faculty come together to worship silently unless some person is moved to speak. Quaker Meeting is not easily accepted by many students who might deny it has any maturing effects. However, the experience of attending Meeting brings students into an intimate relationship with the Friends' values of respect for others, equality of individual worth, individual responsibility, and loving acceptance of others. It encourages the faculty and student community to meet with each other on a far different basis than they do most of the week, to interpret their common problems at a different level of experience than is usually possible in other colleges. Ethical problems and religious insights are explored from different viewpoints and may result in a person's expanded awareness of his own clouded experience and feelings. Meeting permits the entire intellectual community to regress to less rational and more intuitive and emotional forms of thinking, thus providing some legitimate access to unconscious and intellectually suppressed impulses and feelings. Meeting may provide some with the opportunity to experience developing wisdom as well as academic intellectualism. And finally, some alumni claim Meeting provides a deeply meaningful and unifying experience with other people, an experience which they cherish as one of the most central influences of their Haverford education.

What does the College do to its students? One perceptive student claimed it made the mature more mature and the immature more immature. Perhaps the effect can be summarized this way as well. The College encourages maturing in those areas the freshmen are already maturely developed in for their age; it is less effective in helping students to mature in those areas in which as freshmen they are less maturely developed.

The College setting provides a strong value-orientation, the non-doctrinal nature of which can facilitate the *stabilization* of its youths when they are faced by a variety of moral choices. That the students value such an orientation can be seen by their definition of a mature person (Table 1–1, page 6) in which they ranked respecting and valuing others and possessing integrating values much higher than did the experts. The reflective nature of the College's dominant educational pattern, its emphasis on conscious self-determination, its provision for community self-appraisal by means of various institutions (Meeting, unfettered student publications) must optimize the expansion of *self-awareness* and the assimilation of much externally and internally wrought experience into the consciousness of its students. Concomitant with such a developmental influence, I expect the youths develop considerable *autonomy* from situational determinants since such influences are under constant reflective scrutiny and since some of the College's practices (Meeting) deliberately eschew resort to situational props. But it is much less clear that the College, given the type of student it attracts, provides as adequate opportunities for mature *allocentric* self-organization around the personal lives of others. Again, recall from Table 1–1, page 6, the expert psychologists ranked as central the capacity of a mature person to experience personal love, deep friendships, tenderness, and personal involvement in the lives of others whereas the Haverford youths completely ignored this quality in their description of a mature person. Only in highly derivative and group forms, like the Glee Club, are the men able to express such feelings or secure a personal sense of emotional belongingness with others. The lack of a strongly viable or successful football team, for example, dampens and limits opportunities for group emotional identification or expression of such social "belongingness" feelings. It is such experiences that tie youths together, to their College, and to causes beyond themselves.

How effective the College is in assisting its students to develop more *autonomous* behavior from the unresolved, earlier formed and less mature needs (dependency) and conflicts (parental identification) is also not clear. The students consciously value their freedom, their independence and intellectualism. Paradoxically, in describing a mature person it was the experts who ranked self-reliance and independence as central mature traits, and the

Haverford students who failed even to mention them. Certainly, the faculty and institutional expectations and values emphasize independence, intellectual initiative, and provide forms for the development of such initiative in the intellectual and religious areas. But students optimize such initiative and independence primarily in extracurricular activities (which the College also provides in abundance). While difficult to assess, these possible contradictions suggest that the College (and probably other colleges as well) has not been successful in finding appropriate educational patterns by which to encourage its students to become more maturely autonomous.

Finally, the College certainly provides many means for furthering the progressive *self-integration* of its students in the intellectual, extracurricular, and possibly religious areas. However, the intellectual tradition is so commanding, given the students' lack of strong inner or temperamental pushes toward social, emotional, impulse and need expression that many students become even more stretched out of shape at the College than when they entered. While consciously valuing such a tradition and working very hard to fulfill it, many resist this non-integrating distorting effect by unconsciously withholding full emotional commitment to the intellectual way of life and by seeking integration in other ways. Their social, emotional, and tender needs, for love and devotion for receiving and giving friendship, frequently remain unfulfilled and serve to limit and to put a brake on the fuller development of intrinsic academic motives and potentially superb intellectual skills. No human institution speaks to the condition of every man or to all of the growth potential in any one man. Haverford speaks eloquently to some growth trends, but only mutedly to others.

MATURITY AND CONSENSUAL JUDGMENTS

We wish to study the most mature and immature youths of the Haverford population. How are such persons to be reliably identified if we do not yet know what traits define mature persons? Firm valid knowledge about such trait patterns still eludes us, and no convincingly valid and objective methods are available by which to select mature persons to study. Is our dilemma a hopeless one? No, for, as we saw in Chapter 1, considerable agreement does exist about some of the traits that define a mature person. Studies of mature persons must begin at this level of agreement, must explore, probe, and be alert to clues that will push both valid knowledge and methodology into more reliable, precise areas. So we began by relying on consensual judgments about who were and who were not mature in the Haverford population. Hopefully, out of such a bootstrap operation will come suggestions about how to refine both theory and methods more precisely.

The research strategy of using selected criterion groups of mature and immature persons has been vigorously attacked as inappropriate on the grounds that what is discovered is only the criterion for which the groups were selected (value preferences of judges) and only the traits for which the groups were measured or observed. The research can only "come out with distinctions already built into the procedure of investigation, either explicitly or surreptitiously" (M. B. Smith, 1959, p. 680). This criticism is valid *if* judge selected groups represent *only* the value preferences of the judges and *if* the value preferences do not correspond to meaningful psychological congruencies. Furthermore, such a criticism has considerable force if research on mature persons only explored the same level of behavior as that used to select the mature person. The subsequent chapters describe procedures designed to go far beyond the phenomenal criteria the selecting judges used. *If* the context of the results obtained from a great variety of procedures measuring different "levels" of self-organization is internally consistent, is also consistent with theoretical expectation, is replicable over varying samples, and is consistent with results found from other studies using different samples and procedures, *then* perhaps our critic's position becomes less tenable and viable.

The use of criterion groups selected by judges provoked other questions such as "Who is to be a judge?" and "Must different *types* of judges agree about who is and who is not mature?" To what range and types of activities must a person adapt maturely within an institution to be identified as a mature person in that institution? I assumed from the holistic position taken in Chapter 1 that a mature person will reveal this maturity not only in a wide range of socio-cultural settings but also in a range of activities and interpersonal relationships within one institution. This assumption indirectly helped to determine who were to be judges and who were to be the mature and immature persons to study. To identify those persons who maturely adapt in a wide sector of their lives (social, intellectual, authoritative, competitive), it was necessary to use as many different types of judges as possible (student, faculty, administration, and coaches). Reliance on only faculty judges, for example might produce "mature" and "immature" groups extremely divergent in one area such as in the intellectual or on one developmental dimension such as cognitive symbolization but not in other areas such as the social or on other dimensions such as allocentricism (Barron, 1954, 1963). No other study of selected mature and immature persons has used more than one type of judge (Barron, 1954, 1963; Bond, 1950, 1952).

Another issue is, how appropriate is the research strategy for the type of institutional setting in which it is used? To identify persons who are mature in a wide sector of their lives becomes imposingly difficult when the activities of a person take place in many different socio-cultural settings (office, neighborhood, church, country club) or in a large institution such as a university where interpersonal relationships occur on more specialized or narrow bases. Research on mature persons in a self-contained and small social community has some real advantages. Consensual agreement about who is mature and immature should be maximized in a small society in which more of the activities of a person are known to more people. I sought judges who knew a large number of youths of the population and who knew them in a variety of different types of relationships. The identification of mature and immature persons can also be more valid in a small college where situational differences may account for less of the variance in the quality of a person's adaptation than would be the case in a more heterogeneous or multi-institutional society. A small college is like a monastery insofar as it is a comprehensive community. Type of work, relaxation, satisfaction of bodily needs, religious experience and other activities are the same for most members. Differences in the quality of adaptation within such a community cannot be readily attributed just to situational differences since the situational demands are relatively similar for most.

SAMPLES: CRITERION GROUPS AND THEIR SELECTION

Three major and several minor samples were used in the research. (The term "sample" does not imply a randomly drawn sample representative of the Haverford population.) The major samples, called the Maturity, the Organized, and the Standard samples, were each composed of two contrasting criterion groups. The minor samples, called the Case Study, Michigan, and Personality samples, were not divided into criterion groups. Table 3–1 gives an overview of the major and minor samples, their methods of selection, and the principal function they served in the research. I will discuss only the major samples in detail and postpone further discussion of the minor samples until their procedures and data are relevant to the discussion.

Maturity Sample

The ten most and the ten least mature juniors and seniors of the College were selected by eighteen members of the faculty, administration, and student body. These judges independently selected from class lists those most mature and immature men "for their age." *Mature* was defined to be "personal, social, and intellectual effectiveness," not "pleasing appearance, high grades, or popularity." *Immature* was defined as ineffective "personally, socially, and intellectually." The most frequently cited ten mature and ten immature men participated in the study. (Labeling the groups *mature* and *immature* is not meant to imply that the mature men have reached some ideal end point of development. To be more precise, such groups should be called *more mature* and *less mature*. I don't know in absolute

TABLE 3-1: THE RESEARCH SAMPLES[1] AND THEIR PURPOSE

SAMPLE	N	METHOD OF SELECTION	PURPOSE
Case Study	10	Screened Volunteers	Study of traits of normal persons. Data used to check consistency of findings of other samples.
Maturity	20	Judge selected ten most mature and ten most immature	Study of selection and assessment procedures. Data used to check consistency of findings of Organized sample.
Michigan (University of)	16	Volunteers from honors sections	Major pilot study of test procedures for Part III.
Organized	24	Judge selected twelve most and twelve least organized	Principal sample of the research.
Standard	36	Volunteers	Standardization study of tests developed for Part III. Data used to check consistency of Organized sample.
Personality	10	Members of advanced psychology course	Replicate results obtained with self-image test.

[1] Other samples used in the development of specific tests are reported in connection with the tests in question.

terms how far along a continuum of maturity the criterion groups were.)

For later data analysis purposes, the members of the sample were also rank-ordered from most to least mature on the basis of the amount of judge agreement about their maturity. For example, the person most frequently cited to be mature was ranked first; the person most frequently cited to be immature was ranked twentieth; the person in the mature group about whom there was least agreement was ranked tenth.

Some lessons were learned about how to select mature and immature criterion groups from this preliminary study that influenced the procedures used to select the Organized sample. Without giving the detailed data, it was very clear the judges had no difficulty selecting the most mature men of the population; not one mature person in the sample was so identified by *less* than half of the eighteen different judges. But the judges did not agree about those who were immature; not one of the immature persons in the sample was so identified by *more* than one-half of the eighteen judges. Why? First, the number of obviously immature youths is severely restricted not only by very selective screening for immaturity during the admissions process but also by the withdrawal from college of many of the immature and disturbed youths prior to their junior year. Second, the term *immature* may have referred to a broader spectrum of behavior for the judges than did the term *mature,* for more students were identified by the judges as immature than were identified as mature. The immature group was quite heterogeneous. My impression (supported by the Rorschach results) was that it included very rigid and odd character problems, severely disorganized and anxious youths, and some socially naive and inept boys. Obviously, the selection criteria had to clarify the meaning of the term *immature.*

Organized Sample

The twelve most and twelve least well organized upperclassmen of the College were selected by eighteen judges using much more extensive and regularized judging procedures than were used in selecting the Maturity sample. The terms *good and poor self-organization* were used to be more congruent with the language described in Chapter 2 and will be used as synonyms of *mature and immature* throughout the book. The nine students who were judged by the President of the Students' Council to know most of the student body and who were also judged by the Dean and several key faculty to also be of sound judgment served as the student judges. The nine academic and athletic faculty and administration judges were selected who had the greatest opportunity to know a large number of students in a variety of settings.

The selection procedure was as follows. The judges, working independently of each other and of any knowledge of the research program, rated each upperclassman on a scale measuring degree of acquaintance. One to three weeks later, each judge was told the study was about self-organization, that "good self-organization or poor self-organization is manifested in many areas of life (social, academic, extracurricular, athletic, and personal) rather than in just one or two areas." He was given the criteria defining good and poor self-organization listed on page 68. The criteria are general restatements of some of the genotypic developmental trends given in Chapter 1.

Each judge then identified the ten most well and ten most poorly organized persons in each class from lists of the three upper classes. Sophomores were included to increase the number of poorly organized men available to study, although enlarging the population risked reducing judge agreement and increasing the heterogeneity of the criterion groups. If the sophomore year confronts a young male with an "identity crisis" because he must make a tentative vocational decision (choose a departmental major), then even mature sophomores may show considerable temporary disturbance (Sanford, 1957). The population was 289 students. Veterans, married students, and youths whose college career had been interrupted by prolonged absences had been excluded. From the total thirty well and thirty poorly organized men, the judge next named the ten most well and ten most poorly organized youths regardless of class.

To secure some information about the judges' perceptions of the groups, each judge completed a 185 item Adjective Check

WELL ORGANIZED GROUP	POORLY ORGANIZED GROUP
1. Behavior control is reliable and predictable.	1. Behavior control is erratic and unpredictable.
2. Behavior determined by flexible but firm inner controls (manifested by a sense of direction).	2. Behavior determined by impulse or by pressures of social environment (minimal self-defined sense of direction).
3. Unity and harmony between action, feeling, and intellect.	3. Lack of integration between action, feeling, and intellect.
4. Sense of identity.	4. No sense of identity.

DO NOT INCLUDE THE FOLLOWING:

1. Rigid compulsive individuals whose good organization is forced and who are incapable of relaxing their overcontrol (the driven, harried, well organized person).	1. Non-conformists or "odd" individuals who do not meet the above criteria for the poorly organized group (deviant persons may or may not be well organized).
2. Individuals of special talents whose effectiveness may not be due to sound personal organization (intellectual brilliance, good social adjustment, or athletic skill are not necessarily in themselves indices of good self-organization).	2. Ineffective poor students, social isolates, or athletic incompetents whose ineffectiveness may be due to other determinants (handicaps) than those listed above. Such ineffective individuals may not be particularly disorganized persons.

List (ACL) on each of the ten most well and poorly organized men he had selected and then circled the five adjectives that best described why he had selected the youth. The ACL was based on all adjectives suggested by theory and empirical studies to describe mature and immature people, Gough's (1955, 1960) adjective check list, Cattell's (1946) basic personality source traits, and the student definitions of maturity cited in Chapter 1.

Ten months later each judge completed a rating scale (Self-Image Questionnaire described in Chapter 5) for those four youths used in the study whom the judge indicated he knew most intimately. The judge may or may not have initially identified the youth as well or poorly organized.

The men who were most frequently cited by both types of judges as either well or poorly organized were identified. From this larger sample were drawn two groups of twelve men that did not differ in either verbal or quantitative aptitude. The men were invited to participate for pay in the program, the purpose of which was "to determine the characteristics of individuals who differ in their ability to think in organized sequences in a variety of different personal situations." They were told they had been selected on the basis of several criteria, including judge ratings of self-organization. They were also warned that some tests were "novel and challenging," "frustrating and irritating," and they could withdraw from the experiment at any time. All of the twelve well and twelve poorly organized men completed the study.

As with the Maturity sample, the twenty-four members of the Organized sample were also rank-ordered in terms of degree of self-organization on the basis of the amount of consensual agreement about their identification as either well or poorly organized.

To get some preliminary hints about how the well and the poorly organized men were perceived to differ, let us now look at the Adjective Check List (ACL) results of the selecting judges. No argument is made that the ACL results definitively or validly describe either the judges' bases of selection or the organized and disorganized men's "real" trait differences. Most parsimoniously, the judged trait differences between the groups can only be interpreted to define the judge *stereotypes* of organized and disorganized men. In hindsight, the judges' trait descriptions should have been cross-validated by independent ACL ratings from other judges who did not know why the men were selected.

First, what traits did the judges report they used to *select* the organized and disorganized men of the Organized sample? The twelve well organized men were selected, so the judges claim, for possessing the following traits, which are listed in order of decreasing judge agreement: capable, conscientious, clear-thinking, responsible, efficient, good judgment, wide interests, consistent, ambitious, creative, independent, intellectual, and self-controlled. The disorganized men were selected for these traits, also listed in order of decreasing agreement: erratic, disorderly, changeable, purposeless, irresponsible, cynical, impulsive, lacks vitality, apathetic, bottled-up, dissatisfied, and passive. A harsh critic could claim these distinguishing trait lists only tell us that the judges *report* they dutifully followed the research instructions which asked them to select essentially in the terms the judges reported they used. This judgment is technically correct.

However, the two trait lists do make more vividly concrete how the groups were thought to diverge and, in one sense, define operationally what is meant by "socially judged self-organization and disorganization."

TABLE 3–2: JUDGED TRAIT DIFFERENCES BETWEEN
WELL AND POORLY ORGANIZED MEN

WELL ORGANIZED			POORLY ORGANIZED		
.01[1]	.02	.05	.01	.02	.05
adaptable	anticipates	calm		erratic	awkward
alert	consequences	cheerful			disorderly
ambitious	cooperative	deep interests			indecisive
capable	creative	good-natured			moody
clear-thinking	enterprising	insightful			scattered
coherent	fair-minded	intellectual			
common sense	honest	quick (mental)			
completes plans	self-driving	realistic			
conscientious		resourceful			
considerate		well-			
consistent		coordinated			
determined					
efficient					
friendly					
good judgment					
initiative					
logical					
persistent					
reasonable					
reliable					
responsible					
self-controlled					
sincere					

[1] Two-tailed significance level determined by Fisher's exact probability test for two independent samples.

Second, how were the twelve organized men judged to differ from the twelve disorganized men? Table 3–2 reports the traits that significantly (two-tailed) distinguished the organized from the disorganized men. Apparently, judges can agree more readily about the traits that define good than poor self-organization. Surely, at least from the vantage point of the eighteen judges, the organized men were highly effective men, possessing all of the goal-directed traits that form most stereotyped views of what such men are like. These results are remarkably similar to those of Barron (1954, 1963) who found "sound" persons were judged to be efficient, well integrated, adaptable, organized, persistent, and resourceful whereas the unsound persons were considered to be confused, undependable, dissatisfied, and defensive. But in contrast to Barron's findings, the selecting judges did not view the well organized men as completely impersonal, emotionally detached automatons, for they were judged to be more friendly and considerate, cheerful, and good-natured than the disorganized men.

Standard Sample

The Standard sample consisted of thirty-six youths who volunteered (for pay) to participate in a study replicating the design of the Organized sample's study. The purpose of studying this sample was to secure data for developing standard scores (hence the name of the sample) for some new tests, and to check both the validity of some new measures as well as the consistency of the findings of the other samples.

The sample is *not* comparable to the Organized sample, however. I had exhausted the available most well and poorly organized men from three successive classes in securing the Organized sample; consequently, the Standard sample was a much more homogeneous sample and contained no person who was judged to be very well or very poorly organized. Of the applicants for the study, thirty-six met the other criteria used in selecting the Organized sample. Every student completed the six to seven hours of experimental tests.

Even though the Standard sample was not a good cross-validation replicate of the Organized sample, it was desirable for the purposes of data analysis to order the members of the sample in terms of judged self-organization. Accordingly, several months following the completion of the study, independent judgments of the degree of organization of the members of the sample as well as of the representativeness of the sample to the Haverford population were secured. Nine students, members of an advanced psychology class, who had not participated in the major studies and who were reasonably sound and mature persons (judged by Rorschach, college test data, and personal knowledge of them) served as judges. Each judge completed the same type acquaintance scale used by the judges of the Organized sample. Then he assigned each individual to one of five categories of self-organization ranging from very well to very poorly organized. The extreme categories (very well and very poorly organized) were defined as they had been for the judges of the Organized sample. Each judge next rank-ordered the students within each category. The median of the judges' ranks for a particular person were used to order the sample along a continuum from good to poor self-organization as well as to form two (though not very differ-

TABLE 3–3: JUDGE AGREEMENT ABOUT THE TRAITS
OF THE STANDARD SAMPLE

JUDGES CHECKING TRAITS

9	8	7	6
alert	capable	honest	adaptable (5)
clear	friendly (5)[1]	independent (4)	can say no (4)
thinking	wide interests	sincere	cooperative (4)
	mentally quick		critical of others
	verbal		individualistic
			intellectual
			peaceful (2)
			reflective
			spontaneous (4)

[1] The parenthesis gives number of judges less than six checking trait as characteristic of the *student body*. All adjectives not followed by parenthesis were picked as characteristic of student body by more than six judges.

Judge Agreement About the Traits That Do *Not*
Describe the Standard Sample

JUDGES NOT CHECKING TRAITS

9		8	
authoritarian[2]	aggressive		restless (6)
cold (7)	apathetic (6)		scattered
earthy	bland		self-centered (3)
evasive	common sense (5)		self-insight (7)
flighty	considerate		sophisticated (4)
humorless	contented		suspicious (7)
impractical (7)	easily annoyed (7)		tactful (6)
inconsiderate	easily led		tender minded (6)
indecisive	empathic		tense (7)
insightful (6)	erratic (6)		uncritical of
mild	gentle (6)		others (7)
opportunistic (6)	illogical		unrealistic
self-detachment (7)	impulsive (7)		well-coordinated
slow	intense (5)		
suggestible	narrow interests		
tough minded	irresponsible (7)		
undependable	lacks vitality		
understanding	moody		
unemotional	persistent		
unfriendly	purposeless		
vague	religious		

[2] Adjectives not followed by parenthesis were also *not* picked by at least eight judges as descriptive of the Haverford population. Numbers in parenthesis indicate number of judges *not* selecting the trait as characteristic of the population.

ing) criterion groups of good and poor self-organization by dichotomizing the sample at the midpoint. The judges placed very few students in either of the most extreme of the five categories of self-organization.

Because both the representativeness and the psychological stability of volunteers for personality studies have been questioned by psychologists, data about both facets of the sample were also secured. Half of the judges completed the Adjective Check List for the Standard sample as a group and then for the Haverford student body as a group. The remaining judges did the same but for the two groups in opposite order. Table 3–3 gives the traits of the Standard sample about which there was most agreement. Of the nineteen adjectives checked by at least six of the nine judges to describe the sample, twelve of the adjectives (63%) also described the Haverford population. Actually six of the remaining seven adjectives were checked as descriptive of the larger student body by at least four judges as shown in Table 3–3. The judges agreed that thirty-two of the fifty-four traits (59%) *not* characteristic of the student body were *also not* characteristic of the Standard sample. In contrast to the student body, the sample was judged to be less self-centered and less sophisticated.

I next used a direct method of determining the sample's representativeness by asking the judges to list the adjectives that described those Haverford students not represented in the sample. All judges agreed that the sample was representative except for the "way out" creative or bohemian type of student. The adjectives used to describe those not represented were "anti-intellectuals," "the goof-offs," esoteric, rebellious, cynical, unfeeling, unfriendly, sensual, authoritarian, affected, and bottled-up.

Since volunteers for personality studies are sometimes considered to be disturbed persons (Bell, 1962), what evidence is available about the maturity and other trait patterns of the Standard sample? The MMPI, Bernreuter's Personality Inventory, Strong's Vocational Interest test, the Allport-Vernon-Lindzey Study of Values, and aptitude and achievement scores of the sample were compared to those of the remaining student population. The sample not only had higher verbal and quantitative aptitude and English achievement scores but also reported itself to be more psychologically healthy, less defensively controlled, more dominant, self-sufficient, self-confident, and less introversive than the remaining members of its class. The sample was oriented less strongly toward theoretical and religious and more strongly toward political and social values. Its temperamental pattern was also more congruent with its expressed values than was the case for the remaining Haverford population.

In summary, the Standard sample, while judged to be reasonably representative of the student body, does seem to be a homogeneously healthier, less dependent, more allocentric, dominant, and intelligent group of youths. Of what significance is this result? First, the result questions the widely held belief that volunteers for such studies are invariably the more introversive, morbidly self-centered, and neurotic type of student. Second, since the sample seems to be healthier and quite homogeneous, at least on the MMPI, attenuated relationships between the sample's degree of self-organization and its MMPI and other test scales are probable. Finally, the use of the sample's data to develop standard scores for the experimental tests will make the scores more discriminating than would be the case if data had been used from the entire Haverford population itself.

SOME METHODOLOGICAL PROBLEMS ABOUT CONSENSUAL JUDGMENTS

I now return to some questions and findings about consensual judgments themselves. First, how well did the judges agree about who was mature and immature, well organized and poorly organized? From the Maturity sample's study we learned judges agreed more frequently among themselves about who was mature than they did about who was immature. The same result was found for the Organized sample. More judges agreed about who was well organized than about who was poorly organized. While there was near unanimity among the judges about a few persons who were most and who were least well organized, several members of the Organized sample were selected by only about a third of the judges. Analysis of the ratings each judge made of the degree of his acquaintance with each student clearly demonstrated that the moderate judge agreement did not imply conflict in judgment as much as it reflected lack of knowledge by the judges (particularly the faculty) about many students.

Second, does the type of judge used (student or faculty) affect the amount of consensual agreement? In both the Maturity and Organized samples, some students were perceived by the faculty as mature or well organized but were judged by the student judges to be immature or poorly organized—and vice versa. This is not very surprising since the Haverford faculty know the students only within a very limited compass of their lives. From the ACL data it was possible to determine how the two types of judges describe the well and the poorly organized person. While the faculty and student judges did not differ markedly in the type of trait they used to select the men, the two groups of judges did vary significantly in what else they "saw" in the men. The well organized men emerge as more human, expressive, and appealing persons for the student judges than they do for the faculty. Significantly more student than faculty judges rated the well organized youth to be easy-going, empathic, expressive, on the go, to have strong convictions (two-tailed .01), to be adventurous, altruistic, considerate, and modest (.05). On the other hand, significantly more faculty than students judged the poorly organized youths to be illogical (.05). These judge differences support Barron's (1954, 1963) finding that faculty tend to perceive students primarily in terms of cognitive and goal-directed but not emotional and expressive traits (despite the fact the predominant number of faculty judges were from the Humanities Division). Investigators of mature or effective men who rely exclusively on faculty selection judgments must recognize that they may be seriously restricting the operational meaning of *mature* or *effective* to a one-sided emphasis on goal-directed efficiency and completely ignoring the more allocentric-autocentric and spontaneously expressive side of a person. These differences confirm the earlier hunch that a wide range of judges is required when selecting mature persons to study.

Finally, would a different group of judges have selected the same men to be mature and well organized, immature and poorly organized? No direct answer can be given to this question, but my hunch is the answer is "yes." From the Departmental Chairmen ratings of the emotional stability and other traits made of graduating seniors (details are reported in Chapter 6), it is clear that if given the names of each sample, the Chairmen probably would have correctly sorted each person into the appropriate criterion group. What a man is emerges very sharply within the confines of a small institution. My own assessment is that the Maturity and Organized samples were composed of distinct and non-overlapping groups but that the Standard sample's criterion groups were more similar than dissimilar on the criteria used for their identification.

OVERVIEW OF THE RESEARCH PROCEDURE

The following chapters begin to draw together the findings about maturity and self-organization from a variety of tests and other procedures. Now I but briefly preview the research procedures used with the major samples, postponing until the appropriate chapters more detailed descriptions of the rationale, tests, and experimental design that characterized the various studies.

Considerable personality material was available on the men from their college administrative and psychological tests files. In addition to intelligence and grade records, self-report data such as Minnesota Multiphasic Personality Inventory, Bernreuter's Personality Inventory, Allport's Study of Values, Strong's Vocational Interest Blank were also available for all of the samples.

Maturity Sample Procedure

Each person of the sample was seen individually for a total of five to six hours.

DAY PROCEDURE

1 Interview on family, life history, and current problems. The Phrase Association Test (a measure of disorganization to disturbing information)
2 Rorschach
3 Thematic Apperception Test (administered under different instructional conditions)
4 Test of analytic skill efficiency with disturbing information
5 Interpretative interview (optional)

Organized and Standard Samples' Procedure

Each person of the Organized and Standard samples was seen individually for a total of six to seven hours. The Organized and Standard samples' research design paralleled each other with only minor exceptions.

DAY	PROCEDURE
1	Adjective Check List (omitted for Standard sample)
	Self-Image Questionnaire
	Phrase Association Test
	Self-Image Questionnaire
	Terman Concept Mastery Test (completed between sessions)
2	Self-Image Questionnaire (omitted for Standard sample)
	Skill Test experimental procedure (measures of conceptual, analytic, and judgmental efficiency to disturbing information)
3	Skill Test experimental procedure concluded
	Self-Image autonomy procedure (omitted for Standard sample)
	California F scale (completed between sessions and omitted for Standard sample)
4	Self-Image Questionnaire
	Phrase Association Test
	Stroop Color-Word Test (omitted for Organized sample)
5	Rorschach (administered in small groups to Standard sample)
6	Interpretative interview (optional)

SUMMARY

Although it is not possible to say how much more mature one group of youths is than another (or just how mature each youth is), it is possible to determine if a selected group of reasonably mature youths is more maturely developed on the dimensions that define maturity than is a group of less mature youths. Analysis of the research population and institution intuitively suggested the dimensions on which both mature and immature criterion groups might be more and less maturely developed.

The decision to use consensual judgments rather than psychological tests or other procedures to identify who is a mature person provoked questions about the type of information such a research strategy might produce, the types of selecting judges to use, and the types of socio-cultural conditions that limit the appropriateness of such a research strategy.

The principal samples of the research were identified as the Maturity, Organized, and Standard samples. Criterion groups of each major sample were defined by different judgment procedures. The members of each sample were also ordered from most mature to most immature, most well organized to most poorly organized, on the basis of the amount of judge agreement about their identification as mature or well organized.

What has been learned to date about the use of social judgments of maturity and self-organization? Surprisingly, it was easier to get agreement about who was mature and well organized than agreement about who was immature and disorganized. The homogeneity and nature of the population within which the judgments were made accounted in part for the lower agreement about who is immature. Certainly in the Haverford setting it is the exceptional immature or disorganized person who continues to survive, and if he does survive then there is doubt about how severely disorganized he may be. Only moderate judge agreement about who is mature and immature can be expected in larger populations. Judge agreement appears to be limited more by the extent of ignorance about the population than by the vagueness of the selection criteria although idiosyncratic interpretations of such vague criteria surely must play a role. While different types of judges appear to be in essential agreement (faculty and students radically disagreed in very few cases) about who is most mature and who is not, different types of judges do selectively emphasize different aspects of maturity. Maximizing the types of judges may, indirectly, increase the generality of the research conclusions, for if a mature person is maturely adaptable to many types of relationships (authority, peer, competitive, social) in one setting, he may be as adaptable to similar types of relationships in different settings.

CHAPTER 4

Questionnaire and Projective
Measures of Maturity

This chapter begins the exploration of maturity by searching among established questionnaire and projective measures for insights about the meaning of maturity. The following chapter reports procedures specifically developed to investigate our own hunches about maturity. Two problems weave through this and the following chapter: 1) the relation of consensual judgments of maturity to questionnaire (Bernreuter's Personality Inventory, 1935, and the Minnesota Multiphasic Personality Inventory) and projective tests (Rorschach), and 2) the relation between the questionnaire and Rorschach tests. I was forced to examine the second problem as well, not only because the relation of many questionnaire and Rorschach measures has been scarcely investigated (Adams, Cooper & Carrera, 1963; Wylie, 1961), but also because a new and incompletely validated method of analyzing the Rorschach was used to measure some of the central constructs of the research. The use of novel methods demands that whenever possible their meaning be explored by establishing their validity links to other measures. It is, in fact, the network of relationships which the research wove around many new and old measures that increased my confidence about the meanings attributed to our own measures.

QUESTIONNAIRE TESTS

Historically, personality questionnaires have been used more frequently to study the immature and disorganized than the mature and organized person. But degree of *maturity* and *adjustment* have also been inferred from low scores on such tests' scales and from the absence of signs of disorganization and pathology (Golden, Mandel, Glueck, & Feder, 1962). For heuristic purposes, I also assume that low scores on scales of maladjustment such as the MMPI and the Bernreuter indicate maturity although there are obvious limitations to such an assumption. For example, low MMPI (Ma) scores do not imply increased allocentricism, for persons with low Manic scores have been described as seclusive, unpopular, narrow in interests, lacking drive, and difficult to help in counseling (Black, 1953).

My expectation was that those scales considered to measure psychopathological trends (e.g., MMPI Depression (D), Hysteria (Hy), Schizophrenia (Sc), Taylor Manifest Anxiety Scale (MAS) (J. A. Taylor, 1953); Bernreuter Neuroticism, Nonsocial) would be inversely related to maturity. To secure a summary and very crude index of the general amount of immaturity from the MMPI, the MMPI scores of all the traditional psychopathological scales (except the Mf and Si scales) were summed and averaged. Those scales measuring defensive control (MMPI K, Barron Ego-Strength (1953), Block over- but not under-control) and assertive (Bern. Dominance) trends were expected to be directly related to maturity.

But what specific psychological meaning is to be given to the basic scales, particularly those of the MMPI? Several frustrating and unresolved problems arise. First, the failure to replicate factorially the empirically derived scales suggests that they are dimensionally complex which, therefore, makes labeling them an awkward task. Second, the persistent dispute about the relation of the scales to acquiescence, conforming, socially desirable response sets and to some veridical trait property of the person obscures the meaning of the scales (Dahlstrom, 1962; Edwards, 1962; Jackson & Messick, 1962). Third, the clinical labels of the scales have been gradually yielding to more phenomenal trait descriptions but no accepted convenient trait labels adequately summarize each scale. Fourth, most MMPI scales are clinically interpreted within the context of the other scales, so that isolating one scale from its context may affect the meaning of the scale. Given all of these imponderables, I interpreted the scales within the general context of the traits found to be associated with each scale (Black, 1953), but I always report the name of the original scale following the trait description. (The questionnaire scales are occasionally referred to as self-report or self-concept tests, though technically a high MMPI score does not mean the person consciously thought of himself as high on the traits the scale empirically measures.)

It was not expected that the questionnaire tests would be very useful for the study, primarily because the participating youths were mainly juniors and seniors who had taken the Bernreuter and the MMPI three to four years earlier as part of their freshman orientation requirements. The intervening Haverford experience could have produced differential changes in the students and thereby reduced the current sensitivities of the scales. Although only very moderate relationships were expected, the reader may, as I was, be surprised by the many highly consistent results obtained with these scales.

How did the scales of maladjustment correlate with independent judgments of maturity? Recall that the men of each sample were ordered by degree of maturity (or self-organization) in terms of the number of judges who had selected them as mature. Table 4–1 reports the correlations of the questionnaire scales with this consensual measure of maturity. The pattern of the results for each sample is moderately consistent with that of the other samples and generally confirms the expectation that judged maturity is inversely related to questionnaire measure of immaturity (remember these self-reports were obtained three to four years earlier). Specifically, it was consistently and *strongly confirmed* that judged maturity is inversely related to depressive and socially introversive trends.

Although the findings, particularly those from the Organized sample, are encouraging (given the crude method used to order the samples for maturity and self-organization), the differences between the three samples herald some troublesome questions.

Because such questions will pressingly recur in one form or another, I will use Table 4–1 to illustrate these methodological and interpretative problems and indicate some reportorial conventions used throughout the rest of the book.

First, how are results from more than one sample to be interpreted? If the pattern of correlations of each sample is similar (correlations for a scale are in the same direction for all of the samples), the finding is considered *consistent* across the samples. So as not to obscure the major trends in the very extensive data soon to be reported, the *p* values of single scales or samples will rarely be reported or discussed in this chapter. Instead, I evaluate the results from more than two samples as either very strongly confirmed, strongly confirmed, confirmed, weakly confirmed, or not confirmed depending upon the magnitude and consistency of the significance levels obtained. (Appendix A, Table 1 reports the conventions that define the different degrees of confirmation.)

Second, Table 4–1 shows twelve of the twenty correlations of the Organized, none of the Maturity, and two of the twenty correlations of the Standard sample to be significant. To give a quick overview of the degree of relationship between one test and another, I will report the percent of significant correlations found. That is, twenty-four percent of Table 4–1's correlations are significant at least at a one-tailed .05 probability level. But it must be emphasized that such a summary figure is to be interpreted most conservatively. The scales of each test are *not* independent of each other so that the summary figure *cannot* be used as an index of the frequency with which the results were obtained beyond chance expectation. And, until the tests used in the research (including the MMPI) can be reduced to more limited replicable and stable unidimensional factors which can be conveniently summarized into scores whose intercorrelations are known, interpretations of the findings are tentative and may be alternatively interpreted in terms of some mutually related third factor.

Third, the use of rank-order correlations in Table 4–1 does not violate any statistical assumption. But the way I subsequently use the Pearson *r* statistic may cause some concern. Specifically, determining *r* relationships within a sample initially selected to

TABLE 4–1: CORRELATES OF QUESTIONNAIRE SCALES OF MALADJUSTMENT AND CONTROL WITH SOCIAL JUDGMENTS OF SELF-ORGANIZATION AND MATURITY

QUESTIONNAIRE SCALES	SOCIAL JUDGMENTS OF MATURITY		
	ORGANIZED[1] rho	MATURITY[2] rho	STANDARD rho
MMPI			
Total (General Maladjustment)	−.41*	−.39	−.11
Hs (Hypochondriasis)[3]	−.37*	−.04	.10
D (Depression)	−.52***	−.19	−.38**
Hy (Hysteria)	−.30	.13	.09
Pd (Psychopathic deviate)	−.30	−.20	−.15
Pa (Paranoia)	−.38*	.35	−.20
Pt (Psychasthenia)	−.30	−.08	−.10
Sc (Schizophrenia)	−.40*	.12	−.04
Ma (Mania)	−.16	−.30	.10
Si (Social introversion)	−.51***	—[4]	−.31*
Taylor MAS (Anxiety)	−.40*	—[4]	−.03[5]
Bernreuter			
Neuroticism	−.60***	−.21	−.06
Introversion	−.66***	−.29	−.12
Lack self-confidence	−.56***	−.15	.01
Nonsocial	−.45**	−.22	−.14
Control scores			
MMPI K (Defensive control)	.33	−.23	−.16
Barron Ego Strength	.34	—[4]	.25[5]
Block Over-control	−.01	—[4]	−.26[5]
Block Under-control	−.29	—[4]	.01[5]
Bernreuter Dominance	.50***	.07	.07

* p ∠ .05
** p ∠ .025
*** p ∠ .01. Throughout the book, a p ∠ .01 will mean *at least* a p ∠ of .01.
[1] N = 23
[2] N = 17
[3] The names of the scales are given only in this table to familiarize some readers with the meaning of the abbreviations.
[4] Data not available.
[5] N = 26; data not available for remaining men.

consist of extreme groups may violate some statistical assumptions. The samples were too small to determine statistically if the relationships were linearly related. (The graphs of many of the relationships between scales whose linearity I doubted revealed no clear departures from linearity, possibly because the samples were too small or because they may not have represented the full range of variability in a national population.) As far as could be determined from such samples, the distributions of the basic scores of the different measures were not excessively skewed even though several of the samples were composed of selected extreme groups. Finally, the use of extreme criterion groups in the Maturity and Organized samples may tend to inflate their correlations, while the marked homogeneity and essential stability of the volunteers of the Standard sample (thirteen of the fifteen lowest mean scores of the questionnaire scores for the three samples belonged to this sample) probably attenuates its correlations.

PROJECTIVE TESTS: THE RORSCHACH

The Rorschach test places minimal constraints on the responses of a person and these responses can be classified, ordered, and evaluated in many different ways. I first examine the relation of global, impressionistic clinical ratings of self-organization based on the Rorschach and then Rorschach scores of autocentricism and adaptive coordinations to judged and self-reported maturity. Less weight is placed on the more traditional scores as described by Klopfer (Klopfer, Ainsworth, Klopfer, & Holt, 1954) because there is doubt about the meaning and current validity of these scores as well as of the various combinations of scores proposed to index maturity. Some results with the Klopfer scores are reported later, but they were not used as a measure of maturity in this book.

The Rorschach had been individually administered, following the standard procedure recommended by Klopfer (Klopfer, *et al,* 1954) to the Maturity sample in its second test session and to the Organized sample in its fifth test session. The group form of the Rorschach had been given, following the procedures specified by Harrower (Harrower & Steiner, 1951), to small groups of the Standard sample in its fifth test session.

Clinical Evaluations of Self-Organization

An eminent clinical diagnostician, Roy Schafer, evaluated only the Rorschachs of the Organized sample. Working without any knowledge of the research, of the participating youths, or of the psychograms, Klopfer and other scores for each man, he examined each student's responses to the first three Rorschach cards, scanning, where necessary, responses to selected remaining cards. Because he evaluated most of the Rorschachs in one day, he had no time to evaluate the entire Rorschach of each student. Schafer checked along a standard line the degree of that student's self-organization when compared to a male college population. He also categorized the student as well or poorly organized on the basis of the amount and severity of morbid content, quality and rapidity of recovery from having given such regressive schemata, presence of benign, playful, and humorous comments and responses, presence of skill impairment including amount of inadequately combined or integrated schemata, number and quality of M (schemata organized around human activities) and FC (accommodation of more affectively organized schemata to fit the form of incoming information) responses, presence of and quality of popular and originally organized schemata, the accuracy with which a schema was coordinated with the blot (form level), and the constrictedness of the record. As any Rorschach interpreter knows, such criteria only capture the more obvious of all the subtle cues and patterns that defined his final clinical evaluation of the student's self-organization. Later, the distance from one end of the line scale to the checked rating of self-organization was measured so that the entire sample could be ordered from borderline to superior self-organization.

What were the results? Schafer correctly identified ten of the poorly organized and six of the well organized men from their Rorschachs. Of the two poorly organized men he classified as well organized, one withdrew from College because of lack of motivation, sought psychiatric therapy but was judged not to require it; the other student, while an odd character, showed no overt neurotic anxiety or disturbing symptoms. Of the six well organized men whom he categorized as poorly organized from their Rorschachs, one had an ulcer, one had tics and a history of psychiatric difficulty, one eventually withdrew from College because of personal dissatisfaction, one demonstrated a vague schizophrenic type of thinking under the guise of philosophical abstractness, one turned out to be an erratic but driven compulsive, and one had a history of incredibly severe emotional stress. (Despite being categorized by Schafer as poorly organized, these well organized men were generally judged on the line ratings to be more well organized than the selected poorly organized men.)

More sensitive tests of the association between Schafer's ratings and the social judgments of self-organization were more supporting. The difference between the means of Schafer's line ratings of degree of self-organization for the socially judged well and poorly organized men was significant at a one-tailed .05 level (t = 1.75). Schafer's ratings were next rank-ordered in terms of decreasing self-organization and correlated with the consensual judgments of self-organization. The *rho* was .45, p ∠ .05. This significant relation between an expert's Rorschach clinical evaluation and consensual judgments of self-organization was comforting, given the unfavorable judging conditions under which the Rorschach evaluations were made and the crudeness of the consensual ranking procedure.

Eight months following the administration of the group Rorschachs to the Standard sample, the coded Rorschach protocols were ordered for degree of self-organization using Schafer's criteria. The sample's seniors (fifteen) had been given the group Rorschach in their freshman year. Their fifteen freshmen protocols were mixed with the Standard sample's in order to disrupt any judging sets that could influence my judgments of the protocols. The coded fifty-one Rorschachs were preliminarily ordered by degree of self-organization and subsequently twice reevaluated by comparing each to the other similarly judged Rorschachs. There was a small degree of contamination of my judgments because I recognized the Rorschachs of three of the students, although I did not know, at the time, how the men had been ranked for self-organization by consensual judgments.

What were the results of this evaluation procedure? Eleven of the thirty-six men were rated to be at least better and eighteen to be at least worse than the seven who were rated to be average in self-organization. The direction of this ratio is similar to Schafer's categorization of the Organized sample (eight well and sixteen poorly organized). Are the Haverford men more disturbed than other college men? Not according to the questionnaire data from the men, for the samples report themselves on the Bernreuter and MMPI to be no more immature than other college men report themselves to be. Why were more men judged to be more poorly than well organized? The explanation may be contained in Holt's observation that the Rorschach makes "less demand for organizing and synthesizing and less necessity for secondary process thinking" (1960a, p. 267) than do other psychological tests. Consequently, the Rorschach may more readily elicit primary process and pathological types of behavior than adaptive skills (or ego strengths) which may, in fact, mitigate and change the meaning of primary process behavior.

The Rorschach clinical ratings of self-organization of the Standard sample successfully and significantly differentiated the men consensually judged to be well organized from the men judged to be poorly organized. The difference between the Rorschach means of the well and poorly organized men was significant beyond the .05 level (t = 2.01). Similarly, the rank-order correlation between the Rorschach clinical ratings and the judges' ratings of self-organization was also significant beyond the .05 level (rho = .40). Given the differences in sample selection procedure, in clinical skill in evaluating the Rorschach, and in group and individually administered Rorschach forms, these consistently significant results are reassuring about the use of both the Rorschach and social judgments for ordering men by degree of self-organization.

The clinical evaluations of self-organization were also consistently associated in the predicted direction with the questionnaire measures of immaturity secured two to four years earlier. From Table 4-2, which reports the relevant correlations, it is clear that while the general pattern is similar for both samples, clinically identified good self-organization is significantly but inversely re-

TABLE 4–2: CORRELATES OF QUESTIONNAIRE SCALES
OF MALADJUSTMENT AND CONTROL WITH
RORSCHACH CLINICAL EVALUATION OF
SELF-ORGANIZATION

QUESTIONNAIRE SCALES	RORSCHACH EVALUATION OF SELF-ORGANIZATION	
	ORGANIZED[1] r	STANDARD r
MMPI		
Total[2]	−.37*	−.06
Hs	−.12	.40***[3]
D	−.52***	−.18
Hy	−.20	.24
Pd	−.38*	−.03
Pa	−.15	−.39***
Pt	−.27	−.24
Sc	−.31	.03
Ma	−.24	−.13
Si	−.36*	−.24
Taylor MAS	−.46**	−.07
Bernreuter		
Neuroticism	−.40*	−.15
Introversion	−.40*	−.29
Lack self-confidence	−.31	−.13
Nonsocial	−.42**	.12
Control Scores		
MMPI K	.35	−.03
Barron Ego Strength	.26	.01
Block Over-control	.13	−.04
Block Under-control	−.33	.05
Bernreuter Dominance	.15	.25

* p ∠ .05
** p ∠ .025
*** p ∠ .01
[1] N = 23; data not available on one person.
[2] MMPI Total maladjustment score does not include Si score.
[3] In non-predicted direction; significant at two-tailed level.

lated to questionnaire measures of immaturity only for the Organized sample. Poor self-organization on the Rorschach is most closely related to neuroticism (MMPI Total; Bern. Neurotic), social introversion and distinterest in others (MMPI Si; Bern. Introver, Nonsocial), anxiety (Taylor), depressive (MMPI D) and possibly irresponsible impulsive behavior (MMPI Pd). The homogeneity of the Standard sample and its essentially good emotional stability may account for its inconsistent and nonsignificant results.

Measures of Autocentric Schemata and of Adaptive Coordinations of Schemata

The Rorschach data may be more objectively ordered by a variety of other methods. Robert Holt's primary process scoring categories, perceptively derived from psychoanalytic theory, were most appropriate to the theoretical viewpoint of the research. Because his scoring system is relatively unknown, I briefly summarize its theoretical rationale (A more detailed description of its theory and scores has been presented by Holt, 1956, 1960a, 1960b), reinterpret the principal Holt scores into the language of the research, assess the reliability of such scores, and then discuss their relation to our judge and questionnaire measures of maturity. Later chapters will discuss the relation of the Holt measures to other indices of self-organization.

Holt has developed Rorschach indices of primary processes and of defenses used to control or modulate the expression of primary processes. Primary process is revealed in the content of responses organized around drives and in some specific structural characteristics of the response itself. The scoring system also measures quantitative differences in the primitiveness or immaturity of primary processes. Since Holt assumes "*all* thought and perception is organized by drives to some extent" (Holt, 1959, p. 1) he, as well as other contemporary ego psychologists (Gill, 1963; Hartmann, 1955), is able to consider that secondary and primary processes are only opposed portions of the same continuum rather than qualitatively different processes. Despite this assumption, Holt does not assert that his measures of primary processes are conversely *adequate* measures of secondary processes because of the particular structural properties of the Rorschach. A test whose informational properties are ambiguously defined provides little opportunity for behavior to be organized by external determinants. Secondary rather than primary processes are organized around forms and coordinations that match environmental and reality possibilities. The Rorschach does not provide iconic pictures for the person to match nor does its instructional procedure require the person to give "realistically appropriate" responses. Therefore, the test and its administration procedures do not establish optimal conditions for measuring the extent to which a person *can* organize his schemata around reality-given information. But the Rorschach cards are not without some form and informational organization, of course, and for this reason it is still possible to make some inferences about the quality of secondary process thinking or accommodative accuracy. Holt's scoring system also does not directly measure the *effectiveness* of the major adaptive skills of conceptualization, analysis and synthesis, and judgment though some of its scores can be interpreted to indicate degree of impairment of these secondary processes.

In addition to codifying indices of primary process (unstable, autocentric types of schemata), Holt has developed scores that reflect how adaptively the person defends, controls, and recovers from the emergence into awareness of threatening and primitive schemata.

Scoring System

The principal Rorschach scores used in the research can be grouped into those measuring the amount of autocentric schemata[1] (primary process) and the degree to which schemata are adaptively coordinated or controlled.

[1] The term *autocentric schemata* will be used in the major headings and tables only as a convenient label to refer to those types of schemata and coordinations characteristic of the primary process. Primary processes are also unstable, unintegrated (by any conventional standards), nonautonomous, and not readily available to awareness.

A. Measures of autocentric schemata:

1. Drive-Organized Schemata (% Content Score).

Chapter 2 assumed that schemata organized around the self and interpersonal relationships become stabilized and autonomous later than other types of schemata, primarily because such schemata are intertwined with affective and drive derivatives. A person who *persistently* organizes the information given him by the Rorschach around schemata colored by drives and types of relationships found earlier in development (oral, homosexual, sadistic) is assumed to be less mature than a person who gives more highly differentiated and socialized types of schemata. Holt's % Content score codifies the frequency with which a person's schemata are organized around manifest libidinal (oral, anal, sexual, exhibitionistic) and aggressive (sadistic, masochistic) drives.

2. Impaired Skills (% Formal Score).

Schemata can be coordinated and combined in a variety of ways. Chapter 2 identified the major coordinating skills (ego processes) to be conceptualization, analysis and synthesis, and judgment. Holt has identified some thirty-five different indices of skill impairment. For example, impaired conceptual thinking is revealed in condensations and autistic logic. Faulty analysis and synthesis may be seen in compositions or arbitrary linkages of schemata. Or unrealistic judgment is reflected in autistic elaborations, affective contradictions, and attribution of inappropriate activities to objects. Holt's % Formal score refers to the amount of such skill or thought impairment, or more generally, to the amount of autocentric types of thought coordinations.

The % Content and % Formal scores measure different facets of primary process or autocentric thinking, since they are not highly intercorrelated in the Organized, Maturity, and Standard samples ($r = .76, .49$, and $.33$). Because no factor analytic studies have yet identified the major dimensions of the scoring system, the intercorrelations between the different scores for the major samples are reported in Table 2, Appendix A.

3. Degree of Autocentricism (% Level 1, % Level 2, and Sum Defense Demand Scores).

Because of Holt's assumption that primary and secondary processes are the two end points of a continuum, he is able to say some indices of drive-organized schemata or skill impairment are more primitive, unsocialized, or autocentric than other indices. The % Level 1 score refers to the proportion of the total number of primary process responses that represent the most unsocialized types of schemata and the most severely impaired skill coordinations. % Level 2 refers to those intermediate partially socialized types of schemata and skill coordinations. The % Level 1 and 2 scores are not related to each other in the major samples ($r = -.12, .32$, and $.01$).

Holt also assumes that the emergence of more primitive and unsocialized impulses into awareness is a potential threat to the person's self-organization. The stronger such claims are, the more dissonant they are likely to be; thus, greater accommodation is required. The eruption of vulgar, bizarre, odd, unconventional images requires some defensive accommodation (modification, rationalization) to make them more socially acceptable, to tone down their violation of conventional tastes of social communication. The Sum Defense Demand score refers to the total amount of threat internally originating information has for a person. The score is moderately related to the % Level 1 and 2 scores (Appendix A, Table 2).

4. Summary Measure of Autocentricism (% Primary Process).

The % Primary Process is defined as that proportion of the total number of responses given to the Rorschach which reveal either drive-organized schemata and (or) impaired skills. It is the most general measure of the extent to which a person's schemata are organized autocentrically. I expected increasing autocentricism to be inversely related to increasing self-organization. If a person had many unstable and autocentrically organized schemata as well as impaired skills, adaptation to more

socially conventional requirements would have been quite difficult. But this reasoning is incomplete, for mature self-organization
is defined by a combination of developmental trends and not
just by allocentricism. Allocentricism and adaptation are not necessarily coextensive. Adaptation sometimes requires the creative
modification of social institutions and relationships, and such
modification may be facilitated by having autocentric schemata
and unconventional types of coordinations available. Too extensive allocentric development that results in a failure to assimilate
more personal wishes and desires into the self violates the definition of adaptation and is not likely to lead to a stable self-
organization. Therefore, although increasing allocentricism is the
mark of a maturing person, the relation between allocentricism
and self-organization is probably more complex than our linear
hypothesis suggests. A similar argument applies to the other developmental trends as well (e.g., too great stability may mean
rigidity, inability to assimilate new information, and inhibition
of the trend toward progressive integration).

B. Measures of adaptive coordination:

The expectation that measures of autocentricism and self-
organization are inversely related is also limited by the extent to
which a person can successfully adapt to the emergence of threatening information. Holt's scoring system offers several measures
that reflect different facets of the degree to which a person can
adaptively coordinate disturbing information. Our expectation
was that more mature persons would be able to accommodate
their schemata more accurately to the Rorschach information,
would use more effective defenses in mastering disturbing information, and would make many more adaptive regressive and
imaginative coordinations of schemata.

1. Accommodative Accuracy (% Form Accuracy).

There are several different ways to measure the accuracy
of a percept (Beck, Beck, Levitt, & Molish, 1961; Klopfer, *et
al*, 1954), but Holt relies on Mayman's (1960) more differentiated

scoring system of form accuracy. He classifies the accuracy of perceptual accommodation into a graded series from highly accurate to highly unrealistic and arbitrary types of accommodations. The % Form Accuracy score summarizes the average accommodative accuracy of *all* of the person's percepts.

2. Defensive Accommodation (*Mean Defense Effectiveness*).

As a person responds to the Rorschach he himself produces new information. Some of his responses may be dissonant or incongruent with his self-image and unconsciously may provoke defensive means to assimilate and integrate that information with his existing conception of himself. Holt assumes each autocentric type of response may be a potential threat to the person and may lead to some defensive type of accommodation. He has rated various types of defensive controls in terms of how adequately they meet the threat. The *Mean Defense Effectiveness* score (Mean DE) indicates how adaptively the person accommodated to the emergence of autocentric schemata and is moderately related to the % Form Accuracy score in the major samples (.63, .35, and .70).

3. Controlled Regression (% DD x DE and Content DD/Formal DD.)

The Mean Defense Effectiveness score does not measure the degree of threat that different self-produced responses may pose to a person. Holt reasoned that a person who produced maximally autocentric or regressive responses (containing very threatening information in turn to be assimilated) that were accurately accommodated and well controlled had a greater potential for more mature adaptations than did the person who produced rather bland, innocuous or minimally autocentric responses also accurately well controlled. Kris (1952) and Schafer (1958) have suggested that persons of strong egos are "willfully" able to allow more unconscious primary process products into awareness and to use such unstable schemata for more creative adaptations. Presumably, persons who have good controls but who close themselves to the workings of their inner lives have less potential for meeting a wider range of adaptive tasks. Holt tries to capture this ability to "regress in the service of the ego" in his measure of adaptive regression which combines measures of a response's autocentricism (defense demand score) and the effectiveness with which it is defended (defense effectiveness score). A high % DD x DE score means the person has the potential for making adaptive regressive coordinations. Adaptive regression was expected to be directly related to the degree of self-organization, for while a more mature person is more allocentrically organized, his schemata can be autocentrically but reversibly organized if the task requires such regressive coordination. But the relation is likely to be only moderate in samples selected by judges. Self-organization so phenomenally defined is likely to include well-controlled students some of whom may have considerable autocentric schemata available to awareness and others who may have much less.

Holt's scoring system yielded another type of controlled regression score, called adaptive imagination. Skill impairment rather than the amount of unstable schemata has more serious adaptive consequences, if only because coordinating skills (and valuators) are the tools by which schemata are combined to meet different adaptive requirements. Impairment in such skills, regardless of the stability of one's schemata, is, then decisive. Considerable regressive imagery (more drive-organized schemata) combined with minimal skill impairment means a person has available vividly intense and primitive fantasies but that such images can still be coordinated logically and adaptively. Could this not describe a more creative person? The adaptive imagination score was defined by the ratio of the defense demand scores (a measure of the intensity of internal threat) of drive-organized schemata and of impaired skills—Content DD/Formal DD. Adaptive imagination was expected to covary directly with degree of self-organization, but only moderate relationships were expected for the same reasons that applied to the adaptive regression score. The adaptive regression and imagination scores measure two different regressive patterns, for they do not consistently covary in the major samples ($r = .50$, $.15$, and $.07$).

Reliability of Scoring System

The complexity of the scoring system and the sensitive clinical judgment required by many of the scores demanded that close attention be given to the reliability of the scores. Holt (1960a) has reported satisfactory interjudge agreement coefficients for the principal scores for highly trained scorers. Similar reliability coefficients were obtained for the Maturity and Organized samples whose coded protocols had been independently scored by a highly (Lester Alston of the Holt research group) and a minimally trained scorer (myself). The median reliability coefficient of the principal scores used in the research was .91 for the Maturity and .95 for the Organized sample. However, the coefficients of those scores based on much more subtle indices (particularly those for skill impairment) were much lower, due to my limited training with these more complex scores. In reconciling divergently scored indices, the judgment of the more skilled scorer prevailed.

While no stability coefficients have been reported by Holt, my data (based on the data of those men of the Standard sample who had taken the Rorschach in the freshman and senior years) indicate that the principal Holt scores may have moderate stability over four years. The median coefficient was .46, with the scores for skill impairment (Formal) and unsocialized autocentric schemata (Level 1) being most unstable over time. These stability coefficients are similar in magnitude to those found for the standard Rorschach scores in a late adolescent group (Kagan, 1960).

One final index of the reliability of the scoring system was the relation of the Holt scores to the clinical evaluations of self-organization for the Organized and Standard samples (Table 4–3). The pattern of correlations reassuringly agrees for both samples. Good self-organization clinically evaluated from the Rorschach is positively related to all measures of adaptive control and negatively related to all measures of autocentric schemata.

TABLE 4–3: CORRELATES OF RORSCHACH AUTOCEN-
TRIC AND CONTROL SCORES WITH ROR-
SCHACH CLINICAL EVALUATIONS OF
SELF-ORGANIZATION

| RORSCHACH SCORES | RORSCHACH CLINICAL JUDGMENTS OF SELF-ORGANIZATION | |
	ORGANIZED (SCHAFER) r	STANDARD (HEATH) r
Autocentric Schemata		
% PriPro	—.55	—.47
% Content	—.44	—.44
% Formal	—.58	—.27
% Level 1	—.54	—.35
% Level 2	—.13	—.36
Sum DD	—.29	—.52
Adaptive Controls		
% Form Accuracy	.73	.49
Mean DE	.56	.40
% DD × DE	.62	.46
Con DD/Form DD	.46	.07

For Schafer, poor self-organization was most closely associated
with skill impairment, and good self-organization with the ability
to accommodate one's schemata accurately, to regress adaptively
and defend autocentric schemata effectively. My ratings were
similarly related though not as markedly, due either to my lack
of skill and/or the limited usefulness of group administered Rorschach data for securing reliable skill impairment and defense
scores.

Holt Rorschach Scores and Judged Maturity (Self-Organization)

Generally, the Rorschach measures of autocentricism and
adaptive control were related to the judges' ratings of maturity
as predicted. As Table 4–4 indicates, it was *strongly confirmed*
that maturity is inversely related to impaired skills and directly

related to adaptive imagination. It was *confirmed* that maturity is also inversely related to autocentricism, particularly the most unsocialized types of autocentricism. Differences among the samples make the interpretation of the other correlations too risky, although the sample differences are not unintelligible. That some of the Standard sample's correlations are low may be due to the sample's homogeneity, to differences in the types of processes elicited by group and individually administered Rorschachs, or to unreliable skill and defensive control scores. The Maturity sample's reduced adaptive control correlations are perhaps due to the fact it was a more healthy and homogeneous sample than the Organized sample on the Rorschach. (From data not given, the Maturity sample had lower autocentric and better control scores on all but one of the Rorschach scores and was less variable on all but two of the scores.)

TABLE 4–4: CORRELATES OF SOCIAL JUDGMENTS OF SELF-ORGANIZATION WITH RORSCHACH AUTOCENTRIC AND CONTROL SCORES

RORSCHACH SCORES	JUDGED SELF-ORGANIZATION		
	ORGANIZED rho	MATURITY rho	STANDARD rho
Autocentric Schemata			
% PriPro	−.32	−.39*	−.31*
% Content	−.04	−.20	−.23
% Formal	−.50***	−.51**	−.09
% Level 1	−.49***	−.30	−.11
% Level 2	.22	−.37	−.26
Sum DD	−.08	−.33	.01
Adaptive Controls			
% Form Accuracy	.46**	−.03	.07
Mean DE	.33	.14	−.01
% DD × DE	.34	.04	.06
Con DD/Form DD	.62***	.49**	.07

* p $\angle$ .05
** p $\angle$ .025
*** p $\angle$ .01

Holt Rorschach and Questionnaire Scales of Maladjustment and Control

Because the meaning (validity) of Holt's scores has not been firmly established and because I frequently return to both the questionnaire, Holt autocentricism and adaptive control measures in subsequent chapters, some comment about the relation of each measure to the other is imperative. Some of the data upon which the following summary is based are reported in Table 3, Appendix A. To check the consistency of the Standard sample's group Rorschach and questionnaire correlations, I have included the results from the Personality sample (Table 3–1) taken on a group of ten students to whom the group Rorschach had been given. In evaluating the results from the four samples, the samples administered the individual rather than the group Rorschach, and the larger rather than smaller samples were judged to yield more reliable data. The order of sample reliability was judged to be: Organized, Maturity, Standard, and Personality samples.

From the tables emerge some strikingly consistent impressions. The first and most important observation is the singular consistency with which each of the sample's correlations for a single Rorschach score are in the same *and* predicted direction. There are comparatively few contradictory results in the tables (except for some of the adaptive control scores) and when there is a deviant correlation for one sample, the magnitude of that score's correlations in the other samples is usually quite low, thereby indicating no essential relationship between the Rorschach and the score. A second finding is that the correlations of the Standard and Personality samples to whom the group Rorschach procedures had been given are generally nonsignificant though they are usually in the predicted direction. A third general finding is not obvious. That is, of the 620 correlations calculated, 107 were significant beyond the .05 probability level and *only one was significant* (two-tailed) *in the direction opposite to that predicted* (Mat: MMPI Pa-Ror. Con DD/Form DD). It is difficult to evaluate just what this general finding means since none of the questionnaire and Rorschach correlations are independent of each other (the MMPI scales are intercorrelated just as are the Rorschach scores). Of the 290 correlations secured from the Standard and Personality samples, only twenty-three were significant beyond the .05 level. Of the remaining 330 correlations obtained from the Organized and Maturity samples, eighty-four, or twenty-five percent, were significant. Clearly the evidence supports the expectation that the group Rorschach procedure does not differentiate well within a fairly homogeneous sample.

What are the specific findings? Because of incomplete data, the relations between various measures of ego strength and control and Rorschach autocentric and adaptive control scores are more tentative. But of considerable interest is the consistency with which the questionnaire measures of defensive control significantly covary with the Rorschach adaptive control measures for the most reliable sample. In particular, we can say it was *weakly confirmed* that reflective control (MMPI K: Org. p $\angle$ .05) is associated with defense effectiveness and adaptive regression. Ego strength (Barron: Org. p $\angle$ .01) is also associated with the ability to accommodate schemata accurately. (The Block control score correlations were consistently in the predicted direction but were not significant; the Bernreuter Dominance correlations were also in the predicted direction and were significantly positively related (p $\angle$ .025) to adaptive regression and the accuracy with which schemata are accommodated.)

The scales measuring hypochondriacal, hysteric, manic, and lack of self-confidence trends were neither consistently nor very significantly associated with any measure of autocentricism and adaptive control (data not given). However, the correlations of these scales with the Rorschach scores of the more reliable samples were consistently in the predicted direction. It was *weakly confirmed* that anxiety (Taylor) was inversely related to defense effectiveness (Org. p $\angle$ .05) and adaptive regression (Org. p $\angle$ .01).

Instead of a detailed report of the many consistent results found between the remaining questionnaire scales and Rorschach measures, the principal findings are summarized in Table 4–5 which also assesses the degree of confirmation judged to hold for the predicted relationships. (Table 3, Appendix A provides the data supporting the generalizations of Table 4–5.)

TABLE 4–5: CONFIRMED RELATIONSHIPS BETWEEN RORSCHACH AUTOCENTRIC AND CONTROL SCORES AND QUESTIONNAIRE SCALES OF MALADJUSTMENT AND CONTROL

EXPECTATIONS AND GENERALIZATIONS	CONFIRMATION RATING
1. Maladjustment (MMPI Total) is	
a. directly related to autocentricism, particularly skill impairment, unsocialized, autocentric schemata, and (also including the Bern. Neurotic score) is	Strongly confirmed
b. inversely related to adaptive regression	Strongly confirmed
2. Depression (MMPI D) is	
a. directly related to autocentricism, particularly skill impairment, unsocialized and drive-organized schemata, and is	Strongly confirmed
b. inversely related to adaptive regression and accurate schemata accommodations	Confirmed
3. Irresponsible and impulsive behavior (MMPI Pd) is	
a. directly related to autocentricism, particularly skill impairment and unsocialized autocentric schemata, and is	Strongly confirmed
b. inversely related to adaptive regression	Strongly confirmed
4. Paranoia trends (MMPI Pa) are	
a. directly related to autocentricism, particularly unsocialized types of schemata, and are	Strongly confirmed
b. inversely related to adaptive imagination	Confirmed
5. Compulsive trends (MMPI Pt) are	
a. directly related to impaired skills and unsocialized schemata, and are	Strongly confirmed
b. inversely related to adaptive regression	Weakly confirmed

6. Withdrawal trends (MMPI Sc) are
   a. directly related to most measures of auto-   Confirmed
      centricism, and are
   b. inversely related to most measures of adap-   Weakly confirmed
      tive control

7. Introversive trends (Bern. Introver.) are
   a. directly related to skill impairment, un-   Weakly confirmed
      socialized schemata, total defense demand,
      and (including MMPI Si) are
   b. inversely related to good defense effective-   Confirmed
      ness, accurate schemata accommodations,
      and adaptive regression

8. Nonsocial trends (Bern. Nonsocial) are
   a. directly related to most measures of auto-   Confirmed
      centricism, and are
   b. inversely related to adaptive regression and   Confirmed
      accurate schemata accommodations

Summarizing the results in a different way, it can be said
with considerable confidence that impaired skill and drive-
organized schemata are characteristic of immaturity. Persons who
have many regressed and primitively organized schemata are also
likely to be withdrawn, introverted, nonsocial, undercontrolled,
generally disturbed and unhappy people. Controlled regression
and defense effectiveness are inversely related to immaturity,
anxiety, and poor ego strength. Accurate accommodation of
schemata also describes persons of good ego strength.

SUMMARY

The chapter focused on the relationship between social
judgments, questionnaire, and projective test measures of different facets of maturity. The Bernreuter Personality Inventory,
Minnesota Multiphasic Personality Inventory, and the Rorschach
test were used to give indices of maturity. Holt's psychoanalytically derived scoring system for the Rorschach was emphasized
because its rationale seemed to be most congruent with that of
the research presentation. The social judgments, objective ques-

tionnaire, projective test clinical evaluations and Holt definitions of maturity were consistently and frequently significantly related as predicted. Although the significance of the findings varied among the samples, due in part to differences in their selection and test procedures, the results of the more reliable samples consistently supported our expectations. From the *consistently significant* findings emerge the following generalizations. Good self-organization is *inversely* related to self-reported depressive and socially introversive traits, directly related to the Rorschach clinical evaluations of good self-organization, and *inversely* related to the amount of autocentric schemata, impaired skills, and limited adaptive imagination. Less firm evidence tentatively suggests poor self-organization is defined by more unconventional and unsocialized schemata as well as by more inaccurate accommodations of schemata.

The findings also revealed many consistent and significant relationships between different questionnaire measures of immaturity and Rorschach measures of autocentricism and inadequate control. The consistency of the pattern of social judgment, questionnaire, and projective test findings generates considerable confidence about the validity of each of the different measures of maturity.

What is the significance of these findings for the issues raised in earlier chapters? The results demonstrate that social judgments do have some "ecological" validity and can predict scores that objectively measure other levels and facets of personality functioning which could scarcely have served as the phenomenal basis for the initial social judgments.

The findings have another less obvious but important implication. Considering the novelty (and the reliability problems) of the Rorschach primary process scores, the validity of the Holt scores received impressive support from their correlations with more reliable and validated questionnaire scales. These results have implications for the persisting disagreements between the psychoanalytically oriented (Rorschach) and the more empirically and pragmatically oriented (MMPI) enthusiasts about the merits of their respective traditions (Peskin, 1963) and also suggest a tentative basis for conceptually integrating these conflicting viewpoints.

CHAPTER 5

Maturity and the Properties of the Self-Image

For many theorists, the self-image of a person is the most central structure of the self. As a complex superordinate schema it has a decisive selective effect on what information is assimilated and what range of accommodative possibilities can occur. Because of its central role in adaptation, I expected that the developmental trends describing the maturing person would be saliently reflected in a person's self-image. The content of the self-image records the person's past judgmental reactions to himself as a person; therefore, the properties of the self-image as a schema should also record the organizational level of the person. The self-image of a more maturely organized person not only should be composed of manifest traits usually ascribed to a mature person, but also should be more stable, integrated, allocentric, autonomous, and symbolized in awareness.

The previous chapter diffusely explored, in part, some correlates of the (MMPI) content of the " 'published' self-concept" (Cronbach, 1960, p. 454) that had not been systematically related to the developmental trends describing the maturing person. In contrast, this chapter seeks to demonstrate how such elusively defined developmental trends can be translated to describe the

105

maturing self-image. It then presents the Self-Image Questionnaire (SIQ) and the procedures used to define operationally both the maturity level of the phenomenal content and the developmental properties of the self-image. It also explores the validity relations between the SIQ, the social judgments of self-organization, questionnaire procedures, and the Rorschach. The differences in the content and properties of the self-image of the well and poorly organized criterion groups will be summarized in the next chapter.

PROPERTIES OF THE MATURING SELF-IMAGE

No systematic theory or conclusive empirical results enable us to define unequivocally the major properties of the self-image. The most comprehensive theoretical map of the self-image is that sketched by Rogers (1959a) which appeared after the initiation of this research. I drew upon some of his earlier formulations in inducing the developmental trends of Chapter 1. Factorial studies of self-rating scales that claim to isolate fundamental dimensions of the self-image have not been very useful, not only because the obtained factors are limited by the restrictive range of the original self-image data used but also because the factors classify only the phenomenal content and not the structural dimensions of the self-image (Fiske, 1949; P. A. Smith, 1960, 1962). Empirical studies of the content and properties of the self-image also have failed to clarify our understanding of the structure of the self-image as Wylie (1961) very clearly documents.

Our theory about the maturing person suggested what properties of the self-image should be studied. Could the five developmental trends be meaningfully applied to the self-image and could valid measures of each inferred dimension be constructed? Since the five trends defining the maturing person are interdependent, the empirical measures of such properties were not expected to be independent of each other.

Stability of the Self-Image

The self-image becomes more stable over time. While this assertion seemingly contradicts Rogers' definition of the "fully functioning person" whose "*self-structure* will be a fluid gestalt, changing flexibly in the process of assimilation of new *experience*" (1959a, p. 234), the contradiction is perhaps more apparent than real. I prefer to emphasize that there is continuity of structure; Rogers prefers to single out the flexibility and openness of the self-image for assimilating information. For me, stability does not mean rigidity or high assimilatory thresholds to new information. For Rogers, "new *experience*" practically means only minor experiential variations, given the usual constant and familiar internal and external worlds of most people.

Very few studies have explicitly investigated the stability or the identity of the self-image over time and its personality correlates. What data are available come primarily from test-retest correlations computed more to demonstrate the reliability of a self-image test than to explore specific determinants and correlates of the stability of the self-image. The self-image is reasonably stable in young children as well as in adolescents and adults for short intervals of time. Coefficients of the stability of the self-image of fourth to sixth grade children range from .73 to .91 for periods of two (Lipsitt, 1958) to five weeks (Coopersmith, 1959), for adolescents .53 over a two-year period (Engel, 1959), and for young adults .79 for a one (D. M. Taylor, 1955) and an eight week interval (Worchel, 1957). No long-term longitudinal studies of the stability of the self-image have been reported except by Kelly (1955) who found that the self-image of adults to be less stable than other components of the personality, such as valuators, over a twenty year period.

Not much more is known about the personality correlates of the stability of the self-image, primarily because few studies have been reported and none of them have been replicated. Instability of the self-image is associated with self-reported poor adjustment, characterized by insecurity, lack of drive and endurance, poor control, feelings of grogginess and uneasiness (G. M. Smith, 1958) and low self-esteem (McGehee, 1957). I expected the well organized men to have more stable self-images than the poorly organized men and the stability of the self-image to be correlated with measures of good self-organization.

Congruence of the Self-Image

The developmental trend toward integration or coherence and consistency of the self is manifested in the increasing congruence of the self-image. Congruence involves the combination of different, often disparate, incompatible schemata into some integrating larger schema. The limiting example of self-image incongruence is the person who has several complex self-images not previously combined or combinable into a master self-image (e.g., multiple personality). There is considerable disagreement about what measures best define self-image consistency. Bronson (1959) suggests incongruence of the self-image (he uses Erikson's term of identity diffusion) is defined by uncertainty about the relation of one's past and current selves, about one's dominant traits, about one's feelings about oneself, and by greater anxiety. He finds significant intercorrelations between measures of each criterion. Wylie (1961), on the other hand, suggests three different measures of the congruence of the self-image: difference scores between private and ideal selves, between private and social selves, and between both private and social selves and some veridical measure of the person's self. The latter measure I call self-image accuracy. As one might expect, measures of the ideal and of the social self significantly covary with measures of the actual self (Martire & Hornberger, 1957).

What is the most appropriate measure of the congruence of the self-image? The discrepancy between the private and the ideal selves has been most extensively researched. Common sense as well as considerable research indicate that discrepancies between one's private and one's ideal self-image are oftentimes severely painful and are frequently indicative of anxiety and poor adjustment (Bruce, 1958; G. M. Smith, 1958; Turner & Vanderlippe, 1958). But the private-ideal self measure has been severely criticized and its psychological meaning is not clear. The ideal self component of the private-ideal self discrepancy index is alleged to be non-discriminating since most persons share a similar ideal stereotype of what it is to be mature (Wylie, 1961). The obtained private-ideal self research results could be more parsimoniously accounted for by the private self measure alone, as Lipsitt's (1958) results suggest. The meaning of the private-ideal self discrepancy as an inferential measure of the level of self-organization is ambiguous. Not only have some studies found curvilinear relationships between the private-ideal self measure and adaptation (Chodorkoff, 1954; Hillson & Worchel, 1957) but also reflection suggests that the measure favors more drab and contented persons of rudimentary and undifferentiated self-organization levels who have minimal expectations of themselves. Gordon Allport has sagely remarked in conversation that the more "mature" adolescent is the one with vaguely, frequently confused, often unobtainable aspirations and ideals—not the adolescent of low aspirations who presumably would have a minimal discrepancy between his private and ideal self-images.

Given both the empirical and theoretical ambiguities of the private-ideal self-image measure, I sought a more valid measure of the congruence of the self-image in the discrepancy between a person's private and social self-images. A large discrepancy between my view of myself and what I believe others think of me must seriously complicate my adaptation to others. Should I spontaneously act to be consistent with my own valuator hierarchy and "true self" or should I assume the role I believe others expect of me? It is just such a believed discrepancy that leads to feelings of not being understood, of not being able to express one's "real self," of being inhibited and conforming or rebellious and defiant. The conflict between Norma Jean Baker and Marilyn Monroe witnessed the desperation such incongruence can tragically produce. That surprisingly little empirical research has been done on this measure of self-image inconsistency given contemporary concerns about conformity and individualism also encouraged me to explore it. According to Wylie (1961), the meaning of the empirical studies using this definition of congruence is ambiguous because of methodological complications (non-comparable studies, ambiguous measures of the social self). The few results suggest that persons with marked incongruence between their private and social selves master stress less adaptively (Funkenstein, *et al*, 1957), have less accurate self-insight, and report being more maladjusted, insecure, anxious, dependent, and Bohemian (G. M. Smith, 1958). I expected well organized persons to be more congruent in their private and social selves than poorly organized persons, and that the congruence of the self-image would be related to other measures of good self-organization.

Allocentricism of the Self-Image

The self-image becomes more allocentric over time. Colloquially, one might say the self-image becomes less organized around "I" and more around "we." The child's self is initially egocentrically organized around his biological needs and his most immediate world. In time, he identifies with and progressively organizes himself around a wider and wider nexus of other persons, groups, and institutions, including his home town, state, and religion (Mathews, Hardyck, & Sarbin, 1953; Sarbin, 1952). Some theorists such as Mead (1934) suggest the development of the self-image involves primarily the internalization of and accommodation to the expectations of the generalized other. But as the self-image may become too stable or rigid, so it may become too allocentrically organized (as in hysterical identifications) and jeopardize its own stability (or legitimate autocentric needs). Increasing allocentric development seems to depend upon the capacity of the self to accommodate to a wide range of information, particularly that coming from other persons. That a satisfactory measure of the range of information to which the self-image could adaptively accommodate eluded me suggests that the construct of allocentricism has not yet been adequately defined. I measured the allocentricism of the self-image only indirectly by assessing the accuracy of the person's social self. The rationale for such an index was that a person more allocentrically organized should be more objectively aware of the reactions of other persons to his own self than a person whose self-image was more subjectively organized around his own feelings and less around his relationships with others. It was expected that well organized persons would have self-images less centered around their own needs and feelings and more organized around their transactional relationships, allegiances, and social values, and that allocentric self-images would be directly related to measures of good self-organization.

Autonomy of the Self-Image

With growth, the self-image also becomes more autonomous or independent of the coercive effects of information (primarily that from other persons) incongruent with the self-image. The meaning of "autonomy of the self-image" is captured by Rogers' comment that the mature person "will *experience* himself as the locus of evaluation" (1959a, p. 234). The self-image is not slavishly accommodative to either allocentric or autocentric claims. Persons whose self-images are maturely autonomous know who they are and do not necessarily rely on the standards or expectations of other persons to define their private selves. The assumed interrelationship between the properties of the self-image became even more obvious when I sought a measure of the autonomy of the self-image. The most appropriate measure appeared to be the resistance the person showed to changing his self-image when he was confronted by the persuasive information that other persons judged him very differently than he judged himself. But because such a measure also defines one aspect of the developmental trend toward stability, some doubts occur whether the identification of the developmental trends is adequate. I expected that measures of the stability and the autonomy of the self-image would be highly intercorrelated. Autonomy has been found to be related to congruence. Autonomy of the self-image to information that challenged the self-image (faked personality sketches) was significantly related to the congruence of the self-image (congruence measured by the private-ideal self discrepancy score, Gruen, 1960). Research from attitude change studies suggests that persons of high self-esteem are less compliant (more autonomous?) in accepting persuasive information than persons of low self-esteem (Wylie, 1961), though other research indicates variables such as type of information and the personality traits of the communicator complicate the relationship (Debbs, 1962; Leventhal & Perloe, 1962). I expected the self-images of the well organized men would be more autonomous than the self-images of the poorly organized persons, and that autonomy of the self-image would be directly related to measures of good self-organization.

Accuracy of the Self-Image

The fifth developmental trend suggests that more of the self-image becomes available to awareness with increasing development. Such a proposition immediately raises difficult theoretical and methodological issues about the nature of an unconscious or "nonphenomenal" self-image or about attitudes toward and components of the self-image that are not readily verbalizable (Wylie, 1961). I avoided some of these imposing problems by redefining the implications of the developmental trend toward cognitive symbolization to mean that the self-image becomes more accurate with greater maturity. Practically, in what way does one measure directly how much of the nonphenomenal self-image is left to be verbalized? Presumably, the more insight or awareness that a person has of himself the more accurate is his image of himself. Or the more incomplete is a person's self-knowledge the greater is the likelihood that what he knows is only partially accurate. Many measures of self-insight have been used but none are free of severe methodological limitations (Wylie, 1961). Consequently, only a few firmly supported generalizations emerge from self-insight research: "self-ratings show low but significant correlations with the ratings . . . from others;" "self-overestimation is more common than is self-underestimation;" and "there are consistent individual differences in the tendency toward overestimation, underestimation, or accurate estimation across a variety of traits" (Wylie, 1961, pp. 314–15). Of more specific relevance to this study are the findings that well adjusted (Kogan, Quin, Ax, & Ripley, 1957) and sound (Barron, 1954, 1963) persons are more accurate than poorly adjusted and unsound persons in describing their self-images. The perplexing limitation of all such studies, including our own, is that no satisfactory veridical measure of the person's personality has been found against which to compare the person's own self-evaluations. It was expected that the well organized men would have more accurate self-images than the poorly organized men, and that accuracy of self-image would be related to measures of good self-organization.

The Phenomenal Maturity of the Self-Image

Up to this point, I have ignored the affectively evaluative reaction of the person to himself. Such terms as self-regard, self-acceptance and rejection, self-pride, and self-satisfaction refer to the evaluative content but not to the formal properties of the self-image. Self-esteem or self-regard is a complex judgmental consequence of the coordination of a person's valuator hierarchy with the content of his self-image. It is, in part, based on judgments about one's past adaptive successes or competences that go to make up the content of the self-image. As White says, competence, "based on the effectiveness of one's own activity in dealing with the environment, is a vital root of self-esteem" (1956, p. 161). I have suggested that persons more successful in adaptation are more stable, congruent, etc., persons. Therefore, if a determinant of self-esteem is past adaptive success, and if successful adaptation is related to the maturity of a person, then self-esteem should be directly related to maturity. Some support for this expectation comes from the finding that persons who have more differentiated self-images (presumably persons of greater self-organization) also have more positive self-images (Gurin, et al, 1960).

But there are other determinants of self-esteem which distort the simple linear relationship between self-esteem and maturity implied above. Heightened self-esteem levels may be the product of defensive involvement (Block & Thomas, 1955), particularly in severely disorganized persons such as schizophrenics who frequently report excessively high self-esteem (Wylie, 1961). Wylie suggests that the correlation between self-esteem and maturity is curvilinear when the full range of maturity (including that of patients) is studied. Since my research samples were drawn from one portion of the maturity continuum (non-patient population), I held to a linear hypothesis. In this study self-esteem was not measured directly as the youths were not asked to rate the degree of favorableness of their self-images. Instead, a measure of the extent to which they described themselves in terms of those phenomenal traits considered to define maturity was secured. It was assumed a person would regard himself more favorably if he described himself as possessing many more mature traits. The hypothesis was that self-rated maturity was directly related to the stability, congruence of the self-image as well as to other measures of good self-organization and maturity.

THE SELF-IMAGE QUESTIONNAIRE (SIQ)

Structure of the SIQ

The different properties of the self-image were measured using a rating scale, called Self-Image Questionnaire (SIQ), which was administered under varying instructional conditions.

The SIQ has thirty bipolar trait scales, each of which consists of a line with eight boxes along it; four boxes for one defined trait and four for its opposite defined trait. The person selects one of the two bipolar traits that best describes him and checks one of the four boxes of that trait. The boxes at each end of the line indicate the greatest amount of the trait in question. The bipolar mature and immature trait pairs are randomly ordered on the left- and right-hand side of each lined scale to counteract any persistent response sets. An abbreviated form of the SIQ is given below.

The thirty scales were selected from the 185 adjectives of the Adjective Check List. These adjectives were those reported in the theoretical and empirical literature to describe mature and immature, adjusted and maladjusted, effective and ineffective

Self-Image Questionnaire Scales

1. Cautious

Avoids the strange and new. Looks at all aspects of a situation over-cautiously. Plays it safe.

Adventurous

Seeks and readily enters into new experiences and situations. May show a good deal of initiative; enjoys risks.

(Scale and extended definitions omitted hereafter)

2.	Imaginative	Unimaginative
3.	Ordered	Disordered
4.	Aggressive	Gentle
5.	Apathetic	Energetic
6.	Self-perspective	Self-involvement
7.	Empathic	Insensitive
8.	Not anticipate consequences	Anticipate consequences
9.	Strong convictions	Weak convictions
10.	Purposeful	Purposeless
11.	Unpredictable	Predictable
12.	Suspicious	Trustful
13.	Reflective	Unreflective
14.	Accepting of self	Rejecting of self
15.	Open	Defensive
16.	Self-centered	Other centered
17.	Decisive	Indecisive
18.	Overcontrols impulses	Undercontrols impulses
19.	Enthusiastic	Bland
20.	High aspirations	Low aspirations
21.	Dependent	Self-sufficient
22.	Easily upset	Unshakable
23.	Realistic	Unrealistic
24.	Rigid	Adaptable, flexible
25.	Vague thinking	Clear thinking
26.	Placid	Worrying, anxious
27.	Warmth in relationships	Coldness in relationships
28.	Fulfilling potential	Not fulfilling potential
29.	Objective	Subjective
30.	Easy-going	Demanding

persons. The indexed adjectives were classified into thirty scales which seemed to account for most of them.

How can this rather simple measure of the self-image be combined with various instructional procedures to measure the formal properties of the self-image? The self-image dimensions are defined as follows:

Stability is defined by the sum of the differences in scale position for each of the thirty scales between the initial and a successive administration of the SIQ. The smaller the sum of the difference scores, the greater is the stability of the self-image.

Congruence is defined by the sum of the differences in scale position for each of the thirty scales between the private and the social self. The smaller the sum of the differences, the more congruent is the self-image.

Allocentricism is defined by the sum of the differences in scale position for each of the thirty scales between the social self and independent judge ratings of the person's self. Again, the smaller the sum of the differences, the more allocentrically objective is the person's self-image.

Autonomy is defined by the sum of the differences in scale position of the eight most stable traits of the private self and a subsequent private self-rating when persuasive contradictory evidence about the person's personality is given prior to the subsequent private self-rating. The smaller the sum of the difference scores, the more autonomous is the self-image of coercive information.

Accuracy is defined by the sum of the difference scores in scale position for each of the thirty scales between the private self and independent judge ratings of the person. The smaller the sum of the difference scores, the more accurate is the self-image.

Since most scales represented a mature-immature trait continuum, it was possible to secure a summary index of the maturity of the *content* of the self-image, hereafter called "maturity of the self-image." The eight scaled positions on each continuum can be weighted so that the scale positions indicating greatest amount of the mature and immature trait received a high positive and negative score respectively:

Ordered   Disordered

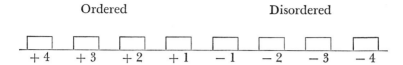

A total maturity score could be obtained by summing the maturity weights for those twenty-six scales most clearly relevant to maturity (i.e., the scores for the traits of aggressive-gentle, over-under-control, objective-subjective, and easy-going-demanding were à *priori* excluded in calculating the maturity scores). The higher the positive score, the more mature the content of the self-image. Similar maturity scores could be obtained for the social self and the judges' ratings of the person.

Samples and Instructional Procedure

The SIQ was administered to the Organized, Standard, and Personality samples.

Organized Sample

Honest self-ratings were encouraged by using code numbers for all SIQ procedures, by guaranteeing that no other person would know his ratings, and, while emphasizing the need for honesty, by presenting the rating tasks in a casual and matter-of-fact way after good rapport had been established. In his first test session, each person completed the SIQ for both private and social self instructions. The private and social SIQs were identical except for their instructions. The written private self instructions, verbally clarified by me, asked the person to describe himself as accurately as possible. The social self instructions requested the person to complete the SIQ as a group of faculty and students might rate him on it. The well and the poorly organized groups were each divided into two replicate groups, and the order of the two ratings was counterbalanced across the replicate groups. The two ratings were separated by the administration of another test in order to reduce contamination of one instructional set by the other.

At the beginning of the second test session, each man rerated his private self on the SIQ. He was told not to recall his earlier ratings since his recollection might be inaccurate; rather, he was asked to rate his current self-image.

At the end of the third test session, each person participated in an experiment designed to measure the autonomy of his self-image. He was told that the selecting judges had completed the SIQ on him and that while the judges agreed with his ratings on most of the traits, they rated him in the opposite direction on eight of the traits. His own rating of the trait and the presumed rating of the judges were then mentioned. Since I wanted a measure of how much the person might change his subsequent ratings on these eight traits as a result of this challenge to his existing self-image, it was imperative that the stabilities of the eight traits (which would certainly vary among themselves and between different persons) be equated among all of the men. The eight most stable traits as rated by the person in the first and second private SIQs were selected to manipulate. No one expressed skepticism of the procedure in a subsequent interview and more than a few said they had brooded about the judges' ratings afterwards.

At the beginning of the fourth test session, each person rerated his private self for a third time, ostensibly to help me out because "my daughter had spilled ink over some of the rating scales and some ratings were not decipherable." He was parenthetically told not to recall his earlier ratings. At the conclusion of the test session, the person's reactions to the self-image procedure were elicited and the entire experiment explained.

Because the stability of the self-image may be affected by the length of the time intervals between the test sessions, the test session intervals of the well and poorly organized groups were matched. The matching was singularly successful for the time intervals between each pair of test sessions were practically identical for the criterion groups. For the entire sample, the mean time interval between sessions one and two was 3.7 days, sessions two and three 4.6 days, and sessions three and four 3.6 days. The correlation between time elapsed and stability of the self-image was .04, indicating time interval is not related to stability of the self-image in this study.

Judge ratings of each person were secured. Ten months following their participation in the initial selection of the sample, groups of those four faculty and student judges who had earlier reported knowing one of the sample's men most intimately completed the SIQ about that man. In retrospect it would have been preferable to have found four different judges who had not participated in the selection process to rate each man, but apart from the sheer difficulty of identifying such campus judges who knew each man as well as the four judges, the ten month time interval mitigated some of the obvious contamination of these judge ratings. Median judge ratings were used in the analysis.

Standard Sample

Some changes in the study of the self-image of the Standard sample were necessary since it was not a selected but a voluntary sample. Also, the test of the autonomy of the self-image was omitted because its results with the Organized sample did not warrant its replication.

The SIQ procedures of the Organized sample were replicated with the Standard sample except that each person was asked to name that fellow student who knew him best and to complete the social self SIQ as that friend would complete it about him. The private and social SIQs were, of course, counterbalanced within the sample. During the second test session, each person rerated his private self-image. The elapsed time interval between the first and second SIQ private ratings did not differ for the well and poorly organized groups (thirteen days). The correlation between time elapsed and the stability of the self-image was .17, indicating again that stability of the self-image is not related to short time interval differences.

In the meantime, data about the person were collected from the designated friend who completed the SIQ on the person participating in the experiment. Each judge was assured no one would learn his ratings and each was asked not to discuss his ratings with anyone else.

Personality Sample

To cross-validate the findings of the major samples, the procedures for measuring the stability, congruence, allocentricism and accuracy of the self-image were replicated on a group of ten students in an advanced course on Personality Theory. At the beginning of the semester, the private and social (defined as the image a group of student judges would have of him) SIQ procedures were given to the class. The alleged purpose was to demonstrate rating scale procedures. Each man had been assigned a code number and the order of the two questionnaires was counterbalanced within the class. The Rorschach was then administered to the group in a second class room, ostensibly to demonstrate its procedure. Several weeks later, I clinically evaluated the coded Rorschach protocols using Schafer's criteria of healthy self-organization, following the same judging procedures used for the Standard sample. I had no knowledge of the coded SIQ ratings which had been locked away unseen and unanalyzed. Fifty-six days following the initial ratings, the private and social SIQs were readministered to the entire class, but this time the ratings were counterbalanced with their first presentation order. Each student selected that set of ordered questionnaires coded with his number. At the end of the semester, each member of the class described each of the nine other members of the course by completing the SIQ on each of them. The code numbers were then identified so that the median judge ratings could be matched with the appropriate person's ratings and the Rorschach.

The SIQ Score Relationships

From the theoretical position of Chapter 1, I expected the measures of the properties of the self-image to be positively intercorrelated but to measure different facets of the self-image. Because most of the SIQ measures, except those of allocentricism and some of the maturity scores, were based on the same private self-report, this expectation strictly cannot be confirmed. But the intercorrelational matrix of the measures can be examined to see if the relationships are positive and if several differently labeled measures may be indexing the same property of the self-image.

Table 5–1 gives the matrix of correlations between the SIQ scores. The pattern was as expected. The measures of the self-image properties do positively intercorrelate and, except for those of the small Personality sample, the magnitude of the intercorrelations suggests that the measures may be tapping somewhat different facets of the self-image. The correlations of the autonomy measure suggest it may not have been a good measure. The high positive relationship between stability and congruence was also found by G. M. Smith (1958) whose suggestion that both may reflect the same underlying dimension our own factor analysis will later question. The moderate positive stability-accuracy correlations do not support other findings that self-image accuracy and stability are not related (Larson, 1959). Finally, the congruence-accuracy correlations confirm G. M. Smith's (1958) finding that the accuracy of self-insight is related to the congruence of the self-image.

As predicted, maturity of the self-image and judge-rated maturity tend to be related directly to increased stability, congruence, etc., of the self-image. For both samples, persons who have more accurate and allocentric self-images are consistently judged to be more mature, although we cannot forget that the accuracy and allocentric measures are not independent of the judge ratings of maturity. Also, the person judged to be more mature tends to have a more stable and congruent self-image. The general pattern of the results fits our expectations reasonably well.

Nothing has been said of the reliability of the SIQ which has not really concerned us. But to complete the record, the test-retest coefficients of the private self ratings for each sample are: Org. $r = .88$ (first-second SIQ) and $r = .81$ (first-third SIQ); Stand. $r = .64$ (first-second SIQ); Person. $r = .63$. The test-retest coefficient of the social self ratings was .58 for the Personality sample, the only one to whom the social self instructions were given at two different times.

TABLE 5–1: INTERCORRELATIONS [1] BETWEEN THE SIQ SCORES OF THE STRUCTURAL PROPERTIES AND MATURITY OF THE SELF-IMAGE

SELF-IMAGE SCORES		STABILITY	PROPERTIES OF THE SELF-IMAGE					MATURITY SCORES	
			CONGRUENCE	ACCURACY	ALLOCENTRIC	AUTONOMY[2]	PRIVATE	SOCIAL
Properties									
Congruence	Org:	.74						
	Sta:	.59						
	Per:	.98						
Accuracy	Org:	.41	.46					
	Sta:	.14	.35					
	Per:	.71	.68					
Allo-centric	Org:	.56	.43	.83				
	Sta:	.18	.37	.66				
	Per:	.79	.81	.81				
Autonomy	Org:	.28	−.04	.10	.26			
Maturity Scores									
Private self	Org:	−.45	−.37	−.09	−.09	−.11		
	Sta:	.07	−.07	−.30	−.39			
	Per:	−.44	−.40	−.37	−.21			
Social self	Org:	−.67	−.69	−.30	−.26	−.04	.83	
	Sta:	−.03	−.19	−.24	−.33		.75	
	Per:	−.65	−.47	−.62	−.42			
Judge	Org:	−.60	−.59	−.61	−.51	.30	.37	.69
	Sta:	.10	−.03	−.46	−.35		.49	.58
	Per:	−.50	−.62	−.45	−.41		.78	.73

[1] Because the original measures of the SIQ scores are not independent of each other, it did not seem advisable to determine the significance levels of the correlations.

[2] The autonomy procedure was not given to the Standard and Personality samples.

SELF-IMAGE QUESTIONNAIRE
PERSONALITY CORRELATES

What is the evidence for the validity of the SIQ? Because of the wide research interest in the self-image, selected personality correlates for most of the self-image scores are reported.

SIQ and Intellectual Skills and Achievement

Quite unexpectedly, twelve percent of the 108 skill and achievement correlations of the three samples were significant at least at a two-tailed .05 probability level. Neither verbal (CEEB), quantitative (CEEB), nor abstract reasoning (Terman) skills were consistently associated with any of the self-image dimensions or maturity scores. All but two of the significant correlations were between the self-image measures and academic grade average. It can be stated with great confidence that high academic achievement in an environment such as Haverford's is very significantly associated with being a mature person, as judged by others (Org. r = .83, p $\angle$ .001; Stand. r = .49, p $\angle$ .01; Person. r = .79, p $\angle$ .01). This remarkable finding is even more startling when the differences in the types of judges and judging procedures used with the SIQ and other differences between the samples are taken into account. Recall that the Organized sample used different groups of four selecting faculty and student judges to make the SIQ ratings; the Standard sample used one student who was selected by the participating person to be a judge; the Personality sample used nine other student class members as judges. This generalization is complemented by the significant though not as consistent finding for persons who believe that others will judge them to be mature (maturity of the social self-image) to have higher grade averages (Org. r = .63, p $\angle$ .01; Stand. r = −.02; Person. r = .79, p $\angle$ .01). Finally, academic achievement significantly (though not consistently supported by the deviant Standard sample) covaries inversely with the instability (Org. r = −.56, p $\angle$ .01; Stand. r = .16; Person. r = −.80, p $\angle$ .01) and incongruence of the self-image (Org.

r = −.48, p ∠ .05; Stand. r = .15; Person. r = −.71, p ∠ .05).
While accuracy and allocentricism but not autonomy are similarly
related to academic achievement, the correlations of no more
than one of the three samples reach significance for either
dimension.

These findings neither confirm nor disconfirm the findings of
other researchers about the relation of the self-image to skill-
achievement measures, primarily because no consistent generalizations emerge from this other research (Wylie, 1961).

SIQ and Social Judgments of Self-Organization

Recall that the men of each sample were ordered from
well organized to poorly organized by the amount of judge
agreement about their degree of self-organization. Does degree of
self-organization covary directly with maturity of the self-image
and the judged maturity of the person and inversely with unstable, incongruent, autocentric self-images as we expected? Table
5-2 which reports the correlations between judged self-organization and the SIQ measures reveals that our expectations were
generally confirmed, except for the autonomy of the self-image.
Consensually judged self-organization is consistently and significantly related to self-judged maturity, beliefs about how mature
one thinks others believe one is, and to SIQ judge ratings of
one's maturity. Also, self-organization is consistently and significantly *inversely* related to autocentric and inaccurate self-images.
Finally, unstable and incongruent self-images may be related to
poor self-organization but sample differences suggest such a relation may not emerge in relatively homogeneous and emotionally stable samples. The significant positive relations between
SIQ judge ratings of maturity and consensual ratings of self-
organization for the Organized sample are not surprising since
some of the same judges participated in both the self-organization
and the SIQ judging procedures (even though their ratings were
made ten months apart). But the Standard sample's parallel finding (which was not so contaminated) does indicate that reliable
agreement about the maturity of a person can be obtained at
a very global level.

TABLE 5–2: CORRELATES BETWEEN CONSENSUAL
JUDGMENTS OF SELF-ORGANIZATION
AND THE SIQ SCORES OF THE
PROPERTIES AND MATURITY OF
THE SELF-IMAGE

SELF-IMAGE SCORES	JUDGMENTS OF SELF-ORGANIZATION	
	ORGANIZED rho	STANDARD rho
Properties		
Stability[1]	−.71***	.10
Congruence	−.62***	−.09
Accuracy	−.62***	−.28*
Allocentricism	−.43**	−.31*
Autonomy	.27	—— [2]
Maturity Scores		
Private self	.44**	.32*
Social self	.71***	.32*
Judge rated	.85***	.45***

* p ∠ .05
** p ∠ .025
*** p ∠ .01

[1] It must be remembered when evaluating the large number of significant findings found with the SIQ, that the SIQ measures are intercorrelated and rely in part on the same private-self ratings.

[2] The SIQ autonomy procedure was not given to the Standard sample.

SIQ and Questionnaire Scales of Maladjustment and Control

Thirty-four percent of the Organized, eleven percent of the Standard, and twenty-seven percent of the Personality samples' MMPI and Bernreuter correlations with the SIQ were significant at least at a one-tailed .05 probability level. One of the Organized but five of the Standard sample's correlations were significant (two-tailed) in the nonpredicted direction, but we do not report them since these results for one sample were not supported by those of the other. Table 5–3 reports only those

TABLE 5–3: CORRELATES BETWEEN SIQ SCORES OF THE PROPERTIES AND MATURITY OF THE SELF-IMAGE AND SELECTED QUESTIONNAIRE SCALES OF MALADJUSTMENT AND CONTROL

QUESTIONNAIRE SCALES		PROPERTIES OF SELF-IMAGE[1]				MATURITY SCORES		
		STABIL. r	CONGRU. r	ACCUR. r	ALLOC. r	PRIVATE r	SOCIAL r	JUDGE r
MMPI Total	Org:[2]	.21	.52***	.24	.00	−.38*	−.52***	−.41*
	Sta:	.08	.14	−.23	−.23	.31	.28	−.06
	Per:	.82***	.77***	.52	.57*	−.31	−.52	−.42
D	Org:	.22	.44**	.28	.03	−.43**	−.55***	−.56***
	Sta:	.04	.00	.09	.18	−.52***	−.46***	−.18
	Per:	.48	.38	.36	.44	.18	.02	−.08
Pd	Org:	.05	.39*	.31	−.03	−.25	−.39*	−.38*
	Sta:	−.04	−.15	.09	−.06	−.24	−.09	−.14
	Per:	.77***	.68**	.46	.44	−.40	−.53	−.49
Pa	Org:	.33	.38*	−.09	.04	−.60***	−.50***	−.11
	Sta:	.36**	.02	−.13	−.08	.25	.45****[3]	.08
	Per:	.65***	.59*	.31	.19	−.38	−.51	−.24
Pt	Org:	.02	.33	.05	−.14	−.34	−.43**	−.30
	Sta:	.29*	.19	−.05	.04	−.29*	−.20	.07
	Per:	.83***	.78***	.53	.56*	−.36	−.52	−.54

126

QUESTIONNAIRE SCALES		Properties of Self-Image[1]				Maturity Scores		
		STABIL.	CONGRU.	ACCUR.	ALLOC.	PRIVATE	SOCIAL	JUDGE
		r	r	r	r	r	r	r
MMPI								
Sc	Org:	.23	.46**	.42**	.21	−.37*	−.47**	−.41*
	Sta:	.09	.20	.23	.11	−.40***	−.15	.02
	Per:	.68**	.71**	.52	.59*	−.59*	−.69**	−.55*
Si	Org:	.15	.30	.08	.03	−.43**	−.59***	−.48***
	Sta:	.12	.17	.05	.21	−.45***	−.46***	−.13
	Per:	Not available						
Taylor	Org:	.22	.50***	−.04	−.03	−.39*	−.57***	−.24
MAS	Sta:	.11	.17	−.05	.06	−.09	.22	.39*[3]
Bernreuter[4]								
Neurotic	Org:	.31	.46**	.11	.07	−.55***	−.69***	−.53***
	Sta:	.17	.13	.00	.15	−.44***	−.40***	.00
Introver.	Org:	.38*	.55***	.17	.14	−.57***	−.71***	−.53***
	Sta:	.11	.27	.09	.12	−.34**	−.28	−.03
Non-social	Org:	.55***	.74***	.51***	.44**	−.21	−.46**	−.44**
	Sta:	−.01	.20	.26	.12	−.15	−.15	−.18
Dom-inance	Org:	−.11	−.19	.00	.00	.46**	.50***	.46**
	Sta:	−.14	−.05	.02	−.20	.50***	.41***	.10

[1] Autonomy correlations omitted because they were not significant and not cross-validated.
[2] N = 23 for all correlates of Organized sample.
[3] Direction opposite from that predicted; significant at two-tailed p level.
[4] Bernreuter data not available for Personality sample.

* p < .05
** p < .025
*** p < .01

significant correlations which were consistently supported by two samples and not seriously contradicted by the third (when test results were available for all three samples).

It is quite clear that accuracy and allocentricism are not as predictive as stability or congruence of either MMPI and Bernreuter self-concept or control scores. Inaccurate and, to a lesser extent, autocentric self-images are most consistently associated with disinterest in (Bern. Nonsocial) and withdrawal from (MMPI Sc) other persons. This pattern is eminently sensible, given theories that emphasize the interpersonal determinants of the self-image (Mead, 1934; Sullivan, 1953). But the relative predictive impotence of difference scores between judge and self ratings is so consistent for the other personality tests I will report that we must wonder (along with many other researchers who have used similar measures) whether such difference scores aren't so complex and so affected by possible artifactual variables that their reliability is very suspect. Since the Standard sample used many different judges, each rating only one person, it was not unexpected to find that few of its judge correlations, based on difference scores, approached significance or formed a consistent pattern.

The measure of autonomy was not consistently correlated with either the questionnaire or the other personality measures. The autonomy experimental procedure was not replicated for the Standard sample because the analysis of the Organized sample's results convinced us that the coercive procedure used to test autonomy was not adequate. It induced very little variance in the subsequent private self-ratings (the difference scores for the eight stable traits departed only minimally from zero). Stable traits may be more central to the self-image and may be too certainly believed to be persuasively changed.

Self-image *incongruence* and not *instability* [1] is associated with greater maladjustment (MMPI, Bern.), although both significantly and consistently covary with intellectualized, obsessionally

[1] The low relation between instability and maladjustment (MMPI Total) is not attributable to any attenuating effect of defensive rigidity. Scatter plots of various stability correlates revealed no curvilinear trends that would support a rigidity hypothesis.

rigid and projective traits (MMPI Pt, Pa) and, less consistently, with socially aloof and introversive traits (Bern. Introver., Nonsocial). But self-image *incongruence* is by far the more powerful predictor of other traits. Highly incongruent self-images are characteristic of persons who report themselves as severely maladjusted (MMPI Total; Bern. Neurotic) and anxious (Taylor). The meaning of the somewhat paradoxical Ma, Sc, and Pd pattern of correlations may better be captured by the example of the agitated and uncontrolled affective, often thinly disguised aggressive, reactions of socially alienated persons. Self-image *inaccuracy* also tends to be associated with this type of social alienation (MMPI Sc).

Some sample inconsistencies rob the self-image maturity correlates of their clarity, but the following generalizations seem warranted. The more mature the person's private self-image, the more socially assertive (Bern. Dom.) and the less disturbed (MMPI Total; Bern. Neurotic), withdrawn and affectively isolated (MMPI Si, Sc; Bern. Introver.) is he likely to be. He may also be less anxious (Taylor) and moody (MMPI D) as well as less obsessionally preoccupied with (MMPI Pt) and more confident of himself (Bern. Lack self-conf.). Those persons judged on the SIQ to be more mature report less general disturbance (MMPI Total; Bern. Neurotic), less social isolation and introversive withdrawal (MMPI Si, Sc; Bern. Nonsocial), and acting out (MMPI Pd) behavior. Similar findings hold for social self-image maturity as well.

These findings agree with those from the studies summarized by (Wylie 1961). Despite different self-image procedures and samples, self-regard (most similar to the maturity of the private self) was, as we also found, consistently and significantly inversely related with MMPI D, Pt, Sc, and Si scores and less consistently with Pd and Pa scores. That persons of more adequate self-regard also report themselves to be relatively nonanxious persons confirms similar results found in other studies (Cowen, Heilizer, Axelrod, & Alexander, 1957).

What is the relation between authoritarianism measured by a self-report type of scale (Calif. F) and the self-image? Although I would assume authoritarianism to be related to more immature and inadequate self-image dimensional development, Wylie (1961) asserts that there is no consistent theoretical basis or pattern of experimental results with the F scale from which to form any directional hypotheses. Given these doubts, I interpreted the results with the scale more conservatively. Authoritarianism was unrelated either to stability, congruence, autonomy, or the maturity of the self-image; but it was significantly related at two-tailed significance levels to both inaccurate (r = .58, p $\angle$ .01) and autocentric (r = .53, p $\angle$ .01) self-images as well as inversely related to judged maturity (r = −.49, p $\angle$ .02). The more authoritarian person is more immature and his self-image is less accurately organized around other persons and is less accurately descriptive of his own self.

SIQ and Rorschach Measures

What new insights about the meaning of the SIQ measures of the self-image does the Rorschach offer? I do not discuss the correlations found for the traditional Klopfer scores, primarily because the findings found to be significant for the Organized sample were not replicated with other samples. Generally, the traditional Rorschach scores of good adjustment (FC, M, Fc) were not related (either linearily or curvilinearily) to the SIQ maturity scores. We will find this to be the case for every subsequent analysis of such scores.

The clinical and Holt methods of analyzing the Rorschach produced more revealing and exciting results. Table 5–4 reports the correlations between these scores and the self-image measures. As predicted, both the stability and the congruence of the self-image are very consistently associated with clinically evaluated good self-organization. The stability of the *social* self-image over a two-month period also tends to be directly associated with clinical evaluations of good self-organization (Person. rho = .46). Finally, clinical judgments of self-organization are inversely related to the immaturity of the self-image, to immaturity as judged by others, and to beliefs that others think one is immature. One

cannot ask for more consistent results than these Rorschach clinical correlates.

The Holt autocentric and control correlates also match some
of our expectations. Thirty-nine percent of the Organized, thirteen and one percent of the Standard and Personality group administered Rorschach correlates were significant at least at a
one-tailed .05 level. Generally, only the stability and congruence
dimensions of the self-image were predictive of Rorschach measures of autocentricism. Greater instability and incongruence of
the self-image are directly linked with more autocentric schemata
(especially the unconventional types), impaired skill, inadequate
defense effectiveness, and inversely with such measures of good
control as adaptive regression and adaptive imagination (Org.
p ∠ .01).

Again, sample inconsistencies blur the meaning of the very
dramatic self-image maturity correlates of the Organized sample.
The more mature a person believes he is and believes others
think he is, the less is his thinking dominated by autocentric
schemata and regressive coordinations and the more is his behavior under adaptive control. Immaturity (determined by the
SIQ judge ratings) tends to be directly related to more severely
regressed schemata, impaired skills, and possibly lessened capacity
to make regressive schemata coordinations that are still adaptively accommodative.

SIQ and Behavioral Measures of Stability

The Stroop Color-Word test had been given to the
Standard sample to secure a measure of the degree to which a
person could resist the disorganizing effects of distracting *but*
nonpersonal types of information. The inability to maintain a
habitual or stable response set (our definition of the trend toward
stability) or to concentrate in the face of such distracting information was directly related to self-image autocentricism ($r = .39$
p ∠ .01) and inversely related to self-judged maturity ($r =
-.45$, p ∠ .005). These self-image results agree with other find-
ings (which I don't report in detail) that instability to even

TABLE 5–4: CORRELATES BETWEEN SIQ SCORES OF THE PROPERTIES AND MATURITY OF THE SELF-IMAGE AND SELECTED RORSCHACH AUTOCENTRIC AND CONTROL SCORES

RORSCHACH SCORES	PROPERTIES OF SELF-IMAGE[1]				MATURITY SCORES		
	STABIL. r	CONGRU. r	ACCUR. r	ALLOC. r	PRIVATE r	SOCIAL r	JUDGE r
% PriPro							
Org:	.25	.58****	.21	.05	–.43**	–.41**	–.21
Sta:	.44***	.43***	.14	.15	–.05	–.19	–.11
Per:	.41	.33	.47	.31	.17	.05	.22
% Content							
Org:	.06	.38*	.08	–.09	–.36*	–.28	–.05
Sta:	.43***	.41***	.12	.23	–.06	–.10	.03
Per:	.53	.48	.60*	.49	.00	–.14	.09
% Formal							
Org:	.46**	.72***	.28	.17	–.42**	–.53***	–.44**
Sta:	.22	.35**	.20	–.01	.01	–.14	–.17
Per:	.11	.04	.11	.07	.35	.24	.36
% Level 1							
Org:	.44**	.63****	.12	.10	–.39*	–.54***	–.39*
Sta:	.14	.18	.30	.09	–.13	–.22	–.39***
Per:	.32	.19	.26	.04	–.01	–.02	.12

RORSCHACH SCORES		PROPERTIES OF SELF-IMAGE[1]				MATURITY SCORES		
		STABIL. r	CONGRU. r	ACCUR. r	ALLOC. r	PRIVATE r	SOCIAL r	JUDGE r
Sum DD	Org:	.14	.38*	−.04	−.02	−.39*	−.39*	−.06
	Sta:	.22	.36**	.00	.13	−.06	−.05	.03
	Per:	.24	.27	.05	.26	.31	.21	.36
Mean DE	Org:	−.49**	−.56**	−.01	−.06	.30	.45**	.27
	Sta:	−.11	−.11	−.18	−.24	.07	−.10	−.07
	Per:	−.38	−.35	−.03	−.23	.00	.14	−.28
% DD × DE	Org:	−.44**	−.66***	−.04	−.03	.39*	.57***	.31
	Sta:	−.23	−.20	−.20	−.23	.11	−.17	.07
	Per:	−.52	−.50	−.16	.43	.04	.22	−.21
Clinical Evaluation	Org:	−.45**	−.55***	−.16	−.03	.56***	.63***	.35*
	Sta:	−.28*	−.32*	−.03	−.18	.15	.30*	.22
	Per:	−.60*	−.60*	−.30	−.36	.15	.30	−.04

* p < .05
** p < .025
*** p < .01
[1] Autonomy correlations omitted because they were non-significant and not cross-validated.

133

nonpersonal information (Stroop) is significantly related to a range of indices of immaturity (e.g., MMPI D; Bern. Neurotic, Introver., Lack self-conf.).

Critique of the SIQ Validity Correlates

Many of the results obtained in previous studies of the self-image may be explained in terms of methodological and statistical limitations and artifacts (Crowne & Stephens, 1961; Wylie, 1961), which we tried to avoid by using explicit instructions about the type of rating required, counterbalanced designs, cross-validation samples, anonymity procedures, matched temporal testing schedules, defined trait continua, and other SIQ checks. But are there other types of limitations and artifacts that may limit the meaning of the many results found with the SIQ?

Relationships found between concurrently given self-report or questionnaire measures may be due to situational or transitory personality factors. But since the MMPI and Bernreuter scales had been given eighteen to forty-two months *prior* to the SIQ, it is unlikely that the replicated findings can be explained just by transitory or situational factors. Parenthetically, it is of some significance for self-theory that verbal reports are found to be as stable as they are even in late adolescence when considerable personality reorganization is allegedly still taking place (Josselyn, 1959).

Many types of response bias have been found to affect self-report scales (Cronbach, 1958; Messick & Ross, 1962), though the psychological significance as well as generality of such response sets across different type tasks is in dispute (Couch & Keniston, 1960; McGee, 1962). Since formal properties rather than the phenomenal content of the self-image were our primary interest, only a few types of response bias concern us directly. Because the measures of stability and congruence are, for example, defined as difference scores between the verbal reports from the *same* person, any factor that affects one report will probably affect the other and thereby tend to reduce the magnitude of the difference between the two. High stability or congruence of the self-image could result from excessively rigid response biases rather than from good self-organization. Persons who have very rigid self-images may have high thresholds for the assimilation of new information, so that relationships between maturity and various self measures of adjustment must be corrected for such rigidity (Brownfain, 1952). One measure used to assess encapsulation to new information is the California F scale, which when correlated with our measures of stability (and congruence as well) produced nonsignificant relationships occurring in the opposite direction from that expected were rigidity a determinant of high stability or congruence. Another indicator of rigidity might be the tendency to give extreme ratings about one's self. Such a tendency was not related to the F scale. Furthermore, the well and poorly organized groups did not significantly differ in the frequency of their extreme self-ratings. The response bias toward rigidity does not seem to account for our results.

Other response biases such as the tendency to select the more socially desirable or "favorable-to-self" traits (Crowne & Stephens, 1961; Edwards, 1957, 1962) also do not seem to be crucial, for the net effect of these tendencies should be to decrease the magnitude of the difference scores and so attenuate the correlations of the dimensional SIQ scores. Actually, the social desirability bias is most relevant to the maturity scores. If critics prefer, I am in fact predicting that more well organized persons will more consistently select the more socially desirable traits and thereby produce a more mature self-image.

Of the statistical artifacts, those associated with difference scores and judge variability must be considered. Cronbach's (1958) forceful and persuasive attack on the use of absolute difference scores, while unsettling, did not convince me that such scores should be abandoned. Some of their suggested limitations were not appropriate to the research's purpose (the formal congruence and stability scores are not affected by the loss of information about the direction of the differences) or were found inapplicable (extreme responses were not related to the relevant measures). The effect of other limitations (e.g., D scores represent errors of measurement rather than real differences) would be to produce inconsistent and nonsignificant effects, but the consistent results found to hold across several samples for some of the self-image scores seem to answer that problem pragmatically.

Finally, critics of self-image and social perception research (particularly that using judge ratings to measure self-insight) suggest that halo and stereotype effects are a major determinant of accuracy correlates (Cronbach, 1955, 1958). Or, they suggest that some of the congruence results might be more parsimoniously interpreted in terms of the lesser variability of the self and social other ratings of the more well organized person. (Of the thirty SIQ scales, the well organized groups were significantly less variable than the poorly organized groups on only one (Standard) and five (Organized) of the private self-ratings and on only one (Standard) and eight (Organized) of their social self-ratings). I do not find these alternative interpretations very satisfying, however. That well organized men perceive themselves (and judges judge them) to have positive and less variable self (and social self) images makes sense theoretically, given the holistic assumptions of the studies. More importantly, that the self-image measures are consistently and significantly related to a variety of other personality measures (and others still to be described), not as influenced by halo and stereotyped effects and other limitations inherent in conscious self-reports, suggests that some meaningful psychological relationships do lurk in the data. It is the holistic context or pattern of all of the results, not just the possible methodological limitations of single isolated findings, that is compelling. Perhaps the critics of previous research have been persuasive just because the criticized studies seldom escaped the confines of self-reports to demonstrate the consistency of their relationships with other types of data.

SUMMARY

The chapter illustrated how the developmental trends hypothesized to describe the maturing person help to define the properties of the self-image of a mature person. The properties of the self-image are stability, congruence, allocentricism, autonomy, and accuracy, and they were expected to be related to maturity. The content of the self-image of a mature person was also expected to include more of those traits which phenomenally define maturity. A Self-Image Questionnaire (SIQ) was designed which, when administered under various instructional and experimental conditions, measured these properties of the self-image. With the exception of the measure of autonomy, the results were generally confirmatory of the hypotheses. The properties of the self-image were related, as predicted, to judged self-organization, self-reported adjustment, and to various Rorschach measures of stable schemata and good control. However, the stability, congruence, and the phenomenal maturity measures of the self-image were more consistently related to the different measures of self-organization than were the allocentric, autonomy, and accuracy measures. I have argued that the pattern of the results cannot be simply explained by methodological and statistical artifacts.

What is the significance of the results? First, the fact that some of the properties of the self-image are related to measures of maturity and self-organization augments our confidence that the developmental trends describing the maturing person may have some validity. Second, the demonstration that properties of the self-image covary with various properties of ego-organization (measured by Holt's Rorschach scores) empirically bridges the gulf that separates the Rogerian-type self-theorists and the psychoanalytic ego psychologists.

It is now time to return to the principal question of this phase (Part II) of the research. How do mature and well organized persons differ from immature and poorly organized persons and are these differences consistent with the theoretically identified developmental trends and earlier empirical studies of mature persons?

CHAPTER 6

The Mature and the Immature
Person Revisited

Who is the mature person? To this question I now return. Is the mature person more stably organized, integrated, allocentric, autonomous, and potentially more aware of his experiences? This chapter examines and summarizes those reliable differences found between the mature and immature, well and poorly organized men.

But first, is a mature person a well-organized person and is a well-organized person a mature person? Are *immaturity* and *disorganization* synonyms or is one term more inclusive than the other? Previously, I have heuristically assumed that the *maturity* and *self-organization* selection procedures were comparable but is this a valid assumption? Our data cannot definitely answer this question since identical cross-validating groups are not available for each of the four criterion groups to check for unreliable and chance differences. However, some hints do emerge from a comparison of the Maturity and Organized samples and from subsequent comparisons between their mature groups and between their immature groups. (Two-tailed significance tests were used in all comparisons and corrective steps were taken when significant differences in score variance occurred.)

The Maturity sample was consistently more homogeneous than the Organized sample not only on the psychological tests but also in academic achievement. All of the Maturity but only four-fifths of the Organized sample graduated from College.

In general terms, the Maturity sample was significantly more theoretically inclined (AVL Theoret. p $\angle$ .02; SVIB Physicist, p $\angle$ .05; had three times as many natural science majors as the Organized sample), and had greater reflective control over its behavior (Ror. FK + F + Fc%, p $\angle$ .05). The Organized sample, on the other hand, was significantly more persuasively and socially inclined (AVL Politic., p $\angle$ .02; SVIB Sales Mgr., p $\angle$ .01, Real Est. Sales, p $\angle$ .05, and Life Ins. Sales, p $\angle$ .02), more dependent upon others for affectional support (Bern. Low self-suff., p $\angle$ .02), more anxious and tense (Ror. m%, p $\angle$ .05), and more strongly, if not compulsively, determined to achieve some organization of its world (Ror. W%, p $\angle$ .025).

What are the sources of these sample differences? The answer led to an examination of the criterion group differences. In comparing the mature with the well organized and the immature with the poorly organized group, it was clear that the greater homogeneity of the Maturity sample was due to the fact that its immature group was not as variable and extreme as the Organized sample's poorly organized group on many measures. As one example, the immature men's grade average was significantly better than that of the poorly organized men (p $\angle$ .01) and did not differ from that of the Haverford population; several of the immature but none of the poorly organized men received national competitive awards for graduate work. On the other hand, the sample differences in social and persuasive values and in the need to synthesize and organize their experience were attributable to the men of the well organized group who were high on these traits.

My evaluation of these few hints is that the mature and well organized groups do not differ so radically as to contradict the assumption that they are roughly comparable. In the Haverford setting, maturity and good self-organization probably denote the same manifest behavior. However, the immature men do not appear to be as disorganized as the disorganized appear to be immature which may raise the question of the conceptual equivalence of the terms *immaturity* and *disorganization.* But for purposes of this chapter, I assume the immature and poorly organized men are basically similar, and I will use *mature* and *immature* as generic terms which include *well* and *poorly organized.*

To return to the main theme of the chapter, how do other judges independently evaluate the mature (including the well organized) and immature (including the poorly organized) men? Following an impressionistic summary of interview data about the men's family and personal expectations and achievements, the chapter describes their college academic, extracurricular, and social accomplishments and then the psychological test differences found between the criterion groups.

INDEPENDENT JUDGE EVALUATIONS

Each Departmental Chairman rates each of his graduating seniors for determination, emotional stability, intelligence, originality, and personality. Since only two of the chairmen had participated in the selection of the youths two years earlier, the chairmens' ratings were, for all practical purposes, independent of any knowledge of the research or of those participating in it.

Table 6–1, which summarizes these independent faculty ratings, reassuringly confirms that the mature groups did differ from the immature groups in the directions predicted. Of the total number of judgments made about each group, the Maturity sample's mature and immature groups received fifty-six percent and six percent of the judgments for excellence, the Organized sample's organized and disorganized men fifty-one percent and thirteen percent, and the Standard's organized and disorganized men fifty-three percent and twenty-three percent respectively. No mature or well organized student was judged to be poor on any of the traits.

Furthermore, the mature and well organized men were generally judged to be more determined, emotionally stable, and to have more attractive personalities, traits which are more closely associated with maturity than either intelligence or originality

TABLE 6–1: DEPARTMENT CHAIRMEN RATINGS OF PERSONALITY TRAITS OF THE MATURE (M) AND IMMATURE (I) MEN OF THE MAJOR SAMPLES

TRAIT	EXCELLENT		GOOD		FAIR		POOR	
	M	I	M	I	M	I	M	I
Maturity Sample								
Determination	5		4	4	1	5		1
Emotional stability	7	1	3	4		4		1
Intelligence	5	2	5	5		1		2
Originality	3		6	6	1	2		2
Personality	8			5	2	4		1
	28	3	18	24	4	16	0	7
Organized Sample[1]	WO	PO	WO	PO	WO	PO	WO	PO
Determination	10		1	2		6		3
Emotional stability	6	1	4	5	1	1		4
Intelligence	5	3	6	3		4		1
Originality	3	2	5	4	3	1		3
Personality	4	1	7	4		5		2
	28	7	23	18	4	17	0	13
Standard Sample[2]								
Determination	9	6	6	4		2		3
Emotional stability	12	4	3	6		3		2
Intelligence	5	3	10	6		6		
Originality	1	1	10	5	4	7		2
Personality	13	3	2	6		5		1
	40	17	31	27	4	23	0	8
Combined summary of all samples[3]								
Determination	24	6	11	10	1	13		7
Emotional stability	25	6	10	15	1	8		7
Intelligence	15	8	21	14		11		3
Originality	7	3	21	15	8	10		7
Personality	25	4	9	15	2	14		4
	96	27	72	69	12	56	0	28
Percent	53%	15%	40%	38%	7%	31%		16%

[1] N = 11 for each group; data incomplete on remaining two students.
[2] N = 15 for each group; data not available on remaining six students
[3] N = 36 students for each group.

on which the criterion groups were not as strikingly differentiated by the faculty. That the mature youths were judged to be more personable warns us that possible halo effects may reduce the validity of the other judgments. We can only buttress our belief that the Chairmen were not unduly affected in their other judgments by citing at the end of this section some of the spontaneous but very discriminating comments of the faculty themselves.

These independent faculty judgments also confirm our failure to secure an extreme and homogeneous group of immature students. Although we have seen from Chapters 1 and 2 that the dimensions of maturity are scarcely well defined, emotional (schemata) stability should surely hover near the central meaning of the term. Whereas the emotional stability of all but one of the mature youths was rated as either excellent or good, the emotional stability of sixty percent of the immature students was also rated excellent or good. This result reinforces our hunch that the immature groups were not very extreme in their immaturity. As Chapter 3 suggested, to survive Haverford's demands requires considerable maturity.

One interesting though tangential result emerges from Table 6–1. MacKinnon has hypothesized that two variables "centrally determinative of effective functioning [are]: (a) emotional stability or personal soundness, and (b) originality or creativity of thought and action" (MacKinnon, 1960 p. 373). There is little doubt from all of our evidence to date that our mature and organized students were some of Haverford's most effectively functioning men. And the evidence from all three samples suggests that such men are emotionally stable persons. But, there is no comparable consistent evidence that the maturely organized person (most effectively functioning person of the Haverford community) is consistently much more original or creative than the immature or disorganized person. Originality or creativity may not be as simply or directly contributory to effective functioning as has been hypothesized—at least in young male adults. Certainly, for the Departmental Chairmen, creativity and emotional stability are not necessarily related and effective functioning does not necessarily imply creativity. Comments such as these were not uncommon:

Of a mature natural scientist: He is more mature than most students of his age, and he has remarkable emotional stability . . . but . . . his one lack is that he has no creativity in the field.

Of a mature humanities student: Has all of his wits about him, a firm mastery of his own abilities and his own time, able to get his clear-headed best into evidence all the way . . . thorough, conscientious and lucid; and I have never seen him do a bad job, no matter what the pressures of other studies or obligations might be . . . lack of any special imaginative flavor or distinctive original character in his work.

Finally, the distribution of the Chairmen ratings also reinforces our confidence in the judging procedures used to identify the well and poorly organized youths in the Standard sample. Its men identified by the student judges to be well organized received ninety-four percent excellent or good ratings from their Chairmen but the poorly organized men received only fifty-nine percent excellent or good ratings from their Chairmen. The Standard sample's well organized men were judged by their Chairmen to have more attractive personalities and to be more emotionally stable but not to be as consistently motivated or determined as the Organized sample's well organized men. Could the Organized sample's well organized group, representing an extreme group in the population, have been a more driven, achieving but conflicted, if not compulsive, and less personable group of youths than the other mature groups?

To garnish and flavor this rather bland statistical summary, and to illustrate how discriminating the Chairmen were, I report the most favorable and the least favorable descriptive phrases from the Chairmen's evaluations about the men. Of the mature youths, the Chairmen wrote: "a very open personality . . . absolutely reliable and trustworthy . . . wears well; mature and capable of taking responsibility far beyond his years . . . no illusions about where his skills lie; wonderful temperament: gay, but fundamentally serious; a young man of great expectations in every respect; a sensitive, respectful regard for human beings. The result is the sort of student one often longs to have, but seldom finds; he strikes me as a man of strong inner character, intellectual and spiritual, who is certain to make a distinctive and valuable contribution in his life work." But the Chairmen also expressed reservations about these mature men: "There is not much chance [he] will develop rapidly into an outstandingly brilliant young [social scientist]; doesn't display the single-minded drive or the type of ability one associates with success in a career; he may develop [originality] more clearly as he gains more confidence; lacked the idealism which one generally encounters in college-age men; I have some feeling that he may devote himself to a pursuit of success, rather than superiority; superficially brilliant, inwardly shy . . . an unpredictable quality. He may do fine things with his life—he may turn out to be a lightweight. I believe he is still too immature for me to make an adequate judgment."

The Chairmen made these unfavorable comments about the immature men: "disorganized, a very poor worker. . . . He was given to act like a petulant child. . . . He seemed to need approval so badly that he sought it constantly; lazy, lethargic; rather too pleased with himself; personality on the brash and opinionated side; he tends to scatter heterogeneously about, rather than penetrate originally or creatively or deeply into any one subject or field; will need . . . a good deal of shaking down of his present mood before he can move with the humility which his gifts would seem to lay upon him; advising him was like moving a sack of potatoes . . . as far as I am concerned he remained a closed book; impresses me as not fully engaged in the life around him . . . simply without sufficient inner fire to drive him to excellence in any one pursuit; is not a very happy person; iceberg character, making one aware not only of a cold and withdrawn reserve on the surface, but of conflicts within which seem to be perplexing to him." The Chairmen also sensed such fine qualities in these immature men as: "A superior person, but needs energizing; a person of great enthusiasm . . . he is not bright but he knows it and is humble about his gifts; solid plodding competence . . . is going to make a good graduate student; a person of extraordinary ability. He is able to maintain an amazing multiplicity of interests all active at the same time. This is his genius and his weakness at the same time; I have enjoyed my association with him; sharp, vigorous person . . . interesting person, with plenty of drive, but not yet centered on any definite goals; able, pleasant, substantial person and a competent student; he may well carve himself a niche of success in the arts—academic failure has no necessary repercussions there; the greatest improvement has been an increasing willingness to admit that knowledge of some subject requires disciplined toil which may not always be interesting in itself."

Now, let us translate these descriptive judgments into actual behavioral data. We let the words and then the lives of the youths speak for themselves—first, in terms of how they looked at their parental and their own achievements and limitations, and second, in terms of their actual achievements in the Haverford community.

SELF-REPORTED EXPECTATIONS
AND ACHIEVEMENTS

In his first test session, each man of the Maturity sample was interviewed for forty minutes following a scheduled set of questions. The interview was recorded. The following analysis was made of the typed transcripts. Unfortunately, because of time and financial restrictions, these interviews were not replicated with the other samples.

Family Emotional Stability

No mature youth reported any emotional instability in either his mother or father, although one reported his parents had separated and four mentioned some form of senility in their grandparents. Three immature youths reported their mothers were either alcoholic (for which one had been hospitalized) or suicidal; one immature youth claimed his father was developing paranoia and one that his father had been married several times.

Paternal Distinctions and Limitations

The men were asked to describe their parents' greatest accomplishments, distinctions, and most important limitations or weaknesses. The fathers of both the mature and immature

men were independent professional or business men with considerable responsibility (doctors, professors, lawyers, and owners
of their own businesses). Two of the immature men's, but five of
the mature men's, fathers had achieved some recognition or
singular distinction for professional achievement. The fathers of
the mature men were described more consistently as determined,
self-driving, and self-educated men and were unanimously
respected by their sons. In contrast, the fathers of the immature
group did not seem to grasp responsibility as actively or strive
for success as frequently (one declined the presidency of his
professional organization, another dissatisfiedly roamed from job
to job, one was casual about his work, ignoring the "American
success ideal"). The immature youths were more critical of their
fathers; a few frankly said they did not respect or "idolize" them
as they used to do when younger. When asked to do so, the
immature youths attributed the following alleged weaknesses to
them: "(1) impractical, absent-minded; (2) volatile temper; (3)
one-sided; (4) no ambition, not settled down to work; (5) stub-
born . . . authoritarian spells, loses temper; (6) reserved; (7) not
understanding; (8) closed mind and alienated himself from
others; (9) paranoia and no ability to see anybody beyond himself; (10) temper and blind to his own faults." The mature
youths, on the other hand, were much more charitable: "(1) too
talkative; (2) small-minded and retiring; (3) none; (4) none; (5)
too competitive with son; (6) none; (7) none; (8) less drive than
his mother who was the leader of the family; (9) distant; and
(10) behind the times."

Maternal Distinctions and Limitations

The mothers of the mature men were reported to be
more achieving and "stronger persons" than the mothers of the
immature men. Seven of the ten mature youths spontaneously
described their mothers as very strong, though not dominating,
persons who had shown great drive, persistence, or accomplishment whether in overcoming a handicap, being a "supersales-
man" and winning national contests, or being a professional who

had won awards for creative research. Of the four immature youths reporting similar maternal accomplishments, three felt their mother's greater personal strength was either "aggressive" and "dominating" or associated with deep personal conflict as shown in excessive drinking or depression. The mature and immature did not differ in their descriptions of their mother's strengths (loving, good mother, gentle, emotional, common sense) nor of their limitations (nervous, underrated self, not abreast with the times, over-exaggerated, touchy, and moody).

Siblings' Distinctions and Limitations

One mature and three immature men had no siblings. Effectiveness and personal soundness apparently runs in families, if we are to believe the reports of our groups. The brothers and sisters of the mature youths were viewed as strikingly effective and maturely stable people. Some positive accomplishment or trait was found for every brother or sister, whether it was completing college in two and a half years, being second in his class at an Ivy League university, achieving excellence athletically, or in just being a mature and stable person. But in very sharp and noticeable contrast, *every* immature youth either reported a sibling to be limited academically (flunked out of Princeton, "not stupid, but does not have a high I.Q."), or when mentioning some sibling's accomplishment overtly or subtly derogated him personally ("he has a complex," "she has bad manners," or "he is twenty-four and still a virgin").

Major Person Influencing Development

The groups did not differ when describing who had the most important determining influence on their lives. For most of the youths, their fathers or some male teacher had been most influential—or so they claimed. Only two of the mature and two of the immature men mentioned either a mother, older female relative, or a girl friend as having shaped their lives decisively.

Self Accomplishments and Outstanding Traits

Both the mature students' achievements and attitudes toward themselves dramatically differed from the achievements and self-images of the immature youths. The mature men reported a long history of successful achievement—academically, athletically, extracurricularly, and socially—culminating, most generally, in outstanding achievements at the College, particularly in academic and extracurricular activities. When asked to tell that about which they were most proud, two cited overcoming very severe physical handicaps, six others mentioned working hard for academic excellence or having been selected for a major student government office, one reported having learned social poise in his relations with others, and the last said having known everyone at Haverford. In contrast, the sporadic and occasional achievements of the immature men, while representing painful and poignant victories by some, would be, by some standards of successful achievement, somewhat inconsequential. Certainly to the immature men, the locus of their less viable sense of accomplishment was in mastering some wilful and capricious part of their own selves—rather than in mastering, as it was for the mature men, some sector of an objective external world. What was the cast of the immature men's achievement and of what were they most proud? The list included such items as, (1) "getting myself to work" and "getting through here;" (2) "not much except some wonderfully warm friendships" (he hinted later they were homosexually based); (3) "becoming aware of things in life of which I never dreamed when I was little;" (4) "little things;" (5) a ninety average in a course in prep school; (6) ". . . sort of being in the middle and not minding it;" (7) "athletically—musically—possibly scholastically, when I want to;" (8) "pulling myself out of the complete slumber I was in in high school and getting myself together here at Haverford;" (9) "After high school I went to my grandfather's funeral against my parents' wishes;" (10) "Nothing. I am pretty much ashamed of myself right now scholastically. . . . It bothers me that I can't make myself do these things."

And what were their self-reported most outstanding traits? Seven of the mature men but *none* of the immature men spontaneously said they enjoyed studying and working hard, concentrating on a task and pursuing it until it was completed. The immature men either ignored such goal-directed achieving traits or explicitly said they were lazy or disinterested in working hard. No mature youth would have said, as one immature student did, "I have a tendency to size up what the minimum is that I have to do to get my eighty or eighty-five and cut down on my work." The mature men thought of themselves in such terms as these: intense concern about time, humble, good mind, extreme enthusiasm, proud of being muscular and well-coordinated, need more self-control, ability to listen to others, steadiness, work well under pressure, and self-sufficient. The immature men used such adjectives as these to describe themselves: practical, moody, arrogant, intolerant of misused intellect, sensitive, judges others correctly, likes people and parties, gets along well with others, outgoing, jealous, rebellious, imaginative, lacking moral sense.

Current Major Problems

The contrast between the more objective and subjective achievements of the mature and immature men respectively finds some parallel in the type of most immediate pressing concern each was currently facing. The mature men were most frequently worried about reality problems: economic, finding a wife, or deciding on a vocation. While three of the immature men directly phrased their current preoccupations similarly, the preoccupations of the remaining seven were more oblique and indefinite, if not vague and shadowy: "security within myself;" "what is true?" "unsure of my capabilities—I fight myself on a lot of things;" "develop ability to get work done;" "fear of failure." In Chapter 3, we suggested that the Haverford milieu provided optimal conditions for academic and extracurricular, but not social and sexual development. While perhaps as applicable to the immature men as well, only the mature men (five of them) explicitly stated, in one form or another, their major problem was not that of (academic) achievement which was so clearly the most pressing problem of the immature youths but that of making an adequate sexual adjustment, dating more frequently or learning how to reconcile their pursuit after excellence with a desire to "help people."

Aim Ten Years Hence

Both groups, when asked to describe the kind of life and person they would like to have and be ten years hence, agreed they wanted to be married, have several children, and be in a profession that kept them in touch with people. The teaching profession had the greatest appeal for four of the mature and five of the immature men. Interestingly, the immature men were more specific about their hopes: one wanted to be a minister, two to be writers, one to be a doctor, one to "not be a scientist," one to do scientific research but maintain an artistic sense, one wanted to be retired so he could go to the theater and travel. The mature men expressed a very different quality in their hopes about their futures—a quality that emphasized excellence, competence, continued growth, and moral leadership to others: (1) "to grow intellectually . . . my mind, I hope, will be still growing;" (2) "Want to advance, but I don't know in which direction;" (3) "I want to be damn good at some profession;" (4) "As great a scholar as I could be . . . find a field of my own . . . be a teacher who could give a lot to my students;" (5) "I think I can do some good especially for high school kids . . . maybe in a really bad school section I could reach one or two bad kids a year;" (6) "I do know I would like to work with people and do something worthwhile but don't know definitely what it is;" (7) "I'd like to be setting an example as to how to live. . . . You should always be doing something; no matter what group you are in, you must be carrying your weight;" (8) "I'm not sure of what field . . . conceivably psychiatry;" (9) "I would put more emphasis on being satisfied personally in the way things are done than in the things themselves. Getting to the top for 'the top's sake' isn't the thing;" (10) "First of all, I would like to be competent in my field and I would like to be effective that way and to interest my students and to do anything I could in that field that would be effective."

ACHIEVEMENTS AT COLLEGE

Intellectual Skill and Achievement

What were the actual accomplishments of the men? I examine their intellectual and extracurricular achievements in detail and then ask if such accomplishment was achieved at the expense of the men's social life and physical health.

The ratings of the Chairmen suggested that the mature groups were slightly more intelligent and homogeneously bright, but these judgments were not supported by the freshmen aptitude scores of the contrasting groups for which no significant differences were found. The mature men of the Maturity sample tended to have higher verbal and quantitative aptitude scores than the immature youths. However, it was not the aptitude scores of the immature but those of the mature men that markedly deviated from the median aptitude scores for the Haverford classes used in the study. The mature group contained some very distinguishedly brilliant youths. However, we cannot say that the more mature person tends to be natively more intelligent than the immature person, for the same factors that make a person immature may also interfere with his aptitude test performance. The Organized sample's groups did *not* differ in aptitude since they were matched in aptitude when selected. The Standard sample's groups, not initially matched for aptitude, also had comparable aptitude scores. The results of the Terman Concept Mastery Test, a test designed to discriminate among people of gifted intellectual ability, also demonstrated that the organized and disorganized groups did *not* differ significantly in general reasoning ability.

More interesting, however, are the dramatic and significant differences found between the mature and immature men's academic achievement. Haverford final grade averages typically hover around eighty-one. The mature groups' final grade averages of eighty-eight, eighty-seven, and eighty-three testify to their high intellectual effectiveness. The immature groups' final averages were seventy-eight, seventy-six, and seventy-nine. One third of the Organized sample's poorly organized students failed out of college during their junior and senior years.

How may such differences in intellectual attainment be interpreted? The difference cannot be understood in terms of just aptitude or general reasoning ability since, as we have just seen, the criterion groups did not differ significantly in aptitude. Could not scholastic achievement be determined more by the personality organization and maturity of the men? This hypothesis cannot be decisively confirmed since intellectual achievement was confounded with (defined as one part of) maturity in the selection process. Moreover, the expectation and value patterns of the Haverford community, as described in Chapter 3, also tend to confound the two. Certainly, exceptional determination and excellent emotional stability (Department Chairmen ratings) aid a person to optimize his natural talents, particularly in settings that value the expression of such talent.

The mature and immature men also differed in the pattern of their major academic interests. The mature men tended to distribute themselves evenly among the humanities, social and natural sciences with a slight predominance in the social sciences. However, sixty percent of the immature men majored in the humanities. (The academic major choices of the larger Haverford population tend to be distributed equally among the major divisions.) We shall shortly see this pattern of academic concentration reflected in the valuator hierarchy differences of the criterion groups.

Extracurricular Achievements

It is clear from Table 6-2 that the mature men were the responsible leaders of the college. For every elective leadership category, whether it was president of the powerful Students'

Council, president of a class or club, chairman of one of the Students' Council committees, or captain of an athletic team, the mature youths received the vote of confidence of the student body much more frequently than did the immature men. Furthermore, except for membership in campus club activities where there was

TABLE 6–2: ELECTIVE AND VOLUNTARY EXTRACUR-
RICULAR ACTIVITIES OF THE MATURE
(ORGANIZED) AND IMMATURE
(DISORGANIZED) MEN

	MATURE (N = 39)[1]	IMMATURE (N = 39)[1]
Elective leadership		
Student Council		
President	3	0
Treasurer-Secretary	2	0
Member	9	3
Class		
President	4	0
Treasurer-Secretary	8	2
College Publications-Editors	14	5
Campus Clubs-President	11	7
Student Committee-Chairman	16	2
Athletic Teams		
Varsity Captain	10	7
J. V. Captain	2	0
Voluntary or appointive memberships		
Campus Clubs	88	92
Student Council Committees	54	23
Athletic Teams		
Varsity Team	22	13
J. V. Team	34	28
Intramural Team	49	42

[1] Data not available on remaining student.

no essential difference, the mature men participated more actively than the immature men in all phases of the college extracurricular and athletic programs. To a very real extent, it was the mature men that set the tone of the College and were responsible for the continuance of the student activities during the period of the research. When one considers that this range of activity and responsibility was held by only thirty-nine men who also maintained grade averages significantly higher than the immature groups and considerably higher than the average Haverford student, one begins to sense the full measure of the effectiveness of these men—not to speak of how effectively they had to learn just to organize their time and energy.

Social Life and Physical Health

As every mortal eventually discovers, not all of life's opportunities can be realized with excellence. Chapter 3 suggested that at Haverford it is likely to be a person's social life that gives way to the College's inexorable demands. Certainly, it would be a rare person who could maintain academic, extracurricular, and athletic excellence, a vigorous and satisfying social life, and sound bodily health in the Haverford setting. Something must give in this setting of potentially competing expectations and strains. Given the pervading values of the student body, were the men's social activities and physical health the areas that suffered?

Unfortunately, I have no regularized measures of the quality or extent of the men's social lives. However, from my own observation, comments by roommates, and the final interpretative interviews held with many of the men, my impression was that in this area as well, the more mature men had many more affectionate and close friendships with both men and women. Many of the immature men lived alone and expressed in one form or another a feeling of loneliness and alienation from the intimate life of another.

What then of the physical health of the criterion groups? Do the strains and tensions of living so close to one's full energy potential erode one's resistance to physical illness? Some researchers have reported evidence that the strongly achieving person may have poorer physical health than more phlegmatic and less insistent personalities (Hinkle & Wolff, 1957; Hinkle, 1959). The frequency of the men's visits to the College infirmary as well as the type of their presenting complaints for the two-year period that overlapped the Maturity and Organized samples' sojourn at the College were tabulated. The data are only suggestive since immature persons may be more hypochondriacal and dependent, and thereby seek medical support more readily. Psychological consultations were not recorded and so are not included in these summary figures. Though the differences are not statistically significant, the mature men averaged 7.4 and the immature men averaged 10.8 visits to the infirmary in the two-year period. Whereas thirty-two percent of the mature men visited the infirmary three or fewer times, *no* immature man visited the infirmary *less* than four times in the two-year period. Also, more immature than mature men were ill for every diagnostic category. The most noticeable differences were for more immature than mature men to report fatigue, headaches, localized pains, and "accidental" types of injuries such as finger, arm, and leg sprains. The data suggest that the effective person does not tend necessarily to achieve his effectiveness at the expense of his bodily health. These results are amplified by Barron's (1963) finding that the personally sound person has a life history significantly more free of physical illness and accident than the more unsound person.

Finally, what happens to these men when they leave college and must accommodate to a different pattern of values and expectations? It is too early to follow up the new circle of achievements that will define whether, as we happen to believe, such mature men would be similarly selected in different environments as highly effective men. With respect to their ties to the College, as one might expect, the mature men retain considerable devotion to the College and are beginning to assume a larger social responsibility for its welfare. Whereas about fifty-five percent of the members of the classes we studied have contributed to the annual alumni fund, eighty-nine percent of the mature men, but only thirty-five percent of the immature men have contributed financially to the College.

PSYCHOLOGICAL TEST DIFFERENCES

Valuator Hierarchy

Chapter 2 suggested that schemata, skills, and valuators were the major "structures and activities" of the self. Although considerable evidence was available about both the skill and schemata organization of the men, no regularized and objective measures directly tapping a person's valuator hierarchy and its stability, autonomy, and integration were designed for the study. Hence, I can gather only indirect clues about the maturity of the criterion group's valuator hierarchies from the AVL Study of Values and the Strong Vocational Interest Blank.

The valuator hierarchy of both the mature and immature groups was similar in major outline to that of the larger Haverford population, for the groups as freshmen held as *one* of their highest values the Haverford ideal of fulfilling a theoretical, intellectual way of life and as one of their lowest values fulfilling a more pragmatic, applied, economic or business type of life (AVL Theoret., Economic). These more consciously held value preferences were generally congruent with the men's temperamental trait patterns as inferred from the SVIB. Like the larger Haverford population, the mature and immature groups do not resonate with successful men in technical, manipulative, applied, outdoor and business types of occupations but they do feel at home with successful men in intellectual, theoretical, and professional types of occupations. The research groups also show the same discrepancies between their expressed values and temperamental patterns that the larger Haverford population does. While not consciously valuing social and altruistic concerns for others as highly as other ways of relating to the world, they are temperamentally similar to those men in the professional social service occupations.

The valuator hierarchies of the mature and immature men do differ, however, in detail, although the differences are not consistent (data not reported). The trend of the valuator differences was for the immature men to value aesthetic and creative types of activities and the mature men to esteem social, altruistic, loving ways of life. (The differences in valuator preferences were eventually manifested in the preponderant academic major decisions of the groups.) These more conscious value differences generally revealed themselves in the SVIB as well. The mature groups preferred more direct persuasive contacts with people (higher on Personnel Director, Sales Manager, YMCA Physical Education Director, Math-Physical Science Teacher) and the immature men either more impersonal intellectualistic (CPA, Chemist) or personal aesthetic occupations (Musician, Artist). Some of these trends reach significance only for the Maturity sample in which the immature men were significantly more temperamentally inclined than the mature men toward such occupations, for example, as that of an artist, musician, or advertising man. Such a high valuation and temperamental congruence of the immature men for the aesthetic does not mean, of course, that the immature men were any more creative or original than the mature men. The Chairman ratings of originality actually tended to prefer the mature groups.[1]

So much for the content of the groups' valuator hierarchies. What can be said about the maturity of the mature and immature men's valuators? If we accept the SVIB measure of Interest Maturity as a general measure of valuator maturity, then we can say all of the mature groups consistently (though not significantly) express greater valuator maturity than the immature groups (Mat. 57.4 vs. 54.3; Org. 56 vs. 52.6; Stand. 55.1 vs. 52.6). With respect to our specific expectations, no data are available about the stability or autonomy of the groups' valuators. I have no direct information about the internal integration or congruence of the valuator hierarchies either; however, if one measure of progressive integration is the increasing differentiated-

[1] It cannot be concluded from the low aesthetic value (AVL) scores of the mature groups that they consciously rejected aesthetic values in any absolute sense for the AVL scale assumes a compensatory model or theory of values. A very high value in one area automatically must result in compensating low value scores in the other areas, even though in reality the person, when compared with others on some absolute scale, may prize that scored lower value more highly than others who score higher on that value on the AVL.

ness of a person's valuator hierarchy, then the number of SVIB occupations the person has that are most highly crystallized (i.e., the SVIB A and B+ categories which indicate interests similar to those persons successfully engaged in that occupation) may give a clue about valuator differentiation. By this measure, except for the well organized men of the Organized sample, the mature men tend to have a more differentiated valuator structure than the immature men (Mat. 10 vs. 8.5; Org. 9.2 vs. 9.7; and Stand. 9.6 vs. 7.3 occupations in the B+ and A categories). One other indirect measure of the differentiatedness of a person's valuator hierarchy may be the California F test of authoritarianism given to the Organized sample only. The well organized men were significantly less (p. $\angle$ .05) authoritarian, held less "black and white" or extremely expressed attitudes, than the poorly organized men, although few of the poorly organized men were very high in authoritarianism relative to many of the college populations for whom normative data are available. As Chapter 3 suggested, a highly authoritarian student would be seriously alienated from the rest of the Haverford student body.

What about the degree of valuator allocentricism? The mature groups by valuing a social way of life much more than the immature groups and by being more temperamentally congruent with professional social and people-centered professions may, in the words of Allport, have a greater "love of people . . . prize persons as ends" and regard "love as itself the only suitable form of human relationship" (1960, p. 5). The immature groups' strong inclination toward the aesthetic may express a more autocentric valuator organization, for a strong aesthetic preference (supported by the SVIB Musician, Artist, and Author scales) suggests that a person enjoys "each single impression . . . for its own sake" and "tends toward individualism and self-sufficiency" (1960, p. 4–5). Certainly, an aesthetic style of life does not in itself necessarily mean immature development, particularly if such aesthetic values can be coordinated with adaptive means to realize such values. But we have no evidence that the immature men had made such an effective coordination (Chairmen ratings) which leads us to suggest that their predominant aesthetic orientation was a symptom of self-absorption about problems of self and bodily expression and may have reflected inadequate allocentric development.

I also had no direct measure of how symbolized and available a person's valuators were to consciousness. But if we assume the SVIB gives a reasonably valid picture of a person's basic temperamental direction and the AVL a more direct conscious report of the direction of that motivational push, then discrepancies between the SVIB and AVL pattern may suggest failure or inability to symbolize correctly in awareness one's inner direction. By this measure, the valuators of both the mature and immature men are reasonably mature, but those of the immature men seem less accurately symbolized. The immature men fail to incorporate into their more conscious value structure their temperamental affinity with some of the professional social type occupations. Their AVL social value is consistently their lowest value, and yet their SVIB occupational scores for psychologist, public administrator, and social science teacher are among their highest SVIB seven or eight scores.

Questionnaire Measures of Maladjustment and Controls

This section draws together the information given in Chapters 5 (Bernreuter and MMPI) and 6 (SIQ) while reporting some new data about how the mature and immature men differed in their self-concept. It then evaluates the differences in the formal developmental dimensions of the self-image (stability, congruence) of the mature and immature youths, relying primarily on the SIQ data.

The Phenomenal Content of the Self-Image

The most simple and direct approach to understanding the self-image is to ask persons to describe themselves, as was done with the Adjective Check List (Organized) and the SIQ (Organized and Standard). On the ACL, significantly (two-tailed for no specific directional differences were predicted in advance) more well than poorly organized men described themselves as adaptable, independent, self-driving (.02), conscientious (.05) and capable of completing their plans (.10), while more disorganized than organized men claimed they were bottled-up, erratic (.01) and hard to convince (.10). Similar results were obtained from the SIQ, the deails of which are given in Table 6–3. The well organized men of both the major samples, in contrast to the poorly organized men, believe themselves to be fulfilling their potential. They also tend to consider themselves to be enthusiastic, purposeful youths of high aspirations. This self-estimate is quite congruent with the personality evaluations of their Departmental Chairmen who found them to be very determined and directed young men.

The social selves of the well organized men do not violate their more private self-images, for they believe others think they are energetic, have high aspirations, and are fulfilling their potential. Others are also believed to think they are ordered and clear thinkers.

Nor do the private and social self-images of the men diverge from the opinions that faculty and student judges have of them. Because of the possible contamination of the Organized judges' ratings, Table 6–3 reports only those *judged* traits of the well organized men which consistently and significantly differed from the traits of the poorly organized men for *both* samples. It is clear that the judges consistently agreed that the well organized man possesses many of the manifest traits claimed by theorists to define mature men (energetic, strong convictions, fulfilling potential, self-acceptance, realistic). These judged trait differences are quite congruent with the trait criteria the judges used to select the extreme groups (purposeful, implied fulfilling potential, self-acceptant or sense of identity, and predictable).

More indirect and therefore more inferential measures of the phenomenal content of the self-image are the MMPI and Bernreuter. The two well organized and, surprisingly, the Standard's poorly organized group have more favorable self-images than the average Haverford student (data not given). Actually, none of the remaining group's self-images were very unfavorable

TABLE 6–3: SIQ Private and Social Self-Image and Judged Trait Differences [1] between Well and Poorly Organized Men

SIQ Trait	Private Self of Well Organized Rated as More		Social Self of Well Organized Rated as More		Judge Ratings of Well Organized	
	Organized p	Standard p	Organized p	Standard p	Organized p	Standard p
Accepts Self			.01	Inconsistent	.01†	.02
Adaptable			.01†	Consistent		
Anticipates consequences			.01	Consistent		
Clear thinking	.01†	Consistent	.01†	Consistent		
Decisive			Consistent	.02		
Demanding	.05	Consistent				
Energetic	.02	Consistent	.01†	.01	.01	.01
Enthusiastic	.05	Consistent	.01	Consistent	.01	.05†
Fulfilling potential	.01†	.05	.01	.02	.01†	.02†
High aspirations	Consistent	.01	.01†	.05	.01†	.05†
Ordered	.05	Consistent	.01	Consistent	.01	.02
Predictable	.05	Consistent	.01†	Consistent		
Purposeful	.05	Consistent	.01	Consistent	.01†	.05†
Realistic					.01	.05†

† F significant at least at .05 level; df halved in evaluating t.
[1] Two-tailed tests of significance, since specific trait differences not predicted in advance.

in comparison with the self-image of the average Haverford youth. Apparently the MMPI distinguished between the Organized sample's groups not because its poorly organized group's adjustment deviated so much from the Haverford modal adjustment but because the well organized men's adjustment was more favorable than that of the average student. In Table 6–5, which summarizes all of the personality differences found between the consensually judged mature and immature groups pages 167–168), we can see that the more mature are significantly and consistently *less* disturbed, introversive, nonsocial, and disinterested in people, and less impulsively and irresponsibly behaved youths than the immature men. Or in comparison to the Haverford population, the mature person tends to be psychologically healthier, more interested in others, and more responsible and restrained in his impulse expression (data not given). These questionnaire differences between the mature and immature men are not inconsistent with those found by Barron (1954, 1963). His sound persons reported themselves to have greater equanimity, to be more self-confident, objective, and virile; his unsound persons reported themselves to have more unstable moods, to be easily bothered and irritated, to be more indecisive, finicky, and effeminate, and to lack internal resources.

The *pattern* of the MMPI differences between the mature and immature groups was explored further by correlating the MMPI patterns of the six criterion groups, the results of which are reported in Table 6–4. The patterns of the self-concepts of the Standard sample's mature and immature groups are the most similar (rho = .61) which reconfirms again that the two groups did not differ much from each other. The Standard sample's poorly organized men were just not very disorganized—if they were disorganized at all; in fact, they probably were not too distinguishable from the modal Haverford student. The low correlation (rho = .37) between the pattern of MMPI scores for the Organized sample's well and poorly organized men confirms much earlier evidence that the sample contained radically divergent groups. Reassuringly, the MMPI pattern of the Maturity sample's mature youths is more similar to the pattern of the two highly organized groups (rho = .83 and .85) than it is to the

TABLE 6–4: CORRELATIONS (rho) BETWEEN THE PATTERNS OF MMPI SCORES OF THE MATURE AND THE IMMATURE MEN OF THE MAJOR SAMPLES

| | MATURITY | | ORGANIZED | | STANDARD | |
	Mat.	Imm.	WO	PO	WO	PO
Maturity						
Mature						
Immature	.52					
Organized						
Well Org.	.83	.49				
Poorly Org.	.42	.66	.37			
Standard						
Well Org.	.85	.45	.93	.45		
Poorly Org.	.51	.56	.56	.33	.61	

pattern of its own contrasting immature group (rho = .52) or to that of the disorganized groups (rho = .66 and .56).

Developmental Dimensions of the Self-Image

The major hypothesis we were pursuing is that well organized men have more stable, congruent, allocentric, autonomous, accurate, and generally more mature self-images than the poorly organized men. A secondary hypothesis was that well organized men would be rated by judges on the SIQ to be more mature than the poorly organized men.

The primary hypothesis was contingently, and the secondary hypothesis fully confirmed. (Table 6–5 summarizes the detailed findings.) That the self-image of the well organized men is significantly more stable, congruent, allocentric, and accurate, but *not* autonomous, was confirmed for the more extreme well and poorly organized men of the population. With respect to the autonomy of the self-image, the poorly organized men tended to resist self-image reorganization as a consequence of the coercive procedure used to measure autonomy more than the well organized men. Why this resulted, I cannot say. It may have been because of chance, the greater rigidity (higher Calif. F) of the poorly organized men (they also reported themselves on the ACL to be harder to convince than the well organized men), greater sensitivity of the well organized men to the opinions of other persons (Higher AVL Social; lower Bern. Nonsocial) or, more likely, to methodological limitations of the defining operations. Interestingly, Barron (1963) also obtained equivocal results when assessing the autonomy of a person's judgment of group consensual (but incorrect) opinions. Those who did shift their judgments to agree with the group rated themselves significantly more personally stable, determined, efficient, and healthy minded, but Barron was unable to validate these self-reports using more indirect measures of healthiness (MMPI). Note our well organized men (described as determined, stable, efficient) also tended, though not significantly, to show less autonomy in their judgments of themselves than did the poorly organized men. The self-image of the well organized men was significantly more stable than the self-image of the poorly organized men over all repetitions of the SIQ (t = 3.43, p $\angle$ .01) despite the intervening autonomy procedure and the consequent change in the well organized men's self-images.

The self-image differences between the Standard's well and poorly organized men tend to support (p $\angle$ .10) the self-image accuracy and allocentric but not the stability and congruence hypotheses. (The well orgnized men are significantly more accurate (t = 2.02, p $\angle$ .05) than the poorly oganized men in their private self-ratings, but only tend to be more accurate (p $\angle$ .10) when an accuracy measure was used that included both their first and second self-ratings.)

Of interest is the comparative magnitude of the self-image scores (Table 6–5) of the two samples. The two well-organized groups are much more similar in their self-image than are the two poorly organized groups. The greater similarity of the Standard's poorly organized group to the other well organized than poorly organized group reconfirms that it was scarcely a very disturbed group and suggests why the Standard sample has not been a good cross-validation sample.

We need not equivocate about the hypothesis of the maturity of the self-image, however. The well organized person has a significantly more mature self-image, believes others think he is mature, and is so judged by other persons. The well organized men of both samples consistently and significantly rated themselves to be more mature than did the poorly organized men for each of the private self-reports. With respect to the judge evaluations of the men, it is true that some contamination of the Organized judges' results occurred because the judges who participated in the selection procedure made the SIQ ratings ten months later. However, one-fourth of the total number of self-image judgments were made by judges about persons they had not initially selected to be either well or poorly organized. Although the Standard's judging procedures were quite different (the many different judges had no knowledge of the purpose of the experiment or of the person's eventual self-organization classification), its significant findings confirm the Organized sample's results.

Rorschach Measures of Schemata and Skill Organization

Turning now to the Klopfer score differences, given in Table 6–5, we encounter some disappointments.[2] Very few of the Klopfer score differences reached significance (even at a two-tailed .10 p level) and of those that did, few were consistently replicated in the other samples. The trends consistent for *all* of the samples were for the mature (including well organized) men to be more productive (Ror. #R), to give more conventional and popular schemata (Ror. #P), and to be more introspective (Ror. FK%) than the immature men. Finally, the mature group of the Maturity sample showed more restlessness and inner tension than its immature counterpart but this result was not consistently supported by the Standard groups' differences. The more traditional Rorschach scores apparently cannot differentiate between

[2] The raw Rorschach scores were converted into percentile scores to control for the wide differences in number of responses given to the Rorschach and to give more reliable scores. Such a procedure was justified for our samples because most men gave more than thirty to thirty-five responses (Cronbach, 1949). Two-tailed tests of significance were used since no advance predictions were made about the direction of the score differences. The more complex ratio scores (W:M) were not examined because they tend to compound the unreliability that marks each of their component scores.

mature and immature men. This important negative result confirms Barron's (1963) findings that the scores did not separate therapeutically improved from unimproved patients or psychologically sound from unsound persons.

The Rorschach clinical judgments of self-organization successfully differentiated (p $\angle$ .05) between the judge-identified well and poorly organized persons of both the Organized and Standard samples, thereby validating, in the large, the judgmental procedures used to identify the criterion groups.

Table 6–5, which also summarizes the Holt score differences for the criterion groups, indicates that most of them are in the predicted direction. The mature person does have a more maturely developed schemata and skill organization than the immature person. The trend, consistent for all of the samples, is for the more mature person to have fewer regressed or unstable schemata (Ror. % PriPro). His cognitive processes are significantly more conceptually integrated and effective in meeting reality concerns. It was *strongly confirmed* that the immature person's coordinating skills are severely impaired (Ror. % Formal) and that his schemata are much more autocentrically dominated (Ror. % Level 1) than is true of the mature person which is consistent with the finding that the schemata of the mature person are more conventionally and reality-oriented. If a valid interpretation of Holt's Level 1 score is that it measures the extent to which more infantile drives still determine and organize a person's schemata, then we can say the evidence consistently supports the hypothesis that the schemata of a mature person are more autonomous than are those of the immature person. The evidence also suggests that the mature person can become aware of his experiences more readily and adaptively than the immature person. The mature group tended to be more introspective (Ror. FK%) as well as significantly better able to imagine or symbolize experience (Ror. Con DD/Form DD). There is the hint that the mature person can also allow more regressively organized and unstable schemata to penetrate his awareness under good control than can the immature person (Ror. % DD x DE data not given). In very gross terms, the Rorschach data certainly favor the hypothesis that the more mature person's skills and schemata are developmentally more mature.

WHO IS THE MATURE PERSON?

At long last, we are now ready to reexamine this question with more perspective and, hopefully, more empirically grounded wisdom. I first summarize in Table 6–5 the empirical data so tediously gathered about our mature and immature men and then compare the results with other published results.

The Haverford Mature and Immature Person

Although the two terms *mature* and *well organized* (and the terms *immature* and *poorly organized*) may not completely intersect, the general tenor of the evidence suggests that we can talk about the mature (including the well organized) and the immature (including the poorly organized) person without violating the denotative meaning of each term too severely.

And the mature person. Who is he? By the measure of his peers, faculty, and Departmental Chairman, the mature person at Haverford was one of the College's most capable and effective young men. He was a highly determined, conscientious, energetic, purposeful, and ambitious person fully in command of his talents. He lived his life not within any limited arena, for his effectiveness played itself out in the academic, extracurricular, athletic, and personal-social spheres. He fulfilled his potential as an excellent student, a responsible leader actively involved in numerous student College activities, and athletic teams. Such heavy involvement was not at the expense of his physical health. Nor were his efficiency and effectiveness bought at the price of consideration, fair-mindedness, personal integrity, or empathy for others—if we are to believe his peer's personality ratings of him. Self-report and impressionistic evidence tend to confirm his peers' ratings, for the mature person (in poignant contrast to the immature men) was deeply involved emotionally in the lives of his close friends—both men and women. He certainly values such involvement and he persists in his devotions, even to his alma mater several years after graduation. His quality as a person

TABLE 6–5: DIFFERENCES BETWEEN MATURE AND IMMATURE GROUPS DEFINED BY CONSENSUAL JUDGMENTS OF MATURITY

Self-Organization and Other Measures	Maturity M	I	t	Organized M	I	t	Standard M	I	t
I. Social Judgments (Dept. Ch.)									
% Total Excel.	56	6		51	13		53	23	
% Determin.	50	0		91	0		60	40	
% Emo. Stab.	70	10		55	9		80	27	
% Personality	80	0		36	9		87	20	
II. Intellectual skill and achievement (2-tail)									
Intell. skill	Mat. consistently higher but not significantly			No difference			No difference		
Grade av.	87.8	78.2	4.45***	87.3	76.3	6.25†***	83.4	78.7	2.40*
III. Self-report (1-tail)									
MMPI Total	53.71	58.4	2.58**	50.32	56.9	2.58***	No difference		
Hs	No difference			48.6	54.8	2.64**	Diff. small but consistent		
D	Consistent			43.6	55.0	2.93***	45.3	51.3	2.08**
Pd	Consistent			49.9	59.5	2.31**	Consistent		
Pt	Consistent			49.2	58.5	1.85*	Consistent		
Sc	Consistent			48.7	58.7	2.30**	No difference		
Si	Not available			41.3	48.4	2.41†***	Consistent		
Bern. Neurotic	Consistent			16.62	51.0	3.15†***	Diff. small but consistent		
Introversion	Consistent			22.5	53.8	3.44***	Consistent		
Lack self. conf.	Diff. small but consistent			33.1	61.8	2.61†**	Consistent		
Nonsocial	Consistent			30.2	50.8	2.48**	Consistent		
Dominance	Inconsistent			74.1	47.8	2.30**	Consistent		

168

Self-Organization and Other Measures	Maturity M	Maturity I	Maturity t	Organized M	Organized I	Organized t	Standard M	Standard I	Standard t
SIQ									
Maturity scores	Not available								
Private				41.1	15.1	2.46**	46.6	32.6	2.74***
Social				40.3	−6.8	4.62****	43.2	25.7	2.44****
Judge				60.7	−18.8	11.22****	43.7	21.0	3.55***
Dimensions	Not available								
Stability				17.3	30.2	4.57****	No difference		
Congruence				23.7	40.3	3.12****	No difference		
Accuracy				36.8	55.4	2.63****	Consistent		
Allocentric				39.3	51.4	1.94*	Consistent		
Autonomy				6.0	4.6		Not available		
IV. Rorschach									
Clin. Eval. (1-tail)	Not available			69.8	51.3	1.75*	63.9	47.9	2.01*
Klopfer (2-tail)									
#R	Consistent			Consistent			41.9	33.4	2.14*
m%	3.6	1.1	2.38†	Difference small but consistent			Difference small and inconsistent		
FK%	No difference			3.8	1.1	2.66**	Consistent		
#P	Consistent			8.1	5.3	3.14†***	No difference		
Holt (1-tail)									
% Formal	15.7	31.1	2.79***	19.6	33.4	2.14**	Consistent		
% Level 1	Consistent			11.2	20.9	1.79*	Consistent		
Other pri pro scores	In predicted direction			In predicted direction			In predicted direction		
Con DD/Form DD	19.5	10.3	3.19***	17.6	10.1	2.87***	Inconsistent		
Other control scores	In predicted direction			In predicted direction			In predicted direction		

† F significant at .05 p level; df halved in evaluating significance; Cochran and Cox formula used when Ns unequal.

* $p < .05$
** $p < .025$
*** $p < .01$

1 N = 7; data not available on remaining men.
2 N = 11; data not available on remaining man.

and as a human being cannot be well hidden in the Haverford community; and, if we are to believe the record and our judges, the mature Haverford person is an emotionally stable, honest, responsible, and personally appealing man.

What impressionistic picture has our mature person painted about his family and early life? He says he comes from a stable family in which both parents and siblings have been models of effectiveness, responsibility, and determination. He respects his parents and siblings and, while strains and arguments occurred within the families, his family seems to have remained a functioning and viable emotional unit whose affectional ties still prevented rancor or rebellion against the basic motivational values of the family. In his own development he fulfilled his familial style of life in many areas of activity. Indeed, what seems to mark the maturity of our mature youth is that his life was centrally organized around a general motivational value to do well with what talents he possessed, not for extrinsic reasons but for the enjoyment and pride that comes from fulfilling himself and from doing well. His motivation appears to be general and not specific and for this reason we see him achieve excellence in most of the areas of life which he touches and in which he becomes engaged.

The self-image of the mature youth is quite stable as well as congruent with the image he projects to his peers and faculty. He has a generally favorable and mature self-image and believes others think of him as he thinks of himself. His social and his personal selves are not in conflict. He not only has considerable self-understanding, but he is more accurate than an immature person in understanding what others think of him. Our mature youth regards himself as adaptable, independent, enthusiastic, self-driving, and as having lived up to his high expectations. He does not think of himself as maladjusted, introverted, or disinterested in others. His intense goal-directedness does not ignore the personal lives of others, for he values sympathy and concern for others. In contrast to the immature man, the life of the mature Haverford man is strongly centered around people. His social allocentricism is also seen in his consistent temperamental preferences for professional social and manipulative-persuasive rather than for nonpersonal, exploitative economic or more solitary aesthetic relationships.

These judge and self assessments tend to be confirmed by the more indirect projective methods. The more mature youth is significantly more productive. His thought processes remain reality-oriented and adaptive even when he must think with or coordinate unstable and drive-involved schemata. His schemata are more socialized, conventional, and less idiosyncratically coordinated. Not only does he tend to be more introspective and better able to symbolize imaginally more of his experience, but he seems to have developed considerable autonomy from being dominated or driven by his inner needs.

The immature person was just that—to others and to himself. His peers and the faculty saw him as erratic, disordered, scattered, illogical, and purposeless. Although the faculty sensed that some of the immature men had the potential for gifted and creative expression, the consensus of all of the judges was that their gifts remained frustratingly, to both the faculty and the immature men themselves, unrealized. Except for an occasional gifted athlete, actor, or musician, the immature man achieved little of distinction during his four years at the College. Despite ability equal to his more mature classmates, the immature youth either barely squeaked through College or left College with his academic hopes in shambles. He was seldom elected or appointed to a responsible office. He just never seemed to get caught up in the academic pulse or the extracurricular and social rhythm of the Haverford community.

Clinically, to interject my own personal judgment as well as that of the diagnostic impressions from psychiatrists (almost one half of the group were in or have subsequently sought psychiatric treatment), the immature group contained three different types of persons: 1) some severely disturbed borderline and obsessional pre-schizophrenic men, 2) inhibited, odd character problems, and 3) uninhibited, compulsive, acting out character neurotics.

Of his family and personal life, the immature person said that his social-economic background was similar to that of the mature person; however, he expressed much more ambivalence about his parents, particularly about his father and his achievement. For the immature youth, the family seemed less cohesive an emotional unit. He reported greater maternal instability. More friction and criticism, if not hostility, mark some of his descriptions of his parents and siblings, which suggest his family was more fragmented and possibly less supportive and less positively tied together than the family of the mature youth. The immature youth has a greater sense of being bound up and limited by his own problems; he does not feel himself to be inwardly free or master of his talents and his will. The arena in which his developmental problems are being fought is an internal one, rather than in the more objective external world in which mastery or achievement is more readily recognized and rewarded. His self-image reflects his spotty and uneven achievement record and his hopes are much more tied to expressive, self-finding, and self-fulfilling (writing, artistic, and theater) interests than are the life styles of the more mature Haverford person. If our immature youth achieves brilliantly, I hazard that his achievement will be more limited in scope and will not be as measurable over a wide range of varying activities as will be the achievement of the more mature person.

If asked, the immature youth would not quarrel with the assessment that he was a disturbed and ineffective person. He too described himself as erratic, bottled-up, impulsively irresponsible, introversive and nonsocial. His singularly high value for aesthetic and expressive activities, while generally congruent with his temperamental sympathy for more individualistic and artistic activities, may have been partially compensatory for his felt inability to give effective expression to his "bottled-up" potentials. Such an aesthetic value not supported by any achieved productivity must always have reminded him of his inadequacy and failure or spurred him on to defensive behaviors shielding him from the discrepancy between his values and his talents. Such shielding prevented the development of a stable and accurate self-image. His view of himself differed from the view he believed others had of him. And his own autocentric self-absorption led him to assess inaccurately what others actually thought of him.

These observations find expression in the Rorschach findings that the immature person was much more severely disturbed, had many developmentally immature or unstable schemata, had more disturbance in his secondary thought processes, was less reality oriented and had less cognitive resistance to the interfering consequences of aroused affect and drive. His control over strong internal disrupting forces was erratic and tenuous and little energy was available for effective accommodation and adaptation.

The first three chapters suggested that social-cultural values and expectations could facilitate or hinder, shape and steer, the maturing or developing self-organization of an individual. Intuitively, I feel the mature men were in "tune," were resonant with the dominant Haverford value and expectation patterns— if, in fact, they were not its major articulators. Such men were sufficiently inwardly free to optimize their talents within a supporting and reinforcing community. On the other hand, the immature men, cast of a mold different from the prevailing values and temperament and simultaneously prisoners of their own drive-dominated thought, were unable to respond adaptively to a not-so-sympathetic or resonating environmental value pattern. Most of these men remained socially alienated from the Haverford community—preserving a fragile and defensive identity either by acting out against the community's value patterns, or by compliantly conforming to its expectations at the expense of achieving a more stable self-organization. In the words of one perceptive student, at Haverford the mature become more mature, the immature more immature. Resumed growth for some of our immature youths probably awaited a more responsive environment.

The Mature Person and Other Empirical Studies of Maturity

Chapter 1 briefly synopsized the results of the few other published studies of mature and effectively functioning persons. Such persons were distinguished not by the absence of conflicts and adjustment difficulties but by the possession of adaptive skills for mastering such conflicts and stresses, particularly those that persisted over time. The mature person had considerable stability and maintained his comparative maturity over several years, largely because his life was directed by persisting goal-directed motives. His behavior was reality-oriented, socially adaptable, and he had confidence in himself.

This picture does not disagree with that just sketched from our data. I have focussed more on assessing the mature person's adaptive skills and the regulating effects of his self-image than on ferreting out types of conflict and adjustment difficulties. But the mature men were not immune to the problems their own continuing development posed, and although the clinical evaluations of the Rorschach identified a number of the judge-identified mature men to be troubled by persisting and focal neurotic conflicts, the severity of their conflicts did not approach that of the immature men. Also, the congruence between the mature person's temperament and values and the Haverford community's value system meant that problems of social and communal alienation, rejection and loneliness were not likely to be his to face. Our mature person also maintained his comparative maturity over several years, for even as a freshman he reported himself to be quite mature compared to the reports of the immature youth. One of the reasons for such stability is probably the more autonomous goal-directed motivation and determination of the mature person. We have seen how frequently such traits as "purposeful, conscientious, high aspirations" and such traits as "scattered, erratic, bottled-up" have distinguished our mature from our immature men. True, many of the mature men, even as seniors, had only vague intuitions about their goals in life, but the quality of their motivation was such as would ensure adaptive excellence in most any area they encountered. So it seems it is not a highly specific need or focalized goal that helps to organize our mature person's life so much as it is to be "damn good" in whatever he does. Finally, our mature person is also more reality-oriented, more socially adaptable, and has a high sense of self-regard as well.

The pattern of the results is also quite consistent with many of the more specific findings of Barron (1954, 1963) whose study of sound and unsound persons is the most comparable study to ours. For example, both studies suggest that more mature persons come from more stable homes, marked by less family friction; they respect their fathers who are considered to be very successful; they express more positive and friendly feelings toward their siblings; and they have a history of successful and responsible participation in a variety of activities, including competitive athletics. These and other similar results found from two studies that differed in method, judging procedures and samples reassure us that our findings may have some validity—and some generality that transcends the possibly limiting effects of consensual judgments made within one type of institutional setting.

As satisfying as these and the many other results (which I now don't resummarize) are, the reader, as I am, may be unable to quell some insistent doubts about the conceptual fit of the developmental theory that ordered and guided the studies with their actual measures, results, and interpretations. True, there are suggestive leads that the more mature person is a more stable and integrated individual whose skills (thought processes), values, and schemata (self-image) are more allocentrically directed. There are even reasonable hints that the mature person's schemata and skills may be more autonomous and that he may have more of his experience cognitively symbolized. And perhaps I have been moderately successful in at least sketching how such a developmental theory could be applied to the study of schemata, valuators, and skills—the principal "structures and activities" of the self.

Can we go beyond these preliminary diffuse explorations in our pursuit of that illusive concept—maturity? I believed it was both possible and compellingly necessary to go beyond the prevalent type of research methodology used in such explorations and pursue one of the hypothesized developmental properties of the mature persons as deeply as possible. In this way, I hoped to give more substance and precision to at least one of the developmental trends, to learn what additional problems may confront research in defining the maturing process, and to emerge with some new understanding of personality structure and development. Part III is devoted to this more technical task.

PART III

Stability of
Self-Organization: Studies of
the Adaptation of Well and
Poorly Organized Persons to
Disturbing Information

CHAPTER 7

Stability of Self-Organization and Disturbing Information

The preceding chapters gave some substance to the developmental dimensions of maturity that guided and ordered the studies up to this point. Mature persons do seem to differ from immature persons as our inductive notions suggested. Would a more carefully controlled definition of one developmental dimension and an intensive but more experimental investigation of how mature and immature men differ on only this dimension also confirm our theory? This chapter asks these questions: "What developmental dimension should be analyzed in depth?" "What type of self-structure should be examined?" These two questions pick up the concerns and themes of Chapters 1 and 2 respectively, and the answers lead to the third question: "What specific hypotheses about the developmental maturity of self-structures shaped the research and what methodological problems do such hypotheses raise?" Finally, we preview the experimental study and its design before entering into the details of the experiments reported in Chapters 8 through 12. Throughout, we explore the relation of our new experimental measures to the measures of maturity discussed in Part II.

ADAPTATION TO DISTURBING INFORMATION

Self-organization and adaptation are reciprocal constructs as Chapter 2 has pointed out. The fundamental task of a person is to maintain and optimize his functional integrity or self-organization while adapting to both changing internal and external demands. A changing internal and external environment requires continuous assimilative and accommodative adaptations to varying information. Such change always contains within it the seeds for producing self-disorganization and overt maladaptation. That is, the organism is never permanently free from the possibility of disorganization. A stable organism requires, therefore, both inborn and learned structural arrangements or skills to coordinate schemata so as either to minimize the possibility of disorganization or to maximize the probability of recovering from schemata disorganization if prior attempts to prevent or tolerate disorganization fail. It is to protect oneself from such potential disorganization that a person develops culturally reinforced habits and idiosyncratic defensive coordinations by which to assimilate disturbing information selectively in order to reduce the magnitude of the accommodation required by such information.

Many different theoretical viewpoints converge on this problem of adapting to disturbing information: the "open system" theorists such as von Bertalanffy (1952a, b) have identified "regulability following disturbances" as a key defining characteristic of the organism; cyberneticists such as Ashby have stressed the role of regulators (the "essential feature of the good regulator is that *it blocks the flow of variety from disturbances to essential variables,*" 1956, p. 201) and of feedback arrangements (negative feedback mechanisms restore stability following some induced disequilibrium in the system); and physiologists such as Cannon (1932) have identified the crucial role of homeostatic mechanisms for the maintenance of organismic stability.

The psychoanalysts have had much more to say about the person's response to disturbing information, particularly that arising from internal sources such as drives and affects related to interpersonal relationships. Countercathexes (e.g., repression) is a central concept of psychoanalytic theory and refers to those regulative structures that block incoming disturbing information. Freud very early identified secondary process skills as the central nondefensive adaptive structures of the person which help him to maintain some accommodation to reality demands and yet, in the long run, guarantee him gratification of his needs. Ego psychologists have extended Freud's structural theory further. For Hartmann, the central criterion of ego strength is found in "how secure . . . the autonomy of the nondefensive functions of the ego [is], and how well . . . they [are] protected against being weakened by the energic demands of the defensive structures" (1960, p. 247). His construct of secondary autonomy or acquired "resistivity against regression and instinctualization" (1955, p. 20) following the receipt of disturbing information opened psychoanalytic theory to the problem we are trying to describe and clarify, a problem phrased in the question: how does a healthy person mature?

Finally, developmental psychologists such as Piaget, defining disturbing information almost solely in terms of external environmental sources, similarly emphasize that the maturing person is increasingly able to maintain his self-organization to disturbing information because he develops the capacity to "reverse" and "decenter" his thought processes from their ties to the phenomenal *hic* and *nunc* of such disturbing information.

Clearly, for a variety of theorists, a major, if not the most important, problem of a maturing person is for him to learn how to maintain some stable, identifiable self-organization, structure, or system in a changing environment. We chose to investigate the developmental trend toward increasing stability, to determine experimentally if the mature well organized person is, indeed, more stably organized than the immature and poorly organized person. Does he resist more persistently the potentially disorganizing effect of personally relevant disturbing information, and, when he does become disorganized, is he able to recover his equilibrium or fashion more adaptive schemata coordinations more rapidly than an immature and poorly organized person is able to do?

We have been talking very abstractly about "stability of self-organization" and "adapting to disturbing information." The discussion must be made more concrete. The self, as we have suggested in Chapter 2, is complexly composed of schemata, skills, and valuators. For research purposes, we measure "stability of self-organization" by measuring the stability of different types of schemata (such as the stability of the self-image), of valuators (such as the stability of a valuator over time), and of skills (such as the resistance of a skill to temporary impairment). Chapter 6 summarized the evidence that well organized men do have more stably organized schemata (Rorschach and self-image data), skills (Rorschach data), and, possibly valuators (e.g., the well organized men were more directed and determined while the poorly organized men were more erratic and purposeless).

However, we have not yet given more concrete meanings to the phrase "adapting to disturbing information" which is to be the focus of Part III. Now, what is "disturbing information" is determined by the schemata organization of the person. What is disturbing information to one person may not be so to another. For us, "disturbing information" must be defined in terms of the stability of the schemata for that information, which leads us to consider how a schema becomes more stably organized. Some of the related theoretical constructs to be presented will be operationally defined in Chapter 8.

Stability is defined as the conservation of a schema's organization or identity during its assimilation of and accommodation to information or during its coordination with other schemata. While a schema may change over time, ordinarily its *essential* structure is preserved within any more limited time. The stability of a schema is defined by the relationship between three thresholds: assimilatory, accommodatory, and anxiety. An example may help to clarify these theoretical constructs before defining them. At the beginning of the academic year, a student begins to develop a schema organized around a professor who is viewed as aloof, demanding, unexpressive, and "out to get the student." The student's schema may also be coordinated with other schemata organized around authority figures, with retaliatory passive negativistic reactions, and with valuators that value a more humane type of person. One day the professor wears a jauntily colored bow tie quite out of harmony with his usual Ivy League somber tie. If the schema is still unstable and not defensively coordinated, it will be poorly differentiated, have a low assimilatory threshold, and will readily assimilate the bow tie without distortion. The bow tie does not fit the schema structure that the professor is unexpressive. The resulting incongruence increases affective tension that may produce more focused affects, some curiosity about the bow tie, as well as accommodatory attempts to figure out why this professor wears a bow tie. Eventually, the student may modify his other views about the professor and accept that he may have a warmer spirit than he first thought. Subsequent behavior of the professor may modify the present or reinstate the earlier schema organization. In time, the professorial schema, now more differentiated and complex, stabilizes so that relatively little additional schema accommodation is required to fit new changes in the professor's behavior. Information is more selectively perceived and assimilated and irrelevancies screened out. However, the assimilatory threshold which is now higher is not so high that the schema is closed to new information or unmodifiable by any marked change in the professor's behavior. Now, what happens if one day the professor wears a toga to class? Affective tension may occur for some who have no immediate schema accommodation available for such drama —or such "disturbing information." Disorganization or defensive behavior may occur. At this point, the anxiety threshold of the schema has been reached.

The term *information* rather than *stimulus* is used to indicate that the person receives data meaningfully patterned or organized by the culture and/or selectively and phenomenally organized by himself. Berlyne (1960) has identified novelty, uncertainty, conflict, and complexity as the central properties of information likely to be selectively attended to. We use the term *amount* of information only to allow us to talk about the disturbing effects of information. What is *disturbing* may be due to the information's complexity, novelty, or its conflictual content. Actually, it is the latter property we investigate in this research.

The assimilatory threshold is defined by the amount, range, or intensity of information required before that information is incorporated into or modified to fit existing schemata structures. Ordinarily, in the absence of specific defensive, neurological or other factors, the differentiated structure (or level of organization) of a schema is the major determinant of the level of its assimilatory threshold. That is, increased schema differentiation results in more effective screening of irrelevant information.

Schemata differ in their thresholds for assimilating information, or, in other terms, in the permeability of their boundaries or barriers (Freud, 1920). Some schemata are so impervious to any information that it takes massive amounts, frequent repetition, or extreme types of information to produce some selective assimilation of this information (psychopathological delusions or culturally reinforced prejudices). Other schemata have such low assimilatory thresholds that they assimilate too much information resulting in fluid, affectively unstable, and unpredictable types of behavior. Such unstable schemata usually characterize new learnings and affectively-involved schemata.

The accommodatory threshold is the amount of information required to produce schema reorganization, modification, or co-ordination with other schemata. In early development, assimilatory and accommodatory thresholds are probably identical but with developing inhibition of behavior and imaginal activity, information may be assimilated without producing schema accommodation. (Piaget's theory develops some of these relationships further.) For example, information may be "recognized" (be congruent with the schema); information may be distorted (denied, misperceived) to fit the existing schema (measured by Rorschach % Form Accuracy score); information may be tentatively assimilated and worked over, but may be rejected without any major persisting schema accommodation. The accommodatory threshold is reached when the bow tie results in tempering the severity of the existing schema to include "a warm spirit hidden by aloofness." Such a modification changes the meaning of "to get the student" to mean "playful teasing or testing of the student." Such schema accommodation now affects the assimilatory threshold which subsequently assimilates a slightly different range or type of information that will confirm or disconfirm the new schema organization.

The stability of a schema also depends upon its anxiety threshold. A schema is limited in the amount of information it can assimilate and accommodate to and yet still conserve its own identity or organization. At the organismic level, this limiting point is popularly called a person's "breaking point." The schema's anxiety threshold is that point at which the schema becomes overloaded by too much, too rapid, or too many irrelevant types of information (or even by the absence of certain kinds of information) to which it has no available accommodative reorganization. It is operationally defined in Chapter 8 by the amount of defensive coordinations or disorganization a person shows to specific types of information. Anxiety is that affective tension which occurs when information is so incongruent with the schema structure that no accommodative means are immediately available for adaptation. Anxiety may or may not be experienced before the anxiety threshold is reached. The construct *anxiety threshold* helps to link Piaget's concern with environmental sources of information to the psychoanalyst's preoccupation with more drive-instigated and conflictual types of information.

To return to the question of what is "disturbing information," we can now define it more precisely to be that information which activates a schema's anxiety threshold. Information which a person can assimilate and accommodate without involving the anxiety threshold of a schema is nondisturbing information. Part III focuses on how efficiently well and poorly organized men find adaptive solutions to disturbing information composed of conflictual interpersonal content that has been independently demonstrated to be anxiety arousing for each person.

SELF STRUCTURES AND ACTIVITIES FOR ADAPTING TO DISTURBING INFORMATION

The process of adaptation usually requires not only the modification of schemata through the processes of assimilation and accommodation but also the coordination, the linking and unlinking, of different schemata to form new combinations of schemata. Both skills and valuators interactively coordinate schemata in the adaptation process. We only investigated how adaptively mature and immature persons can *skillfully* coordinate disturbing information.

What type of skillful coordinations of disturbing information most centrally contribute to maintain the stability of a person's self-organization? In the language of the psychoanalysts, the question is what are the principal activities and structures that define "ego strength," or the ego, when that term is used (as it frequently is) to mean adaptation to disturbing information. (Chapter 2 suggested that the type of disturbing information most likely to threaten the stability of self-organization was that dealing with interpersonal relationships, the schemata of which are usually the last to become stabilized.)

Psychoanalytic theories of ego structure were of little assistance in identifying specific self structures for no adequate systematic or comprehensive classification, or even listing of the most important adaptive skills exists. Ego psychologists such as Hartmann (1950) have even disclaimed any attempt to so systematize ego functions. We cannot ignore, however, a major empirical effort, guided by psychoanalytic theory, to clarify the meaning of ego structure (Klein, 1958). Klein and his associates,[1] taking a clue from Freud that the ego is composed of controls as well as defenses (and other countercathetic structures such as derivative drives or valuators), have empirically identified a number of cognitive controls that appear to be factorially independent, are relatively stable over several years, and that mediate adaptation to a limited range of adaptive tasks (Gardner, Holzman, Klein, Linton, & Spence, 1959; Gardner, Jackson, & Messick, 1960). Such cognitive controls as field-articulation (originally identified by Witkin as field-independence, Witkin, Lewis, Hertzman, Machover, Meissner, & Wapner, 1954), sharpening, and tolerance for unrealistic experience have not been found to be related to the types of adaptation or adjustment measures most personality psychologists (and ourselves) are interested in. Klein has suggested that different patterns of cognitive controls may constitute

[1] Unfortunately, the major summary of Klein's theory and research became available to us following the inception of the research, so that, except for the Standard sample to whom was given one of Klein's specific tests (Stroop Color-Word test), we have no measures directly related to his cognitive control constructs.

a cognitive style which may, in turn, be related to more general adaptational criteria. While we will discuss the significance of his and Witkin's (1954) work for our results in Chapter 14, the major burden of his work has not been very useful to our studies because the relevance of the identified cognitive controls to the mastery of disturbing information is unknown, the predictive power of the cognitive controls is limited to fairly specific psychophysical and cognitive tasks, the factorial studies (done on small and heterogeneous samples) of the empirically derived cognitive control measures are ambiguous about the most reliable measures of such controls, and, except for field-articulation, the relation of the cognitive controls to other cognitive skills is as yet minimal or undetermined. Finally, the personality correlates of only the field-articulation control have been researched thoroughly (Witkin, et al, 1954).

But Freud did have something to say to our problem about the types of coordinating skills for which to search. He identified secondary thought processes as the core regulating and coordinating processes of the ego. Secondary process "thinking must concern itself with the connecting paths between ideas, without being led astray by the *intensities* of those ideas" (1900, p. 602); that is, a more well organized or mature person, whose thought processes are more allocentrically developed (secondary processes are reality-oriented) will be able to isolate (Klein's field-articulation control) the disturbing cathetic charge of a memory from the thought coordinations to be performed with those memories in the adaptive process.

We then searched for evidence about the relation of thought operations to adaptation as well as for a theory identifying the most important secondary processes. Most such theories of thought processes take the form of theories about intelligence, but little of the work on intellectual abilities helped us. True, some evidence suggests that more intelligent persons are more socially adapted and mature (Stalnaker, 1961; Terman, 1954; Warren & Heist, 1960) and that personally sound graduate students are better in abstract reasoning than their more unsound counterparts (Barron, 1954, 1963). Also, clinicians have long used differences in thought performance for inferring to the quality of a person's adaptation (Wechsler, 1958). But the major limitation of most intelligence theories was that they and their operational measures defined adaptation very narrowly to involve primarily nonpersonal and usually nondisturbing types of information. Schafer (1946) long ago called for the conversion of intelligence tests into true measures of adaptation by including a greater range (interpersonal conflict themes) of disturbing information. Another limitation of such theories is that little agreement exists about the most appropriate classification of thought operations (Tuddenham, 1962). Guilford's (1959b) comprehensive theoretical model of intellectual abilities may clarify the problem eventually, for he takes explicit account of the types of adaptational problems for which different skills are most relevant.

We eventually relied on Piaget's (1947) developmental theory of thought operations as a model of the major allocentric or secondary process skills. Logical conceptualization, analysis and synthesis, and associative judgment were identified to be the skills most relevant to the widest range of interpersonal or, more generally, adaptive problems. There is no question that many other skills are more important for particular types of adaptation, but we wanted a manageable number of skills that would encompass the basic types of schemata coordinations an adaptive problem was likely to present.

One way to define adaptive problems is in terms of the amount of information they make available for the solution of a problem. Thinking involves completing the informational gap, according to Bartlett (1958). Some problems present all of the information necessary for their solution. For example, in logical reasoning problems, "all the items to be used are theoretically definable before they come to be used in any particular instance" (Bartlett, 1958, p. 23).[2] The skill of logical conceptualization (hereafter called conceptual skill) requires noting logical similarities and dissimilarities, abstracting and ordering similarities into

---

[2] Incidentally, our term "skill" has been taken from Bartlett who suggests that "thinking is an advanced form of skilled behaviour, . . . that it has grown out of earlier established forms of flexible adaptation to the environment and that the characteristics which it possesses and the conditions to which it submits . . . are related to those of its own earlier forms," namely bodily skills (1958, p. 199)—a view similar to that of Piaget (1947).

some more abstract hierarchic combination. The ordering or coordinating principle is determined by the definitions given and the rules of transformation allowed by the task information itself. The solution is invariant—right or wrong. Logical consistency in thought has been considered by some to be the hallmark of secondary process thinking.

Other problems do not present all of the information necessary for their solution and therefore demand different thought operations. The person, out of his own social experience, provides additional information, usually the coordination and transformation rules. He must construct his own ordering principles. The skill of analyzing and synthesizing requires breaking up and rearranging the problem's information into combinations of schemata according to some induced coordinating principles. Several alternative schemata recombinations may be possible, but the criterion of the most adequate solution is more a conventional social one than one of logical necessity.

Finally, other types of problems to which a person must adapt present even less information and therefore place even fewer restrictions on the solution process. As in the case of associative judgment with interpersonal types of content, the person must provide much of the necessary information out of his own knowledge and experience. Given minimal information, can he select other information that "fits," that is "appropriate" to the minimal information the problem presents. Such judging problems typically involve constructing, comparing, evaluating and selecting according to some social criterion of *appropriateness* which the individual has internalized rather than according to some logical or conventional criterion of "right" or "wrong." This type of problem involves valuations, the coordination of means to goals, the selective guidance by valuators and affects. Most of the more important adaptive problems a person encounters (his relationships with others) are just those in which minimal or unreliable information is available ("What is his motive?" or "How does she really feel towards me?"). For this reason, impairment in judgmental skills is frequently diagnostic of severe social alienation as one sees in schizophrenics (Bleuler, 1911). Unfortunately, psychology has no adequate measure of realistic judgment. We will return to our measures of this and the other skills later.

SELF-ORGANIZATION AND SKILL EFFICIENCY TO DISTURBING INFORMATION

Hypotheses

Thinking must concern itself with the connecting paths between ideas, without being led astray by the *intensities* of those ideas—Sigmund Freud, *The Interpretation of Dreams,* 1900, p. 602.

Part III explores some determinants and correlates of "the autonomy of the nondefensive functions [skills] of the ego" (Hartmann, 1960, p. 247). When confronted by ideas of strong affective intensity or, in our language, by disturbing interpersonal information, can a person skillfully coordinate such ideas, connecting one with another, "without being led astray by the *intensities* of those ideas?" Developmental theory says skills become more stable in development. Our hypothesis asserts that more mature (or well organized) persons will have more stabilized skills and will, therefore, be more skillfully efficient in coordinating disturbing information than will more immature (or poorly organized) persons.

The second formal hypothesis asserts that more mature persons will *resist* skill impairment or, in the terminology of Hartmann, "regression and instinctualization" more persistently, and if their skill efficiency is impaired, they will *recover* their efficiency more rapidly than immature persons will be able to do. Both hypotheses test whether well organized persons do have and can maintain a more stable self-organization when forced to adapt to disturbing information.

Our holistic premise that stability, integration, allocentricism, autonomy, and cognitive symbolization are *organismic* developmental dimensions and are manifested in schemata, skill, and valuator development led to other expectations. We expected that schemata, skill, and valuator developmental maturity would be positively intercorrelated. Not only did we expect low to moderate positive intercorrelations between the adaptive skills, but we also expected persons of more stable, congruent, and mature self-images, for example, to be more skillful in coordinating disturbing information. We expected, then, that skillful coordinations of disturbing information would be positively related to other personality traits indicative of maturity and good self-organization.

Some Methodological Problems

The hypotheses were tested by presenting to each well and poorly organized youth especially designed skill tests that had as their content disturbing information or ideas of strong affective intensity. A youth had to solve:

1) logical concept problems by concentrating on the formal "connecting paths" between the concepts and ignoring the affective connotations of the anxiety-arousing conceptual content (Chapter 9),

2) analytic-synthetic problems by analyzing and combining words and phrases to meet certain formal grammatical and meaning standards "without being led astray" by the affective content of the material (Chapter 10), and

3) judgmental problems by associatively using the anxiety-arousing content but following reality-oriented and not regressive (primary process) principles of appropriate coordination (Chapter 11).

But deceptively hidden in such hypotheses and the above procedure was a Pandora's box of so many tangled methodological difficulties that we despaired more than once of ever concluding the research. Our first dilemma was that the major hypothesis might not be testable. Why? If it is confirmed that well organized men do coordinate disturbing information more skillfully than the poorly organized men, a critic will claim that the information which he coordinated was not as phenomenally disturbing to him as it was to the poorly organized person. So he was not more skillfully efficient; he only had higher anxiety thresholds for the problem's information. Obviously, then, we must equate how disturbing the information is for the two criterion groups. But how can we do that? What is disturbing depends upon the stability of the relevant schemata and our developmental theory says that for the same interpersonal-type information the well organized person's schemata will be more stable than those of the poorly organized person. So we must select different types of information that have the same anxiety threshold to present to the criterion groups. But to do that, we must equate the difficulty level of different types of information and that poses its own formidable methodological problems.

To anticipate the solution and some results, we did try to equate the difficulty level of problems of different content. Chapters 9 through 11 describe how this was done. We also did find a way of reliably measuring a schema's anxiety threshold. That solution is reported in Chapter 8. And when we compared the anxiety threshold values for different types of information for the two criterion groups we found that although the well organized men did tend to have more stable schemata than the poorly organized men for the same information, their anxiety threshold values were not significantly more stable. So it was possible to confront the criterion groups with the *same* information to coordinate and to be assured the information was about equally disturbing to each group.

A second but similar dilemma plagued the research. Even if the amount of disturbing information were equated for the criterion groups, if the well organized men were more skillfully efficient, their superiority could be due to just being more intelligent persons. So the groups were selected (Organized) or found (Standard) to be not significantly different on three different measures of intelligence (Verbal and Quantitative CEEB and Terman Concept Mastery Test). Any contribution that intelligence made to the variance of a particular skill test could be statistically controlled—if necessary—by partial correlation or covariance analysis.

Such experimental and statistical controls did not wish away the underlying theoretical issue which was this: we expected the skills of a well organized person to be more maturely developed than those of an immature person. The skills measured are probably moderately related to intelligence. Does this not mean theoretically that the well organized person has to be more "intelligent?" Further, what is the meaning of each term? The issue cannot now be solved. We ourselves are trying to explore the meaning of "maturity," and some sixty years of research on intelligence has not resolved many central questions about intelligence (Hunt, 1961). The only points we dare make are those most relevant to the hypothesis. Intelligence testers have distinguished between a native and an effective (i.e., that actually used for adaptation purposes) intelligence (Wechsler, 1958). The two criterion groups may be no different in native intelligence as the tests indicate, but the well organized groups, as we predict, may realize their potential more effectively to a much wider range of information. The poorly organized groups are not so disorganized that their intellective skills are radically impaired or immaturely developed—otherwise, they would not have been admitted to Haverford. But, following the suggestions from other research on thought impairment (Cameron, 1939; Schilder, 1938; Winder, 1960) and our notions, it may be that the instability of a person's thought processes first manifests itself with more personally threatening information. Accordingly, we expected that the well and poorly organized men would differ more to the most disturbing than to the least disturbing information. To check such an expectation, each skill test was composed of disturbing information ranging from less threatening to more threatening ideas.

Other methodological problems did not so challenge the assumptions of the research and could be solved when constructing the skill tests or planning the experimental design of the study.

Test Construction and Experimental Design

The thematic content of the three skill tests was identical. Each skill test was composed of replicated problems for each type of information. To check the hypothesis that well organized men would recover more rapidly from induced disorganization, two matched forms of each skill test were developed and administered on different days. Since considerable adaptive learning occurs to disturbing information (D. H. Heath, 1954), the item sequence within each test form was also systematically randomized in each test session. The skill tests were so physically designed that at the time of testing, their forms and individual items could be readily reordered to follow an à priori prescribed sequence that had been randomly assigned to each man. Table 1, Appendix B gives the different samples used in the development of the skill tests and the test of the hypotheses. Fewer samples were used in the development of the test for measuring conceptual skill (TCT) because it was modeled on Bruner's test of concept formation about which a great deal of procedural and other information was available, (Bruner, Goodnow, & Austin, 1956).

The three skill tests could be administered in one of six possible sequences on either test day. Therefore, the two criterion groups of the Organized sample were each randomly divided into two six man replicate groups. Each of the six men received one of the test sequences on day one and a different sequence on day two. A well organized man was randomly paired with a poorly organized man and both received identical experimental treatments. Since the degree of self-organization of the men of the Standard sample was determined only after the experiments, its men were randomly paired with each other and divided into three paired replicate groups. To control for varying recall and adaptation rates to the content of the skill tests, the length of the time intervals between the two days of testing was matched for each well and poorly organized replicate pair.

What did the men know of and how did they react to the experiment? Each was told he was to take tests measuring the efficiency of his thought processes in a variety of situations and that some tests might be disturbing to him; he was to feel free to stop participating in the experiment at any time. Several students who showed signs of too great anxiety were encouraged to stop, but each insisted he wanted to complete the research. No student ever tested on the skill tests has failed to complete them. Many students reported that the tests were "rough" but, when asked, none said other students should not take them.

The excellent student cooperation and favorable response to the project may have been due to several factors. First, each student was guaranteed anonymity by the use of code numbers and other procedures. Second, the ethos of a student body that values honesty about one's self, combined with the challenge that the tests were likely to be disturbing, probably generated more openness and cooperative interest than might be the case in other studies. Finally, I as the experimenter was not unknown in the community. To what extent experimenter attitudes and styles of reaching students affect the amount of test score variance in personality studies is largely unknown (Milam, 1954). It may be considerable, but no objective evidence is available to assess its influence in this study.

SUMMARY

The chapter introduces the experimental studies that illustrate how one developmental trend was investigated in depth. The developmental trend toward stabilization suggested that mature and well organized men were more stably organized. Part II has defined "more mature and well organized." Part III identifies "more stably organized" to mean that well organized persons more skillfully adapt to disturbing information. They both resist schemata disorganization more persistently and recover from such disorganization more rapidly than the poorly organized person. In the absence of any detailed theory of the skills that facilitate adaptation to the widest range of disturbing information, Piaget's theory of operational thought was used to identify conceptual, analytic and synthetic, and judgmental skills as the core secondary thought processes. We expected these skills to be moderately and positively intercorrelated as well as related to the developmental maturity of other self-structures, such as the self-image.

The hypothesis that well organized persons more skillfully adapt to disturbing information posed troublesome theoretical and methodological problems. To test adaptation to "disturbing information" required identifying and controlling how "disturbing" the information to be used in the experiment was for each criterion group. Our solution is given in the next chapter. To measure "more skillfully adapt" required basal intellectual skill be controlled, but the theoretical relation of maturity to intelligence was left unclarified. Chapters 9, 10, and 11 describe the tests measuring skillful coordinations of disturbing information and their intellectual and personality correlates. Chapter 12 discusses the interrelationships of the three skills, a combined summary measure of cognitive skill efficiency to disturbing information and its personality correlates, and then examines the hypothesis that more mature persons are more stably organized persons.

CHAPTER 8

Disturbing Information:
Definition by Anxiety Thresholds

The first order of business is to demonstrate that the information which the well and poorly organized persons must subsequently conceptualize, analyze, and judge is indeed disturbing. How is "disturbing information" to be measured? What is disturbing to a person depends upon his anxiety threshold for such information, and so a way must be found to measure independently his anxiety thresholds for different types of information. Once we find a reliable and valid method of determining a person's anxiety thresholds, we can also ask, for example, whether well organized persons have higher anxiety thresholds for disturbing information than poorly organized persons. Or do the samples have higher anxiety thresholds for information organized around developmentally earlier than later types of relationships?

Following a brief discussion of the behavioral criteria of anxiety thresholds, this chapter presents a reliable and partially validated test, called the Phrase Association Test (PT), that measures the anxiety threshold values of different schemata. The relation of PT-defined anxiety thresholds to our notions about self-organization is then re-examined. Because of the novelty of the PT, its reliability and validity correlates are summarized in some detail to clarify just what the test measures. Finally, we

return to demonstrate that the information used in the conceptual, analytic, and judgmental tasks was disturbing for the
men, and to examine if the well and poorly organized men
differed in their anxiety thresholds for different types of information.

BEHAVIORAL CRITERIA OF ANXIETY THRESHOLDS

Chapter 7 suggested that anxiety occurs when a person
cannot accommodate or fails to accommodate to information. At
some point the need to reduce the anxiety becomes more imperative than the need to persist in seeking an adaptive solution.
Regressive and defensive coordinations of schemata occur and
are the signs that the person's anxiety threshold for tolerating
anxiety has been reached. However, *not* all maladaptive behavior
necessarily indexes that it is the informational content that has
triggered off the nonadaptive behavior. Maladaptive behavior
may be due to informational ambiguity, novelty, or difficulty, or
to limited accommodative capacity, fatigue or other non-disturbing variables (D. H. Heath, 1958). It is therefore necessary when
measuring anxiety thresholds to control for such variables if one
intends to talk of the anxiety threshold of particular types of
schemata.

How are regressive and defensive behaviors to be understood
within the language framework of the research? Regressive
coordinations of schemata are defined more by autocentric
(primary process) than allocentric (reality-oriented) types of
coordinations. Responses are linked together not on the basis of
their conventional, socialized, and conceptual relevance to each
other but on the basis of affect and drives as is seen in condensations, fusions, and interpenetration (Cameron, 1938) and as
measured by Holt's % Formal score. Regressive behaviors
reveal impairment in coordinating skills such as conceptualization and realistic judgment. Defensive coordinations or controls,
on the other hand, are not as well understood theoretically.
Different defenses and controls have been clinically and empirically identified but no theory has yet been proposed by which to

derive, classify, and systematically order defensive coordinations. What behavioral criteria define regressive and defensive behavior? Diagnosticians have typically inferred disorganized or defensive behavior from (1) response deviations from a person's persistent accommodative style when the test conditions remain relatively constant (deviation in response length, number, content, or quality from his modal response); (2) response deviation from *patterns* of responses typical of the person's reference group; (3) failure to comply with the task instructions; and (4) specific irrelevant and inappropriate responses that indicate an inability to maintain a conceptually relevant set (Rapaport, Gill, & Schafer, 1945, 1946).

Despite considerable clinical agreement about *specific* behavioral indices that may define anxiety, no test exists that reliably measures the anxiety thresholds of different schemata. I have argued elsewhere (1958) that an adequate measure of anxiety thresholds must (1) use meaningful (highly structured) information that permits comparison of inter-individual accommodative differences; (2) consist of replicated informational items to control for factors other than the content of the schema such as item position, ambiguity, difficulty, and novelty that produce disorganization; (3) present a range of disturbing types of information in order to elicit different amounts of disorganized and defensive behavior; and (4) provide an objective and reliable scoring system of the amount of response disorganization and deviance that differentiates between information that is threatening and nonthreatening to a person. Such criteria defined the structure not only of the PT anxiety threshold test but also of the tests of conceptual, analytic, and judgmental efficiency.

THE PHRASE ASSOCIATION TEST[1]

Structure of the Phrase Association Test (PT)

The Phrase Association Test used in this study consists of thirty-six five word phrase-sentences each of which is presented verbally to a person who responds as quickly as possible with

[1] A more complete description of the test has been published elsewhere (D. H. Heath, 1960).

the first phrase or sentence that occurs to him. It is called a *Phrase Association Test* to distinguish it from its more diffuse and less objectively scored ancestors, the word association and sentence completion tests. Phrases and short sentences were used to secure better control over the meaning of the test information. Although the word association test yields clues about thought disorganization and conflict, it is of little use for any detailed specification of anxiety thresholds. One word items are not restrictive enough to give both the uniformity and the specificity in meaning required. The typical incomplete sentence test, on the other hand, permits more specification but restricts the form of the accommodative response to fit the existing grammatical structure of the sentence. I know of no sentence completion test that controls grammatical differences, sentence length, or other informational variables that may affect the type of response elicited to the different types of information used in the test.

By using meaningful five word phrases, it was possible to control the specificity of item meanings for all persons and yet to exercise minimal constraint on the *form* of the accommodative response. By making the structure of the phrases that define different schemata comparable, it was also more likely that deviant and disorganized responses to the phrases of one schema were due to the content than to any peculiar structural properties of the phrases themselves.

For research purposes, the anxiety threshold values of the following schemata, representing central tasks young male adults must master in development were measured: separating from mother and from father, aggressing toward mother and father, sexually relating to men and to women, receiving affection, cooperatively working with others, and relaxing and playing with others. The latter three types of schemata were assumed to be more stable and to have higher anxiety thresholds than schemata organized around being deserted, aggressing, and sexually relating toward others. Except for the desertion and the receiving affection information, the themes were used as the content of the skill tests as well. Selected sample PT items of each schema are:

Schema	PT item
Mother desertion	Mother bird left babies behind
	Mother sent neglected son away
Father desertion	Father lions desert their cubs
	He rejects his own son
Mother aggression	Young fox snapped at mother
	He cursed the old lady
Father aggression	Young tigers attack their fathers
	He angrily struck his father
Heterosexual relations	Male monkey pursued the female
	He seduced her last night
Homosexual relations	Frustrated male dogs mate together
	Young man seduced him yesterday
Receiving affection	Mother cat nursed her young
	Father helped him with homework
Playful relaxation	The two puppies sunned themselves
	People relaxed at the show
Cooperative work	Two beavers built the dam
	Both men worked well together

Since our focus is the effect of conflictual interpersonal content on skill efficiency, the term *disturbing* information will now be restricted to the interpersonal type of information found in the PT and skill tests. Such information varies in degree of threat to the person's self-organization; or, in other words, the anxiety thresholds of a person's schemata for such information will vary among each other. For research purposes, we *à priori* say *threatening* information refers to the PT desertion, aggression, and sexual themes. Less threatening (which from now on we call *nonthreatening*) information is defined by the PT receiving affection, cooperative work, and playful relaxation themes.

To meet the requirement that the PT consist of replicated items, each of the nine thematic areas was represented by four differently phrased but similar thematic examples. Two of the four phrases relevant to each schema used animal content. Replicated phrases should give a more stable measure of the anxiety threshold of a particular schema. For example, an individual could give a nonadaptive response to one phrase because it was novel or awkwardly phrased rather than because its content aroused anxiety; however, if he became disorganized to other similar phrases, occurring at different positions in the test and less awkwardly phrased, then the experimenter could have greater confidence that neither item position nor awkwardness but thematic content elicited the disorganization. Of course, more items for each schema type are necessary to insure adequate internal consistency for a schema measure, but too long a test had other undesirable effects that outweighed the requirement for maximizing internal consistency. The order of the PT phrases was so controlled that split-half reliability checks could be obtained. Item position and sequence were also controlled.

The PT is easily administered. The examiner tells the person the test measures "how quickly . . . [he] . . . can react in a number of different situations." He is told to respond with the first phrase or sentence that comes to mind, but he is not told to respond relevantly or appropriately to the phrases. The examiner then reads each phrase and records the time and content of the person's response as well as any behavioral signs of anxiety to each phrase. Almost all persons, even chronic schizophrenics, quickly learn from the practice items to respond with a phrase or sentence within several seconds.

Scoring System of the Phrase Association Test

The scoring system is based on clinical and experimental evidence (Rapaport, *et al*, 1946; Rotter, 1951) and extensive experience with ten different samples about the behavioral and verbally deviant and disorganized indices that suggest a schema's anxiety threshold has been activated. Each response to a PT phrase is scored for the presence of any of twenty indices that now define the scoring system. For example, to the phrase "One bull mates many females" a poorly organized man responded in one-half second "That is why they buy them. A good man is hard to find" (laughs). This response was scored for the presence of four anxiety indices: more than one substantive response, abstract categorization ("A good man is hard to find" is on a different level of generality than the PT phrase), excessive length (more than ten words), and behavioral affect (laughs). Some other anxiety indices are criticism of phrase, fragmented response, and failure to hear phrase. The most adaptive response will not be scored for any anxiety index. To the same phrase, a well organized man responded in two seconds "He is vigorous." This response contains no anxiety indices.

The anxiety threshold score for a particular schema, such as the heterosexual one of which the phrase just mentioned is an example, is the sum of the number of anxiety indices given to each of the four phrases that define that schema.

It is then possible to rank-order the schemata in terms of their anxiety thresholds. The schema with the highest score is assumed to have the *lowest* anxiety threshold, to be the most unstable schema, to be the most conflictual interpersonal relation for the person. The assumption is that the indices can be summed to produce an interval score for each schema type. Such an assumption means the anxiety thresholds of two different persons can be directly compared (one person's maternal schema is more unstable than another person's). Linearity and additivity are assumed in this scoring system and not yet demonstrated.

The anxiety threshold scores of all the schemata can also be added to give a Total PT score. High PT scores suggest that the person has generally low anxiety thresholds for disturbing information. Similar type scores can be found for the threatening (PT Threat score) and the less threatening (PT Nonthreat score) information.

An unexpected dividend of the PT scoring system was the possibility of classifying the twenty indices of response deviance into defensive groupings. Other researchers have inferred defense types from similar verbal and behavioral measures (Carpenter, Wiener, & Carpenter, 1956), but no studies have yet successfully classified or thoroughly explored the personality correlates of different types of defenses. Mandler and his coworkers (Mandler, Mandler, Kremen, & Sholiton, 1961) have classified the PT anxiety indices (as well as several other indices identifiable from their records) into five groupings that can be ordered from minimal to extreme involvement with the PT information. A person may *avoid* a phrase, *recode, rationalize,* or *personalize* its meaning or react with response *interference* or disorganization. Measures of these defensive patterns were routinely secured from the samples.

The Phrase Association Test and Self-Organization

I now want to reexamine the response of a person to the PT and the meaning of "anxiety threshold." The PT instructions require an immediate accommodation to a phrase, but, as with the Rorschach, no conceptually relevant accommodation is demanded. Although it is unlikely that a person has previously encountered the PT information exactly in the form in which it is presented, it is very likely that the general content of the information (sex, aggression, work, play) is schematically represented for most adults. For this reason, it is not surprising that most persons assimilate the PT information to conceptually relevant schemata and very rapidly (within several seconds) accommodate adaptively to the phrases. Only in severely disorganized persons such as chronic schizophrenics whose schemata are autocentrically organized is information likely to be consistently assimilated to idiosyncratic, non-conventional, and conceptually irrelevant schemata. But when an adult whose schemata for such information should be developmentally mature or stable blocks and fails to accommodate appropriately to some phrases, then it is assumed that such interference of the assimilation-accommodation process is due to anxiety about the theme.

Chapter 7 described the theoretical relation between the assimilation, accommodation, and anxiety thresholds. The PT does not measure the assimilation and accommodation thresholds. And it measures a schema's anxiety threshold only indirectly. Why? To measure an anxiety threshold directly, one could present increasingly more threatening phrases about the same schema to the person until signs of disorganization occurred. The PT does not systematically vary the amount of informational incongruency for each schema. All it measures is the amount of response disorganization to four different examples of one type of information. The assumption is then made that the amount of response disorganization is an indicator of how incongruent the information was for the person's schema.

We can now turn to a second question: What is the relation between amount of anxiety shown to all of the PT phrases (Total

PT score) and self-organization? A maturing person becomes more and more stably organized because, in part, an increasingly larger number of his schemata for different interpersonal relationships become more stable. It was expected that the more disorganization a person shows to a variety of such interpersonal relationships the more immature or unstable is his self-organization. The magnitude of the relation between PT Total score and poor self-organization is limited, however, by several factors: 1) The PT anxiety threshold measures are only partial indices of the stability of schema. Schema stability is also a function of its other thresholds. 2) The PT taps only a limited, though we hoped important, segment of the total domain of schemata that may define a person's self. 3) Theoretically, the stability of a schema is not necessarily directly and simply related to increasing self-organization, for extreme "stability" may be the product of rigid types of defensive coordinations. Few signs of disorganization (high anxiety threshold) could mean either a stably or a defensively rigid person. To be able to separate out such rigid persons, the PT scoring system included indices of defensively perseverative, stereotyped, and minimally compliant and evasive behaviors that might describe such rigid but stable-appearing persons. But it is an empirical question how adequately such persons can be distinguished from the maturely stable person by the PT.

Summarizing then, the PT anxiety threshold is a measure of how much anxiety a person has for specific types of information. And the more anxiety (PT Total score) a person shows to several different types of information the less stably organized he is assumed to be.

Reliability of the Phrase Association Test

The Total PT score is a highly reliable measure. All judge scoring of the PT has been done independently of any knowledge of the scores of other judges and of the men involved. Interjudge reliability coefficients vary from .86 to .99 (median coefficient for seven samples was .95) and intrajudge consistency coefficients over a six month time interval vary from .89 to .99 and over a five year interval .95. The PT has considerable internal consistency, for the equivalence (split-half) coefficients of the PT Total score range from .88 to .97 (median coefficient of fourteen different split-half coefficients was .94). Finally, the PT Total score is reasonably stable over a three to four week time interval. Stability coefficients for three samples are .75, .80, and .92.

How reliable are the anxiety threshold scores? Judges agree very well in assessing the anxiety thresholds of different schemata, for the interjudge reliability coefficients (determined by the Hoyt analysis of variance method) for a variety of samples vary from .81 to .99 with most reliability coefficients ranging in the mid-nineties. The anxiety thresholds are less stable over the intervening three to four week intervals than the PT Total score. The median stability coefficients for the thresholds of the nine schemata ranged from .61 to .84. The maternal desertion, maternal aggression, and homosexual anxiety thresholds were the most variable or unstable over time.

Of less direct relevance to the research, but not of less importance to diagnosticians, was the reliability of the specific anxiety indices that served as the basis for determining the threshold scores. Generally, there was high interjudge agreement about most of the anxiety indices (coefficients were in the eighties and nineties). However, the stability of the different behavioral indices varied markedly. Several of the indices of anxiety most favored in diagnostic practice (reaction time and intensity of emotional response) were the most unstable for the short time interval used in the reliability studies. These tentative findings should warn diagnosticians to investigate more closely the reliability of their preferred indices. The structure of the PT and its scoring system may help to facilitate such investigations.

Interjudge reliability of the Mandler-defined defense scores was moderately satisfactory. Because of judge disagreement on such behavioral indices as evasiveness and affective intensity, the reliability of the recoding and personalization defenses was minimal.

These results and those reported elsewhere (D. H. Heath, 1956, 1960) demonstrate the consistently good reliability of the PT.

Considering the essentially projective nature of the test and the judge discretion involved in scoring verbal responses, the major reliability problems of such a test seem to be under reasonable control.

Validity of the Phrase Association Test

The much more difficult and challenging problem is to determine what the anxiety threshold scores measure. The PT posed difficult validity problems because it was designed to measure reliably certain facets of the person no other tests were believed to measure as reliably and validly. Ebel, in his dissection of the validity concept, scolds psychologists for scandalously failing to develop validity criterion "measurements 'clearly superior' to those . . . [their] . . . test[s] will yield," (1961, p. 644). In one sense, the skill measures which are composed of the same disturbing information used in the PT are one type of validity criterion but whether they are "clearly superior" measures is a moot question. We expected that persons who are very disorganized to disturbing information (high PT Total score) would also be inefficient in conceptualizing, analyzing, and judging similar disturbing information. (Chapters 9 through 12 present the evidence that supports this prediction.)

Reassuringly, the PT scores have been found to be related to a variety of measures, including physiological, Rorschach, and other tests. The next sections briefly summarize the validity coefficients of the PT Total, the PT anxiety threshold, and the defense scores.

Correlates of PT Total Score

The PT Total score is not a measure of associative productivity, for it is related neither to the number of words given to the PT (Heath, 1960) nor to the number of responses given to the Rorschach (Mat. $r = -.17$; Org. $r = .20$; Stand. $r = .04$; Mandler's (1961) Harvard $r = -.12$). Similarly, PT

Total score is not significantly related to verbal intelligence as measured either by Wechsler-Bellevue vocabulary (D. H. Heath, 1954) or by CEEB verbal scores (Mat. r = .19; Org. r = .26; Stand. r = .04).

The PT measure of amount of anxiety is significantly related to high cardio-vascular but not GSR activity (Mandler, *et al*, 1961). Mandler found that both the GSR and the Taylor anxiety scale (MAS), while significantly related to each other, were unrelated to PT Total score. To account for the different PT-cardio-vascular and Taylor-GSR patterns, Mandler offered the *ad hoc* hypothesis that the PT measures emotionality whereas the Taylor MAS test measures drive activation:

Activation is associated with individual differences in the galvanic skin response and scores on Taylor's Manifest Anxiety scale. Emotionality is associated with signs of verbal disorganization, situational awareness of bodily reactions, and physiological arousal in channels other than the GSR . . . (1961, p. 18).

Even though anxiety may be defined by both emotionality and drive activation, it is not clear that the PT Total score and the MAS are unrelated. While the Standard sample's PT and MAS correlate did support Mandler's earlier result (r = −.10), the Organized sample's PT-MAS correlate was significant but positive (r = .49, p ∠ .01). Differences in PT and MAS administration (Mandler used a modified PT and scoring system and the MAS without buffer items) may account for some of the difference but additional research is obviously required about the relation of the MAS to the PT.

PT Total score was consistently but only occasionally significantly related to various questionnaire measures of immaturity or SIQ measures of immaturity. Table 8-1, which reports the correlations between the PT Total score and the questionnaire scales, illustrates that while the pattern is consistent with theoretical expectation only a few significant findings were obtained. Of particular interest is the finding that irresponsible acting out and possibly under-controlling one's behavior (MMPI Pd; Block Under-control) are directly related to increasing amounts of PT response disorganization.

The SIQ and PT Total score pattern of correlates was unclear

TABLE 8-1: CORRELATES BETWEEN PT AFFECTIVE INSTABILITY (TOTAL SCORE) AND QUESTIONNAIRE SCALES OF MALADJUSTMENT AND CONTROL

QUESTIONNAIRE SCALES	PT AFFECTIVE INSTABILITY		
	ORGANIZED[1]	MATURITY[2]	STANDARD
	r	r	r
MMPI			
Total	.29	.39	.08
Hs	.04	.19	—.11
D	.24	.24	.10
Hy	.07	.00	.08
Pd	.41*	.49**	—.05
Pa	.09	.04	.15
Pt	.23	.32	—.07
Sc	.21	.34	—.01
Ma	.29	.20	—.20
Si	.32	—[3]	.08
Taylor MAS	.51***	—[3]	—.10[4]
Bernreuter			
Neuroticism	.22	.21	—.01
Introversion	.32	.29	—.02
Lack self-confidence	.15	.10	.01
Nonsocial	.20	.48*	—.04
Control scores			
MMPI K	—.42*	.15	.04
Barron Ego Strength	.02	—[3]	.05[4]
Block Over-control	—.22	—[3]	.25[4]
Block Under-control	.60***	—[3]	—.16[4]
Bernreuter Dominance	.09	.07	—.06

* p $\angle$ .05
** p $\angle$ .025
*** p $\angle$ .01
[1] N = 23
[2] N = 17
[3] Data not available for these scores.
[4] N = 26

because of sample differences. The only noticeable trends in the data were for the increasing PT Total score to be associated with greater instability and incongruence of the self-image.

The Rorschach validity coefficients of the PT Total score just as consistently agree with our expectations. Clinical evaluations of good self-organization based on the Rorschach are consistently but not significantly inversely related to PT response disorganization (Org. r = −.23; Stand. r = −.19). Although the PT Total score was significantly related to a few Klopfer scores such as amount of inner tension (Ror. m%: Org. r = .63, p ∠ .01), the correlates are not reported because none were consistently supported across the major samples.

Is PT Total score associated with Holt's measures of autocentricism and adaptive control? Table 8–2, which gives the results, also includes data from the Case Study sample which were used to check the Maturity sample's results. The Case Study volunteers had been given the individual Rorschach form and a PT form comparable in content to that given the Maturity sample. The samples are ordered in the tables from most to least reliable.

Several prominent and consistent trends emerge from Table 8–2.

First, the expected relations between the PT and Rorschach autocentric schemata and adaptive control are generally confirmed. That is, amount of PT response disorganization is correlated directly with the amount of Rorschach autocentricism and is inversely related to Rorschach indices of well-controlled coordinations and adaptive regression. Twenty percent of the correlates in Table 8–2 are significant and all of them are in the predicted direction.

Second, although the Organized and Maturity samples' results generally parallel each other, the Organized sample's less sparkling performance is puzzling since it was considered the most reliable sample. But its findings were more encouraging when its PT correlates were analyzed separately for the first and second PT administrations. (Neither the Maturity nor the Case Study sample had been given the PT twice.) Its PT correlates for the second administration (Table 8–3) reach significance and now are more consistent with those of the Maturity sample in Table 8–2. How is this shift in fortune to be understood? The PT test-retest coefficient of the Organized sample was the lowest obtained from any sample (.75) and this, in combination with the differences between Tables 8–2 and 8–3 suggests that the Organ-

TABLE 8–2: CORRELATES BETWEEN PT AFFECTIVE INSTABILITY AND RORSCHACH AUTOCENTRIC AND CONTROL SCORES

RORSCHACH SCORES	PT AFFECTIVE INSTABILITY			
	ORGANIZED	MATURITY	STANDARD	CASE STUDY
	r	r	r	r
Autocentric Schemata				
% PriPro	.20	.57***	.11	.39
% Content	.23	.26	.07	.39
% Formal	.20	.73***	−.07	.33
% Level 1	.25	.48**	−.04	.61*
% Level 2	−.03	.46**	.15	.46
Sum DD	.39*	.30	.06	.40
Adaptive Control				
% Form accuracy	−.08	−.32	−.11	−.18
Mean DE	−.27	−.15	.13	−.32
% DD × DE	−.40*	−.33	−.09	−.48
Con DD/Form DD	.03	−.59***	.04	−.38

* p $\angle$ .05
** p $\angle$ .025
*** p $\angle$ .01

ized sample's first PT may not have been as valid as its second. Of course, we cannot ignore the possibility the Organized men approached the initial PT differently than the Maturity men did. There is no doubt, however, that the PT Total score predicts Rorschach autocentricism, but the exact conditions (type of person, PT content and test form, and administration order) under which this relationship could be consistently replicated are not yet known.

What generalizations can now be made from Tables 8–2 and 8–3? It is *confirmed* that the PT Total score is directly associated with autocentricism, impaired skills, and amount of internal threat and is inversely related to measures of controlled regression. It was *strongly confirmed* that PT Total score is directly related to amount of unconventional and unsocialized schemata.

We now are in a position to review what the PT Total score measures. Defensive and disorganizing responses to the PT dis-

TABLE 8–3: CORRELATES BETWEEN PT AFFECTIVE
INSTABILITY AT TIME 1 AND TIME 2
AND RORSCHACH AUTOCENTRIC AND
CONTROL SCORES

RORSCHACH SCORES	PT AFFECTIVE INSTABILITY			
	ORGANIZED TIME 1 r	ORGANIZED TIME 2 r	STANDARD TIME 1 r	STANDARD TIME 2 r
Autocentric Schemata				
% PriPro	—.03	.33	.10	.10
% Content	.00	.36*	.09	.05
% Formal	—.04	.34*	—.12	—.02
% Level 1	—.05	.42*	—.04	—.03
% Level 2	.03	—.05	.15	.14
Sum DD	.14	.53***	.08	.03
Adaptive Control				
% Form accuracy	.11	—.17	—.17	—.04
Mean DE	—.05	—.38*	.16	.09
% DD × DE	—.16	—.50***	—.10	—.07
Con DD/Form DD	.09	—.01	.06	.01

* p ∠ .05
*** p ∠ .01

turbing information are associated with aroused cardio-vascular
activity, increased autocentrically organized and unstable schemata, reduced capacity for inhibition and for control of regressive coordinations. The PT score seems to measure the affective
instability of a person whose inhibitory controls are impaired
or inadequately developed.

Correlates of PT Anxiety Threshold Scores

Does the PT threatening information actually cause more
response disorganization than the PT less threatening information? Do schemata organized around separation, aggression, and
sexual themes have lower anxiety thresholds than schemata organized around receiving affection, working, and relaxation
themes? The answer is very emphatically "yes." The threat

phrases have elicited significantly more anxiety than the non-threat phrases not only for every sample to whom the PT has ever been given but also to every person in each sample (D. H. Heath, 1954; Mandler, *et al*, 1961). Mandler (1961) has also reported that nonthreatening information evokes significantly less physiological activity than threatening information.

More precisely, what do the specific anxiety threshold scores measure? Although persons who show disorganization to one type of information also tend to show disorganization to other types, thereby suggesting "that a subject's overall anxiety level in response to the task may be more important in determining degree of response disorganization than specific anxiety reactions aroused by some particular subject matter" (Mandler, *et al*, 1961, p. 6), the PT anxiety threshold patterns have proved to be diagnostic of a variety of different behaviors. The PT anxiety threshold pattern is significantly related to 1) the pattern of conflicts schizophrenics manifest in their pre-morbid personal histories; 2) a similar pattern of *analytic* skill inefficiency with the same information (D. H. Heath, 1954, 1956); and 3) a similar pattern of aroused physiological activity (Mandler, *et al*, 1961). In considering validity differences among *just* the PT *threatening* types of information, it has been found that 1) analytic skill efficiency is poorer for the *phenomenally* most threatening than for the phenomenally least threatening information (D. H. Heath, 1954, 1956), and 2) sexual and aggressive information elicited significantly more disorganization and physiological activity than did dependency and competitive information (Mandler, *et al*, 1961).

It is now time to cease ignoring the Rorschach which has been widely used by clinicians to make comparative statements about different anxiety thresholds ("The patient is more anxious about expressing hostility toward maternal than toward paternal figures"). I describe very briefly how Mandler used the Rorschach to validate the PT anxiety threshold scores, my own attempt to replicate his results with Holt's % Content scores, and then a third study using Holt's Rorschach defense effectiveness scores.

Mandler hypothesized that low PT anxiety thresholds of aggressively and sexually organized schemata would be negatively correlated with similar *manifest* but positively correlated with similar *latent* Rorschach images. Persons anxious about sexual information, as measured by the PT, will avoid giving manifest sexual images to the Rorschach but will project many such latent images. He tabulated the frequency of manifest and latent sexual and aggressive schemata given to the Rorschach and correlated the totals for each person with his appropriate PT schemata scores. No significant relationships were found between latent imagery and the various PT scores; however, significant relationships were found for the manifest Rorschach scores. The PT sexual anxiety threshold score correlated $-.39$, p $\angle$ .05, with Rorschach manifest sexual imagery; PT sexual plus aggressive threshold scores correlated $-.39$, p $\angle$ .05, with their Rorschach counterparts; and Total PT score correlated $-.45$, p $\angle$ .02, with Rorschach manifest sexual plus aggressive imagery. Mandler concluded "that anxiety as expressed in the PT is negatively related to the appearance of manifest threatening imagery on the Rorschach" (1961, p. 10).

Generally, I was unable to replicate these suggestive findings over several samples using the number of Holt defined oral, sexual and aggressive schemata, although the trend of the results was as predicted. If PT Total score and number of responses to the Rorschach are controlled by using percentile scores, then the trend for the PT anxiety threshold scores to be inversely related to the number of similar Rorschach images becomes more consistent and pronounced, reaching significance only for the PT sexual anxiety thresholds of the Maturity sample ($r = -.42$, p $\angle$ .05). This result agrees with Mandler's finding that the number of sexual images given to the Rorschach is significantly and inversely related to the PT sexual anxiety thresholds.

A more direct test of the relation between the PT anxiety threshold and Rorschach schemata patterns can be made using Holt's defense effectiveness (DE) score. The anxiety threshold score measures how *well* the person has accommodated to the disturbing information. Accordingly, the appropriate Rorschach validity criterion is some measure, such as Holt's defense effectiveness score, that indexes how *well* the person controls or coordinates his schemata with the ink blot "forms." The DE scores for the oral, sexual, and aggressive Rorschach images were determined and respectively summed and then correlated with their corresponding PT anxiety threshold scores for our most reliable sample, the Organized sample. Poorly controlled desertion, aggression, and sexual responses on the PT were, in fact, significantly inversely related to well controlled oral ($r = -.41$, p $\angle$ .025), aggression ($r = -.40$, p $\angle$ .05), and sexual ($r = -.41$, p $\angle$ .025) images in the Rorschach. When both the PT Total score and the Rorschach number of responses were partialled out of the correlations, the respective correlations became $-.34$, $-.33$, and $-.39$ (p $\angle$ .05), indicating that PT anxiety thresholds may still be predictive of the effectiveness with which Rorschach schemata are controlled. In other words, disorganization to the PT sexual information seems to be prognostic of poorly controlled sexual imagery in the Rorschach. This one validating demonstration requires careful replication, particularly because of the important implications for diagnostic use of the Rorschach. From these and previously reported results, we predicted that PT anxiety thresholds should be directly related to the inefficiency with which a person conceptualizes, analyzes, and judges similar disturbing information.

Correlates of Defensive Coordinations

Explorations of the correlates of the PT defensive patterns are relatively recent and the only published data available to summarize come from Mandler's studies (1961). He reports that the pattern of correlates between the different defenses is theoretically consistent, that persons can be distinguished by their consistent use of certain defensive patterns, that "subjects who react with more anxiety to the areas of Sex and Aggression also show more use of the response modes [interference and avoidance] which indicate generalized disturbance" (1961, p. 8), that particular types of information do not elicit predominantly one type of defense rather than another, and that physiological involvement is associated with the different defensive groupings as was theoretically predicted (interference and avoidance were accompanied by greater and recoding by lesser amounts of physiological activity). Since no explicit hypotheses about such defensive patterns were pursued in our research, and since the PT measures of defenses were generally not related to Holt's measures of adaptive controls, their correlates are not discussed in detail.

DISTURBING INFORMATION AND SELF-ORGANIZATION STABILITY

We have proposed well organized persons are indeed more maturely and stably organized than poorly organized persons, and that stability can be defined by the person's ability to adapt skillfully to disturbing information with a minimum of disorganization. Our demonstration that the information used in the research was, in fact, disturbing involves proving that different types of information (threatening) were more anxiety-arousing than other types (nonthreatening) for the persons used in this study. We have already demonstrated that the threatening information is more disturbing than the nonthreatening information for a variety of other samples. Table 8–4, which summarizes the samples' anxiety threshold scores for the PT information, demonstrates that the à priori defined threatening information produced more anxiety than did the à priori defined nonthreatening information for the current samples as well. The anxiety thresholds for the different types of threatening information were, with only a few exceptions, consistently lower (more anxiety) than the anxiety thresholds for their comparable nonthreatening types of information. Only one person of the eighty men used in the major samples gave as many disorganized responses to the nonthreatening as to the threatening information.

Now that we have a reasonably reliable and valid method of determining anxiety thresholds, we examine the relation between social judgments of self-organization and the PT measures of affective instability and anxiety threshold patterns.

TABLE 8–4: PT ANXIETY THRESHOLDS OF THE MATURE AND IMMATURE MEN OF THE MAJOR SAMPLES

| PT SCHEMATA | MATURITY[1] | | PT ANXIETY THRESHOLDS | | | |
| | | | ORGANIZED | | STANDARD | |
	MATURE	IMMATURE	WELL	POORLY	WELL	POORLY
Desertion	7.1[2]	12.7	13.0	13.4	12.1	11.8
Aggression	10.3	13.3	14.1	14.8	10.2	12.5
Sexual	11.5	16.2	15.7	16.9	13.5	16.9
Receiving Affection	5.7	8.4	8.2	10.5	9.4	11.9
Working	5.0	10.2	7.8	8.8	7.2	8.4
Relaxing	8.9[3]	8.9	8.0	7.1	5.8	6.2

[1] Scores adjusted to be comparable to PT scores of other samples.

[2] The threatening scores of all samples have been adjusted to be directly comparable to the nonthreatening scores.

[3] Score is for the schema of constructive activity for the Maturity sample only.

Self-Organization and PT Affective Instability (Total Score)

The maturely and immaturely organized men did not differ significantly in affective instability, although the more mature persons of all the samples consistently responded with less disorganization to the PT information than the more immature persons (Mat. p ∠ .10; Stand. at time two, p ∠ .10).

Funkenstein (1957) has suggested that it is not the quality of adaptation (or amount of affective instability) to immediate stress (which the PT measures) but the amount by which the induced (physiological) disorganization is reduced following repeated experiences with stress that differentiates between mature and immature persons. Those personality traits found by Funkenstein to describe adaptive improvement to stress over time were similar to those we found to describe maturely organized persons: good personality integration, accurate assessment of reality, and congruence of the self-image. And when adaptive improvement to the PT (defined by the percent of *decrease* in amount of disorganization from the first to the second PT administration) was correlated with our various measures of maturity, we did find adaptive improvement to covary as predicted with maturity. For example, adaptive improvement to the PT is consistently inversely related to self-reported maladjustment (MMPI Total $r = -.32$ and $-.25$ for the Organized and Standard samples respectively). Adaptive improvement was found for the Organized sample to be significantly inversely related to depressive, compulsive (MMPI D, Pt), neurotic, and introversive (Bern.) trends and to be directly related to good ego strength (Barron). Funkenstein's finding that adaptive improvement was inversely related to incongruent self-images was replicated by the Organized sample ($r = -.44$, p $\angle$ .05). Adaptive improvement was also impressively related to Holt's primary process Rorschach scores. While the Standard sample's results were consistent but not significant, eight of the ten Organized sample's correlates were significant and most of them beyond the .005 level. The results suggest that adaptive improvement to disturbing information is inversely related to the amount of drive-organized schemata and impaired skills (Ror. % Content $r = -.53$, p $\angle$ .005; % Formal $r = \angle .59$, p $\angle$ .005, etc.), and directly related to the ability to make adaptive but regressed coordinations of schemata (Ror. % DD $\times$ DE $r = .65$, p $\angle$ .005) and to make accurate accommodations to external information (Ror. % Form Acc. $r = .50$, p $\angle$ .01). Finally, clinical judgments of self-organization based on the Rorschach were consistently though not significantly associated with adaptive improvement. The tenor of the evidence confirms Funkenstein's finding that adaptive mastery of stress is associated with personality integration, accurate reality accommodation, and self-image congruence.

Second, do the well and poorly organized men differ in their adaptive improvement to disturbing information? The answer is "yes" if we look at the Organized sample and "no" if we consider the Standard sample. The well organized men of the Organized sample improved (plus ten percent) but its poorly organized men actually got worse over time (minus ten percent).

Both criterion groups of the Standard sample improved, but the poorly organized improved 32.6 percent while the well organized improved 20.1 percent. In view of these persistent sample differences, we must conclude that the relation between judged self-organization and PT Total score is just not clear.

Self-Organization and PT Anxiety Thresholds

The last principal question to be answered concerns the sample and criterion group differences in their specific anxiety thresholds for different types of information. First, do the samples show less anxiety for developmentally earlier than later types of conflicts? From Table 8–4 emerges a clear and consistent trend for developmentally earlier (desertion) schemata to be more stable than developmentally later (sexual) schemata. This pattern was also confirmed with a fourth sample of sixteen University of Michigan men who were members of special academic honors sections. Their mean anxiety threshold scores were: Desertion 6.8; Aggression 7.8; Sexual 9.1.

The sexual schemata, particularly homosexually organized schema, are the most consistently unstable ones for every sample. This is not very surprising since the most pressing adaptive task for unmarried male youths in their late teens in our culture is the management of their sexual and affectional needs. That homosexual information evokes more defensive and disorganizing signs than the heterosexual information is also not unexpected in our culture. At Haverford, at least, homosexual activity is strongly disapproved and as a topic of conversation among the men is usually avoided. Therefore, heterosexually organized schemata may, through persistent student conversation, fantasy, imaginal and behavioral rehearsal, achieve some stabilization that is not as possible for homosexually organized schemata that are kept on the fringe of self-awareness. (These results are not limited to the Haverford samples; they also apply to a sample of University of Michigan men as well. Their mean anxiety threshold scores for heterosexual information was 8.3 and for homosexual information 9.9.)

Second, do well organized men have higher anxiety thresholds for developmentally earlier schemata than the poorly organized men? Table 8–4 indicates this question must be answered negatively. None of the specific anxiety threshold scores of the well organized groups significantly differed from their anxiety threshold counterparts of the poorly organized groups.

Self-Organization PT Defensive Groupings

The well and poorly organized groups did not differ significantly in their use of any of the Mandler-defined types of defensive groupings.

SUMMARY

Lest the complexity of the results have overwhelmed even the most diligent reader and obscured the major trends of the research, we now abstract and summarize the most important points to remember about the PT.

1. The PT, with reasonable reliability, gives an independent measure of response disorganization or affective instability and of the anxiety threshold values of different schemata.

2. The PT Total score measure of affective instability is significantly related to other measures of unstable schemata and anxiety including selected Rorschach, questionnaire, and physiological indices, and inversely related to measures of good adaptive control.

3. The PT pattern of anxiety threshold values is predictive of the patterns of physiological involvement, of analytic skill efficiency with similar disturbing information, and defense effectiveness to similar types of Rorschach schemata. These findings, in particular, are rather tentative and need to be replicated.

4. The threatening information used as the content of the skill measures has been independently shown to be phenomenally more threatening than the nonthreatening types of information.

5. Adaptive improvement to the PT disturbing information

over time may be related to good ego strength and to the amount of stable schemata and of well controlled and accurate accommodative responses.

6. There is no significant relation between PT measures of affective instability and social judgments of maturity or self-organization. In failing to confirm this hypothesis, we have inadvertently insured ourselves against a very telling possible criticism of the studies to be reported in the next chapters. Namely, if well organized persons are found to conceptualize, analyze, and judge disturbing information more adaptively than poorly organized persons, such a result cannot be alternatively explained by the hypothesis that the disturbing information was phenomenally less disturbing to the well than to the poorly organized persons. In other words, the nonsignificant PT differences between the criterion groups demonstrate that the disturbing information used as the content of the skill tests is anxiety-arousing to about the same extent for each of the groups.

Generally, the PT is less efficacious than Holt's primary process scoring system in predicting to a wide range of validity criteria. The PT may be quite useful, however, in economically and reliably identifying amount of disorganization to disturbing information and possibly important anxiety threshold differences between schemata. It may or may not hold some promise for reliably identifying patterns of defensive coordinations.

CHAPTER 9

The Thematic Concept Test (TCT)

Efficiency in conceptualizing disturbing information was measured by the Thematic Concept Test (TCT). The TCT consists of three test boards on each side of which are mounted different sets of sixty-four pictures or instances. When shown one instance of an unidentified concept, a person must find as efficiently as possible the three other instances that also define the concept of that set.

Before expanding this glimpse into the structure of the TCT, we very briefly look at the two experimental traditions that sired the TCT: research on concept formation and on cognitive efficiency with thematic material. Since our focus is not the concept process itself, it is not necessary to review the results in this area (Vinacke, 1952) except to mention one relevant line of research. Some researchers have explored personality differences associated with conceptual efficiency, although their major effort has been to demonstrate that such efficiency is impaired by pathological (schizophrenic) processes (Hanfmann & Kasanin, 1942; Kasanin & Hanfmann, 1938; Vigotsky, 1934). This chapter will later summarize our findings about the personality traits of conceptually efficient and inefficient *healthy* persons.

We are more vitally concerned with the problems of cognitively using thematic materials efficiently; yet, because of the

historical bias against the use of meaningful content, little research pointedly speaks to this problem. Investigators of cognitive processes *qua* cognitive processes consider the content of the
cognitive task a complicating variable that confounds and obscures the solution processes which are assumed to be similar
for both meaningful and meaningless content. From those cognitive studies using thematic content, and most relevantly using
disturbing information, what generalizations emerge? Very few;
in fact, only one major generalization can be stated. For a variety
of different cognitive skills, cognitive efficiency is impaired by
the inclusion of meaningful content in the test problems, particularly of themes personally relevant to the needs or social
attitudes of the person. Impaired logical reasoning (Janis &
Frick, 1943; Lefford, 1946; Morgan & Morton, 1944; Morgan,
1945; Thistlethwaite, 1950), abstract thinking (Meadow, 1950;
Richman, 1953), associative learning (Laffal, 1952); associative
speed (Dolinko, 1957), and code translations (Combs & Taylor,
1952) have been reported. The results measuring recall or
memory efficiency, frequently reinterpreted as repression experiments, are ambiguous (Betlheim & Hartmann, 1951; Levine &
Murphy, 1943; Meadow, 1940; Rapaport, 1950). Although few
of these experiments are immune to methodological criticism, the
generalization that "emotional" content disrupts cognitive efficiency agrees with clinical experience. For example, the Stanford-
Binet intelligence test has been criticized for its use of strongly
affective content (killing a man, hanging, railroad accident) alleged to cause cognitive inefficiency in children and thereby
obscure their "true" intellectual level (Friedline & Berman, 1941).
Or, as another example, clinicians have noted that conceptual
(ego) impairment first appears in personally conflictual areas
(Schilder, 1938). To the clinician, such impairment frequently
means some ego decompensation is in process.

Few researchers have investigated exactly what uniquely specific, if any, cognitive effects are produced by meaningful or
affective content that is not also produced by meaningless or
nonaffective content. Furthermore, few studies have investigated
thematic concept attainment and none have explored the relation of personality variables to conceptual efficiency with such

information. Bruner's (1956) analysis of the differential effects
of thematic and nonthematic content on concept attainment is
the only major study of this problem. He found the inclusion
of thematic content produced an increased number of errors and
of redundant choices, an increased variability of choices, the
choice of some attributes as cues more frequently than other
attributes, and the increased use of continuous successive scanning rather than other types of strategies. He concludes that to

attain concepts with materials that are meaningful and amenable to
familiar forms of grouping leads to several difficulties. In the first place,
the problem solver is likely to fall back upon reasonable and familiar
hypotheses about the possible groupings. In so doing, he may be led
into a modified form of successive scanning; the strategy par excellence
for going through a list of hypotheses. In the second place, the thematic
material will, more readily than abstract material, lead certain attributes to have nonrational criteriality: the subject will 'hang on' to
these and will formulate hypotheses around them (1956, p. 111).

Our measures of skill efficiency have been designed to tempt
the person to resort to "nonrational criteriality," to solve prob-
ems on the basis of the idiosyncratic and personal meaning of
the thematic content rather than on the basis of what Bruner
calls the "ecological validity" or formal task requirements. We
hypothesize that the person's degree of self-organization and his
anxiety threshold for the schema content determine, in part,
whether he yields to the temptation. It was expected not only
that some information contained in the content would serve as
nonrational criteria, but also that its association with unstable
schemata of low anxiety thresholds would induce disorganizing
and defensive reactions to the formal problem. For example, a
youth with a low anxiety threshold for information about paternal aggression may become so disorganized to such information that he fails to note the orderly pattern in which the test
instances are arranged, or fails to remember the correct instances
he may have identified; or he may become so defensive that he
rigidly fixates on only one hypothesis (the father must be striking the son) or fails to "see," or denies some of the crucial
attributes. To save some youths considerable embarrassment and

not complicate the controls of the experiment, they were not asked to report the hypotheses they were entertaining. It was therefore not possible to determine whether well-organized persons used a different pattern of solution strategies and defensive coordinations than poorly organized youths.

STRUCTURE OF THE THEMATIC CONCEPT TEST

Let us return now to the structure of the TCT. The content of the TCT was modeled on the Phrase Association Test themes of interpersonal aggression, sex, and general activity (working and relaxing). Each theme was represented by a different set of thematic cards. A set consisted of sixty-four different instances that represented all the combinations of three basic attributes characterizing each of the two people of the theme. Similar attributes were varied for each schema type: sex, dress (or some aspect thereof), and type of interaction. The sixty-four aggressive cards pictured all combinations of an adult and child (father-son, father-daughter, mother-son, and mother-daughter) each either holding or not holding a stick and each either threatening the other or protecting himself from the other. The sexual cards showed two adults (male-female, female-male, male-male, or female-female) each either dressed or nude and each either actively embracing or passively not responding to the other. Finally, the general activity cards pictured two adults (male-female, female-male, male-male, female-female) each either dressed in work or play clothes and each either cooperatively working or playfully relaxing.[1] Figure one presents examples of each type of theme.

It was possible to test conceptual efficiency for a variety of different types of interpersonal relations with these sets of concept cards. The six interpersonal schemata tested were mother-son aggression, father-son aggression, heterosexual relations, homosexual relations, cooperative and playful relaxation. Of the two test problems developed for each schema, one was an easy (defined by only two of three possible attributes) and one

[1] I am grateful to Sonia Schwartz who drew the pictured instances.

TCT SAMPLE CARDS

1 Mother-Son aggression
2 Father-Son aggression
3 Heterosexual relations

4 Homosexual relations
5 Cooperative work
6 Playful relaxation

227

was a difficult (defined by a pattern of three attributes) concept. To illustrate an easy concept, consider the heterosexual test concept. The person was shown a nude man embracing a dressed but passive woman. The task was to locate the three other instances of the concept of a man embracing a passive woman. Dress or nudity was an irrelevant cue. Concept problems for the six different interpersonal relations were selected to be equal in difficulty. The resulting twelve test concepts were divided into two test forms of six concepts, each concept representing one of the six different schemata types. Three of the six concepts for a test form were easy and three were difficult.

How was the TCT presented? The sixty-four thematic cards of a schema type were numbered and displayed on a pegboard. The display pattern was identical for each of the six easy problems. A different display order was used for the difficult concepts. To control for adaptation effects, the presentation orders of both the test forms and of the individual test concepts were systematically varied according to a prearranged and randomized schedule for each person, following the procedure described in Chapter 7. The TCT is presented individually. The ordered cards of one thematic set are displayed in full view. An instance of a concept is given and the process of discovering the concept, by identifying the other instances that define the concept, is demonstrated. The task is, when given an instance of a concept, to discover as quickly as possible the three other correct instances of that concept, making as few incorrect choices as possible. Although he has five minutes to discover the three correct instances, the person is required to select an instance every thirty seconds. He is told whether the selected instance is correct or not. Since only the initial sample instance is marked, some additional cognitive strain is involved in remembering which selected instances are the correct and incorrect ones. The next set of test cards is presented when the three correct instances have been identified or five minutes have elapsed. The amount of time taken to get the concept and the number of correct and incorrect instances used is recorded.

Optimal conceptual efficiency is defined by a rapid solution of the test problem, using a minimal number of clues. Conceptual efficiency scores for each problem, for the two problems of the same schema, for the *à priori* defined threatening and nonthreatening information (called Threat and Nonthreat scores, respectively), or for all of the schemata (called Total TCT score) are easily secured. A high Total score means greater conceptual efficiency for all schemata. An error score, defined by the number of incorrect instances given, was also used in the data analysis.

How reliable are these scores? For all of the skill tests, we were most concerned about their interjudge agreement coefficients (not relevant to the TCT because of its objective score system), rather than about either their equivalence or stability coefficients. Too few items for each of the test forms and schemata types, and the use of different schemata content, to which we were predicting differential efficiency, seriously limit the magnitude of equivalence coefficients, which were .00 and .34 for the Organized and Standard samples respectively. Similar considerations apply to the stability coefficient. We were, in fact, predicting attenuation of such sample coefficients due to differential improvement of the well and poorly organized men. The coefficients between the first and second administration were .13 and .44 for the Organized and Standard samples.

The samples' conceptual efficiency varied for the different schemata as Table 9–1 indicates. Why? Very suggestively, the order of increasing skill efficiency for the different schemata is related

TABLE 9–1: CONCEPTUAL EFFICIENCY SCORES FOR
EACH SCHEMA TYPE

SCHEMA TYPE	CONCEPTUAL EFFICIENCY SCORES			
	ORGANIZED		STANDARD	
	Mean	SD	Mean	SD
Mother-son aggression	28.2[1]	7.1	26.2	8.4
Father-son aggression	31.5	9.0	35.8	8.1
Heterosexual relations	24.4	5.6	25.3	9.5
Homosexual relations	23.4	7.9	25.8	8.5
Cooperative work	33.4	9.8	36.7	9.2
Playful relaxation	33.7	8.5	33.8	7.2

[1] The maximum score possible for a schema type is sixty.

to the sample's anxiety threshold pattern for the schemata (Org. rho = .90, p ∠ .05; Stand. rho = .66). While persuasive, this evidence is not conclusive that the samples' greater conceptual inefficiency with the sexual information, for example, was due to the greater anxiety-arousing potential of that type of content. Other factors of which we are not aware may have produced the differences in conceptual efficiency.

THEMATIC CONCEPT TEST RESULTS

It is now time to place the TCT within the public context of more familiar psychological tests. The TCT, as each of the skill measures, is too untried to ignore whatever data are available about its interlacing validity network with more established psychological tests. Such information is of pressing pertinence to ego psychologists who are interested in the personality correlates of specific ego controls, and to clinicians who infer personality traits from ego inefficiencies with disturbing thematic information (Rapaport, et al, 1945). With what facets of the personality is conceptual efficiency to personally relevant thematic material associated? (The analysis of the TCT results for the formal hypotheses about the stability of the well and poorly organized men is postponed until Chapter 12.)

At this point, our reportorial conventions change slightly. To economize on space and the reader's patience, the tables include only those correlates that are significant and (or) consistent across several samples. One-tailed significance levels are used to evaluate those relationships predicted from our expectations (questionnaire, SIQ, Rorschach autocentric and control, and some PT scores); two-tailed significance tests are used to evaluate those relationships for which no prediction about directionality was explicitly made prior to the data analysis (intellectual skill and achievement, Klopfer Rorschach scores, and the PT schema and defense scores). Since none of the personality correlates in this book have been corrected for attenuation, they are all underestimated. Given the inaccuracy of our reliability coefficients (for the reasons stated and because of the small size of the samples) that may underestimate test reliability, correction for attenuation could well have overestimated the validity coefficients. Also, no measure of the reliability of the principal validity criterion (consensual judgments of maturity) was available. We preferred to err on the conservative side with respect to corrective statistical operations on the data.

TCT and Intellectual Skill and Achievement

Conceptual efficiency with disturbing information is not significantly related to any measure of intellectual skill (CEEB Verbal, Quantitative, or Terman Concept Mastery Test), or to either achievement in English (CEEB) or academic grade average. However, there is a consistent trend in the samples for conceptual reasoning with nondisturbing information (Terman) as well as final grade average to be positively correlated with conceptual efficiency to disturbing information, particularly that which is most threatening (Terman: Org. $r = .22$; Stand. $r = .16$; Grade av.: Org. $r = .27$; Stand. $r = .21$). These low positive but nonsignificant relationships do not so seriously confound conceptual reasoning (Terman) and conceptual efficiency with disturbing materials to push us to partial out the Terman (or CEEB) scores from the personality test correlates, to which we now turn.

TCT and Questionnaire Scales of
Maladjustment and Control

The correlations between the questionnaire measures of maturity and conceptual efficiency are largely nonsignificant. Of the total number of correlations between conceptual efficiency and the MMPI and Bernreuter scales (160), only nine percent were significant at the predicted one-tailed five percent level. (The summary percent score is only a convenient convention to describe the results; no statistical interpretation of the percent is warranted because of the non-independence of the correlations.) Furthermore, the results are occasionally inconsistent be-

TABLE 9–2: SELECTED CORRELATES BETWEEN CONCEPTUAL EFFICIENCY AND QUESTIONNAIRE SCALES OF MALADJUSTMENT AND CONTROL

QUESTIONNAIRE SCALES		CONCEPTUAL EFFICIENCY SCORES			
		TOTAL SCORE	THREAT	NON-THREAT	# ERRORS
		r	r	r	r
MMPI					
Ma	Org.	.39	.44* [3]	.18	−.58* [3]
	Sta.	.26	.25	.20	−.19
Pd	Org.	.18	.33	−.11	−.40
	Sta.	.29	.21	.34* [3]	−.25
Si	Org.[1]	−.24	−.15	−.27	.06
	Sta.	−.31*	−.28*	−.26	.23
Taylor	Org.	−.18	−.15	−.15	.00
MAS	Sta.[2]	−.26	−.23	−.22	.30
Bernreuter					
Neurotic	Org.	−.16	−.16	−.13	.06
	Sta.	−.24	−.18	−.27	.26
Lack self-	Org.	−.10	−.25	−.13	.03
confidence	Sta.	−.24	−.17	−.30*	.26
Control Scores					
MMPI K	Org.	.34	.43**	.08	−.38*
	Sta.	.20	.18	.21	−.27
Barron Ego	Org.	.43**	.31	.44**	−.28
Strength	Sta.[2]	.21	.15	.22	−.16
Block Under-	Org.	−.17	−.01	−.31	.13
contro	Sta.[2]	−.18	−.17	−.15	.36**
Bern.	Org.	.07	−.06	.14	.04
Dominance	Sta.	.31*	.27	.29*	−.36*

* p ∠ .05
** p ∠ .025
[1] N = 23 for all Organized correlates.
[2] N = 26
[3] Direction opposite from that predicted; significant at least at .05 two-tailed significance level.

tween the two samples and do not sketch a theoretically convincing canvas.

Several trends seem to run through the data reported in Table 9–2. First, and fitting our expectations, conceptual efficiency (defined by high Total, Threat, and Nonthreat TCT scores and a low Error score) is positively related to measures of reflective control or ego strength. Persons who make many incorrect choices report themselves to have inadequate emotional control (Block Under-control). Second, and again not violating our expectations, conceptual efficiency with disturbing information is consistently, though not significantly, inversely associated with socially introversive (MMPI Si), inhibiting, inadequate (Bern. Neurotic, Lack self-conf.), and anxious (Taylor) feelings. Finally, and quite unexpectedly, good conceptual efficiency appears to be associated with self-assertive and a strong outward, if not an uninhibited, push of energy (MMPI Ma; Bern. Dom.). The results suggest that excellent conceptual adaptation to a range of information may occur within persons who can actively marshall their energy and attention to be "all there" and yet, at the same time, have such energy under good reflective and defensive control. To solve the TCT, one must mentally explore many possibilities actively and quickly, keep in touch with the material, and not just passively respond, indecisively waiting for the solution to appear.

Skill in solving thematic concepts is generally not related to either the dimensionality (stability, congruence) or the maturity of the self-image (SIQ). Only self-image autonomy significantly and inversely covaried with conceptual inefficiency with disturbing information ($r = -.36$, p $\angle$ .01) but because the autonomy procedure was not replicated with the Standard sample, we have no check on the consistency of this result.

TCT and Rorschach Measures

Conceptual efficiency with disturbing information cannot be predicted from any method of analyzing the Rorschach. None of the traditional Rorschach scores (Klopfer) were associated consistently across both samples with any measure of conceptual efficiency. Similarly, clinical evaluations of self-organization from the Rorschach, as well as most of Holt's autocentric and control scores, were not correlated with the TCT measures highly enough to warrant being reported. The one significant and consistent finding was that conceptual efficiency is related to accuracy of schema accommodation or good reality testing (p $\angle$ .05). While only five percent of the Holt correlations reached significance, the pattern of the autocentric and adaptive regression scores was congruent with our expectations. That is, conceptual efficiency, particularly to threatening information, was directly related to adaptive regression and good defensive control, and inversely related to various expressions of autocentric thinking.

TCT and Anxiety Thresholds

The expectation that the Phrase Association Test would predict conceptual efficiency was confirmed. Table 9–3 indicates that conceptual efficiency is consistently and negatively related to

TABLE 9–3: CORRELATES BETWEEN CONCEPTUAL
EFFICIENCY AND PT AFFECTIVE
INSTABILITY

PT SCORES		CONCEPTUAL EFFICIENCY SCORES			
		TOTAL	THREAT	NON-THREAT	# ERRORS
		r	r	r	r
Total	Org.	−.25	−.07	−.38*	.16
	Sta.	−.38**	−.33**	−.33**	.30*
Threat	Org.	−.19	−.01	−.35	.13
	Sta.	−.38**	−.34**	−.34**	.33**
Nonthreat	Org.	−.37*	−.20	−.44**	.22
	Sta.	−.35**	−.30*	−.32*	.25

* p $\angle$ .05
** p $\angle$ .025

affective instability or low anxiety thresholds and that this relationship most consistently holds for less threatening types of information. Or, to phrase the conclusion differently, persons with low anxiety thresholds are more conceptually inefficient, particularly when they must coordinate less threatening but disturbing information. Neither basal conceptual reasoning (Terman) nor conceptual efficiency with disturbing information (TCT) was related to the ability to adapt to distracting information composed of nonthematic content (Stroop).

Personality Correlates of TCT Improvement

We had assumed that increasing self-organization meant, in part, increasing resistance to the disrupting effects of disturbing information and increasing ability to recover from induced disorganization. One measure of such recovery is the amount of improvement a person shows in skill efficiency from an initial to a subsequent encounter with disturbing information. Since the TCT scores had also been converted into standard scores, it was possible to define skill improvement by subtracting the Total TCT score of time one from that of time two. High scores mean greater improvement in conceptual efficiency. Now, what personality traits covary with improvement to the disturbing information of the TCT? Of all the personality measures, the only consistent and significant finding was that improvement is related to increasing ego strength (Barron: Org. r = .39, p ∠ .05; Stand. r = .24). Since Barron's ego strength measure was originally designed to identify those who improve in therapy, such a result is eminently understandable.

SUMMARY

The Thematic Concept Test (TCT) measures a person's conceptual efficiency in solving problems composed of disturbing information. To summarize the personality traits associated with conceptual efficiency and inefficiency, the samples were divided into two contrasting groups on the basis of their total TCT score and the personality differences between the two groups were then determined (See summary Table 2, Appendix B). Men who are conceptually efficient to disturbing information are likely to be more proficient in conceptually reasoning with non-disturbing information as well (Terman), to have good ego strength (Barron), and to show considerable reflective (MMPI: K) and imaginative control (Ror. Con DD/Form DD) over their behavior. They may be less inhibited and more assertive (MMPI Pd; Bern. Dom.). They are not retiring, passively introversive (MMPI Si), unconfident (Bern. Lack self-conf.), highly anxious (Taylor) or neurotic (Bern. Neurotic) persons. They tend to have higher anxiety thresholds for both threatening and nonthreatening information (PT) and are able to make sensible pragmatic (Ror. D%) and realistic (Ror. % Form Acc.), if not less unusual (Ror. A + Ad%) accommodations to such information. More specifically, they may have high anxiety thresholds for information organized around sexual-affectional impulses toward other men and, perhaps, for aggressive impulses toward paternal figures (PT).

CHAPTER 10

The Thematic Analysis-Synthesis Test (TA-S)

Efficiency in analyzing and synthesizing disturbing information was measured by the Thematic Analysis-Synthesis Test (TA-S) which consists of twenty-four different scrambled sentences. Each sentence's words must be rearranged to make a meaningful and grammatically correct sentence.

Again, before discussing the TA-S test in detail, a few words are necessary to place the test within its historical context. Psychologists preoccupied by individual intellectual differences have long sought to find such differences in verbal combinatory processes. Ebbinghaus in 1897 defined intelligence as a combinatory process and sought to separate the bright from the less bright children of Breslau by the use of his well-known incomplete sentence procedure (Peterson, 1925). In the revision of the Binet-Simon intelligence test, Terman included as one item a scrambled sentence problem and defined its solution process as relating "the given parts to a meaningful whole" (Terman & Merrill, 1937, p. 276). But to "relate the given parts to a meaningful whole" requires the prior formation of an anticipatory schema of the whole—often an only vaguely and intuitively expressible schema—that serves as a scaffolding into which to fit or relate the individual words. Little is known about how anticipatory schemata are constructed or synthesized despite the long but sporadic history of research into the problem (Bartlett, 1932; Getzels & Jackson, 1962; Goldstein & Scheerer, 1941; Humphrey, 1951; Piaget, 1936, 1937, 1945, 1947; Stein & Heinze, 1960.) But our focus is not "mental construction" *qua* "mental construction"; instead, it is the relation of personality traits to the ability to construct certain types of anticipatory schemata, or, more specifically, in Goldstein's terms, to the ability "to grasp the essential of a given whole [schema]; to break up a given whole [schema] into parts, to isolate and to synthesize them" (Goldstein *et al.*, 1941, p. 4).

The Thematic Concept Test measured this hypothesis-formation process with respect to problems whose solution was invariant (only one correct combination of schemata defined the correct solution) and could be systematically and logically arrived at by testing different schemata combinations. The TA-S test, as a measure of combinatory activity, is similar to the TCT. Both tests require the selection of one appropriate combination of schemata from a larger number of possible combinations. But there are some fundamental differences between the two tests. The task required by the TCT is to find the one common attribute pattern that correctly coordinates only four of the sixty-four different pictorial schemata when given only one of the four as a clue. The TA-S test, however, consists of words that do not differ systematically from each other on the basis of some logical ordering principle. The words of a set are not unrelated, because the task instructions define them to be "meaningfully" related and because the words are part of a language whose grammatical structure establishes certain anticipatory schemata for certain types of word patterns (e.g., the pronoun "he" sets up the anticipatory schema that a singular rather than a plural verb is to follow). When given several scrambled words, the person must construct a new superordinate schema that combines all or most of the words given him. The words of one TA-S sentence can be combined most adaptively in only one way; they can also, in contradistinction to the TCT, be combined in a number of less appropriate patterns that are still adaptive. Because different schemata combinations may be more or less adaptive, we say the solution process is not as invariant as that of the TCT. The TA-S requires analyzing (discovering various "meaning" and grammatical combinations) and synthesizing (combining) schemata to meet the task requirements.

How may the threatening information contained in the sentences disrupt analytic and synthetic processes? In contrast to the TCT, a TA-S scrambled sentence does not confront a person with immediate, palpable, and defined threatening information. Of a sentence's words, none or only one or two may be "emotional" ("attack," "love"). The person does not know whether the sentence when rearranged will speak excitedly or calmly to him, for the full import of the sentence emerges only as a result of his own coordinating activity. He constructs his own "threatening" world, so to speak. This troubles very anxious men. They are not certain whether the emerging disturbing theme is correct, and therefore the responsibility of the examiner, or incorrect, but their responsibility for "thinking" or revealing such disgusting thoughts. The ambiguity of the "real" meaning of the sentence, until it has been solved, may push the person deeper into disorganized and defensive behavior, many varieties of which are played out in the different combinations of words a person makes. Disorganization of an anticipatory schema is seen in the resort to random juxtapositions of the words and in the perseverative coordination of obviously incorrect combinations. Defensive coordinations are varied: breaking up or undoing a correctly coordinated sentence to search for some other less disturbing combination, omitting key words or forming a sentence with less than the required number of words whose meaning then explicitly denies the correct but more threatening meaning, accusing the examiner that he has slipped in some unsolvable sentences, rationalizing grammatical infelicity by claiming some people speak that way, or actually changing the structure of some words to fit an incorrect anticipatory but defensively organized schema (A student said of the word "was," "This is a printing error. It should be 'were,' " and proceeded to use the word as if it were "were").

STRUCTURE OF THE THEMATIC
ANALYSIS-SYNTHESIS TEST

The TA-S has twenty-four sentences composed of the same thematic content used in the PT and TCT. Each of the six specific schemata types is represented by four sentences. Like the TCT, the sentences are divided into two equivalent test forms of twelve sentences each. A sample test sentence for each schema and its most adaptive solution is as follows:

SCHEMA TYPE	TEST SENTENCE
Mother-son aggression	boy between often her his stupidity the for has head criticized mother (the boy has often criticized his mother for her stupidity)
Father-son aggression	death some was old on herd challenged the males leader by young (the oldest herd leader was challenged by some young males)
Heterosexual relations	horses vigorous were with wagon the female harness receptive stallion a mated (the receptive female horses were mated with a vigorous stallion)
Homosexual relations	another between lured man search sometimes his the has room student into (the student has sometimes lured another man into his room)
Cooperative work	helped an assisted who him three engineer chart apprentices was above by (an engineer was assisted by three apprentices who helped him)
Playful relaxation	friends has with was the entertained boy funny glass often his jokes (the boy has often entertained his friends with funny jokes)

Although each scrambled sentence consisted of twelve words, the person was informed the correct solution required exactly ten words. The inclusion of two nonrelevant "red herrings" that could not be coordinated with any combination of eight other words to make the correct solution forced a person to entertain more complex and alternative anticipatory schemata, and provided additional opportunity for the person to evade defensively the task requirements by using eleven rather than ten words. The words of each sentence were linotyped on white cardboard. No capitalized words or punctuation were used. Each word was numbered on the back for identification and presentation order purposes.

The current form of the TA-S is the product of studies on nine different samples (listed in Table 1, Appendix B). Considerable effort was made to identify and control the task variables that made some sentences more difficult to solve than others. All sentences were of the same length. A different grammatical form was used for each of the schema's four sentences; each of the four sentences of the other schemata also was composed of one of the four basic grammatical forms. The four sentences in a schema varied in active or passive voice and in structure of adverbial and prepositional phrases and clauses. Two of a schema's sentences used animal and two human content. The presentation order of the twelve scrambled words for one schema's sentence was matched with that of its grammatically parallel sentence in each of the other schema. Because it was impossible to match the number of alternative correct word combinations of each sentence with its parallel sentence for every other schema to our satisfaction, we resorted to corrective scoring methods, and eventually to standard scores, to control this variable. Since practice effects and anxiety reactions to a threat sentence may affect subsequent performance on other sentences, the twelve sentences in each test form were systematically randomized and each person in one of the six-man replicate groups received a different prearranged presentation order. Again, as with the TCT, the order of the two test forms was counter-balanced across the replicate groups.

When given the TA-S, the person was told that twelve scrambled words would be placed in front of him and that he was to select and rearrange ten of the words to make the most meaningful and grammatically correct sentence as quickly as he could. He was to be sure he had two unused words left over. He had two minutes to solve each problem. The prearranged scrambled words of a practice sentence were then placed in front of him. Time to rearrange each test sentence and the proposed solution were recorded. Only one reminder was given to make a ten word sentence. No hints were given about the correctness of any sentence solution.

Analytic efficiency was defined by a basal meaning score to which a time bonus was added for very rapid solutions. The basal meaning score of a sentence was established by comparing each sentence solution to score criteria that took into account the number of words used, meaningfulness and grammatical correctness of the sentence. For example, the solution given by one person to the heterosexual example cited earlier was "the vigorous horses were mated with a receptive female stallion." Out of a possible seven score points, this sentence was given four points. The meaning is not quite sensible, and he has misplaced a major phrase or key word (a stallion is neither female nor as passive as the word *receptive* implies).

Analytic efficiency scores could be obtained for the four sentences of a schema, the threat and nonthreat schemata, all of the schemata (Total score), as well as the basal meaning score. A more efficient performance received a higher score for every score category. A critic will say a schema score based on only four items is not reliable. He is correct, but he is not faced by the realistic motivational and other research exigencies that force undesirable compromises. Schema scores based on few items will be interpreted cautiously.

Just how well do judges agree in judging the meaningfulness and grammatical structure of a rearranged sentence? As for all of the skill tests, the judges worked independently of any knowledge of each other's scores and of the name of the person whose sentences were being scored. Furthermore, the same sentence in a schema type was scored for all persons before the next sentence was scored. To help control for differences in number of alternative correct solutions between the matched sentences, one judge kept a record of all alternative solutions for the more discrepant sets of six matched sentences in order to score adverbial and adjectival placements similarly between the six sentences. In the early studies, judges agreed on about ninety-five per cent of both the threat and nonthreat scores. The interjudge reliability coefficients for the revised test forms and scoring system used in the current studies were, for the Total TA-S score, .97 for the Michigan, .89 for the Maturity, and .94 for the Organized sample. (Because of the history of high interjudge agreement and the detailed specificity of the scoring system examples, only one judge scored the Standard sample's sentences.) Detailed analyses of the discrepancies in the scores of the judges showed that they agreed exactly in seventy-one percent of their scores and in ninety-two percent when disagreements involving a discrepancy of one score unit were included as agreements.

We were not as concerned about the equivalence (.73 and .85 for the Organized and Standard samples) and stability (.50 and .43 for the Organized and Standard samples) coefficients of the TA-S for the reasons given in discussing the reliability of the TCT.

Table 10–1 gives the schemata scores for the Organized and Standard samples. Both samples are more efficient when analyzing

TABLE 10–1: ANALYTIC EFFICIENCY SCORES FOR
EACH SCHEMA TYPE

SCHEMA TYPE	ANALYTIC EFFICIENCY SCORES			
	ORGANIZED		STANDARD	
	Mean	SD	Mean	SD
Mother-son aggression	29.3[1]	5.2	28.6	4.6
Father-son aggression	30.5	4.9	32.1	3.7
Heterosexual relations	25.0	6.2	28.3	5.7
Homosexual relations	27.7	5.2	28.5	5.0
Cooperative work	32.9	4.9	32.0	4.9
Playful relaxation	36.8	5.1	37.1	3.9

[1] The maximum score possible for a schema type is forty-eight.

the nonthreatening information. As with the TCT, the pattern of analytic skill efficiency for the different schemata was highly correlated with the samples' pattern of anxiety thresholds (Org. rho = .81; Stand. rho = .77), indicating that the samples did more poorly with that information about which they were more anxious.

THEMATIC ANALYTIC-SYNTHETIC
TEST RESULTS

Because the TA-S has not been used in studies other than the one for which it was designed, its links to other more familiar psychological procedures must be generated from our own studies. Actually, the scrambled sentence procedure, while well known, has scarcely been investigated, either as revelatory of problem solution styles (probably because of American psychology's historical resistance to studies of "higher mental processes"), as a measure of behavior sensitive to the effect of other variables such as stress (Alper, 1946), or as a means by which to measure need strength such as aggression (Watson, Pritzker, & Madison, 1955).

Early TA-S Results

Before describing the intellectual and personality traits associated with efficient analytic performance, we will briefly summarize results obtained from our earlier TA-S research.

Since the TA-S requires considerable verbal combinatory skill, its correlations with other measures of verbal or combinatory skill and achievement may affect our subsequent interpretations. Analytic skill was not related in the initial studies to measures of conceptual ability (Goldstein Object Sorting Test) and verbal intelligence (Wechsler-Bellevue Vocabulary Score) for a schizophrenic sample nor to verbal or quantitative reasoning skill

(CEEB) and English (CEEB) or academic achievement for a small volunteer sample of college men (Case Study sample). Schizophrenics of high conceptual skill, though not of high verbal intelligence, were significantly more efficient (p $\angle$ .05) in analyzing and synthesizing threatening information than those of low conceptual skill when analytic efficiency for nonthreatening information was held constant (D. H. Heath, 1954, 1956). Both schizophrenics and college men (Case Study) were significantly more efficient in analyzing the less threatening than the more threatening information (p $\angle$ .001 and .01). Furthermore, the analytic efficiency for different types of information significantly covaried (p $\angle$ .05) with the schizophrenics' and the college males' anxiety thresholds for such information. Finally, analytic efficiency was significantly better (p $\angle$ .025) for less threatening information when the degree of threat was determined by each person's PT anxiety threshold scores.

TA-S and Intellectual Skill and Achievement

Although the initial studies suggested analytic efficiency was not related to intellectual skill, it is very clear from Table 10–2 that Terman was wise to include scrambled word tasks in his test of intelligence. Analytic efficiency, even with disturbing information, is consistently associated over the four samples with verbal skill but less consistently with quantitative skill. Analytic skill is also significantly associated with achievement, particularly grade average.

These results demand that basal verbal skill (CEEB Verbal) be partialled out of our correlations between personality measures and analytic efficiency since any significant relationships between the two could be due to basal verbal skill rather than to just personality differences. Partial coefficients are reported for every TA-S correlate in this chapter unless mentioned otherwise. When the partial coefficient resulted in a shift from nonsignificance to significance (to p ∠ .05) or vice versa, the direction of the shift is footnoted in the table.

TABLE 10–2: CORRELATES BETWEEN ANALYTIC
EFFICIENCY AND INTELLECTUAL
SKILL AND ACHIEVEMENT

INTELLECTUAL   ANALYTIC EFFICIENCY SCORES
SCORES

		TOTAL	THREAT	NON-THREAT	MEANING
	Sample	r	r	r	r
Skill Measures					
Verbal CEEB	Mich.[1]	.28	.47	.59*	.41
	Mat.	.41	.33	.41	.48*
	Org.	.24	.23	.20	.19
	Sta.	.39**	.45***	.26	.39**
Quantitative					
CEEB	Mich.[1]	.50*	.46	.36	.41
	Mat.	.35	.17	.61***	.46*
	Org.	—.09	—.03	—.16	—.03
	Sta.	.15	.21	.20	.22
Terman	Org.	.25	.22	.21	.22
	Sta.	.33*	.38*	.18	.16
Achievement Measures					
English CEEB	Mat.	.41	.37	.31	.37
	Org.	.35	.31	.30	.24
	Sta.	.47***	.43***	.46***	.46***
Final Grade					
Average	Mat.	.51**	.33	.69***	.59***
	Org.	.41*	.41*	.27	.32
	Sta.	.15	.19	.15	.06

* p ∠ .05
** p ∠ .025
*** p ∠ .01

[1] Michigan intellectual skill scores were available only for the ACE. Its ACE Language and Quantitative scores were substituted for the CEEB Verbal and Quantitative scores.

TA-S and Questionnaire Scales of Maladjustment and Control

Questionnaire scores were not available for the Michigan sample. Of the 220 correlations calculated for the Maturity, Organized, and Standard samples collectively, twenty-four percent were significant at least at a one-tailed .05 probability level. However, not one significant finding was found for the basic TA-S scores of the Standard sample, possibly because of its severely restricted variability on both the self-report and TA-S measures (its TA-S total score was the least variable of all the samples). Thirty-two percent of the Maturity and Organized samples' TA-S correlations were significant at a one-tailed .05 level.

Table 10–3 reports those significant and consistent findings used for interpretative purposes. In contrast to the personality correlates found for conceptual efficiency, analytic efficiency is not consistently or significantly related to defensive control or ego strength but is quite consistently associated with a variety of maladjustment scores. This intriguing finding may be a harbinger that analytic and conceptual efficiency do not covary as we expected.

Analytic efficiency, particularly to threatening information, is inversely associated most strikingly with maladjustment (MMPI Total; Bern. Neurotic), characterized most consistently by an inability to refrain from expressing, if not obsessionally (MMPI Pd, Pt), hypochondriacal complaints (MMPI Hs), inadequacy and depressive feelings (MMPI D), and possibly introversive trends (MMPI Sc, Si; Bern. Introver.). The analytically efficient person also experiences less anxiety (Taylor) and reports that he adequately controls (Block Under-control; MMPI Pd) his behavior. The wide range of uniformly moderate MMPI and TA-S correlations blur any more detailed analysis.

Although only eight percent of the TA-S and SIQ dimensional and maturity correlations were significant at the .05 level, the pattern of the scores (except for self-image autonomy) was as predicted. In particular, analytic efficiency with disturbing in-

TABLE 10–3: SELECTED PARTIAL CORRELATES BE-
TWEEN ANALYTIC EFFICIENCY AND
QUESTIONNAIRE SCALES OF MALAD-
JUSTMENT AND CONTROL

QUESTIONNAIRE SCALES		ANALYTIC EFFICIENCY SCORES			
		TOTAL SCORE	THREAT	NON- THREAT	MEANING
		r	r	r	r
MMPI					
Total	Org.[1]	—.38*	—.36*	—.28	—.29
	Mat.[2]	—.66***	—.52**	—.58***	—.59***
Hs	Org.	—.39*	—.36*	—.32	—.19
	Mat.	—.52**	—.44*[3]	—.25	—.60***
D	Org.	—.48***	—.46**	—.33	—.30
	Mat.	—.52**	—.47*	—.30	—.51**
Pd	Org.	—.46**	—.42**	—.37*[3]	—.28
	Mat.	—.60***	—.47*	—.52**	—.46*
Pt	Org.	—.24	—.27	—.11	—.21
	Mat.	—.43*	—.36	—.33	—.59***
Sc	Org.	—.34	—.34	—.23	—.25
	Mat.	—.43*	—.46*	—.09	—.39[4]
Si	Org.	—.48**	—.54***	—.26	—.49***
	Mat.		Not available		
Taylor MAS	Org.	—.39*	—.35*[3]	—.36*[3]	—.43**
	Mat.		Not available		
Bernreuter					
Neurotic	Org.	—.36*[3]	—.29	—.21	—.31
	Mat.	—.34	—.41*	.07	—.17
Introversion	Org.	—.31	—.23	—.29	—.25
	Mat.	—.40	—.43*	—.07	—.23
Control Scores					
Block					
Under-	Org.	—.42***	—.37*[3]	—.36*[3]	—.31
control	Mat.		Not available		

* p ∠ .05   ** p ∠ .025   *** p ∠ .01

[1] N = 23 for all scores.   [2] N = 17 for all scores.

[3] Correlation not significant at .05 probability level prior to partialling out verbal skill.

[4] Correlation significant beyond .05 probability level prior to partialling out verbal skill.

formation was directly related to judged maturity (Org. $r = .54$, $p < .005$).

TA-S and Rorschach Measures

Rorschach data were available for the Maturity, Organized, and Standard samples, but we focus on the data of the former two samples whose Rorschach administration conditions were comparable. Only seven percent of the uncorrected Klopfer and TA-S correlates were significant at a two-tailed probability level and of those that were significant for one sample, the comparable correlates were usually in the opposite direction for the second sample. For this reason, we saw no need to calculate all of their partials. The traditional Rorschach scores give remarkably and consistently little solace to us. The only significant correlation consistently found in both samples was for analytic efficiency to covary with the number of conventionally organized and commonly shared schemata (Ror. # P: Org. $p < .05$). This is a most sensible finding, for adaptive solutions of the TA-S problems do require a firm grasp of the conventional language and meaning patterns of the culture.

Good analytic efficiency was directly related to Rorschach clinical evaluations of good self-organization (Org. $r = .38$, $p < .05$) but again most prominently for the more threatening information ($r = .42$, $p < .025$).

Fourteen percent of the eighty correlations between the autocentric and adaptive control and TA-S scores were significant for the Organized and Maturity samples. But very dramatically, the Maturity sample accounted for all but three of the significant correlations which are reported in Table 10–4. All of the correlations are in the predicted direction. *Poor* analytic efficiency, particularly with the more threatening information, tends to be related to impaired skill and poor defense effectiveness. Good analytic efficiency is consistently associated with the ability to make adaptively imaginative and (less consistently) good regressive schemata coordinations.

TABLE 10–4: SELECTED PARTIAL CORRELATES BE-
TWEEN ANALYTIC EFFICIENCY AND
RORSCHACH AUTOCENTRIC AND
CONTROL SCORES

RORSCHACH SCORES		ANALYTIC EFFICIENCY SCORES			
		TOTAL SCORE	THREAT	NON-THREAT	MEANING
		r	r	r	r
% PriPro	Org.	−.02	−.19	−.14	−.12
	Mat.	−.28	−.25	−.19	−.14
% Formal	Org.	−.32	−.29	−.24	−.21
	Mat.	−.51**	−.41*	−.29	−.34
% Level 1	Org.	−.23	−.25	−.12	−.11
	Mat.	−.23	−.17	−.20	−.14
Mean DE	Org.	.15	.11	.16	−.01
	Mat.	.40*	.48**	.04	.44**
% DD × DE	Org.	.16	.12	.19	.05
	Mat.	.60***	.65***	.13	.41*
Con DD/Form	Org.	.44*	.34*	.47**	.34
DD	Mat.	.23	.17	.27	.20

* p $\angle$ .05
** p $\angle$ .025
*** p $\angle$ .01

TA-S and Anxiety Thresholds

The Phrase Association Test was very consistently related
to analytic efficiency in the expected direction. Of the forty-eight
partial correlates calculated for the four samples, nineteen percent were significant beyond the one-tailed .05 probability level
and all of the others were in the predicted direction. We can
summarize the data, which we don't report in detail, as follows:
it was confirmed that analytic efficiency with disturbing information (both threatening and nonthreatening) was consistently but
moderately associated with high anxiety thresholds for similar
types of information.

Analytic efficiency with nonthreatening information was also directly related to the ability to maintain stable schemata in the face of nonpersonal but persuasive external distractions (Stroop, p $\angle$ .05).

Personality Correlates of TA-S Improvement

Improvement in analytic efficiency tends to be associated with good defensive ego control (MMPI K: Org. r = 18; Stand. r = .45, p $\angle$ .005; Barron r's: .26 and .32). Improvement was also associated for the Organized sample with the ability to make accurate schemata accommodations (Ror. % Form Acc. r = .39, p $\angle$ .05) and adaptively regressed schemata coordinations (Ror. % DD $\times$ DE r = .42, p $\angle$ .025). Persons who improve analytically certainly do not retreat into themselves when confronted with disturbing information (MMPI Si: Org. r = $-$.27; Stand. r = $-$.31, p $\angle$ .05; Ror. M%: Org. r (two-tailed) = $-$.42, p $\angle$ .05). Instead, they appear to use their energy assertively and aggressively to keep in contact with the external world (MMPI Ma: Org. r (two-tailed) = .37, p $\angle$ .05; Stand. r (two-tailed) = .34, p $\angle$ .05; Bern. Dom. consistently high for both samples; MMPI Pa: Stand. r (two-tailed) = .46, p $\angle$ .01). This pattern of traits associated with meeting disturbing information must be replicated of course, but it is not inconsistent with notions of ego strength and empirical studies of traits associated with the mastery of stress (Funkenstein, et al., 1957).

SUMMARY

The Thematic Analysis-Synthesis Test (TA-S) measures a person's analytic and synthetic efficiency in solving problems composed of disturbing information. Analytically efficient and inefficient persons (defined by dividing each sample at the midpoint of its Total TA-S score distribution) consistently differ in a variety of personality traits (See summary Table 3, Appendix B).

Persons who are highly efficient in analyzing disturbing information are consistently better in verbal reasoning or combinatory skills (Verbal CEEB) and have acquired a more adaptive working knowledge of English as well as higher academic averages in college. Such persons may have better control over their behavior (MMPI Pd) than do persons who are poor in analyzing such material. This good control is reflected in their significantly higher anxiety thresholds for a range of disturbing information, particularly information about maternal aggression, heterosexual relations, receiving affection, and relaxation (PT) and in their ability to preserve their schemata organization in nonpersonal stressful situations (Stroop correlates). Good analytic efficiency is also associated with possessing a predominant amount of conventional (Ror. # P correlates) and more socialized schemata (Ror. % Level 2).

Even more tentatively, poor analytic efficiency occurs in persons judged to be more immature (SIQ), to show more bizarre, unrealistic, and regressive schemata coordinations (Ror. % Formal correlates) and to handle anxiety by withdrawing and internalizing defenses (MMPI Si, Sc, D). More tentatively still, some correlational evidence suggests that those persons who analytically master new and potentially disturbing information most rapidly deny inner conflicts (MMPI K), actively and aggressively assert or seek contact (MMPI Ma, Pa; Bern. Dom.) with the incoming information to which they can accurately accommodate (Ror. % Form Acc.).

CHAPTER 11

The Thematic Associative
Judgment Test (TAJ)

The last skill we investigated was associative judgment which was measured by the Thematic Associative Judgment Test (TAJ). Briefly, the test consists of pictures each depicting a different type of interpersonal relationship. The person's task is to give as many different *but* realistic interpretative stories about the portrayed relationship in each picture that he can.

Historically, the Thematic Associative Judgment Test has many tributaries though the primary streams flow from the holistic concern about individual differences and from imaginative methods for assessing personality. Binet first identified good judgment to be the central skill distinguishing high intelligence (Peterson, 1925), and his early intelligence tests were composed of many judgment problems. While Binet restricted his first judgment tests to more impersonal and nonverbal types of problems, the Stanford-Binet and the Wechsler-Bellevue intelligence tests use verbal problems some of which tap the operation of judgment with more personally affective content. For example, one Wechsler-Bellevue item is, "Why does the state require a license in order to get married?" Clinicians from Bleuler on have consistently identified one of the key ego deficiencies of neurotic and psychotic persons, particularly schizophrenics, to be unrealistic judgment or poor reality testing. Both the intellectual and the clinical traditions converged in the work of Rapaport (1945) who demonstrated how patterns of cognitive skill differences, measured psychometrically, could be used for differential diagnostic purposes. Nowadays, no sensitive clinician ignores the contribution qualitative analyses of intellective patterns can make to his understanding of the control and defensive structure of the person he is assessing, even though the validity of the meaning of the alleged intellective patterns is still a moot question (Cronbach, 1960). But most surprising, given the centrality of the construct in clinical theory, is the paucity of good research on judgment, or, more ubiquitously, reality testing. It has been the psychophysicists and social psychologists, rather than the personality psychologists or clinicians, who have investigated the judging process—though not without much effect on either personality theory or clinical practice, the fields which are more concerned about individual differences in judgment and their personality correlates. One inhibiting factor to such personality research has been the absence of objective means by which to assess judgment and its impairment as it is understood by the clinician.

The other tributary contributing to the TAJ is the use of imaginative procedures, particularly Murray's Thematic Apperception Test, to assess the personality (Henry, 1956; Murray, 1943). Such procedures have been used in research to measure motives such as N achievement and N affiliation (Atkinson, 1958; Johnston, 1957; McClelland, Atkinson, Clark, & Lowell, 1953) rather than ego strength or skill efficiency. Holt (1958) tried to develop a TAT measure of ego strength but it has not received wide acceptance. While the perceptive clinician is able to make inferences about the quality of a person's self-organization and skill efficiency from the fabric of his imaginative themes, the TAT and other similar fantasy measures are neither administered nor designed to optimize such inferences.

The TAJ is the product of the confluence of the concern for individual differences and the imaginative assessment traditions. Constraints have been imposed on the imaginative process to convert it into a judging process—so we hoped.

What defines judgment? Within the clinical tradition, the meaning of good judgment is defined by the quality of adaptation to information that has social, affective, and valuational implications, or, in Piaget's terms, by "operations concerned with values, i.e., those expressing the relations of means and ends which play an essential part in practical intelligence . . ." (1947, p. 47). This type of information is complex, configurational, and certainly not unidimensional.

Furthermore, the meaning of judgment, as used by us, is not touched by problems that can be answered by one correct or right answer; its meaning is approached by those problems for which several solutions are more or less appropriate. But what is "appropriate" is contingent upon some type of social validation of the solution's appropriateness. In this sense, the TAJ is more similar to, and should be more closely correlated with, the Thematic Analysis-Synthesis than with the Thematic Concept Test.

Finally, and already implied, we do not believe "good" judgment can be assessed by procedures whose *only* measure is a final product (e.g., the degree of match of two illuminated discs). Persons of good judgment are able to entertain a variety of more or less appropriate solutions. Our measure of judgment must assess this breadth. Since valuational problems do *not* permit a single correct solution, discoverable within the structure of the problem itself, their solution is closely dependent upon the skill with which a person can fashion many alternative solutions, test each out, not for "match," but for "fit," and then select that which is the best "fit." To make tentative reversible schemata coordinations requires that schemata relevant to the valuational problem be available for coordination. That is, the judging process is not independent of the memory organization of the person. Freud (1900) has asserted that one of the distinguishing characteristics of secondary process thinking, including judgment, is that memories (schemata) are readily available for tentative coordinations. Furthermore, good judgment depends on some "looseness" in the memory organization of imaginal schemata to permit other than stereotyped or habitual coordinations to problems (Humphrey, 1951, p. 287).

The TAJ test is labeled an "associative judgment" rather than "realistic judgment" test, not because we ignore the appropriateness of the solutions given, which we don't, but because we believe a measure of good judgment must assess the range of realistic schemata coordinations a person associatively creates in the judging process itself. (The TAJ was initially designed to measure Piaget's (1947) operation of associativity as it was manifested in the judging process.) The breadth of realistic combinations is not unrelated to imaginative skill, which was one reason we eventually settled on a modified imaginative procedure to assess associative judgment, hereafter referred to as judgment.

Summarizing these test criteria of judgment then, we required a test composed of affectively meaningful problems, relevant to the person's valuator and memory organization, of such complexity that a range of alternative appropriate solutions could be given which could be ordered for degree of realistic fit to the problem requirements.

The Thematic Associative Judgment Test (TAJ) was designed to meet these criteria. How does the TAJ differ from the Thematic Analysis-Synthesis Test which also seems to meet these requirements? The thematic "meaning" of the TAJ picture was portrayed directly; that of the TA-S scrambled sentence only indirectly. The tests required different types of responses to cope with these different types of meaning. While the TA-S required one recombination of the given information, the TAJ required many adaptive recombinations of the same information, which made it more difficult to evade the given meaning. Evasion of the intended "meaning" of the picture or the sentence was penalized by lower skill efficiency scores. The number of recombinations possible for the TA-S sentence was, in effect, pragmatically limited by immediately verifiable requirements external to the personal standards of the person (grammatical and conventional standards of meaningfulness). While he did not "discover" the solution, as was true for the TCT, neither did he create the TA-S sentence solution out of whole cloth. An externally given pattern, essentially irrelevant to his own valuators, was present which guided his recombinations. But in the TAJ, the information given the person, while already organized meaningfully, did not exercise the same type of constraints. The person, rather than relying on conventional and verifiable standards, had to establish for himself his own criteria of what was a realistic interpretation of the picture. True, the portrayed interpersonal action oftentimes was unambiguous and very constraining; yet, and this is a crucial difference between the TA-S and TAJ, when required to give a number of different alternative interpretations of the action, the initial "ecological" constraint had to be stretched. In addition, the way in which it was stretched reflected the person's own judgment about what constituted an appropriate extension. The source of the recombination possibilities was not an externalized set of words that could be, at the least, mechanically recombined to fit nonpersonal standards; the source was the person's own schemata organization and valuator hierarchy. In this sense, the TAJ shares some of the properties of other projective measures. Another difference between the skill tests is that the Thematic Concept Test, and, to a lesser extent, the Thematic Analysis-Synthesis Test could be most effectively solved by isolating the affective connotations of the test content from the solution process itself. But similar defensive isolation in the TAJ robs the person of a source of hypotheses about other possible combinations of themes. The clinician has long recognized that the obsessive person, whose primary defense is isolation, shown in intellectualization, often shows poor judgment. He has lost contact with the affective context or emotionally relevant considerations that are frequently so decisive in human judgmental situations. The most adaptive response to the TAJ will rely upon and use rather than deny or isolate the affective suggestions contained in the information. For this reason, we expect that any measures of control, that depend upon intellectualizing and denial defenses (MMPI K), may not be related to judgmental efficiency as measured by the TAJ.

STRUCTURE OF THE THEMATIC ASSOCIATIVE JUDGMENT TEST

The TAJ has two parallel test forms of six different photographs each. Each of the six photographs of a test form depicts one of the schemata types used in the PT and the other skill tests. A brief description of the two pictures that define each schemata type is as follows:

Schema	Test Form I	Test Form II
Mother-son aggression	I. Woman with hands upraised in front of a young boy who is holding a stick over his head; Quonset hut in background.	VII. Boy has arm upraised as if to throw an object, and woman in front of him has hands to her face; takes place in room.
Father-son aggression	II. Boy has arm raised toward older boy who has hands in front of his face; takes place outdoors.	VIII. Young man with arm raised and older man holding raised arm of young man; takes place in a room with desk.
Heterosexual	III. Woman is clutching the bare back of man in an embrace.	IX. Young man clothed only in pants embracing and kissing a young woman on a playing field.
Homosexual	IV. Man in dark suit kissing a man in a light suit.	X. Nude young man with hands on back of neck with second nude young man in back of him.
Cooperative work	V. Man with upraised mallet and man watching metal which first man is about to pound on an anvil.	XI. Woman dressed in white at cash register watching grocer working at potato chip rack.
Relaxation	VI. Man slumped over on park bench and young woman also sitting on bench looking at something in lap.	XII. Man in work clothes lying on park bench and old man in overalls sitting on the bench looking into the camera.

258

The use of photographs immediately raises the problem of inter-picture cue differences that may make one picture more difficult to respond to than another. Only photographs could realistically capture the dramatic quality and complexity of the schemata types necessary to measure judgment as we defined it. Although the pictures were selected to be comparable in difficulty, we later relied primarily on scoring procedures to remedy the effects of cue differences between the pictures.

The pictures were photographed to be of similar size and were then photostated to make all pictures achromatic and to blur many of the less essential details. Each picture was mounted on 8″ × 10½″ white cardboard. A demonstration picture was used to which the most anxiety arousing theme, homosexual relationships (as measured by the PT), for young males could be given as one of the illustrative themes in order to give the men "permission" to imagine disturbingly and socially unconventional but appropriate themes. Generally, the men did not seem to be imaginally inhibited, either in the content or the number of their stories (Mean number of stories given to each picture was 3.5 for the Michigan, 4.6 for the Organized, and 3.7 for the Standard samples).

The other standard controls were also maintained. The order of picture presentation within each set was systematically randomized, as was the order of test form, for the replicate groups. And the order of presentation of the three skill tests was also randomized as outlined in Chapter 7.

In the early development of the TAJ procedure, the Maturity sample was given three different TAT cards three different times and asked to give a different story to each picture at each presentation. The Michigan sample was given the TAJ set of pictures and asked to give many different stories to each. It was given only two minutes per picture which very drastically limited the thematic richness of its stories. On the basis of these and other studies, each man of the Organized and Standard samples was asked instead to give as many different but realistically appropriate stories that he could to each picture in five minutes. Each story was to be organized around the interpersonal relationship portrayed between the persons, their relationship to each other,

or role in society, and their vocation. He was then shown the
demonstration card and told a variety of short stories that could
be given to the picture. How each story was realistically appropriate to the picture was briefly mentioned. The first test picture
was then presented.

Each person was urged to be more interpretative if he persisted
in literally describing only the picture itself, to give very different stories following his first story to a picture, to give more
stories if he stopped before five minutes had elapsed, or to go
on to another story if his stories started to exceed five or six
sentences in length. Although the men had a clock in front of
them indicating how much time they had left for a picture, they
were also given a thirty-second warning prior to the end of five
minutes. All men were stopped if they had not completed their
stories by fifteen seconds following the five-minute time interval.

The men's stories were either recorded or typed verbatim. The
Maturity sample's protocols were recorded and subsequently
transcribed for data analysis purposes. The Michigan sample's
protocols were typed verbatim as they were reported. The Organized sample's stories were simultaneously recorded and typed
verbatim. Subsequent comparisons of the transcribed recording
with the initial typed version revealed so few inaccuracies that
affected the scoring of the protocols, that the Standard sample's
stories were only typed as they were given by each person.

The Measurement of Associative Judgment:
Scoring System

Two problems troubled us: the measurement of breadth
or associativity and of the realistic appropriateness of a person's
judgments. Interindividual comparisons of judgment require the
identification of the range and type of thematic components
given to the TAJ photographs and a method that evaluates the
realistic appropriateness of those components to the actual information given to the person.

A classification of the thematic components that recurringly occurred to the TAJ pictures was empirically developed after no

published classification model had been found completely applicable to the type of material elicited by the TAJ. Of the varied affect (Woodworth & Schlosberg, 1954), hormetic and valuator (Atkinson, 1958; Edwards, 1954; Guilford, 1959a; McClelland, *et al*, 1953; Murray, 1938), traits and values (Allport, *et al*, 1960; Cattell, 1957), occupational (Roe, 1956) and other schemes, only Murray's and Roe's seemed most appropriate. A frequency analysis of the themes of some five thousand stories given to the TAJ (collected in preliminary pilot studies) suggested that the thematic variability of the stories could be accounted for by three components: 1) need inferred from the interpersonal interaction given in the story, 2) occupation, and 3) familial and social role of the major persons in each story.

Valuator (Need) Classification

Drawing persistently on Murray's classic and enduring set of needs and our own data, we constructed twenty-eight need categories each ordered on the dimensions of affect (negative-neutral-positive) and self-other interpersonal orientation. Each valuator was closely defined by examples and expressions drawn from the themes of preliminary studies. For example, the need of vegetating was defined this way:

need to loaf, nonachieve, wait (when no goal specified), sit but not know what to do, waste time, rest (but not to rest to recover energy which would be scored Health-maintaining), retire (but not to separate self socially from others which would be scored Separation), be indolent, passively inactive, anergic, resigned, fail due to inactivity. If any of the above are accompanied by positive affect, then score for Enjoyment (e.g., sunning self in park).

The valuators were grouped into five categories: positive affect toward others (loving opposite sex, loving same sex, affiliating, nurturing, rewarding, cooperating, expositing, and cognizing others), positive affect toward self (depending, exhibiting, playing, and enjoying), neutral affect toward self (cognizing self, working by self, health maintaining, and achieving), negative affect toward others (defending self, autonomy, possessing, rejecting, dominating, punishing, verbal aggression, and physical aggression), and negative affect toward self (vegetating, health destroying, submitting, and separating).

Occupational Classification

Roe's (1956) vocational classification economically ordered thousands of existing occupations into six major types of vocations (service, business-government, technical, outdoor, cultural, and art-entertainment), each of which was further ordered into levels defined by educational and responsibility criteria. To increase interjudge agreement, we simplified and redefined her levels using specific examples drawn from the early studies with the TAJ preparatory to the use of the classification with the major samples (e.g., Service: professional, semi-professional, skilled, and semi- or unskilled).

Familial-Social Role Classification

Since all of the pictures portrayed two persons, the relationships of a person, whether familial (father, sister) or societal (intimate personal, intimate social, nonsocial, anti-social toward persons, and anti-social toward non-persons) were similarly classified.

From the map of the content of a person's stories comes an embarrassingly large number of scores, as a moment's reflection about the TAJ and its associative instructional procedure reveals (e.g., *Imaginative breadth* could be defined by the number of different needs, roles, or occupational categories used in the stories). We report only the results of the *Imaginal productivity* score, defined by the total number of stories given to all the pictures. While similar to the Rorschach score of total number of responses, the two scores are not identical since the TAJ instructions require the person to give as many different *but* realistic stories as possible.

The next problem was to measure the degree of realistic appropriateness of each classification category for each person pictured in each TAJ card. Historically, realistic appropriateness to the Rorschach, for example, has been defined either by the frequency of a response (Beck, *et al.*, 1961) or by the judgment of a trained examiner (Klopfer, *et al.*, 1954; Rorschach, 1921). But neither is a completely satisfactory definition of appropriateness. An infrequent response is not necessarily inappropriate and, given the type of disturbing information used in the TAJ, evasive or denial responses to its information reduces the frequencies of even the most realistic types of responses. Judgments of realistic appropriateness by skilled clinicians were likely to be as unsatisfactory, as suggested by our own earlier studies on judge agreement (summarized in Appendix C) in rating the anxiety thresholds of schemata from imaginative information. But we patently could not escape using social judgments of appropriateness. The real problem was how to optimize the conditions under which objective and valid judgments of the realistic fit of a category to a person in a story could be made by judges. Very briefly, our solution was as follows. Using regularized procedures, ten judges independently rated and then ranked the degree of realistic fit of each need and each occupation-role category to each person in each of the twelve TAJ pictures. The judges determined the realistic fit of the need categories and of the occupational and role categories separately in two four-to-six hour judging sessions. Despite the prolonged and tedious judging procedures, the judges were conscientiously cooperative and made few notational errors, which was remarkable given that they made 15,560 and 20,800 need and role judgments. The median rank-order for each need and each occupation-role category for each character in each picture was then determined from the judges' ranks. The resulting medians of the twenty-eight needs and of the forty occupations-roles were each ranked in turn from most to least realistic for each character in each picture. Positive and negative weighted scores were then assigned to those more realistic and unrealistic categories. (Because of some restrictions placed on the judge ratings, it was possible to control statistically for some of the inter-picture differences in difficulty when assigning the weighted scores.) After a person's stories had been classified into the need and other categories, each category for each story's principal actor was routinely assigned its weighted score for degree of realistic fit. Analysis of the reliability of the judging procedures used to define realistic appropriateness indicated the judges agreed surprisingly well among themselves about the degree of appropriateness of each category to each picture (data not given). The judged ranks of the need categories were also compared to the *frequency* with which the different needs had been assigned to the pictures in the five thousand themes of the pilot studies. The ranks of only seven of the fifty-five more reliably determined needs differed noticeably, and most of these differences were due to the women who interpreted certain pictures differently than did the men in the pilot studies.

We now can secure a measure of associative judgment which we defined by the sum for the twelve pictures of the weighted scores for every *different* need, role and vocation given to each person in a picture (if a person gave five stories all about the *same* theme to one picture, his Associative Judgment score for that picture would be the weighted score for that theme for only *one* of the five stories). The higher the score, the better associative judgment (the more realistically varied judgment) the person has for information varying in anxiety arousing potential. Partial associative judgment scores were also obtained. The Need Associative Judgment score measures the appropriateness of the range of need images given to the pictures; the Threat Associative Judgment score gives a clue about how associatively realistic the person's judgment is when confronted with threatening information; the Associative Judgment Schemata Hierarchy tells us how realistic the person's judgment is for different types of information.

Methodological Properties of the TAJ

Two trained judges, working independently of any knowledge of the other judge's scores and of the identity of the authors of the stories, scored the Organized sample's 1298 and the Standard sample's 1606 stories some sixteen and five months respectively following their collection. The protocols of the well and poorly organized men were coded and randomly mixed. For the major samples, all of the stories given to a picture by all of the men were scored before the stories to a different picture were scored. As the researchers on N-ach and other motives have found (Atkinson, 1958), many scoring conventions had to be developed in the pilot studies to regularize judgments about ambiguous themes. These conventions were indexed and served as a reference file for each judge. Score disagreements between the judges were later reviewed and resolved, though not without considerable dispute. Persistent judge disagreement focused on certain recurring themes that represented a fusion of certain needs.

Although not as extensive reliability studies have been done with the TAJ as were done with the PT, for example, its reliability seems to be reasonably satisfactory. The median inter-judge reliability coefficients for three samples (Michigan, Organized, and Standard) of the Associative Judgment score was .91 and of the Need Associative score .79. As expected, the reliability coefficients for the individual TAJ cards were lower. The median coefficient of the twelve cards was .81 and .71 for the two samples respectively. Combining the scores for the two pictures of each schema resulted in higher coefficients. More sensitive measures of the interjudge agreement that took account of all of the scored categories in a protocol yielded median coefficients of .94 for a total associative type score and .90 and .82 for the individual TAJ pictures of the Organized and Standard samples respectively. The TAJ classifying system can be applied to other types of imaginative information with moderate judge agreement as well. The reliability coefficient of a comparable Need Associative Score for the Maturity sample was .77. The TAJ equivalence coefficients of the Associative Judgment score are .55 for the Organized, .63 for the Standard, and .66 for the Michigan samples when corrected by Spearman-Brown's formula. The stability coefficients were the lowest of all the skill tests, that is .19 and .08.

What about inter-schemata differences in judgmental efficiency? Table 11–1 lists the judgment scores for the six schemata types and shows considerable variability in judgmental appropriateness to the information. All three samples are judgmentally most inefficient with heterosexual information and most efficient with cooperative work information. Again, we are puzzled by how to interpret such variability. On the one hand, the weighted score system was so developed as to equalize the opportunity to get equivalent scores for the different pictures; yet, on the other hand, the *rho* coefficients between the TAJ judgmental efficiency and PT anxiety threshold patterns were only .03, .60, and .59 for the Organized, Standard, and Michigan samples respectively. These results indicate no or only a moderate association between the anxiety arousing potential of the information and judgmental inappropriateness. More than with the TCT and TA-S, TAJ inter-schemata differences may be due primarily to structural differences in the pictures and not to the anxiety thresholds for the varied information.

What types of needs does the TAJ evoke most readily? It is quite clear from Table 11–1 that despite the threatening and unpleasant tone of many of the TAJ pictures, the test evokes

TABLE 11–1: JUDGMENTAL EFFICIENCY SCORES FOR EACH SCHEMA TYPE AND THE VALUATOR SCORES FOR THE MAJOR SAMPLES

SCHEMA TYPE	JUDGMENTAL EFFICIENCY SCORES							
	MICHIGAN		ORGANIZED		STANDARD		MATURITY	
	Mean	SD	Mean	SD	Mean	SD	Mean	SD
Mother-son aggression	47.5 [1]	13.2	59.5	16.0	54.5	13.3	Not relevant	
Father-son aggression	36.4	16.4	57.6	18.8	50.4	15.7		
Heterosexual relations	29.8	17.4	34.0	20.9	33.5	17.5		
Homosexual relations	47.8	12.7	60.9	19.5	56.2	18.7		
Cooperative work	59.0	12.6	62.3	20.3	63.3	18.0		
Playful relaxation	53.9	13.3	52.5	19.6	56.3	22.2		
Valuator Type	Frequency of Expression of Valuator Types							
+Affect Others %	35.3	5.2	31.8	4.3	33.2	5.1	27.1 [2]	5.5
+Affect Self %	10.1	6.0	12.6	4.4	11.6	3.9	4.9	3.8
Neutral %	19.4	6.6	14.4	4.0	15.7	4.7	29.0	7.6
−Affect Self %	11.9	4.4	14.0	3.2	12.3	4.0	24.6	7.2
−Affect Others %	23.3	5.6	27.2	4.8	27.3	5.8	14.6	4.7

[1] High score means greater realistic judgment.

[2] Valuator scores based on imaginative responses to the TAT cards VIII, XII, and XIII.

positively and, to a lesser extent, negatively toned needs, organized around and oriented toward other people more frequently than any other type of need. This pattern holds for the three samples to whom the TAJ was given. For the Organized and Standard samples, the most frequently expressed needs were, in order, Physical Aggression towards others, Play, Cognizing Others, and Heterosexuality; for the Michigan sample, the needs were Maintaining Health, Cooperating, Play, Physical Aggression, and Heterosexuality. Now contrast this evocative pull pattern with that of the interpersonally structured cards of the TAT used with the Maturity sample in which self-oriented needs of neutral and negative affect are evoked most frequently (Cognizing self, Maintaining Health, Health Destroying). These results tend to support clinical hunches that the TAT evokes depressing and self-involving themes. The data also support N ach research (Birney, 1958) and common sense: informational structure is an important determinant of elicited need images.

Given the difficult problems involved in reliably assessing judgmental relevance to complex types of information, and our own reasonably reliable methods, the TAJ may be a useful measure in some types of personality research, particularly because it requires more than one response to information whose thematic meaning can be controlled. Just as thematic sequence analysis of responses to a Rorschach card (Schafer, 1954) has enriched Rorschach interpretation, so does thematic analysis of the progressive schemata reorganizations to a TAJ picture deepen one's insight into the self-organization and defensive coordinations of a person confronted with specific types of information whose thematic content has been controlled. If space and our purpose allowed, many examples of the process of "unlayering defenses" could be given. Some evidence exists that when asked to give opposite stories to the same TAT card, patients reveal more of their unconscious needs and conflicts in the second than in the first story (R. M. Jones, 1956). The TAJ procedure also permits a glimpse into the stability of a response or need. How frequently and how inappropriately does a need obtrude itself to the same or similar information? Too few studies have assessed the reliability of N ach measures, for example, overrepeated stories to the same thematic information. It is a dangerous theoretical question to ask, but what are the differences in, and the determinants of, N ach imagery to a first, and to a second, and to a third story to the same picture? The test also yields several potentially useful objective scores: measures of imaginative breadth, variety, productivity, judgmental measures, etc. How useful such scores will be to other researchers depends, of course, on what they produce. We now examine the surprising and occasionally quixotic validity correlates of the TAJ.

THEMATIC ASSOCIATIVE JUDGMENT TEST RESULTS

TAJ and Intellectual Skill and Achievement

Ten percent of the Organized and Standard samples' fifty judgmental efficiency and verbal skill and achievement correlations were significant beyond a two-tailed .05 significance level; but we refrain from presenting them in detail since some of the significant results were inconsistently supported across the samples.[1] The judgment findings were perplexing. The Organized sample's judgmental efficiency, particularly with threatening information, was significantly but *negatively* related to high verbal reasoning skill (CEEB Verbal r = −.57, p ∠ .01) but the Standard sample's judgment was not so related (r = .09). Judgmental efficiency with nonthreatening information is not correlated with verbal skill. Apparently, the use of threatening thematic content modifies and changes the relationship between judgment and verbal skill, which we had assumed would be positive. Because of the erratically significant though negative verbal skill and judgment relationships, verbal skill was par-

[1] The one consistent finding found to hold across three samples for whom we had roughly comparable measures was that imaginative breadth (page 262) was positively correlated with academic grade achievement (Org. r = .42, p ∠ .05; Stand. r = .24; and Mat. r = .52, p ∠ .05).

tialled out of the judgment correlations in order to control for whatever effect verbal reasoning had upon the relation of personality traits with judgment. All TAJ correlations reported in this chapter are partial correlations. One urgent statistical question must be answered before interpreting the TAJ and the personality test results. Since the TAJ, just as the Rorschach, requires many responses, should not the TAJ scores be corrected for the number of TAJ stories given, just as the Rorschach scores were corrected for total number of responses by using percentile scores? This question is even more compelling in view of the significantly high relationship found between Rorschach # R and TAJ productivity (p $\angle$ .001). The basic TAJ score we derived is, in part, an imaginal productivity score and controlling such productivity by the use of percentile scores defeats the purpose of our labors. A person was instructed and ever-pressed to be as productive as possible (and encouraged to give many different stories) although his productivity was instructionally limited by the associative and judgmental requirements. A compulsively banal person could give one maximally appropriate story to each picture and get a higher judgmental efficiency percentile score than a person who accommodated himself to the instructions. Since only one of several stories to a picture could receive the maximal score (because of the distribution of weighted scores for the different alternatives), no one following the instructions could achieve the same maximal percent score as our compulsive example. To measure the associative breadth of a person just requires that he give many different stories. So we do *not* report the correlations of the percentile judgment scores which we did calculate and which were, as we expected, moderately attenuated.

TAJ and Questionnaire Scales of Maladjustment and Control

Twenty-one percent of the Organized and sixteen percent of the Standard samples' MMPI and Bernreuter partial correlates were significant, either in the predicted direction at a one-tailed or in the nonpredicted opposite direction at a two-tailed significance level. All of the Organized sample's significant correlates (as well as most of its nonsignificant correlates) were in the predicted direction. Although four of the Standard's significant correlates were in the opposite direction from that expected (those for the MMPI Hs scale), we do not report them since the comparable Organized sample's correlates were in the opposite direction. Table 11–2 reports only those significant findings which were either supported or, at most, not contradicted by the other sample's results.

Imaginal productivity is much less consistently predictive of various personality traits than is judgmental appropriateness. Table 11–2 suggests, though not too convincingly, that persons who are disinterested in other people (Bern. Nonsocial) and who use repressive (MMPI Hy) controls may be imaginally unproductive to interpersonal types of information. Persons who undercontrol their behavior may be more imaginally productive persons (Block Under-control).

Interestingly, the judgment scores are very significantly and consistently related to a variety of self-image but not control indices, a pattern similarly found for the TA-S but not for the TCT. Poor judgment (and the findings hold for judgmental appropriateness in describing interpersonal needs as well) occurs in persons who have neurotic self-images (MMPI Total), characterized by poor emotional and inhibitory control (Block Under-control; MMPI Pd), alienation and withdrawal from others (MMPI Sc; Bern. Nonsocial), obsessive ideational push (MMPI Pt, Ma), and general anxiety and tension (Taylor). Table 11–2 shows that this pattern applies almost exclusively when the person must make many realistic judgments to threatening information. The finding that personality trait differences are not associated with judgments about nonthreatening information supports our biases that traditional intellective procedures are not adequate measures of adaptation—particularly that type of adaptation with which ego psychologists are concerned. As clinicians have found, responses to threatening items in the standard intelligence tests are peculiarly diagnostic of a wider

TABLE 11–2: SELECTED PARTIAL CORRELATES BE-
TWEEN JUDGMENTAL EFFICIENCY AND
QUESTIONNAIRE SCALES OF MALAD-
JUSTMENT AND CONTROL

QUESTIONNAIRE SCALES — JUDGMENTAL EFFICIENCY SCORES

		TOTAL r	THREAT r	NON-THREAT r	NEED r	IMAGINA-TIVE PRO-DUCTIVITY
MMPI						
Total	Org.	−.45**	−.42**	−.30	−.44**	−.12
	Sta.	−.19	−.32*	.10	−.25	−.16
D	Org.	−.29	−.26	−.22	−.33	−.12
	Sta.	−.07	−.21	.18	−.15	−.23
Hy	Org.	−.30	−.36*	−.13	−.34	−.35*
	Sta.	−.01	−.04	−.04	−.04	−.14
Pd	Org.	−.48***	−.47**	−.28	−.39*	−.10
	Sta.	−.14	−.22	.00	−.06	−.03
Pt	Org.	−.37*	−.22	−.33	−.26 [4]	.08
	Sta.	−.28 [3] *	−.39***	.06	−.27 [4]	−.18
Sc	Org.	−.55***	−.57***	−.26	−.44**	−.10
	Sta.	−.28*	−.40***	.04	−.33**	−.22
Ma	Org.	−.40*	−.31	−.28	−.29	.11
	Sta.	−.39***	−.36**	−.20	−.37**	.15
Taylor MAS	Org.[1]	−.42**	−.36 [3] *	−.30	−.40*	.26
	Sta.[2]	−.02	−.12	.15	−.16	−.10
Bernreuter						
Nonsocial	Org.	−.61***	−.74***	−.23	−.52***	−.43**
	Sta.	−.19	−.16	−.08	−.16	.01
Control Scores						
Block Under-	Org.[1]	−.27	−.20	−.16	−.11	.41* [3]
control	Sta.[2]	−.37*	−.26	−.33*	−.32	−.06

* p ∠ .05
** p ∠ .025
*** p ∠ .01
[1] N = 23
[2] N = 26
[3] Correlation not significant at .05 probability level prior to partialling out verbal skill.
[4] Correlation significant beyond .05 probability level prior to partialling out verbal skill.

domain of personality characteristics and, inferentially, quality of adaptation.

Seventeen percent of the SIQ self-image dimensional and maturity partial correlates were significant beyond the .05 level. The pattern of correlates was as predicted, with judgmental efficiency about threatening information being most significantly and consistently inversely related to the *in*congruence of the self-image (Org. $r = -.51$, p $\angle$ .01; Stand. $r = -.28$, p $\angle$ .05). The ability to make realistic judgments about the needs of others was also consistently and significantly inversely related to self-image *in*congruence (Org. $r = -.44$, p $\angle$ .025; Stand. $r = -.41$, p $\angle$ .01) as well as directly related to judged maturity (Org. $r = .49$, p $\angle$ .01; Stand. $r = .20$). Imaginal productivity was consistently inversely related to both self-image *in*congruence (Org. $r = -.35$, p $\angle$ .05; Stand. $r = -.26$) and autocentricism (Org. $r = -.16$; Stand. $r = -.31$, p $\angle$ .05), and directly related to judged maturity (Org. $r = .47$, p $\angle$ .05; Stand. $r = .26$).

TAJ and Rorschach Measures

We will not discuss in detail the Standard sample's *group* administered Rorschach results which were generally nonsignificant and, with a few exceptions, barely discrepant from zero. Since we have no comparable data from other samples to replicate the Organized sample's results, we must heed, however, some Standard sample's results in passing.

Fourteen percent of the Organized sample's Klopfer and TAJ imaginal productivity and eleven percent of its TAJ judgmental correlates were significant at the .05 two-tailed significance level. TAJ imaginal productivity is significantly related to Rorschach imaginal productivity (Ror. #R: $r = .71$, p $\angle$ .001) and, in particular, to the ability to give more popular conventional percepts (Ror. #P: $r = .42$, p $\angle$ .05). This result is quite sensible since the TAJ productivity score is derived from a procedure that requires many adaptive or realistic (frequently given) responses. But why is imaginative productivity *inversely* associated with emotional sensitivity and (tactful) accommodation to others (Ror. Fc%: Org. $r = -.50$, p $\angle$ .02; Stand. $r = -.31$), particularly when the TAJ information being judged contained dramatically emotional and interpersonal themes? We don't know. We turn now to the correlates of associative judgment. Good judgment, particularly to threatening information, is significantly associated with the ability to give conventionally realistic (Ror. #P: $r = .41$, p $\angle$ .05), if not more stereotyped (Ror. A + Ad%: Stand. $r = .33$, p $\angle$ .05; Org. $r = .25$) percepts. The results suggest that the more idiosyncratic the person's schemata organization is the less realistic will his judgment be for threatening information. (We will see this result replicated with the Holt measures of impaired skills.) A somewhat different personality pattern is associated with good judgment to *nonthreatening* information. In this case, appropriate judgment occurs in persons who are not intellectually rigid or constrictive (Ror. F %: $r = -.50$, p $\angle$ .02) but are more reflective (Ror. FK %: $r = .42$, p $\angle$ .05); these persons have schemata that are not meticulously detailed (Ror. Dd + S%: $r = -.42$, p $\angle$ .05), and they have, paradoxically, considerable amounts of earlier formed or more regressive schemata available to be organized (Ror. FM %: $r = .44$, p $\angle$ .05). Unfortunately, we lack a good cross-validating sample to check the consistency of these interesting findings.

The global Rorschach clinical evaluations of self-organization were not significantly related to either the imaginal productivity or judgment measures, although good judgment for the Standard sample tended to be directly related to clinically rated good self-organization ($r = .27$).

Of the Holt Rorschach and TAJ imaginal productive and judgment correlates, twenty and five percent respectively were significant at the .05 one-tailed level. Imaginal productivity to the TAJ is consistently and significantly inversely associated with impaired skills or disorganized thought processes (Ror. % Formal: Org. $r = -.37$, p $\angle$ .05; Stand. $r = -.46$, p $\angle$ .005)[2] and consistently tends to be inversely related to the extent to

---

[2] This finding was also supported by a parallel imaginative productivity correlate of the Maturity sample, $r = -.42$.

which a person's schemata organization is autocentrically organized (Ror. % PriPro and % Level 1). High TAJ imaginal productivity is very significantly and consistently related to good adaptive imagination (Ror. Con DD/Form DD: Org. r = .67, p ∠ .005; Stand. r = .38, p ∠ .025).[3] Although the TAJ judgmental and Holt Rorschach correlates were only erratically significant, they tended to be in the predicted direction. Judgmental efficiency, particularly to threatening information, tends to be inversely associated with impaired skills (Ror. % Formal: Org. r = −.24; Stand. r = −.28, p ∠ .05). Realistic judgment was positively correlated with good adaptive control, particularly the ability to coordinate unstable schemata imaginally (Ror. Con DD/Form DD: Org. r = .27; Stand. r = .36, p ∠ .025). These consistent though generally nonsignificant results across at least two (and occasionally three) samples using different Rorschach (and TAJ) procedures were moderately encouraging about the utility of the TAJ classification system.

TAJ and Anxiety Thresholds

From preliminary TAJ studies with the Michigan sample, it was found that PT affective instability to disturbing information was very significantly *inversely* related to TAJ Associative Judgment (r = −.55, p ∠ .025) as well as to TAJ Need Associative Judgment (r = −.58, p ∠ .01). These relationships held for both the PT threatening and nonthreatening information as well. This evidence that increasing affective instability or anxiety is inversely related to skill efficiency is consistent with the PT relationships found for other skill measures.

In contrast to these earlier Michigan findings, good judgment was not significantly inversely related to affective instability for the Organized and Standard samples, although their judgmental correlates tended to be in the predicted direction. (If the number of stories given to the TAJ is held constant, then realistic judgment is significantly, p ∠ .05, and inversely associated with most of the PT

[3] This finding was also supported by the Maturity sample's comparable correlate of r = .54, p ∠ .05.

measures of affective instability.) However, TAJ imaginal productivity was unexpectedly found to be significantly related (two-tailed) to *increased* affective instability (Org. r = .45, p ∠ .05). Just why imaginal productivity should be directly related to anxiety in the Organized and no other sample we don't know. Our hunch is that when made anxious by disturbing information, the highly verbal men of the Organized sample resort to counterphobic or counteractive types of defensive operations, which tend to invalidate measures of realistic judgment based in part on verbal productivity. Summarizing, the evidence (including that of the Michigan sample) suggests that increasing anxiety may be directly related to inappropriate judgmental responses to disturbing information but the conditions under which such a relation will be consistently obtained are unknown.

Finally, neither judgment nor imaginal productivity was significantly related to the ability to maintain a stable schemata organization in the face of nonpersonal but distracting information (Stroop).

Personality Correlates of TAJ Improvement

Improvement in judgmental efficiency is related to a pattern of personality traits that is somewhat different from that which described improved conceptual and analytic efficiency. Except for improvement in judgment, to be significantly and consistently *inversely* associated with increased autocentric and inaccurate self-images (Org. r's were −.45, p ∠ .025 and −.35, p ∠ .05 respectively) and directly associated with imaginal productivity (Ror. #R: Org. r = .41, p ∠ .05), all of the other consistent and significant (two-tailed) personality correlates were unpredicted. The data suggest that improvement in judgment tends to vary directly with the strength of a person's wishes and impulses (Ror. Sum DD: Org. r = .24; Stand. r = .35, p ∠ .05) and inversely with degree of schemata stereotypy (Ror. A + Ad %: Org. r = −.44, p ∠ .05; Stand. r = −.29) and obviousness (Ror. D %: Org. r = −.42, p ∠ .05; Stand. r = −.27). The few other consistent trends made less theoretical sense and are not reported. Considering that the TAJ encourages more reflective imaginal than immediate controlled motoric adaptations, the differences in the personality patterns between the skill tests may make some psychological sense.

SUMMARY

The Thematic Associative Judgment Test (TAJ) was designed to measure the range of realistic and appropriate judgments a person can give about personally disturbing information. Judgmentally efficient and inefficient persons (defined by dividing each sample at the midpoint of its TAJ Associative Judgment score distribution) do consistently differ from each other on a variety of personality measures (See summary Table 4, Appendix B).

Persons of poor judgment while not less intelligent than persons of good judgment (Intellectual skills) do significantly poorer college work (Grade average). They are immature and maladjusted (MMPI Total), obsessionally moody (MMPI D, Ma, Pt), and tend to act out rather than inhibit such feelings (MMPI Pd). Poor judgment is associated with aloof disinterest in other people (MMPI Sc; Bern. Nonsocial) and a congruent valuator preference for more nonpersonal and intellectualistic occupations (SVIB).

The pattern is consistent with clinical observation that obsessional and schizoid persons frequently show poor judgment in their social relationships. Their self-image is generally less congruent and probably less stable than persons of good judgment (SIQ). They tend to think others think they are immature which, in fact, is the case. The person poor in judgment also tends to be more anxious and tense (Taylor correlates) and may (given all our reservations) have lower anxiety thresholds (PT correlates). His thinking is disorganized, likely to produce regressive and idiosyncratic schemata coordinations (Ror. % Formal). The person of good judgment is able to accommodate himself more conventionally and realistically (Ror. #P) but not at the expense of allowing a wide range of imaginally adaptive schemata (Ror. Con DD/Form DD) to emerge into awareness.

CHAPTER 12

Cognitive Skill Efficiency
and Skill-Organization

This chapter completes Part III—the investigation of the developmental trend of stability and its relation to maturity. Before assessing the formal hypotheses that framed this investigation, we must complete the soffits and nail down the last shingles. We examine the interrelationship of conceptual, analytic, and judgmental efficiency, devise a combined measure of cognitive skill efficiency, and then determine its personality correlates. After speaking directly to the major hypothesis that well organized men are more stably organized than poorly organized men, we examine the hypothesis that cognitive skill efficiency is greater to less, than to more, threatening information.

THE INTERRELATIONSHIP OF SKILL EFFICIENCY TO DISTURBING INFORMATION

The expectation that the three skills would be positively, though minimally, intercorrelated was generally confirmed. The pattern of intercorrelations (details of which we don't report) between the three skill tests for both the Organized and Standard samples can be briefly summarized this way: seventy percent of the total number of correlations (170) between the basic scores of successive pairs of skill tests were positive; twenty-eight percent of the total number of correlations were more than $+.15$ but only five percent were more than $-.15$. Less than two percent of all the correlations were significant (two-tailed) and these were all positive. As expected, analytic and judgmental efficiency were consistently and positively related and conceptual and judgmental efficiency were consistently unrelated. The relation between conceptual and analytic skills was not interpretable because of sample differences. It seems clear that although the skills tend to be positively intercorrelated it is not possible to predict performance on one skill test from performance on a different skill test. The skill tests obviously measure different facets of the coordinating process, but it is not known if some other type of skill than the three selected would account for more of the individual differences in adaptively coordinating disturbing information.

Adaptation involves the continuing and simultaneous coordination and recoordination of many different schemata and skills. Conceptual, analytic, and judgmental skills are inextricably fused in most adaptive tasks. And while the preceding analyses of the skills and their more consistent personality correlates were necessary steps in our efforts to explore the component "structures of the ego," some more manageable general measure of skill organization might predict to more complex adaptive tasks. Complex statistical combinatory procedures seemed premature in our search for such a general measure of skill organization, particularly since some of the criterion measures of adaptation like social judgments were basically ordinal judgments. The most direct and expedient solution was to develop standard scores for each skill problem (using the Standard sample's raw skill scores), weight each skill test equally, and combine the total standard scores for each of the three tests into one common score. This we did and called the score *cognitive skill efficiency*. Cognitive skill efficiency scores to threatening (Threat score) and nonthreatening (Nonthreat score) information were also secured. Although the relative position of a person's raw skill scores to that of other persons was not changed by the standard score conversion of each skill problem, the pattern of his *intra-schemata* efficiency scores was changed drastically. Converting the skill scores to the threatening and to the nonthreatening information into a common scale statistically eliminated the significant skill efficiency differences based on raw scores earlier found to the threatening and nonthreatening information.

We now turn to a most intriguing question: what personality traits are associated with cognitive skill efficiency to disturbing information?

PERSONALITY CORRELATES OF COGNITIVE SKILL EFFICIENCY TO DISTURBING INFORMATION

Cognitive Skill Efficiency and Intellectual Skill and Achievement

One suggestive and consistent finding buried in the three preceding chapters' mass of results not heretofore highlighted must now be made more publicly visible because of its relevance to the research on factors producing high achievement and academic success. While conceptual, analytic, and judgmental efficiency have been only erratically associated with intellectual measures such as CEEB or Terman Concept Mastery scores, they have been consistently and significantly associated with measures of achievement such as final grade average. The correlations between cognitive skill efficiency and achievement sharpen that pattern. Cognitive skill efficiency to disturbing information does *not* covary significantly with any measure of intelligence (CEEB or Terman), but it does covary significantly and consistently with academic achievement (Org. $r = .49$, p $\angle$ .02; Stand. $r = .24$). These findings suggest that more successful predictions of academic success and failure in college may wait not upon finding "purer" measures of basal intellectual skill but upon developing more adequate measures of personality organization and, concomitantly, (ego) skills in mastering meaningful but disturbing information.

Cognitive Skill Efficiency and Questionnaire
Scales of Maladjustment and Control

Table 12–1 reports selected MMPI and Bernreuter correlations of cognitive skill efficiency. Whereas twenty-seven percent of the total correlations of both samples were significant beyond a .05 one-tailed probability level, most of the significant correlations belonged to the Organized sample (Forty-five percent of its correlations were significant).

One obvious finding is that personality traits are more closely associated with cognitive efficiency to threatening than to nonthreatening information. From data not reported, impaired skill efficiency covaries most regularly with a pervasively negative if not neurotic self-image in the *first* encounter with the threatening information. This finding agrees with those research results demonstrating that aroused needs and anxiety impair cognitive performance before practice effects adapt out or overshadow the motivational variable (D. H. Heath, 1958). Telling personality differences may not be discoverable from procedures that do not require the person to coordinate threatening information.

What were the more specific findings? Persons of poor skill efficiency, particularly to threatening information, report they are moody (MMPI D, Ma), anxious (Taylor), lack self-confidence (Bern. Lack self-conf.), are socially aloof and isolated (MMPI Si, Sc; Bern. Nonsocial), introversive (Bern. Introver), and tend to have poor control over their impulses (MMPI Pd; Block Undercontrol). Persons who skillfully coordinate disturbing information report good reflective control over their behavior (MMPI K).

Cognitive skill efficiency was also consistently related to more mature and dimensionally developed self-images (SIQ). Twenty percent of the Organized's but none of the Standard's SIQ and skill relationships were significant; however, except for self-image accuracy, the Standard sample's results consistently supported those of the Organized sample. The more skillfully a person accommodates to disturbing information (and it makes no difference whether it be threatening or nonthreatening), the more mature is he judged by others to be (Org. r = .51, p ∠ .01). And

TABLE 12-1: SELECTED CORRELATES BETWEEN COGNITIVE SKILL EFFICIENCY AND QUESTIONNAIRE SCALES OF MALADJUSTMENT AND CONTROL

QUESTIONNAIRE SCALES		COGNITIVE SKILL EFFICIENCY SCORES				
		TOTAL SCORE	THREAT	NON-THREAT	TIME 1	TIME 2
		r	r	r	r	r
MMPI						
Total	Org.[1]	−.43**	−.46**	−.32	−.49**	−.27
	Sta.	−.08	−.14	.10	−.20	.10
D	Org.	−.43**	−.38*	−.38*	−.45**	−.26
	Sta.	−.30*	−.38**	−.02*	−.26	−.29*
Pd	Org.	−.45**	−.44**	−.35*	−.48***	−.30
	Sta.	.07	.02	.16	−.05	.22
Sc	Org.	−.50***	−.54***	−.31	−.51***	−.33
	Sta.	−.11	−.13	−.02	−.21	.05
Ma	Org.	−.25	−.33	−.20	−.45**	−.10
	Sta.	−.02	−.05	−.02	−.14	.15
Si	Org.	−.56***	−.67***	−.27	−.53***	−.37*
	Sta.	−.20	−.23	−.06	.00	−.42***
Taylor MAS	Org.	−.49***	−.53***	−.40*	−.51***	−.37*
	Sta.[2]	−.12	−.17	.01	−.01	−.23
Bernreuter Introver.	Org.	−.38*	−.36*	−.34	−.34	−.29
	Sta.	−.11	−.14	.00	−.04	−.18
Nonsocial	Org.	−.40*	−.53***	−.14	−.26	−.30
	Sta.	−.08	−.04	−.15	−.18	.07
Control Scores						
MMPI K	Org.	.32	.38*	.12	.16	.41**
	Sta.	.04	.05	.03	−.15	.29
Barron Ego Strength	Org.	.26	.23	.21	.21	.19
	Sta.[2]	−.08	−.02	−.16	−.22	.12
Block Under-control	Org.	−.37*	−.35*	−.38*	−.36*	−.30
	Sta.[2]	−.27	−.26	−.22	−.18	−.33*

* p ∠ .05   [1] N = 23 for Organized sample correlates throughout table.
** p ∠ .025   [2] N = 26
*** p ∠ .01

skill efficiency to disturbing information after some adaptation to it (time two) is inversely related to unstable ($r = -.51$, p $\angle$ .01), incongruent ($r = -.44$, p $\angle$ .05), and autocentric ($r = -.44$, p $\angle$ .025) self-images. These results support previous findings that youths identified as able to master *successive* stresses also have significantly more congruent self-images (Funkenstein, *et al.*, 1957). But the finding that different personality traits do covary with skill efficiency in an initial encounter with stressful information suggest that the temporal variable cannot be ignored in personality and stress research.

Cognitive Skill Efficiency and Rorschach Measures

No method of analyzing the Rorschach predicted cognitive skill efficiency as well as the questionnaire scales did. Only five percent of the Klopfer scores were significant at a two-tailed .05 probability level, and, as has been seen so often, the pattern of results was erratic and frequently inconsistent between the samples. From those findings consistent for both samples, it can be said that persons who skillfully master the threatening information are reflectively introspective (Ror. FK %: Org. $r = .35$; Stand. $r = .37$, p $\angle$ .05) and possess many conventionally organized schemata (Ror. #P; Org. $r = .49$, p $\angle$ .02; Stand. f = .17).

The Rorschach clinical evaluations of self-organization and skill efficiency were consistently related in the predicted direction but not significantly.

Finally, only seven percent of the Holt autocentric and control scores were significant at the .05 one-tailed level. While the direction of the correlations was as predicted, their magnitude, with only a few exceptions, was scarcely comforting. Cognitive skill mastery of threatening information was most consistently associated with the ability to imagine adaptively many schemata coordinations (Ror. Con DD/Form DD: Org. $r = .44$, p $\angle$ .025; Stand. $r = .27$). Consistent with the findings of the separate skill measures, skillfully efficient persons tend to make more adaptively regressed schemata combinations (Ror. % DD × DE: Org. $r = .35$, p $\angle$ .05) and well-controlled coordinations

(Ror. Mean DE: Org. r = .36, p ∠ .05), particularly after some adaptation to the disturbing information, and tend not to show the illogical and disorganized formal thought linkages that characterize more severely disturbed persons (Ror. % Formal).

Cognitive Skill Efficiency and Anxiety Thresholds

The PT findings are very dramatic as Table 12–2 illustrates. Sixty-three percent of the PT correlations are significant at least at a one-tailed .05 probability level and all of them are in the predicted direction. The generalization can be firmly made that the lower a person's anxiety thresholds are, the greater will be his difficulty in skillfully adapting to disturbing information. The conclusion that greater anxiety is inversely related to cognitive skill efficiency is not inconsistent with the results from the other personality measures.

The ability to maintain stable schemata when confronted by nonpersonal but distracting information (Stroop) is also directly related, though not significantly, to skill efficiency, particularly to nonthreatening information.

TABLE 12–2: CORRELATES BETWEEN COGNITIVE SKILL EFFICIENCY AND PT AFFECTIVE INSTABILITY

PT SCORES		COGNITIVE SKILL EFFICIENCY SCORES				
		TOTAL SCORE	THREAT	NON- THREAT	TIME 1	TIME 2
		r	r	r	r	r
Total	Org.	−.34*	−.21	−.55***	−.26	−.37*
	Sta.	−.33**	−.31*	−.23	−.30*	−.29*
Threat	Org.	−.36*	−.20	−.59***	−.29	−.35*
	Sta.	−.34**	−.32*	−.25	−.30*	−.32*
Nonthreat	Org.	−.30	−.22	−.44**	−.21	−.35*
	Sta.	−.30*	−.29*	−.19	−.30*	−.22

* p ∠ .05
** p ∠ .025
*** p ∠ .01

Personality Correlates of Cognitive
Skill Improvement

Chapters 9 through 11 reported that the personality traits associated with improvement in skill efficiency over time were very tentative. Does a more general summary measure of skill improvement (defined as cognitive skill efficiency at time one subtracted from that of time two) clarify what personality traits covary with the ability to improve to disturbing information? We report primarily the Organized sample's results and only those not contradicted by the Standard sample's results which were generally nonsignificant. Skill improvement is associated with good reflective control (MMPI K: Org. r = .31; Stand. r = .43, p $\angle$ .005), with good defense effectiveness for ambiguous information (Ror. Mean DE: r = .38, p $\angle$ .05), with accurate accommodation to the form of externally given information (Ror. % Form Acc.: r = .41, p $\angle$ .025), and with good adaptive imagination (Ror. Con DD/Form DD: r = .41, p $\angle$ .025). Improvement in the skillful mastery of disturbing information is inversely related to unstable (SIQ r = −.51, p $\angle$ .01) and autocentrically organized (SIQ r = −.37, p $\angle$ .05) self-images.

It is now time to pull together these and other personality traits that distinguish cognitively (ego) efficient from inefficient men. Since the three preceding chapters have emphatically told us that the quality of adaptation to threatening rather than to nonthreatening information is more diagnostic of the quality of a person's self-organization, we chose to summarize the personality traits associated with skillful mastery of *threatening* rather than of disturbing (including nonthreatening) information. (See summary Table 5, Appendix B).

The person more skillful in adapting to threatening information, while not more intelligent than the person less skillful, consistently demonstrates superior achievement in the mastery of his culture and its language (CEEB Eng. Ach.) as well as in his formal academic work (Grade Average).

He is nonauthoritarian, open to information from both his external (Calif. F) and internal worlds (MMPI Hy). He is not a socially isolated or withdrawing type of person, uninterested in others (MMPI Sc, Si; Bern. Nonsocial), nor, on the other hand, is he an energetically aggressive and demanding person (MMPI Ma). He tends to think of himself as more objective (SIQ p ∠ .025). This more skillful person has a stable and perhaps more accurate self-image (SIQ). He rates himself on the Adjective Check List to be significantly (two-tailed) more self-driving (.02) and flexible (.05) than the less skillful person. He is judged by others (ACL) to be more self-sufficient (.02) while the less skillful person is judged to be impractical (.02), flighty, rebellious, tactless, and to have stronger needs (.05). On the SIQ, judges consistently rated the very skillful person to be more mature and to be significantly (two-tailed) more realistic (.02), ordered, objective, to have higher aspirations, and to think more clearly (.05). The Departmental Chairmen also consistently rated the more skillful person to be more determined and to be more emotionally stable.

Congruent with the greater achievement is the greater imaginal productivity and adaptiveness of the more skillful person (Ror. #R, Con DD/Form DD). He has more stable schemata, possessing higher anxiety thresholds for both threatening and nonthreatening information. The less skillfully efficient person's schemata organized around maternal-separation and homosexual themes are significantly more unstable than are the comparable ones of the more skillfully efficient person.

COGNITIVE SKILL EFFICIENCY AND SELF-ORGANIZATION

It is now time to confront the hypothesis that well organized men are more stably organized than poorly organized men. *Stably organized* was defined in two related ways: the skillfulness with which a person accommodated to disturbing information and the capacity to resist and recover from induced disorganization. We have already noted that the well and poorly organized men did not differ in their skill in mastering nondisturbing information (CEEB and Terman Concept Mastery test results). Chapter 8 suggested that the thematic content used in the skill tests did produce disorganization and defensive behavior and that some of the disturbing information was much more threatening than other types of information.

The principal hypothesis was *confirmed*. First, the well organized men were consistently, and significantly so for one sample, more efficient than the poorly organized men in skillfully adapting to disturbing information (Org. $F = 6.97$, p $\angle$ .025; Stand. $F^1 = 2.67$, p $\angle$ .20).

The Organized sample's Task × Organization F of 2.11, p $\angle$ .20, suggests that the well organized men were not significantly better than the poorly organized men in every skill. It is reasonable to expect that personality disorganization will affect some skills more severely than others, though we have only clinical hunches to rely upon for predicting what skills are more readily disrupted by disturbing information. Separate analyses of the skill efficiency tests suggest that although the well organized men of both samples were consistently more skillful than the poorly organized men on every skill test, they were only significantly more skillful on the conceptual (Stand. $F = 6.98$, p $\angle$ .025) and the analytic tasks (Org. $F = 8.73$, p $\angle$ .01).

The samples showed considerable improvement in skill efficiency, although only the Standard sample significantly *improved* in its second encounter with the disturbing information (Org. $F = 1.46$; Stand. $F = 23.74$, p $\angle$ .001). Improvement in skill efficiency occurred for both samples on the conceptual problems (Org. $F = 5.14$, p $\angle$ .05; Stand. $F = 16.37$, p $\angle$ .001) but only for the Standard sample on the analytic problems ($F = 16.0$, p $\angle$ .001).

The second definition of *stably organized* (resist disorganization or *recover* from induced disorganization) turned out to be too complex to measure unequivocally with the combined scaled skill scores. (The necessary use of standard scores in such a combined score washed out the consistently significant differences

---

[1] The F is based on the Standard sample's extreme twelve well and twelve poorly organized men who are a little more comparable to the consensually selected extreme criterion groups of the Organized sample. Parenthetically, the results with the Standard's twelve man groups did, in fact, parallel those of the eighteen man groups.

between the threat and nonthreat raw scores of the three skill tests; hence, it was impossible to test statistically specific *resist* and *recovery* sub-hypotheses predicting differential efficiency to the threat and nonthreat information. Appendix D reports the results for the raw scores of each skill test separately.) But very generally, to *resist* the potential disrupting effects of disturbing information was defined to mean that the well organized men were more skillful in their first encounter with such information than the poorly organized men and that their increased resistance would be seen most clearly with the more threatening information. Table 12–3, which reports the summary scaled threat and nonthreat scores, informally confirms that the well organized men of both samples did resist the disorganizing influences of the disturbing information, particularly the threatening information, more successfully than did the poorly organized persons.

The *recovery* meaning of *stably organized* was in turn defined in two ways. First, the *mastery* sub-hypothesis predicted that the well organized men would at time two be more skillful to the nonthreatening and significantly more skillful to the threatening information than the poorly organized men. Comparison of the appropriate scores in Table 12–3 shows the well organized men tend to master the disturbing information better. However, the well organized groups were much better than the poorly organized groups in mastering the nonthreatening information (22.7 and 16.0 scaled points) than they were better than the poorly organized groups in mastering the threatening information (15.3 and 7.2 scaled points). The second prediction of the recovery hypothesis was that the well organized men would *improve* more than the poorly organized men over the test periods. Only the well organized men of the Organized sample informally confirmed this *improvement* hypothesis for they improved 20.6 points while the poorly organized men improved only 4.3 scaled score points.

Given our present vantage point, what conclusions can now be stated that will not blur too many of the important details? First, judge identified well organized men are significantly better than poorly organized men in skillfully adapting to disturbing information, but their superiority is not equally as prominent among different skills, nor is it as evident when they are not

TABLE 12–3: IMPROVEMENT IN COGNITIVE SKILL EFFICIENCY FROM FIRST TO SECOND PRESENTATION OF DISTURBING INFORMATION

SAMPLE GROUPS	DAY 1			DAY 2			GRAND TOTAL	MEAN IMPROVEMENT TO		TOTAL MEAN IMPROVEMENT
	TH	NT[1]	TOTAL	TH	NT	TOTAL		TH	NT	
Organized										
WO	181.6[3]	179.0	360.6	189.7	191.5	381.2	741.8	8.1	12.5	20.6
PO	169.9	169.0	338.9	174.4	168.8	343.2	682.1	4.5	–.2	4.3
Standard[2]										
WO	176.0	174.8	350.8	192.5	201.0	393.5	744.3	16.5	26.2	42.7
PO	161.3	168.3	329.6	185.3	185.0	370.3	699.9	24.0	16.7	40.7

1 Nonthreat (Nt) doubled to be comparable to Threat (Th) score.
2 12 extreme WO and PO.
3 Higher scores means greater cognitive skill efficiency.

the most well organized men of the type of population we have described. The key hypothesis we consider to be confirmed. Second, the hypothesis that the well organized men resist more persistently and recover more rapidly from schemata disorganization than the poorly organized men was neither statistically confirmed nor disconfirmed. The hypothesis proved to be too complex to be settled unequivocally. If forced to make a summary assessment, the weight of the results do suggest well organized men resist disorganization better and recover from induced disorganization more rapidly than poorly organized men. We conclude that well organized men are more stably organized than poorly organized men.

COGNITIVE SKILL EFFICIENCY AND
SCHEMATA ANXIETY THRESHOLDS

Is skill efficiency significantly more impaired to threatening than to nonthreatening information? The answer is a strong though not quite unequivocal "yes" for every skill test. Both the Organized and Standard samples were more efficient in conceptual (p $\angle$ .001), analytic (p $\angle$ .001) and judgmental efficiency (p $\angle$ .20, p $\angle$ .025) with the nonthreatening than the threatening information. Since Chapter 8 demonstrated that the aggressive and sexual information (à priori defined as "threatening") was in fact more threatening than the relaxation and the working types of information for every person but one used in the two samples, the hypothesis that skill efficiency is more impaired to threatening than nonthreatening information has considerable phenomenological validity as well.

The phenomenological validity of the hypothesis was tested further by comparing the skill efficiency for the least and most threatening types of information for each person when least and most threatening information were defined by each person's own PT anxiety threshold scores. For both the Organized and Standard samples, the prediction that skill efficiency would be significantly better (two-tailed) with the PT defined least than with the most threatening information was significantly confirmed for the conceptual (p $\angle$ .01) and the analytic (p $\angle$ .05, p $\angle$ .01) but not for the judgment skill. Similar results were found for the PT-defined two and three least and two and three most threatening types of information. When skill efficiency for the PT-defined least and most threatening information was determined for the well and the poorly organized groups separately, similar results were found, except that now some of the differences for the judgment test approached or were significant for the poorly organized groups.

But can we now demonstrate that the *particular* anxiety threshold hierarchy of a person is significantly related to how skillfully efficient he is with that same information? We have already seen that the pattern of a *sample's* anxiety thresholds for different information does consistently (and occasionally significantly) covary with its skillfulness in mastering that information (pp. 229ff, 243, and 266). And earlier research has demonstrated the same relationship in a sample of schizophrenics (D. H. Heath, 1956). Now, let us look at the relation between an *individual's* anxiety thresholds for and his skill in solving problems containing different types of information. There was a consistent trend in both samples for cognitive skill efficiency to one type of information (the sum of a person's three skill scaled scores for one type of information) to be inversely related to his anxiety threshold for that same information. For example, a person with very little anxiety (when compared to others in his sample) about cooperatively working with others was more skillful (than the others in his sample) in solving problems composed of cooperative work themes (Org. r = $-.47$, p $\angle$ .025; Stand. r = $-.34$, p $\angle$ .025). Some further evidence suggests that a person's self-organization affects the degree to which his anxiety about information may be related to his efficiency in mastering that disturbing information. Whereas the anxiety threshold level for sexual information of the Organized sample's poorly organized men was significantly (two-tailed) inversely related to their efficiency in mastering sexual information (r = $-.60$, p $\angle$ .05), for example, the relation of its well organized men was opposite in direction (r = $.45$). Do very well organized persons when faced with very personally disturbing information aggressively counteract by marshalling and concentrating their energies to master the disturbance instead of passively reacting by becoming disorganized and impaired? Such findings suggest that researchers investigating the cognitive effects of anxiety might well pay attention to the degree (particularly the extremes) of self-organization of the persons they are studying.

Concluding, then, we can say skill efficiency is greater with phenomenally less than more disturbing information. However, the generality of the hypothesis may be limited by the type of skill, by the degree of threat in the information, and possibly by the degree of the person's self-organization.

SUMMARY

This chapter concludes Part III which has explored the developmental trend of stabilization in detail. What does our preliminary map tell us about self-organization and its stability? Of the skills that compose the self's "structures and activities," conceptual, analytic and synthetic, and judgmental skills were à priori identified to be the skills most relevant to the widest range of adaptive problems. These skills are moderately intercorrelated but not so highly interrelated as to measure similar coordinating processes. The efficiency with which these skills are used tends to be inversely related to the amount of anxiety the information phenomenally has for a person. When the stability of a person's self-organization is defined by a measure combining conceptual, analytic, and judgmental skill efficiency to disturbing (particularly threatening) information, stability is found to be directly related to academic achievement, strength of motivation, imaginal productivity, non-defensive openness to disturbing information (higher anxiety thresholds), degree of social interest in others, accuracy and stability of the self-image, and other traits predictable of more mature persons.

Keeping in mind all of the qualifications that the differences between the samples and the skill measures must inevitably stake around any concluding statement, it appears that well organized men are more stably organized men. They are able to maintain the stability of their self-organization and adapt more successfully to disturbing information than poorly organized men are able to do. In psychoanalytic terminology, we believe we have demonstrated that well organized men, in contrast to poorly organized men, tend to show more "resistivity against regression and instinctualization" (Hartmann, 1955, p. 20), and that their "thinking . . . concern[s] itself [more] with the connecting paths between ideas . . . and is not as . . . led astray by the *intensities* of those ideas" (Freud, 1900, p. 602).

PART **IV**

Measures of Maturity and Theoretical Implications

CHAPTER 13

Measures and Dimensions
of Maturity: A Comparison
and Assessment

It has been claimed the construct maturity (or mental health) is an inherently evaluative term. Furthermore, the use of consensual judgments to identify who adapts maturely and immaturely to a particular institutional setting only makes more transparent the prescriptive and subjective nature of the term. While not able to refute such arguments decisively, the research findings do at least moderate the severity of such claims. Consensual judgments of maturity do consistently and significantly covary with a variety of more traditional objective and validated measures of good self-organization and maturity. Chapter 6 demonstrated that the judge-identified mature and immature men differed consistently on measures tapping different "levels" of personality organization and Chapter 12 showed that they differed in their capacity to resist the disorganizing effects of disturbing information. The research has pushed our knowledge of *how* such men differ beyond what the judges could report determined their personal judgments of the difference between those who were, and those who were not, *mature*. The differences found between men who maturely and immaturely adapt to the

Haverford setting were not inconsistent with those found from other studies using different judges with different samples in different settings. Moreover, the results hang together meaningfully and theoretically. Very few significant results were found that violated our expectations. True, many of the expectations were not consistently or significantly confirmed; yet, the direction of the great weight of the results was congruent with theoretical expectations. These results suggest that consensual judgments did reflect some underlying psychological "reality," some set of trait congruences that were just not the product of the socially shared value standards of the selecting judges.

Two questions now arise: first, was it a wise decision to have used consensual judgments rather than more objective psychological measures to select mature and immature men? Would other more objective selection procedures have yielded more discriminating answers to the question of who is a mature person? Second, can the many complexly related trait congruences reported in the earlier chapters be clarified and organized into more fundamental personality dimensions? Would such dimensions approximate the major developmental trends hypothesized to define maturing persons?

Neither question can be answered definitively by this research. We did not measure the entire population on each of the tests of self-organization and identify criterion groups most extreme on each measure. So we can not fairly compare the discriminating power of the test measures to the consensual judgments of maturity. Nor can factor analyses of the data satisfactorily clarify the results, for our samples were too small, many of the scores of each personality test were not independently measured, several independent measures of each developmental trend were not available, and two of our more sensitive indices of maturity (social judgments and Rorschach clinical evaluations) were basically ordinal and not interval measures. However, in a book titled *Explorations of Maturity*, we dare to violate some statistical assumptions (and perhaps good judgment) to seek clues about ways in which each question could be answered if more extensive studies were conducted in the future. Those not interested in this more technical exploration will find an evaluative critique of our conclusions at the end of this section (page 308).

PSYCHOLOGICAL TEST DEFINITIONS OF MATURITY

The men of each sample were divided into two contrasting groups on the basis of those personality test scores that seemed to be the most powerful indices of maturity. We have already explored how consensually judged mature and immature groups (Chapter 6) and skillfully (ego) efficient and inefficient groups (Chapter 12) differ on many other personality measures. How do contrasting groups differ when they are defined by dichotomized MMPI total maladjustment scores, Rorschach clinical evaluations of self-organization and impaired skill scores, SIQ instability and incongruence measures, and PT affective instability scores? Although our aim is to compare the adequacy of different measures of maturity, the results can be alternatively viewed as summarizing the major validity relationships our studies have generated about each principal measure.

MMPI Adjustment Score

The men in each of the major samples were assigned to a mature or immature group on the basis of their MMPI Total score which is the best index of the tenor of the MMPI sub-scales. To enable other researchers to compare the results with their own test-defined samples, Table 13-1 shows just how extreme and homogeneous the two comparison groups are. Clearly they are not very extreme groups for their scores are within the range defining healthy personality adjustment. Furthermore, college educated males tend to score higher on the MMPI than the normal standardization sample so that, in comparison to male college samples (Bier, 1948; Goodstein, 1954), the immature groups (particularly that of the Standard sample) are scarcely very deviant. Actually, the mean MMPI scores of the mature groups are comparable to those of Golden et al. (1962) who selected their "normal" men from a population pool of 1953 male students, but our groups show more sub-scale variability.

Given the above reservations, what can now be said? The fol-

TABLE 13–1: MEAN MALADJUSTMENT SCORES OF
MMPI-DEFINED MATURE AND
IMMATURE GROUPS [1]

SAMPLE	MATURE		IMMATURE	
	MEAN	SD	MEAN	SD
Maturity	53.0 [2]	1.9	60.0	2.9
Organized	48.6	3.6	58.9	5.3
Standard	45.9	3.3	55.1	2.7

[1] Maturity sample: 8 men in each group; Organized sample: 11 men in each group; Standard sample: 14 and 15 men in mature and immature groups. Incomplete and overlapping test scores at the median resulted in reduced Ns.

[2] Low scores indicate greater maturity or better adjustment.

lowing generalizations are based on Table 1, Appendix E. The MMPI consistently discriminated in the predicted direction between good and poor performance on the other personality measures. As expected the MMPI groups were most consistently described by the other questionnaire scales (Bern.; SIQ), which demonstrates the men were consistent in their responses to the scales as well as consistent over several years in describing themselves as more or less mature. The MMPI-defined immature men of the Organized sample were rated by the judges to be significantly (two-tailed) more dissatisfied (.05) persons on the ACL. The men judged themselves to be more bottled-up (.05), intense (.05), and reflective (.02). While both the Organized and Standard samples' mature men rated themselves on the SIQ as reflective, their immature men rated themselves to be significantly (Org. p $\angle$ .02) and consistently more reflective. This finding, in view of the immature men's consistent SIQ self-ratings indicating high self-rejection (Org. p $\angle$ .01), may mean they are using more introversive methods to master internal disturbances. The MMPI-defined groups did not differ in the dimensionality of their self-image.

The Departmental Chairmen ratings were retabulated for the men now defined by the MMPI as mature and immature. The trend was for the mature men of the two samples composed of the more extreme groups (Maturity and Organized) to be rated as excellent more frequently than the immature men—and most noticeably for emotional stability, personableness, and determination.

Of greater interest are the differences in the personality measures in which the person has less control over what he reveals about himself. The MMPI-defined mature groups consistently had fewer autocentric schemata (Ror. pripro scores), fewer socially unconventional schemata (Ror. % Level 1), higher anxiety thresholds (PT), and were judged to be much more well organized persons from their Rorschachs (Clin. eval.) than the immature groups. With the exception of the immature men's greater introversive orientation (Ror. M %), the few significant differences found for the Klopfer Rorschach scores were inconsistently supported across the samples.

How discriminating is the MMPI of cognitive skill efficiency to disturbing information? The MMPI-defined mature men were significantly more skillful in their initial accommodation to disturbing information, particularly to the most threatening types of information. This superior accommodation to threat was consistently and significantly maintained for the analytic and judgmental but not for the conceptual skills (data not given).

Rorschach Clinical Evaluation of Organization

Both the Organized and Standard samples were divided into well and poorly organized groups on the basis of their clinically evaluated Rorschachs. (The means and SDs not given.) Given the differences between the individual and group administered forms of the Rorschach and the restricted variability of the Standard sample, the consistency of the results between the samples (summarized in Table 2, Appendix E) was unexpected.

Of considerable interest are the self-image differences, because these are not directly tapped by the Rorschach. The clinically defined poorly organized men generally are more maladjusted (MMPI; Bern.)and significantly more immature (SIQ). They tend to believe others think they are immature. The men differ most noticeably from the clinically defined well organized men by being more introversive (Bern.) and obsessionally self-critical and projectively critical of others (MMPI Pt, D, Pa). The ACL data of the Organized sample amplify this description. The well organized men judged themselves to be significantly (two-tail) more cheerful, reliable, and clear-thinking (.02), friendly and thorough (.05); the poorly organized men judged themselves to be more unemotional and worrying (.02), cynical, self-conscious, and resentful (.05). These self-image differences between the Rorschach-defined well and poorly organized men were supported by the following SIQ (two-tail) findings. The well organized men of both samples consistently rated themselves to have greater perspective about themselves (.01 and .02), to be more empathic, unshakable, realistic, and objective (.01 for one sample), to be more predictable, trustful, and adaptable (.02 for one sample), and to be other-centered as well as more calm (.05 for one sample).

What did the judges say? On the SIQ, the judges rated the Rorschach-defined well organized men to be significantly more predictable (.02) and, generally, more mature. The Department Chairmen tended to judge the well organized men to excel in emotional stability. Not one of the numerous and significant self-image trait differences violates what might have been expected. If the Rorshach gets at "deeper recesses" of the personality and if it is relatively refractory to conscious verbal distortion, then these self-image validity differences are remarkable, particularly in the face of the many studies questioning the validity of Rorschach clinical evaluations.

The clinically-defined poorly organized men do not have as differentiated and detailed a schemata organization (Ror. W %, d %, Dd + S %), as good control over their affectional needs (Ror. c(cF) %), and have higher assimilatory thresholds for emotion-inducing types of information (Ror. R to VIII–X %) than the well organized men. But the poorly organized men do tend to have significantly lower anxiety thresholds for both threatening and nonthreatening information, particularly for information organized around heterosexual and affectional relationships with others (PT data not given).

Not surprisingly (since the same data were used for the Holt scores as for the clinical evaluations), the poorly organized men have more autocentric schemata (Ror. pripro scores) and impaired skills (Ror. % Formal). They accommodate less accurately to information (Ror. % Form Acc.) and have less adequate control over their autocentric schemata (Ror. % DD × DE).

The clinically rated well organized men were neither significantly nor consistently more cognitively efficient in mastering disturbing information than the poorly organized men, which may suggest Rorschach clinical evaluations are not highly predictive of specific ego strengths or deficiencies in men from relatively homogeneous and highly intelligent populations.

Rorschach Measure of Impaired Skill (% Formal)

One of the more prominent and consistent findings reported in Chapter 4 was the discriminating power of Holt's % Formal score. Table 13–2 gives the groups' means and standard deviations of the Rorschach score for impaired skills defined by the % Formal score. In contrast to the MMPI-defined groups, the three samples' extreme groups are more clearly distinguished from each other.

TABLE 13–2: MEAN IMPAIRED SKILL SCORES OF ROR-SCHACH % FORMAL-DEFINED WELL AND POORLY ORGANIZED GROUPS

SAMPLE	WELL ORGANIZED		POORLY ORGANIZED	
	MEAN	SD	MEAN	SD
Maturity	11.9 [1]	5.4	34.9	10.0
Organized	13.9	3.9	39.1	14.9
Standard	7.5 [2]	3.7	27.7	9.6

[1] Low scores mean minimal impairment in thought processes.

[2] Group Rorschach results are not directly comparable to those of the other samples.

The division of the samples into well and poorly organized groups defined by unimpaired and impaired skills produced a wide range of significant differences (summarized in Table 3, Appendix E). How might the individual who reveals little or minimal thought disorganization to the Rorschach be described? Most descriptive is the quality of his self-image. His self-image is significantly more congruent, accurate and, perhaps, stable (SIQ). He reports himself to be significantly less immature (MMPI Total) than the youth who has impaired skills on almost every sub-scale of the MMPI. Most prominently, he consistently and significantly reports much better control or restraint over his behavior (MMPI Pd) and much less social alienation from others (MMPI Sc; Bern. Nonsocial). On the SIQ he reports himself to be significantly more energetic (two-tailed p $\angle$ .01). On the ACL the well organized male reports himself to be significantly (two-tailed) more logical, persistent, and mentally quick (.05). The general tenor of these self-reported traits is confirmed by the judge ratings of the men. The well organized men were judged on the SIQ to be more predictable (.02) and on the ACL to be more creative, enterprising, planful, precise, realistic and well coordinated (two-tailed p $\angle$ .05). The poorly organized men were judged to be more evasive, rebellious, and tactless (two-tailed p $\angle$ .05).

The flavor of these test differences finds support from the Department Chairmen judgments of only the Maturity and Organized samples. These samples' well organized men were more frequently judged to excel in determination, emotional stability, and personableness.

Men who have more stabilized skills are more imaginally productive (Ror. #R). Their schemata are more impersonally organized (Ror. % F) and are much more differentiated. They maintain control of their fantasy (Ror. FK + F + Fc %). The men with more skill impairment had a significantly higher Rorschach M % score, which is, at first glance, somewhat surprising, particularly in view of the common interpretation that such responses suggest greater imaginativeness, empathy, and resiliency to disrupting information. However, excessive M % is clinically interpreted as withdrawal into fantasy and, depending upon its quality, incipient delusional trends. What empirical evidence do we have about the meaning of M % in our samples? Increasing M % was significantly associated with stronger aesthetic values, lower SVIB scores for pragmatic and applied occupations, higher Rorschach W %, and more primary process thinking. These correlations suggest that persons of excessive M %, as our poorly organized men, may have a more global or less differentiated cognitive structure in which schemata coordinations are dominated more by affect than by logical or social conventions. The high M % of the poorly organized men apparently did not suggest greater originality to the Department Chairmen either. Only one poorly organized *but* eight well organized men from all the samples received ratings of excellence for originality.

The PT results were equivocal although the Maturity sample's results tentatively suggested men with thought impairment may have lower anxiety thresholds for both threatening and nonthreatening information and may consistently use rationalizing defenses (two-tailed p ∠ .05) more frequently than men with minimal thought impairment.

Somewhat disconcertingly, given the discriminating power of the % Formal score, only the well organized men of the organized sample were consistently more cognitively efficient to disturbing information. However, and possibly because of the Rorschach and TAJ test similarities, the men with greater skill impairment were significantly and consistently less imaginally productive (Org. p ∠ .01) than the men with less skill impairment which confirms the just reported Klopfer Rorschach results. The content of the poorly organized men's imagination was significantly (Org. p ∠ .05) and consistently less centered around other persons (+ and − affect needs towards others) just as their values (AVL Social) were significantly (.01) and consistently not socially oriented.

SIQ Stability and Congruence Scores

Chapter 5 reported the pattern of correlates of the SIQ stability and congruence scores to be similar but not identical. We investigated the personality differences between groups defined by stable and unstable as well as by congruent and incongruent self-images. From Table 13-3, which compares the mean stability and congruence scores of the contrasting groups, it is clear that the Standard sample's SIQ-defined groups were more similar to each other and less variable than the Organized sample's contrasting groups. The greater heterogeneity of the immature (unstable and incongruent) groups is consistent with the pattern we have seen when the immature groups are defined by other types of test scores.

Both the SIQ-defined stable and congruent groups differed *similarly* from their unstable and incongruent groups on several personality measures (summarized in Tables 4 and 5, Appendix E). For example, the stable and congruent persons are more emotionally healthy and well organized persons (questionnaire; Ror.). Their energy and talents are not constrictedly bound up by inner conflicts but are available for effective adaptation, par-

TABLE 13–3: MEAN AMOUNT OF STABILITY AND CONGRUENCE OF SIQ-DEFINED WELL AND POORLY ORGANIZED GROUPS

SAMPLE	STABILITY [1]				CONGRUENCE			
	WELL ORG.		POORLY ORG.		WELL ORG.		POORLY ORG.	
	Mean	SD	Mean	SD	Mean	SD	Mean	SD
Organized	16.3 [2]	4.5	31.2	6.3	26.3 [2]	9.0	56.8	15.1
Standard	18.8	3.2	28.9	3.7	19.6	3.1	33.2	4.8

[1] Standard sample: 17 and 16 men in well and poorly organized groups. Overlapping test scores at median resulted in reduced *Ns*.
[2] Low scores mean greater stability and congruence of the self-image.

ticularly for superior academic work (.02) and a willingness to become involved with other persons (Bern. Nonsocial). They have many maturely organized schemata (Ror. % PriPro, % Content) which can be imaginatively coordinated to make effective accommodations (Ror. Con DD/Form DD). They are more frequently judged on the ACL to be planful, realistic, and well coordinated persons (.01). On the SIQ, the stable and congruent groups, judged by others to be more mature on many traits, were most consistently and significantly judged to be unshakable, adaptable, open, and self-perspective persons (.01). Persons of unstable and incongruent self-images, on the other hand, more frequently report themselves to be dissatisfied and are judged by others to be apathetic and purposeless (ACL, .01).

More specifically, persons of *stable* self-images may have more reflective control over their behavior (MMPI K; Ror. FK %) but this does not mean they are introversively inhibited persons unable to act spontaneously and emotionally (Ror. CF %). They are less authoritarian (Calif. F, .05) and value altruistic-loving rather than manipulative and controlling types of relationships (AVL Social, Politic. .05). Judges, using the Adjective Check List, significantly differentiated between the men with stable and unstable self-images on so many maturity traits we can only highlight some of the more significant differences. The stable person was judged to be more considerate, dedicated, efficient, empathic, logical, planful, realistic, responsible, self-insightful, (ACL, .01) and (for both samples) more ordered, easy going and less aggressive (SIQ, .05). The person with an unstable self-image was judged to be disorderly, distractible, irresponsible, purposeless, scattered, undependable, unrealistic, and vague (ACL, .01). The Department Chairmen's ratings of the stable and unstable men were inconsistent for the samples. Finally, men with more stable self-images cognitively master disturbing information consistently and significantly more efficiently than men with less stable self-images (Org. $F = 28.8$, $\angle$ .001; Stand. $F = 5.9$, p $\angle$ .025), largely due to their more skillful analytic performance (data not given).

Persons of very *congruent* self-images are less neurotic and introversive (Bern. Neurotic, Introver.), and are more frequently judged by others to be realistic, planful, competitive, and well-coordinated (ACL, .01) as well as more adventurous (SIQ, .05) young men. In contrast, persons whose private self-images are sharply discrepant from what they believe others think of them report being dissatisfied (ACL, .01), withdrawn (MMPI Sc), and depressed (MMPI D). They are judged by others to be unambitious and slow as well as apathetic and purposeless (ACL,

.01). They highly value aesthetic harmony and manipulative control of others (AVL Aesth., Politic., .05) but this may be compensatory for their own lack of internal harmony (Ror. Clin. eval.) and for their alienation from others (Bern. Nonsocial; MMPI Sc). The internal world of such persons is moved by many unstably and primitively organized schemata (Ror. % PriPro), not autonomous of strong regressive wishes and drives (Ror. % Level 1, Sum DD). Their thinking, as is their self-image, is illogical, inconsistent, and occasionally bizarre and unconventional (Ror. % Formal). Their defensive control of such disorganization may be fragile (Ror. Mean DE); they are less able to rely on regressively adaptive coordinations to meet stress than persons of more congruent self-images (Ror. % DD × DE).

PT Affective Instability

As with the other tests, the men in each sample were dichotomized on their PT Total score, the means and standard deviations of which are reported in Table 13-4. Apparently, the three groups of affectively stable (called well organized) and the three groups of unstable (called poorly organized) men are each reasonably homogeneous, although the PT-unstable groups are much more variable than the stable groups.

While the PT results (summarized in Table 6, Appendix E) are less impressive than those reported for the other personality measures, they do suggest persons who have low anxiety thresholds have less adequate control (Block Under-control; Ror. c(cF) %; Holt control) and report themselves to be more anxious (Taylor) as well as more maladjusted and immature (Bern., SIQ). Their greater maladjustment is confirmed by the clinical Rorschach ratings. On the SIQ, the PT-defined well organized men consistently and significantly (two-tailed) reported themselves to be more easy-going (.01) and empathic (.05). But neither the SIQ judge ratings nor the Adjective Check List differentiated between the PT-defined well and poorly organized groups.

TABLE 13-4: MEAN AMOUNT OF AFFECTIVE INSTA-
BILITY OF PT-DEFINED WELL AND
POORLY ORGANIZED GROUPS

SAMPLE	WELL ORGANIZED		POORLY ORGANIZED	
	MEAN	SD	MEAN	SD
Maturity	61.7[1]	17.0	153.4	49.5
Organized	62.1	25.9	165.0	47.4
Standard	55.7	14.4	147.2	59.0

[1] Scores adjusted to be comparable to those of other samples. Low scores mean less affective instability or higher anxiety thresholds.

Although some inconsistencies marred the map of the Department Chairmen ratings, PT-defined well organized men were consistently and more frequently rated to be emotionally stable than the poorly organized men. A closer analysis of the PT and Department Chairmen ratings revealed a very intriguing finding. Nine men or twenty-six percent of the PT-defined affectively unstable men but only one man or three percent of the PT-defined stable men were rated excellent in originality. Since I have no independent measure of originality or creativity other than the Department Chairmen ratings, I cannot track down what this finding may mean. But two possibilities immediately come to mind: 1) Let us assume good self-organization is directly associated with originality (i.e., stable schemata coordinations are more reversible, combinable, etc.). Then the facile use of the PT as an index of schema stability (and hence self-organization) may either be incorrect or the PT may be complexly related to good self-organization (extremely high anxiety thresholds may index overly rigid but *not* stable schemata). 2) Let us assume the PT is one measure of schema stability. Then, good self-organization may *not* be simply or directly related to creativity as I have already suggested in Chapter 6.

The PT was more predictive of cognitive efficiency. Well organized persons, defined by higher anxiety thresholds, are generally and consistently more cognitively efficient to disturbing information than poorly organized men. They are significantly more skillful in mastering the nonthreatening information following some accommodation to the task. The superior cognitive efficiency of the PT-defined well organized men is due primarily to their analytic and conceptual rather than their judgmental mastery of disturbing information (data not given).

Comparison and Assessment of Measures of Maturity

Was it a wise strategy to have used consensual judgments rather than psychological tests to identify the more mature and immature men of the Haverford population? A "wise strategy" to discover and predict what? This is our dilemma for we have no independently defined criterion against which to compare whether social judgments or MMPI scores or Rorschach evaluations were the better predictors. Ideally, if we had such an independent criterion, we could determine statistically just what the best predictor or combination of predictors was. Practically, we must rely primarily on our intuition to answer the question.

Our hunch is that in exploratory studies where the dimensions of that which is to be predicted are not firmly known and where methods of their assessment are not yet constructed, the most global type of selection criterion is the most appropriate. Consensual judments were the most economical as well as the best predictors of the widest range of other personality measures indexing facets of good self-organization (Chapter 6). The social judgment definition of self-organization or maturity successfully predicted self-image dimensionality, maturity, and various components of the content of the self-image, Rorschach measures of schemata organization, and cognitive efficiency to disturbing information. Only the consensual judgment criterion separated out the skillfully efficient from the inefficient person *and* covaried with a wide range of other personality measures as well.

The above hunch subsequently received some support when I sought a more objective (though approximate) method of evaluating the predictive power of the different measures of maturity. The men of the Organized sample were ranked on each of the eight measures we have summarized in detail: social judgments (Chapter 6), Rorschach clinical evaluations, Holt's % Formal score, MMPI Total score, SIQ stability and congruence scores, PT Total score, and cognitive skill to threatening information (Chapter 12). Each person's general median rank on all of these measures was obtained, and then the median ranks of the entire sample were in turn ranked to give a general rank measure of maturity. I was surprised by the great consistency in rank position on the different indices, given the very disparate types of measures used. For example, the ranks of the most mature man (defined by the lowest rank on the general measure of maturity) were, in order: 2, 1, 1, 7, 3, 1, 3.5, and 8; the ranks of the most immature man were 24, 24, 24, 24, 22, 24, 24, and 24. Of course, greater variability in rank position occurred for those toward the middle of the distribution, but such consistency across a variety of measures was still surprising. The rank order correlations between each index of maturity and the general maturity measure were then determined and in order of predictive efficacy were: SIQ congruence (.85), social judgment (.80), Holt % Formal (.77), Rorschach clinical evaluation (.75), SIQ stability (.75), MMPI Total (.47), PT Total (.20), and cognitive skill efficiency (.15). Out of curiosity, the entire procedure was redone, but scores for cognitive skill efficiency at time one and at time two were included instead of the score for cognitive efficiency to threatening information. The correlations were higher by some six to ten points for most of the other measures and cognitive efficiency at time two was significantly related to the general maturity measure (.76), indicating that quality of mastery of disturbing information after an initial accommodation to it is an important aspect of maturity as Funkenstein also found (1957). These informal and tentative results suggest that other researchers interested in exploring the area of maturity may want to use social judgments as an economical preliminary screening method and then subsequently may deem it fit to refine their groups using self-image dimensional and selected Rorschach measures.

Partisans of either the questionnaire or the projective test methods may be disturbed by the comparative validity of the other type of measure, for the research does demonstrate that the questionnaire (including the SIQ) and the projective type of methods are related to each other and that both probably complement each other. Given the gloom that hovers around the Rorschach (Meehl, 1954), its results were most impressive. Both Rorschach clinical ratings of self-organization and Holt's measures of thought disorganization (and some of his other scores as well) significantly predicted to a large number of personality traits. What makes the Holt scoring system so attractive and potentially superior to other Rorschach ordering procedures is that it codifies actual clinical interpretative practice into theoretically meaningful categories. In comparison, the traditional Rorschach scoring procedures (Klopfer) were just not as useful in our research. The scores that reputedly index emotional maturity (M, FC, Fc) did not relate to any of the large number of other indices of maturity and good control available on the men. If sampling limitations account for such a result, then much closer attention must be given in the future to the types of populations to which the standard Rorschach scores apply. Our results, of course, do not invalidate the use of the Klopfer scores which when sensitively *combined* with other methods of analysis may produce insightful and valid judgments. This specific Rorschach problem we did not investigate. The research suggests that neither the Rorschach procedure nor the questionnaire scales are hopelessly antiquated, and are perpetuated only by dogmatic prejudice or inadequate methodology.

The selection of maturely organized persons demands a complex multidimensional judgment. The complexity of the assessment criterion, whether it be quality of adaptation, ego-strength, or scholastic efficiency must be captured by procedures which approach the multidimensional structure of the adaptive criterion. This is the lesson of factor analytic ideas of test validity (Fruchter, 1954), of many empirical assessment studies (Stern, Stein, & Bloom, 1956) and of our research. For example, the PT which was the best predictor of the stability of cognitive skills was only occasionally related to a wider nexus of personality measures. These focused tests may come more into their own when research such as that illustrated in Part III, which intensively investigates a specific developmental dimension, becomes more frequent.

FACTORIAL DIMENSIONS OF MATURITY

Developmental and personality theory have suggested that a map of five developmental trends describes the maturing person. Such a map has directed and ordered our exploratory venture into the world of the mature person. But such preliminary charts must be redrawn and redrawn again after explorations like ours. Just how the chart should be drawn is not yet clear. Could factor analytic procedures clarify where we have been as well as suggest a more manageable and comprehensive view of the personal worlds of our maturing youths? This question can only be explored by playfully abandoning a number of assumptions that factor analytic procedures require must be met. The more somber reader should skip these next few pages, for I will now violate several practices that define good factor analytic procedure. The size of the samples is much too small; most of the MMPI, Rorschach, and SIQ subscores were not empirically independent, although most were linearly independent; some of the trends were not represented by more than one measure and therefore could not be identified as factors; and, in spite of our holistic assumption which hypothesizes correlated factors, an orthogonal rather than an oblique rotation of the factor matrix was used. (Given these and other limitations, it scarcely seemed worthwhile to go to the trouble of getting involved in the more complex oblique rotations, higher order factors, or too detailed descriptions of our procedures and results.)

The procedure and results will be only cursorily summarized. Selected scores of the two major samples (intelligence and achievement, MMPI and Bernreuter, valuator, etc.) were analyzed using Thurstone's centroid method. Very briefly, the major findings were that five interpretable factors accounting for thirty-six percent of the total variance of the Organized sample's scores were identified. In describing these dimensions, I will concentrate most centrally on only those measures most highly correlated with the dimension. (Table 1, Appendix F, lists those measures loaded on the factor at least at a .05 two-tailed significance level, the most convenient objective criterion available for identifying the correlates to report.)

Factor I: Allocentricism-Autocentricism (12.4% of the variance)

The allocentric pole of the factor is described by adaptively regressed and imaginative coordinations of schemata, adaptive improvement to disturbing information over time, and by conventionally and commonly organized schemata. Autocentricism is defined by skill impairment, unsocialized and bizarre drive-organized schemata, an incongruent self-image, poor defense effectiveness, self-reported withdrawal, and depressive trends. The dimension appears to represent more a primary-secondary process type of dimension than one just of immaturity-maturity or disorganization-organization, primarily because the more holistic measures of immaturity and maturity are not loaded as highly on this factor as are the Holt measures of autocentric thinking.

Factor II: Competence-Incompetence (7.3% of the variance)

This dimension seems to involve the turning of energy away from self-absorbing activities to mastering actively and assertively one's external environment. Competence is defined by a high grade average, judged maturity and effectiveness, self-assertive, dominant interpersonal relationships, high verbal and abstract skills, the ability to make skillful adaptations to disturbing information. Incompetence is most clearly related to the failure to achieve a stable identity, to neurotic incapacities, and to failure to participate in socially responsible activities. The dimension might otherwise be labeled stability-instability but the relatively low loadings of the Rorschach measures of unstable schemata and cognitive skill inefficiency convinced us that adaptive competence in fashioning a stable identity, developing rewarding social responsibilities, and achieving intellectually seems best to describe the dimension.

Factor III: Symbolization (internalization) of Experience-Behavioral (externalization) Surgency (6.1% of the variance)

The name of this factor attempts to capture more than just the traditional introversion-extroversion distinction, for the factor seems to be one in which reflective imagination or the capacity to symbolize imaginally one's experience is used for adaptation rather than just self-involving purposes. Reliance on symbolizing experience for adaptive purposes is described by adaptive imagination, intellectualization, imaginal productivity, depressive and self-blaming traits, and improvement in associative judgment to disturbing information. Behavioral surgency refers to the externalization of a person's energy into self-assertive, commanding social relationships that seek approval of others primarily through impersonal and practical uses of power in the manipulation and direction of others. The relation of this dimension to maturity seems to be more ambiguous than is the case for the other dimensions.

Factor IV: Reflective Control-Affective Instability (6.1% of the variance)

This dimension seems to organize those measures dealing with the ability to control inner tension or anxiety and perhaps to isolate it from interfering with adaptation. Some of Klein's and Witkin's measures of field-articulation or field-independence might be related to this or the following dimension.

Factor V: Emotional Receptivity-Intellectual Constriction (4.6% of the variance)

This factor refers to the readiness with which aroused impulses and affects are assimilated into the self. Persons high in emotional receptivity are sensitive to emotional stimulation, have strong appreciative aesthetic values, and are more open to more earthy if not primitive and unrefined impulses.

Another principal finding was that only two of the Standard sample's obtained factors were theoretically interpretable (data not given). Its first factor was defined by unstable and autocentric (drive-organized) schemata. That the sample had no severely disorganized persons in it may account for the low loadings of other measures of autocentricism such as impaired skills on the factor. The second factor was a more restricted version of the competence factor of the Organized sample. Verbal abstract ability and cognitive skill efficiency to disturbing information as well as greater imaginal productivity were its major defining measures.

The last major finding is primarily an impression. The mature person cannot be comprehended only by one general dimension or factor. If social judgments of self-organization are one of the more valid indices of maturity, as the chapter has earlier claimed, then it is clear from the data of both samples that at least two, if not more, dimensions are required for understanding a mature individual. Both the consensual judgments of self-organization and the SIQ judge measure of maturity were primarily related to allocentricism and competence. Almost eighty percent of the variance of the consensual judgments of self-organization was accounted for by the first two factors in the Organized but not in the Standard sample. Both consensual measures of maturity were loaded most highly on competence.

These results are not very decisive, for our interpretative labels do seem arbitrary, given the imprecise meaning of many of the measures. Yet, the analysis has been fruitful for it does suggest that the term *maturity* is multi-dimensional, that the results of the research cannot be collapsed into one general factor, that there are some very consistent but different patterns of correlates among the many new measures the research has introduced, and that perhaps our developmental map must be modified to include a dimension like competence. To the theoretical implications of these and other findings we now must turn.

SUMMARY

The results of this summary chapter must be taken casually and lightly for we have too frequently trespassed beyond the boundaries of good statistical judgment. Nevertheless, the results hint that many of our measures of maturity have considerable validity and are quite discriminating. Our impression is that social judgments of maturity need not be just value judgments. And if personal preferences and standards did creep into the judgments of who was well and poorly organized, the judgments still reflected an empirical order that made a great deal of psychological sense. The determinants of the social judgments of self-organization may have been primarily two: competence in adapting to one's environment (including forming a stable identity) and allocentricism.

Was it a wise decision to have used consensual judgments to define the criterion groups? Yes, though in hindsight we could have increased the homogeneity of the groups if criteria of allocentricism had been given the judges. The question of the adequacy of our developmental map is more complex; we return to it in the next chapter.

CHAPTER 14

Some Reflections
About Maturity

Our exploration produced an abundance of interesting findings and hypotheses for future research about maturity and psychological health. Undoubtedly some of these findings will not be confirmed in subsequent validation studies, if only because of sample idiosyncracies, test and statistical artifacts. But the entire pattern of the results does make psychological sense. The variety of judging and selection procedures, the number of diverse types of psychological processes measured, the variety of samples, the congruence between disparate psychological tests such as the questionnaire MMPI and projective Rorschach measures, as well as the internal consistency of the complex pattern of results guarantee that the findings cannot be simply explained by some combination of artifacts or uncontrolled variables. Accepting that the findings are reliable what do they imply for personality theory? Following this question, I ask another: do our assumptions about maturity affect the generality of our findings? I conclude by returning to the themes of Chapter 1 to reflect about the meaning of maturity.

SOME THEORETICAL IMPLICATIONS

Implications for Psychoanalytic Ego Psychology

From the ego psychologist's view, the book could well be titled *Explorations of Ego Structure*. The ego, as it matures, becomes a more stable, differentiated and integrated, autonomous, allocentrically organized structure which allows memories and experience to be more readily assimilated into consciousness. The burden of the book has been to pin this conception of ego development down to empirical measures. The research has woven a loose but highly interrelated web of findings that is consistent with the leading ideas of contemporary ego psychologists.

Certainly, a central and continuing focus of psychoanalytic ego psychology has been the study of the adaptation of a person to internal sources of disturbing information (usually dependency, sexual, and aggressive needs) and the ways in which regulating structures, such as defenses, are elaborated to reduce the disorganizing consequences of such information in order to maintain the continued survival of the organism. Hartmann has modified Freud's theory to suggest that some structures may be constitutionally given and not the product of a person's adaptation to disturbing information (i.e., do not develop out of frustration of basic needs), that any structure (even that which develops primarily in response to disturbing information) may achieve and maintain its functional effectiveness (its autonomy) to the most disturbing information. One measure of the strength of a person's ego is his capacity to resist regression to defensive or maladaptive behavior when he must adapt to disturbing information. Or, in the language of Hartmann,

Developmentally speaking, one main trend can be characterized as away from instinctualization of ego functions toward greater [secondary] autonomy, that is, better protection against instinctualization and regression. The degrees of autonomy vary, of course, from individual to individual, according to the developmental stage, and to different functions of the ego. If we take an over-all picture of an individual ego, the degree of autonomy is correlated with what we call ego strength, though it is not its only source (1955, pp. 11–12).

The research supports this theoretical statement in most respects, for persons more maturely developed (of greater ego strength) were able to adapt to personally disturbing and threatening information more competently than persons less maturely developed. Furthermore, we found that resistance to regressive thinking (our measure of stability but for Hartmann an index of ego autonomy) did vary as a function of the type of ego function or skill. Finally, ego autonomy was found to be not the "only source" of ego strength. That is, cognitive skill efficiency to disturbing information did not predict as well to a general measure of ego strength (maturity) as did other measures of ego function (self-image congruence). However, ego autonomy is more "correlated with . . . ego strength" following some knowledge of the disturbing information.

A topic of lively concern in contemporary ego psychology is the type of energy used by the ego (Hartmann, 1955; Lustman, 1957; White, 1963). For Freud, ego structures develop as the result of the neutralization of libidinal energy (and for Hartmann, countercathexes like defenses as the result of the neutralization of aggressive energy, 1950), thus reducing the amount of libidinal cathexes (and aggressive energy) available (1923). For White (1963), the ego has its own independent sources of non-instinctual energy, so that increased ego development does not necessarily reduce the amount of libidinal cathexes available. Two contrasting (but over-simplified for we ignore that extensive defenses of disorganized persons may inhibit manifestations of drive energy) predictions seem to follow from these positions. Freud should expect the unsocialized drive strength (amount of cathexes) of the more maturely developed men to be less than that of the immaturely developed men. On the basis of just his independent ego energy theory, White would predict no difference. What do our findings suggest about the predictions? The mature and immature men did not differ significantly in the amount of drive-dominated fantasies (Ror. % Content) nor in the degree of the demand their drives made for assimilation and accommodation (Sum Defense Demand). Also, the mature men were not significantly less disturbed by conflictual and drive-involved information than the immature men (PT). Not only is there no evidence to support the hypothesis that the mature men have less unsocialized drive energy available for adaptation, but as Chapter 6 demonstrated, the mature men seemed to have an enormous amount of energy (more socialized?) available for all kinds of adaptive tasks. But other problems so complicate the interpretation of these results (the groups may differ in constitutionally determined amount of energy) that no decisive answer can be given about either prediction.

Both theorists would, however, predict that the more mature person's ego, regardless of its energy source, would be more socialized, would be less impaired by formal primary process condensations and autisms (White, 1963, p. 190). This prediction was very consistently confirmed (Ror. % Formal).

The research findings and procedures may also help to clarify some aspects of ego psychology theory, the abstractness and imprecision of which has made it refractory to direct and clear test. That several new procedures developed to measure some psychoanalytic constructs (Holt's primary process and adaptive regression and the anxiety threshold and cognitive skill measures) are moderately valid opens up new possibilities for testing theoretical propositions. For example, Holt's measures of formal thought (% Formal) and of unsocialized memory or idea (% Content) regression may help to clarify the meaning of regression. If such scores do measure different types of regression, we could ask "How unitary is the process of regression?" Freud suggested that topical, temporal (perhaps Holt's % Content score), and formal (possibly Holt's % Formal score) regression "are, however, one at bottom and occur together as a rule; for that which is older in time is more primitive in form and in the psychical topography lies nearer to the perceptual end" (1900, p. 548). In data from five samples (cf. Table 2, Appendix A for the data of the major samples), formal and content measures of regression covaried only moderately, thereby suggesting that the unitary theory of regression or the meaning of Holt's scores (or both) need further clarification.

The close interdependence between the efficiency with which

a particular skill is used to process disturbing information and various personality traits provokes questions for both the ego psychologist and the intelligence theorist. Do similar types of personality traits covary with skill (ego) efficiency in dealing with nondisturbing information? That personality traits are more closely and consistently related to the mastery of threatening than to less threatening information suggests the answer will be "no." Perhaps this is why diagnosticians have not found the more factorially pure measures of intelligence composed of "nonmeaningful" content useful for predicting to any range of adaptive tasks. Long ago, Thorndike (1927) and, more recently, Guilford (1956, 1959b) recognized that the efficiency with which abilities were used varied with different types of information, whether concrete, mechanical, symbolic, or social. Do our results suggest that to measure ego strength, tests must use phenomenally relevant disturbing information that require for their solution not only intellectual skills but also personality capabilities such as the inhibition of affective responses?

Let us briefly explore the relationship between the most sophisticated psychoanalytic attempt to identify more fundamental cognitive (ego) controls and our own findings. Chapter 7 reported that Klein and his coworkers have sought to identify more basic "mediating structures [than secondary process skills] that take their form from drives, from constitutional characteristics of the relevant ego apparatuses, and from the adaptive problems the individual has encountered" (Gardner, *et al.*, 1960, p. 3). Can the relationships between our more complex cognitive skills and various personality traits be understood in terms of such cognitive controls? For example, efficient skill performance (certainly to the TCT and TA-S type of information) requires the person to isolate any anxiety induced by the disturbing information from interfering with the processes of solving the problem. To isolate, to attend focally, to concentrate, to ignore competing irrelevant (affective) cues seems to be similar to Klein's (1958) field-articulation (formerly called field-independence, Witkin, *et al.*, 1954). Field-articulation has been described this way: ". . . that persons adept at field-articulation . . . also inhibit response[s] to irrelevant embedded *items* while attending to relevant *surrounds* support[s] the interpretation of the dimension as representing generalized individual differences in the selectiveness of attention" (Gardner, *et al.*, 1960, p. 19).

Complex cognitive skills may be higher order organizations of field-articulation and other cognitive controls (Gardner, *et al.*, 1959). If so, it is then understandable that cognitive skills are more closely related to criterion measures of maturity than the cognitive control tests have been reported to be (Gardner, *et al.*, 1959). That the cognitive skills may be "higher order" organizations of various cognitive controls is suggested by the similarity between Witkin's findings (1954) and our own conclusions. He discovered that persons unable to resist the effects of competing cues were more passive and immature. They had low self-esteem and poor emotional control. We found that persons who are inefficient in processing disturbing information (which presumably requires resisting the disruptive effects of irrelevant cues) also have the same personality traits. Since our research did not include measures of field-articulation or of the other cognitive controls, we cannot check these hunches.

While the leading empirical edge of ego psychology is the effort to identify basic cognitive modes of assimilating and accommodating to information, some theorists have begun to reconsider the relation of the ego to the self (Jacobson, 1954; Rubins, 1958) or to self-esteem (White, 1963). It is a peculiar anomaly in the history of personality research and theory that researchers interested in the self-image and self-esteem, and theoreticians preoccupied with psychoanalytic constructs have found so little in each other's work to stimulate efforts to find either theoretical or empirical links between the two traditions.

Both "ego" and "self" are sufficiently vague and ambiguous terms to make any extended discussion of their relation at that level of generality futile. I prefer to talk in terms of schemata (including the self-image), cognitive skills, and valuators whose developmental maturity is described by their stability, integration, allocentricism, autonomy, and availability to awareness. The self-image (taken by Rogers and others as a representation of the self) and cognitive skills (understood by us as one index of the ego) were assumed to be related, since both were structures whose level of organization is defined by the same developmental dimensions.

What do our findings about the self-image imply for ego psychology theory? Like valuators (ego interests), the self-image can be considered to be either a derivative or an autonomous ego structure which selects and regulates what information is assimilated, and initiates and determines what accommodations are made. It has the same developmental properties that define any ego structure. For example, the developing self-image may be initially organized by primary process types of coordinations and drive content (omnipotent fantasies) and only later by reality demands (more allocentric considerations). The research results do suggest that self-image immaturity (defined by the SIQ developmental dimensions) covaries directly with ego immaturity (defined by Rorschach primary process and cognitive skill measures). Just as the ego eventually becomes a coherent stable organization ruled by the reality principle, so does its component (from the view of the ego psychologist) self-image become more stable, congruent (integrated), allocentric, and accurate. Could not the dimensional maturity of the self-image then be one index of the level of ego organization? This is not to claim that the analysis of the self-image is *the* royal road to understanding ego strength, for the developmental maturity of the self-image is only moderately correlated with that of the ego's cognitive skills and schemata organization.

However, the ego psychologists are not alone in seeing only part of a person. Just as they have ignored the conceptual relation of the self-image (and the associated empirical research results) to other ego structures, so have the self theorists such as Rogers ignored the conceptual relation of the cognitive skills or secondary processes to other self-structures and activities. By showing that the major concerns of the ego psychologist and the self-theorist can be theoretically understood in terms of similar developmental dimensions and by producing some empirical evidence that links the level of ego organization (primary process and cognitive skills) and the self-image together (as well as the related projective and questionnaire assessment traditions), perhaps an adventurous theorist will soon bring some greater conceptual integration to what appear to be really complementary and not divisive theoretical and methodological traditions in personality theory.

Implications for Other Cognitive Viewpoints

In as much as the research was heavily centered on cognitive constructs and the focus of Part III was on personality differences in processing disturbing information, the research may be relevant to other cognitive models of adaptation. Cognitive theorists such as Festinger (1957) and Miller, Galanter, and Pribram (1960) have been concerned with how information that is dissonant or incongruent with a person's cognitive structure or Images (schemata) and Plans (possibly valuators?) affects his adaptation. Dissonance is aversive or anxiety arousing. The person strives to reduce dissonance by a variety of methods, some of which may involve the defensive assimilation of the information or the use of operations (TOUT) to modify Images or schemata to be more congruent with the information. While the language of our research seems to be similar, its precise relation to these other cognitive theories may be little more than verbal. The experimental operations that define the basic terms of this research on maturity differ from those most frequently used in research on cognitive dissonance. The strategy of the research is also different: ours can be interpreted to be a correlational study of individual differences in resolving dissonance, not an experimental study manipulating variables that affect, for example, the amount of dissonance. Only the procedure for exploring the autonomy of the self-image approximates the typical methods of cognitive dissonance research. We have not explored the process of reducing dissonance *qua* dissonance; instead, we have used the phenomenon of mastering dissonant information as a means to investigate maturity. However, the research may be pertinent to such questions as these: what are the personality traits of persons who can tolerate dissonance without resorting to defensive types of maneuvers or premature decisions; what traits characterize persons who can operate on dissonant (threatening) information without regressive impairment in the efficiency of their operations? If one measure of dissonance is the amount of anxiety and disorganization induced by incongruent information, does the Phrase Association Test offer an independent method by which to identify what types of interpersonal information are likely to be more dissonant than other types for an individual? Just as personality variables such as self-esteem have been explored in order to understand the effects of persuasive information, so other personality variables such as incongruence of the self-image may be useful in refining predictions of how individuals will respond to dissonant information. The time appears to be approaching when experimentally based cognitive theory may help to clarify the domain of personality and ego psychology just as drive reduction learning theory, in the hands of Dollard and Miller (1950), helped to clarify some aspects of psychoanalytic theory. Levy's (1963) enlightening analysis of the clinical process of interpretation in cognitive dissonance terms is a harbinger of such a trend.

Implications for Motivational Theory

Motivational theory remains in a state of disarray. No one theory of human motivation has won general acceptance. The psychoanalytic theory of motivational development lingers on as the most influential theory, and it, in fact, guided the selection of the types of disturbing information to use in the research. But as a comprehensive theory, it is seriously wanting and has not led to a substantial body of firm research findings (White, 1959, 1963). Psychoanalytic motivational theory does not seem to be adequate for clarifying the many differences found between mature and immature men. For example, how would traditional psychoanalytic theory further our understanding of this fact: as far as we can tell from the lives of our mature men, their dominant motive was neither aggression nor sex but achievement. The mature and the well organized men were highly achieving persons by any imaginable standard. They had significantly higher grade averages, sought out and shouldered much more responsibility in the community, were significantly more imaginally productive on the Rorschach and the TAJ, were rated by their Department Chairmen to be highly determined and ambitious men, and considered themselves to have high aspirations, to be conscientious, hard workers who enjoyed doing well whatever they did.

It is true that we have no direct measure of the comparative strengths of the different motives of the mature and immature men. The only indirect clue we have from psychological tests about motive strength is the frequency with which different motives are given in stories to the TAJ disturbing information. The only significant (two-tailed) difference found between the criterion groups of *both* the Organized and the Standard samples was for the well organized men to give more stories about punishing others. The well organized men of the Organized sample also tended (p $\angle$ .10) to have stronger needs to verbally aggress and to achieve while the poorly organized men had stronger needs to enjoy bodily pleasures.

I suppose there is some psychoanalytic interpretation of these results (the well organized men are sublimating strong aggressive and punitive needs into achievement), but let us explore the relation of our results to more recent work on motivation. We have noted that the mature men were highly achieving persons. Should not the title of the book be *Explorations of achieving and nonachieving youths?* Have we only been exploring in great depth the personalities of men high and low in need achievement? Not only the life patterns but also the manifest personality traits of the mature and immature men seem to resemble those of high and low need achievers. For example, high need achievers come from homes in which achievement and adventurousness were highly rewarded very young in life (Winterbottom, 1958). And our mature youths reported that they were surrounded by both highly achieving mothers and fathers who presumably reinforced them for achievement. Also, the personality traits found for persons high in achievement (but low in N affiliation) seem to describe our mature men (though it is not clear the men were low in N affiliation): facility in and preference for working with people, ambitious, consistent, and predictable (Groesbeck, 1958).

But despite these and other similarities between mature and

immature men and high and low need achievers, I doubt whether the mature youths can be understood solely in terms of a strong need to achieve. Since intensive personality studies of selected high and low need achievers using measures similar to ours have not been done, only wisps of evidence support our doubts. For example, high need achievers have incongruent self-images, particularly about N achievement-related traits, and are dissatisfied with themselves (Martire, 1956)—a pattern we did not find. Also, the exploratory factor analysis of our data (Chapter 13) suggested that at least two dimensions—competence and allocentricism—might be centrally defining dimensions of maturity. It is conceivable that high need achievers when defined by fantasy measures might not be very competent persons and might be strongly dominated by autocentricism. Or some high need achievers when defined by behavioral accomplishment could well be utterly ruthless, self-seeking, and opportunistic persons, characteristics not found in our mature men.

Let us now look at the relation of maturity to achievement from a broader perspective. In his review of the drive-reduction and psychoanalytic motivational models, White (1959) marshalled an impressive and convincing array of evidence to suggest both models are incomplete, if not invalid, for understanding the motivation of human beings, particularly that of maturing persons. He proposes that a man's motivation can be more adequately understood in terms of how competently he interacts with his environment. Specifically, man has an "urge toward competence" (1959, p. 323), characterized by needs to explore, to be curious, to seek novelty and change in stimulation, to construct, to master, and to achieve. The consequence of action (an achievement) is less important than the *process* of achieving the consequence. The aim of competence motivation is a "feeling of efficacy, not . . . the vitally important learnings that come as its consequence" (1959, p. 323). Self-esteem and competence are correlated (1956); "self-esteem has its deepest root in the experience of efficacy" (1963, p. 192). Both self-esteem and competence are "clearly related" to ego strength or maturity, for effectance develops "adaptive capacities that help in coping with dangers, and a sense of competence that opposes the development of anxiety" (1963, p. 193).

Perhaps the title of the book should also be *Explorations of Competence!* If our criterion groups are distinguished by the traits that define competence (achievement, self-esteem, self-assertion, active intrusion into the environment), then the findings fill a major empirical void in White's theory as well as demonstrate the interaction of competence motivation with ego strength, self-esteem, and ego psychological measures of allocentricism. Our playful factor analytic excursion into the dimensions of maturity also suggests some operational measures of competence. Recall that a portion of the variance of our samples was accounted for by a competence, effectance, or achievement dimension, indexed by a stable self-image (SIQ), active penetration into the environment (high Dominance and low Social introversion scores), judged maturity, skillfully adaptive coordinations of disturbing information, as well as by more conventional measures of achievement such as grade average.

Sorting out the relationships between achievement, competence, and maturity will not be easy. Our hunch is that achievement as it has been defined by McClelland (1953) and Atkinson (1958) is one manifest component of competence. But the relation of competence to maturity is more complex. I return to that problem later.

MATURITY: ADAPTATION AND SELF-ORGANIZATION

Since the research findings can be placed within a theoretical framework formed from the observations of persons from varying social and cultural settings, perhaps the results have considerable generality. To the issue of the generality of the results I now turn by examining the relation of the maturity to the adaptation and to the self-organization concepts.

Maturity and Adaptation

We are interested in the mature person—not just the mature male, certainly not just those reasonably mature young males to be found in a small American college, or not just the mature female whom we haven't even studied. Let us be very clear about what we have *not* done. We have not studied *the* mature person, some ideal prototype. We have only studied several young men, some of whom were more maturely developed than others. Now, to what population (or cultural situations that have different adaptive requirements) can the results be generalized? I risk provoking many to suggest that I can speak generally about any maturing person, whether male or female, aged twenty, thirty or sixty, lower, middle, or upper class, American, Italian, Chinese, Protestant, Catholic or Hindu.

How can such a radical hypothesis be defended? Such an assertion follows from the assumption that the genotypic developmental trends describe any maturing person, regardless of his sex, age, class, culture, or religion. The most appropriate question is whether more maturely developed persons within one population are more stably organized, allocentric and autonomous than less maturely developed persons within that *same* population. Would not the more mature person of that population show less disorganization on the Rorschach, better inhibitory controls on the MMPI, a more stable and congruent self-image on the SIQ, and more skill efficiency to disturbing information on the cognitive skill tests? This is *not* to assert that the most mature persons of two different populations are equally mature. It is to assert, however, that the self-images of more mature twenty-year old Italian or Moslem male students, for example, may be more *or* less congruent than those of more mature American students, but they will be more congruent than their immature counterparts within their own population. This assertion is testable. Until more or less mature persons in very different populations are as intensively studied as the Haverford youths were, we cannot establish the validity of our developmental assumptions or the limits of the generality of the findings. In fact, comparative cross-cultural studies have demonstrated a parallel similarity in the pattern and prevalence of psychiatric syndromes among such diverse socio-cultural (North American and African) groups (Leighton, Lambo, and others, 1963) that it may not be radical at all to hypothesize such generality to our own findings.

Maturing self-organization is revealed in increasingly effective adaptations. To adapt effectively is to find some equilibrium between one's own internal demands and structure and the claims of the environment. To adapt is not necessarily to adjust, to accommodate to environmental requirements. Consensual judgments of maturity probably do, in fact, assess adjustment more than adaptation, just because the person's own demands and self-structure are not as visible or determinable. (One contribution of our exploratory study has been to identify psychological measures of self-organization that when used with consensual judgments of "adaptive" effectiveness can help future researchers on maturity, ego strength, or competence purify their criterion groups.) Since we did not know what were valid measures of self-organization when our exploration into maturity began, we relied exclusively on consensual judgments that probably ignored some aspects of self-organization and over-weighted adjustment to the college's requirements.

How may the adaptive requirements of the institution within which a study of maturity is done limit our understanding of maturity? The requirements most relevant to the maturity construct are those involving a person's relationships to himself, to others, and to his particular socio-cultural world. These are universal adaptive requirements even though their manifest forms may be highly particularistic or even unique. The success of a Peace Corps assessment program is possible despite the very varied adaptive requirements of different countries just because the underlying psychological dimensions of the requirements must have had considerable universality (Hobbs, 1963; Kelly, 1963). Now, a college like Haverford is a reasonably comprehensive community in which a very wide range of needs and interactions are met: bodily, social, authority, competitive, affective, achieving, religious. I would argue that its adaptive requirements are not so psychologically (though they may be sociologically) peculiar as to limit drastically our understanding of who is mature in most situations. I expect that if the more mature and less mature men of the study were suddenly transported to Uganda, Nepal, or Spain, the mature youths would still adapt more effectively than would the immature youths.

This is the assumption practically every institution makes when it seeks to select reasonably mature members, whether for a position in a business or a job with an overseas relief agency. But the analysis of the college and its population in Chapter 3 did suggest that the college emphasized achievement and competence at the expense of emotional and social expression. We must admit, therefore, when we come to assess the adequacy of our developmental map of maturity that we may overemphasize the role of achievement, or, more broadly, competence, and underemphasize the role of autocentricism.

Maturity and Self-Organization

Other issues about the generality of the findings are best approached by considering the relationship of maturity to self-organization. It is frequently asserted that a person may be very mature in some relationships but quite immature in others. This assertion probably describes some persons, perhaps more immaturely developed ones. We have assumed, on the other hand, that a more maturely developed person is likely to express his maturity more consistently in many more relationships than an immature person is able to do. The research has generated considerable informal support for this assumption both at the action level (Chapter 6) and at the psychological test level (Chapter 12).

At a more abstract level, two interrelated issues stand out. First, how closely do the developmental trends covary? Second, how closely do the maturities of a person's self-structures covary? Our holistic orientation led us to expect considerable positive covariation among the developmental trends as well as the developing self-structures.

Can one predict from a measure of self-stability to a measure of self-accuracy? True, in describing the typical Haverford youth (and the College) we mentioned that he (and the College) was more mature on some developmental dimensions than others. Different institutions and cultures may value some dimensions of maturity more than other dimensions. But we do expect that excessive development along one dimension will eventually be braked or impeded by retarded development along other dimensions. Could not the resistance of many Haverford students (seeming lack of strong autonomous intrinsic intellectual curiosity) be an unconscious response to being stretched too far out of shape, too far away from their more impulsive and autocentric needs? To extend Jung's point, an inordinately extended development on one personality dimension may create its own inhibiting forces on further development.

Also, must we speak only of a Mature stable self-image or a Mature stable skill person? Again, I may provoke some theorists (and perhaps apparently ignore contradictory evidence) to suggest—as a hypothesis—that the maturity of different self-structures is likely to be positively and moderately correlated. It is the person who matures, not just his body, intellectual skills or social relationships. A principal developmental tendency of the maturing person is to integrate and unify his self-structures. Freud described this progressive integration this way:

> What, however, especially marks the ego out in contradistinction to the id, is a tendency to synthesize its contents, to bring together and unify its mental processes which is entirely absent from the id. . . . It is this tendency alone that produces that high degree of organization which the ego needs for its highest achievements. (1933, p. 107).

This thesis is not inconsistent with research evidence suggesting that within limited temporal periods differential development of self-structures may occur (Mussen, Conger, & Kagan, 1963). Temporary imbalances in structure development certainly do occur. But the thesis appears to be inconsistent with other evidence, particularly factor analytic, which demonstrates the progressive independence of different self-structures, such as intellectual skills. Hunt (1961) has critically reviewed the evidence about the organization of intellectual skills and concludes that intellectual organization is not heterogeneous and factorially independent. Longitudinal evidence about the covariation between the developing self-image, schemata, and cognitive skills is lacking (Kagan & Moss, 1962; Mussen et al., 1963), but given our evidence about the interrelationships of the maturity measures we continue to hypothesize that development is organismic, that within broad limits we can predict from the self-image congruence of a person to his cognitive skill efficiency. We do not expect to be able to predict from self-esteem to more peripheral and segmental skills such as typing or musical skill.

Finally, can it be claimed that the more mature person today will continue not only to mature but also to maintain his greater maturity relative to that of the less mature youth? It is too early to follow the trail of the students we tested in order to determine how prognostic their degree of maturity in college is of their maturity as an older adult who has faced occupational, marital, familial, and community responsibilities. Our hunch is that the criterion groups will differ similarly but not as much, and that of those who may mature most rapidly some will be those less immature men of the immature group who find a more supporting environment than that of the college. Some more mature youths may cease maturing as well. Just what determines differential rates and spurts of maturing in young adults is another area of exploration just opening up (Sanford, 1964).

MATURITY—A REEVALUATION

Maturity and Psychological (Mental) Health

If we answer the question "Who is a mature person?", do we also answer the query "Who is a psychologically healthy person?" If the terms point to the same phenomena in *adults* and are actually used as synonyms by most professional persons and if the research has stirred doubts that more than consensual wisps of air define maturity (that the maturity concept is not just an evaluative or normative fiction), then the growing wave of opinion that the mental (psychological) health concept is a myth or an inherently normative term may be only foam and froth (M. B. Smith, 1961; Szaz, 1960, 1961). Certainly, a person, society, or entire culture may prefer or value a way of life that does not promote the maturing or health of its members which it may consider to be irrelevant. But from this does not follow the idea that naturalistically and empirically verifiable criteria do not exist for defining the direction of healthy growth. The issues, semantic and philosophical and others, are indeed more complex than I intimate, but until many of the empirical problems this book raises are settled, debate over such issues may be only a terminological game. For example, Sanford seems to identify the developmental trend toward stability ("potential for dealing with strain," 1962, p. 620) with *psychological health*, the trend toward allocentricism with *maturity*, and the trend toward progressive integration with *development*. He then carefully and perceptively describes how health, maturity, and development do not necessarily covary in, I would say, the less mature person. Presumably, when health, maturity, and development are simultaneously optimized, an ideal type is approached which I happen to call maturity. It may be necessary to use Sanford's labels for more careful thinking about practical concerns, but such labels should not obscure the possible fundamental systemic and psychological relationships between the developmental dimensions that describe the maturing organism. Only more empirical studies will show whether such dimensions covary to the extent our holistic stance assumes.

The research only explored the edges of the complexities associated with the maturity and psychological health concepts. For example, what is the relation of conflict to maturity? One might conclude (as Barron also concluded, 1963) that the more mature person, while not without inner conflict and adjustment difficulties, does have more effective means to adapt to such difficulties. Our evidence for such a conclusion might be that although the criterion groups differed on measures of ego strength, they did not differ on measures of conflict. The more mature men were almost as conflicted about different interpersonal relationships as were the less mature men (PT results). Or half of the well organized men were judged by an eminent diagnostician to be poorly organized and conflicted on the basis of their Rorschach data. But this evidence is not unambiguous. The relationship between maturity and conflict is more complex. For example, the PT findings also suggested that the amount of conflict elicited initially by disturbing interpersonal relationships is not as predictive of maturity as subsequent reactions to the same type of relationship. Or the diagnostician's ranked judgments of self-organization covaried significantly with the community's appraisal of the men's maturity, suggesting that his criteria of mature self-organization were either unduly severe or that the community-selected well organized group, while more mature than its poorly organized counterpart, did not contain many men who approached the maturity region of the developmental continuum. Perhaps a more accurate way of stating the relationship between conflict and maturity is to say increasing maturity means decreasing conflict as well as increasingly more effective ways of dealing with potential conflict. Subsequent studies of groups selected from different portions of the maturity continuum may help settle the issue. In the meantime, all we can minimally suggest is that maturity or psychological health does not necessarily mean an inner clarity unstreaked by persisting conflicts or a state so distilled of conflict as to guarantee appropriate adaptations to whatever the internal or external world produces, particularly if the external world makes immature demands on the person (Hartmann, 1939b).

Toward a Definition of Maturity

The research demonstrates that there are trait congruences that do consistently describe the maturing person. But it does not speak as forcefully about the number of dimensions that most parsimoniously define maturity. The complexity of the results (supported by the exploratory factor analysis) indicate that the maturity construct is certainly not unidimensional. Even those like Maslow (1962), long considered to advocate an unidimensional definition of maturity (self-actualization), specify its meaning by many dimensions.

How closely do the provisional five developmental trends fit the major seams of the results? The mature person is more stably organized. His schemata are more stably organized (Rorschach); his self-image is more stable over time. He skillfully adapts to disturbing information with less disorganization and tends to recover from disorganization rapidly. And independent judges say he is a more emotionally stable and predictable person.

The mature person appears to be a more consistent and integrated person as well. We have noted the greater congruence of his self-image, the close fit of his more conscious valuator and less conscious temperamental pattern, and the integrating effects of his strong motivation that produced such outstanding achievement in a wide range of activities.

Generally, mature persons are more allocentric, for their thought processes are more reality-oriented and less frequently coordinated by affect and drives (less primary process). They are more aware of what other people think of them. Their valuators are centered around loving and caring relationships with others, and they are judged by their peers to be more empathic, altruistic, and considerate of others. Chapter 6 amply confirmed their greater allocentricism and Chapter 13's tentative factor analysis supports the existence of such a dimension as well. I return shortly to discuss the relationship between autocentricism and maturity.

Less evidence confirms that increasing maturity is defined by an increasing potential for bringing experience into awareness. Again, definitional imprecision and difficulty in finding univocal measures of such a trend presented imposing problems. The evidence more or less surrounds but does not penetrate into the meaning of the trend. The mature men tend to have more accurate self-images. They make significantly more adaptive imaginal responses to the Rorschach and give more imaginal stories to the TAJ. While significantly less introversive socially, the mature men of every sample used introspection to gain perspective more frequently than the immature men (Ror. FK %).

Finally, the evidence that the mature person has greater autonomy from both the persuasive control of external information and the determination of his behavior by earlier experience and more infantile drives is not clear. The self-image of a well organized person is neither more nor less autonomous (as we measured it) of another person's opinion than that of a poorly organized person. However, the mature person is less burdened by more primitive and unsocialized types of schemata and to that extent may be freer of more infantile conflicts. The meagerness of these results is due not only to the fact that we did not develop specific tests of autonomy but also due to a theoretical dilemma and a terminological confusion. The dilemma is a product of the holistic assumption that the components of the self can not be adequately studied by splitting them into mutually exclusive parts. The maturing person should be studied as a fine painting is studied by a connoisseur who sees "it now in this organization (as a whole), now in that. Each 'aspect' discussed can be considered a partial explanation of each of the other 'aspects' " (Maslow, 1962, p. 98). The developmental trends are interdependent facets of growth much as the operations of identity, combinativity, associativity, reversibility, and tautology are inseparable but different facets of Piaget's (1947) formal thought operations.

Thus, a measure of one developmental dimension reflects to some extent every other dimension and obscures, therefore, the clarity of the measure. The tests used to measure the stability of cognitive efficiency are an example. The studies reported in Part III on stability could be interpreted by Piaget (1947) and Hunt (1961) to illustrate that the thought processes of more maturely developed persons function autonomously or independently of the concrete but irrelevant meanings of a problem, that the thinking of such persons is not tied to the phenomenal *hic* and *nunc* of irrelevant content. Hartmann (1955) would also interpret measures of a person's capacity to resist regressive thinking to disturbing information as an index of ego autonomy. If this autonomy interpretation of the skill study is more accurate, the meager findings supporting the hypothesis that the mature person is more autonomous would be powerfully supplemented.

Although the research only barely captured the developmental trends by its translations into concrete measures, the general tenor of the findings suggests the developmental map does clarify the meaning of maturity. But to others the provisional map must appear incomplete, perhaps even drab and unexciting. And it may well be. The theory probably errs on the side of omission. Comparing the map to the definitions of the mature person given by the experts and nonexperts in Chapter 1, one could ask "What provision is made for strong values and convictions that so obviously guide and integrate some people's lives? How does the theory deal with the fact that the mature person is more determined, energetic, self-driving, insistent and dominant, or, in

more general terms, that competence may be a crucially important motivational component of maturity?" Admittedly, the
theoretical framework of the research has not adequately dealt
with valuator intensity (which most of these findings seem to
involve), and until the valuators of the mature and immature
men are explored in the same way that their self-images were
explored, we have no basis for claiming that our developmental
map is complete. I do not know if a motivational dimension like
competence must be added to the conception of maturity. More
parsimoniously, could not competence motivation be a valuator
that becomes more prominent in the valuator hierarchy of a
person as he matures? Its increasing dominance may be due to
growing organismic autonomy from more biologically based
drives, to greater allocentric interest in the environment, to
greater organismic stability and integration permitting openness
to novelty without producing disorganization, and to increasing
symbolization stimulating cognizing and curiosity behavior.

Some other theorists may also be discontented by the silence of
our provisional theory about creativity. Although only five of the
thirty-five experts and one of the forty-three non-experts said
that mature persons were creative, some psychologists forcefully
claim creativity to be closely related to maturity (MacKinnon,
1960; Maslow, 1962). For Maslow, creativity is only one example
of a larger network of phenomena any adequate conception
of a mature person must include: primary process "cognition
and archaic or mythological thinking" (1962, p. 171), the more
passive, receptive, meditational, and transforming "peak" types
of experiences. Maslow vigorously rejects equating maturity
with adaptation and allocentrism.

To identify the whole psyche with these tools of coping with the
environment is to lose something which we no longer dare to lose.
Adequacy, adjustment, adaptation, competence, mastery, coping, these
are all environment-oriented words and are therefore inadequate to
describe the *whole* psyche, part of which has nothing to do with the
environment (1962, p. 172).

Lest our theoretical emphasis on adaptive efficiency and allocentricism and the empirical findings that primary process thinking directly covaries with poor self-organization lead to a

misunderstanding, I restate the issue. Does maturity imply sacrificing or ignoring legitimate autocentric claims in accommodating to external sources of information? Clearly, for Maslow, adjustment to the environment is synonomous with adaptation. This is *not* my viewpoint. Adaptation is a more comprehensive term. It is the process of assimilating information from both external *and* internal (one's own being) sources and finding some accommodation to that information which does not violate the integrity of one's self-organization. One method of adapting is to "regress" temporarily to use more autocentric coordinations of schemata in order to create more novel accommodations. With such insights, a person may creatively modify his external environment to be more congruent with his valuator hierarchy or he may reintegrate his own schemata (self-image, philosophy of life) in a way that may or may not be adjustive but which may be the most adaptive solution for him.

The term "organized" (selected to pinpoint Freud's emphasis on the synthesizing function of the ego, 1933) unfortunately may connote to some that we ignore the constructive role disorganization experiences or autocentric coordinations may have in the maturing process. Although unemphasized, it follows from our theoretical notions of development that a more mature person, just because of his greater stability, integration, allocentricism, autonomy, and symbolization, is able to allow himself to become temporarily unstable, disintegrated, autocentric, less autonomous and conscious if adaptation requires such regression (i.e., to adjust temporarily with less mature behaviors when confronted with less mature situational requirements, Hartmann, 1939b). The distinction is that he is master and not a prisoner of such regression.

Now, what evidence do we have that the more mature person is capable of such controlled regression? Degree of maturity consistently and significantly covaried with adaptive imagination which was one of two measures we used to measure controlled regression. It and our measure of adaptive regression covaried (and frequently significantly so) with other measures of maturity, including self-report, self-image, and cognitive skill tests. (Parenthetically, the College's religious form of worship which encourages regressive thinking may promote maturing by helping students to learn how to use autocentric thinking for adaptive purposes.)

Insofar as creativity depends in part upon the ability to regress adaptively (Barron, 1963; Kris, 1952; Pine & Holt, 1960) and such controlled regression covaries moderately with different measures of maturity, we may expect some minimal relation between maturity and the ability to make novel but useful schemata coordinations. We did not study creativity directly nor did we include good measures of it. Our evidence does not clarify the relation between maturity and creativity. The well organized person was more imaginally productive on the Rorschach and adaptively imaginative on the Thematic Associative Judgment test, but he was not judged by his Department Chairman to be singularly more original or creative than the poorly organized person.

Creativity and maturity may intersect because they share some similar psychological processes (productivity, controlled regression), but the evidence does not support the notion that creativity is a central or necessary defining dimension of maturity. Some of the most mature persons of the college whom I knew well could scarcely be called creative or original—at least not at this point in their developing lives.

SUMMARY

The research findings can be located within the context of both cognitive and motivational theory albeit somewhat imprecisely. The research has demonstrated, for example, the validity of the ego theory about the relation of ego strength and resistance to regression. It has also shown that several tests may validly measure some core psychoanalytic constructs and so open up the possibility of empirically and thence theoretically clarifying ego theory. One pressing task is to determine the relation of our cognitive skills to measures of cognitive controls, such as field-articulation, and in this way indirectly to link the work on cognitive controls to a wider nexus of adaptive criteria than such work has yet been able to produce. The findings also provide an empirical foundation for White's theory of competence, because our criterion groups seem to be sharply distinguished on almost every index of competence he might use.

The generality of the findings is a complex, unresolved but empirical problem. Given the assumptions about the genotypic developmental properties of the maturing person, the pattern of the results should be replicated with any groups of more and less maturing persons. However, the results do hint that the generality of the findings may be most crucially challenged by mature and immature groups from cultures that value competence less and autocentric impulse expression more. Given the general confirmation of the relationships between the self-structures, an intensive exploration of the valuators of mature persons should reveal not only that they are more stable, integrated, and allocentric but also that the maturity of a person's valuators covaries with the developmental level of his schemata and skills. To advocate that the research findings have such generality runs counter to most contemporary psychological currents, but the merit of such a position will be decided not by opinion but by relevant research.

We can now answer the question "Who is a mature person?" with more confidence. He does seem to be a more stable person who masters disturbing information more efficiently; he is a more integrated and allocentrically organized person, though he also is able to use regressive or autocentric types of thinking more effectively than the immature person. He may have more memories available to awareness, particularly those organized around his self-image which is more accurately symbolized. While his cognitions are less dominated by more primitive motives, it is still not clear just how autonomous he is of the influence of coercive external information. Our developmental theory seems to offer a reasonable description of the maturing person, though it may be incomplete. The capacity for involvement and commitment, the strength of a person's purpose, may be a missing dimension. But creativity does not seem to be a centrally defining dimension of maturity.

Now that the work is done, the plan completed, what did our

exploration of maturity accomplish? The venture certainly produced many intriguing findings that not only were consistently
cross-validated but also were eminently sensible and related to
larger patterns of meaningful findings. Scattered throughout the
book are firm as well as suggestive findings about the personality
correlates of academic achievement and intellectual (ego) efficiency in adapting to disturbing information, about new validity
relationships between the MMPI and the Rorschach, about new
methods of using the Rorschach for exploring heretofore in-
tractible psychoanalytic hypotheses, about promising empirical
links between self-theories and psychoanalytic ego psychology,
and about the comparative usefulness of different test measures
for identifying mature and immature persons.

As interesting as such findings are, they are only peripheral to
the main aim of the book which was to demonstrate that a
socially and psychologically important construct such as maturity
(or mental health) could be explored in depth with some
objectivity and discipline. It is our hope that our exploration has
identified and clarified some important issues that may have
inhibited studies of mature persons in the past; that it may
provide a theoretical map that orders some major dimensions of
personality development and offers a basis for synthesizing and
systematizing self-image, valuator, and skill research; that it has
developed new personality measures that will encourage others
to take a fresh look at old refractory problems; and that it
has reflectively demonstrated the potency, as well as the problems,
of the research strategy of using selected criterion groups in
initial explorations.

Appendices

APPENDIX A

Table A–1: Definition of Degrees of Confirmation

Degree of Confirmation [1]	Criteria
Very strong confirmation	When tested on two or three of the major samples (Organized, Mature, and Standard), at least one sample, usually the Organized sample, $p < .005$ and other sample(s) usually at least $p < .01$.
Strong confirmation	At least one major sample $p < .025$—$.01$, usually Organized sample, and other sample(s) at least at .05 or, in rare instances, approach significance, depending upon total context of results.
Confirmation	At least one major sample, usually Organized $p < .05$—$.025$, and other sample(s) approach a $p < .05$ significance level. No contra-indicative results from other samples.
Weak confirmation	At least one major sample $p < .05$ with some other samples supportive. No contra-indicative results from major samples.

[1] Considerable judgment has been required in some cases when assigning *degree of confirmation* to take into account inter-sample differences in test forms, test reliability, appropriateness of experimental controls, and number of samples for which the finding is relevant. The Standard sample's results were not weighted as heavily because Holt's scoring system is not well adapted to group Rorschach procedures.

TABLE A–2: INTERCORRELATIONS OF HOLT RORSCHACH SCORES FOR THE ORGANIZED, MATURITY, AND STANDARD SAMPLES

		% PriPro	% Content	% Formal	% Level 1	% Level 2	Sum DD	% Form Accuracy	Mean DE	% DD×DE
% Content	Org.	.91								
	Mat.	.83								
	Sta.	.86								
% Formal	Org.	.91	.76							
	Mat.	.84	.49							
	Sta.	.70	.33							
% Level 1	Org.	.79	.73	.89						
	Mat.	.72	.65	.62						
	Sta.	.49	.28	.53						
% Level 2	Org.	.51	.46	.24	−.12					
	Mat.	.89	.71	.74	.32					
	Sta.	.88	.83	.51	.01					
Sum DD	Org.	.71	.72	.63	.71	.16				
	Mat.	.62	.65	.29	.63	.42				
	Sta.	.63	.65	.43	.32	.55				
% Form Accuracy	Org.	−.50	−.42	−.49	−.54	−.04	−.52			
	Mat.	−.12	−.10	−.19	.08	−.17	.07			
	Sta.	−.35	−.39	−.12	−.16	−.31	−.41			
Mean DE	Org.	−.49	−.30	−.69	−.74	.23	−.47	.63		
	Mat.	−.02	.01	−.19	−.02	.00	−.09	.35		
	Sta.	−.15	−.20	−.15	−.32	.02	−.43	.70		
% DD×DE	Org.	−.56	−.38	−.72	−.78	.18	−.56	.64	.93	
	Mat.	−.31	−.11	−.39	−.21	−.28	−.27	.41	.63	
	Sta.	−.34	−.37	−.19	−.33	−.21	−.45	.74	.76	
Con DD/ Form DD	Org.	−.42	−.15	−.64	−.45	−.06	−.11	.24	.58	.50
	Mat.	−.54	−.14	−.83	−.37	−.50	−.08	.07	.14	.15
	Sta.	−.38	−.20	−.60	−.30	−.26	−.45	.22	.30	.07

TABLE A–3: CORRELATIONS BETWEEN RORSCHACH AUTO-
CENTRIC AND CONTROL SCORES AND SELECTED[1]
QUESTIONNAIRE SCALES OF MALADJUSTMENT
AND CONTROL

MMPI	ORGANIZED[2]	MATURITY[3]	STANDARD	PERSONALITY
Total General Maladjustment[4]	r	r	r	r
Autocentric Schemata				
% PriPro	.47**	.23	.23	.38
% Content	.46**	.14	.11	.42
% Formal	.57****	.44*	.31*	.18
% Level 1	.57****	.53**	.04	.30
% Level 2	−.02	.01	.24	.33
Sum DD	.26	.05	.07	.02
Adaptive Control				
% Form Accuracy	.00	−.45*	−.11	.17
Mean DE	−.23	−.49**	−.13	−.30
% DD × DE	−.42**	−.59***	−.01	−.34
Con DD/Form DD	−.20	−.35	−.25	−.16
D (Depression)				
Autocentric Schemata				
% PriPro	.48***	.27	.12	.41
% Content	.46**	.12	.01	.24
% Formal	.59****	.41*	.13	.54
% Level 1	.60****	.46*	−.01	.20
% Level 2	−.08	.10	.15	.46
Sum DD	.33	−.12	−.04	−.17
Adaptive Control				
% Form Accuracy	−.24	−.45*	−.39***	.31
Mean DE	−.33	−.14	−.16	.06
% DD × DE	−.47**	−.26	−.21	−.06
Con DD/Formal DD	−.21	−.16	−.09	−.39

	ORGANIZED r	MATURITY r	STANDARD r	PERSONALITY r
Pd (Psychopathic deviate)				
Autocentric Schemata				
% PriPro	.44**	.37	.13	.34
% Content	.40*	.36	.03	.40
% Formal	.54****	.44*	.19	.09
% Level 1	.47**	.56***	.17	.47
% Level 2	.07	.17	.05	.14
Sum DD	.15	.37	−.03	−.21
Adaptive Control				
% Form Accuracy	.00	−.27	.12	−.01
Mean DE	−.24	−.38	−.07	−.41
% DD × DE	−.40*	−.64****	.06	−.41
Con DD/Form DD	−.20	−.25	−.08	−.21
Pa (Paranoia)				
Autocentric Schemata				
% PriPro	.40*	−.24	.28*	.56*
% Content	.35*	−.09	.14	.57*
% Formal	.47**	−.25	.27	.27
% Level 1	.48***	−.05	.08	.63**
% Level 2	−.03	−.29	.28*	.34
Sum DD	.42**	−.18	.07	.23
Adaptive Control				
% Form Accuracy	−.15	−.31	−.18	.11
Mean DE	−.28	−.31	−.18	−.58*
% DD × DE	−.40*	−.35	−.09	−.50
Con DD/Form DD	−.19	.41	−.29*	−.17
Pt (Psychasthenia)				
Autocentric Schemata				
% PriPro	.32	.00	.20	.28
% Content	.35*	−.13	.09	.35
% Formal	.43**	.24	.29*	.05
% Level 1	.51***	.12	.16	.26
% Level 2	−.19	.10	.14	.20
Sum DD	.25	−.17	.20	.05
Adaptive Control				
% Form Accuracy	−.07	−.50**	−.28	.16
Mean DE	−.22	−.47*	−.23	−.28
% DD × DE	−.40*	−.37	−.14	−.30
Con DD/Form DD	−.05	−.23	−.40***	−.07

	ORGANIZED r	MATURITY r	STANDARD r	PERSONALITY r
Sc (Schizophrenia)				
Autocentric Schemata				
% PriPro	.47**	.18	.12	.28
% Content	.44**	.12	.09	.45
% Formal	.58****	.37	.19	−.10
% Level 1	.48***	.35	.09	.20
% Level 2	.08	.03	.08	.25
Sum DD	.17	.12	.11	.43
Adaptive Control				
% Form Accuracy	.08	−.51**	−.05	−.07
Mean DE	−.13	−.79****	−.07	−.42
% DD × DE	−.27	−.70****	.03	−.44
Con DD/Form DD	−.22	−.30	−.17	−.27

	ORGANIZED r	STANDARD r
Si (Social introversion)[5]		
Autocentric Schemata		
% PriPro	.05	−.01
% Content	.02	.05
% Formal	.20	−.19
% Level 1	.22	−.04
% Level 2	−.24	.02
Sum DD	.06	.04
Adaptive Control		
% Form Accuracy	−.21	−.36*
Mean DE	−.14	−.10
% DD × DE	−.32	−.34*
Con DD/Form DD	−.12	.19

BERNREUTER	ORGANIZED r	MATURITY r	STANDARD[1] r
Neuroticism[6]			
Autocentric Schemata			
% PriPro	.18	.14	−.03
% Content	.15	.03	−.05
% Formal	.33	.15	−.02
% Level 1	.39*	.22	−.16
% Level 2	−.26	.07	.06
Sum DD	.31	.24	.05
Adaptive Control			
% Form Accuracy	−.35	−.37	−.38**
Mean DE	−.27	−.47*	−.13
% DD × DE	−.45**	−.33	−.29*
Con DD/Form DD	−.21	−.09	−.01
Introversion			
Autocentric Schemata			
% PriPro	.26	.20	.02
% Content	.21	.10	.04
% Formal	.42**	.18	−.01
% Level 1	.45**	.29	−.10
% Level 2	−.22	.10	.07
Sum DD	.40*	.31	.16
Adaptive Control			
% Form Accuracy	−.33	−.39	−.38**
Mean DE	−.35*	−.45*	−.17
% DD × DE	−.51***	−.39	−.29*
Con DD/Form DD	−.26	−.12	.02

	ORGANIZED	MATURITY	STANDARD
	r	r	r
Nonsocial[6]			
Autocentric Schemata			
% PriPro	.33	.57***	.10
% Content	.08	.58***	.16
% Formal	.49***	.40	.03
% Level 1	.27	.53**	−.14
% Level 2	.15	.46*	.20
Sum DD	.02	.44*	.10
Adaptive Control			
% Form Accuracy	−.24	−.46*	.06
Mean DE	−.49***	.00	.04
% DD × DE	−.49***	−.38	.07
Con DD/Form DD	−.68****	−.09	.12

* p ∠ .05   *** p ∠ .01
** p ∠ .025   **** p ∠ .005 (Listed only for this table)

[1] Only those scales are reported that are referred to in Table 5, Chapter 4.
[2] N = 23 for all tables.
[3] N = 17 for all tables.
[4] Higher MMPI General Maladjustment and other questionnaire scores mean greater immaturity.
[5] Data not available for the Maturity and Personality samples.
[6] Data were not available for the Personality sample for the Bernreuter scales.

APPENDIX B

TABLE B–1: SAMPLES USED IN THE DEVELOPMENT OF SKILL TESTS

SKILL	SAMPLES	N	FORM	ADM.	PURPOSE
Conceptual (Thematic Concept Test-TCT)	Adv. Psych. V.	13	Final 12 item	Ind.	Pilot study to develop score system
	Organized	24	Final 12 item	Ind.	Test hypotheses
	Standard	36	Final 12 item	Ind.	Test hypotheses
Analysis-synthesis (Thematic Analysis-Synthesis Test-TA-S)	Schizophrenic Case Study	24	48 item	Ind.	Test hypotheses
		10	48 item	Ind.	Pilot study
	Three Advanced Psychology Classes, I, II, III	46	48 item	Gp.	Study correlates of gp. adm. with personality tests
	Maturity	20	24 item	Ind.	Study revised items and scoring systems; tests later rescored with final score system
	Michigan Honors	16	24 item	Ind.	Study new test items and score system
	Adv. Psychol. IV	9	24 item	Gp.	Pilot study of revised test items and score system
	Adv. Psych. V	13	Final 24 item	Gp.	Pilot study to complete development scoring system
	Organized	24	Final 24 item	Ind.	Test hypotheses
	Standard	36	Final 24 item	Ind.	Test hypotheses

SKILL	SAMPLES	N	FORM	ADM.	PURPOSE
Associative Judgment (Thematic Associative Judgment Test-TAJ)	Maturity	20	4 TAT cards	Ind.	Pilot study to develop method testing judgment; data later rescored with final score system
	Three Univ. Michigan classes	100	12 item	Gp.	Secure data to develop scoring system
	Michigan Honors	16	12 item	Ind.	Pilot study of instructions, items, and methods of analysis
	Adv. Psych. IV	9	Final 12 item	Gp.	Pilot study on revised test items
	Selected judges	10	Final 12 item	Gp.	Develop method of analysis and establish scoring procedures
	Organized	24	Final 12 item	Ind.	Test hypotheses
	Standard	36	Final 12 item	Ind.	Test hypotheses

TABLE B–2: Personality Traits of High and Low TCT Conceptually Efficient and Inefficient Persons

Personality Trait	Organized Efficient Mean	Organized Inefficient Mean	t	Standard Efficient Mean	Standard Inefficient Mean	t
Basal skill (2-tail)						
Terman	Consistent			127.4	113.8	2.11*
Self-reports (1-tail)						
MMPI Pd	Difference small, but consistent			52.6	45.6	2.16*1
Si	41.4	48.3	2.27†**	Consistent		
Taylor MAS	9.5	14.9	1.81†*	Consistent		
K	59.1	52.3	2.03†*	Consistent		
Barron Ego Strength	51.1	46.9	2.41**	Consistent		
Bern. Neurotic	22.8	46.3	2.04*	Consistent		
Lack self-conf.	37.8	58.3	1.83*	28.4	46.1	1.85*
Dominance	Consistent			75.2	57.7	1.73*

354

Personality Trait	Organized			Standard		
	Efficient Mean	Inefficient Mean	t	Efficient Mean	Inefficient Mean	t
Rorschach						
Klopfer (2-tail)						
D%	Inconsistent			46.4	31.8	2.29*
A + Ad%	Difference small, but consistent			40.8	33.2	2.19*
Holt (1-tail)						
% Form Acc.[2]	Consistent			15.2	11.1	2.24**
Con DD/Form DD[2]	16.3	11.3	1.74*	Inconsistent		
PT						
Anxiety (1-tail) Total	Difference small, but consistent			83.0	119.9	1.78*
Schema Type (2-tail)						
Father-son agg.	Inconsistent			8.7	15.6	2.58**
Homosexual	Consistent			13.2	18.7	2.40††

† F significant at least at .05 level; df halved in evaluating t.
* p ∠ .05
** p ∠ .025
1 Direction of mean difference opposite from prediction; two-tailed significance level.
2 All Holt adaptive control and Sum D scores have been arithmetically adjusted. High adaptive control scores mean greater maturity.

TABLE B-3: PERSONALITY TRAITS OF TA-S ANALYTICALLY EFFICIENT AND INEFFICIENT PERSONS

PERSONALITY TRAIT	MATURITY[1]			ORGANIZED			STANDARD		
	EFFICIENT Mean	INEFFICIENT Mean	t	EFFICIENT Mean	INEFFICIENT Mean	t	EFFICIENT Mean	INEFFICIENT Mean	t
Basal skill (2-tail)									
CEEB Verbal	653	561	2.35*	Difference small, but consistent			Consistent		
CEEB Quantitative	690	592	2.13*	Inconsistent			Difference small, but consistent		
Achievement (2-tail)									
CEEB English	650	563	2.73**	Consistent			Consistent		
Grade average	86.8	78.6	2.99***	Consistent			Difference small, but consistent		
Self-reports (1-tail)									
MMPI Pd	Consistent			50.1	59.8	2.48**	Consistent		
Sc	Consistent			49.4	58.4	2.16**	Difference small and inconsistent		
Ma	Inconsistent			49.3	57.5	2.00*	Difference small and inconsistent		
Si	Not available			41.8	47.8	1.95†*	Difference small, but consistent		
Block Under-control	Not available			7.9	12.3	2.50**	Inconsistent		
SIQ Maturity Judge	Not available			70.6	43.2	2.13**	No difference		

PERSONALITY TRAIT	MATURITY[1]			ORGANIZED			STANDARD		
	EFFICIENT Mean	INEFFICIENT Mean	t	EFFICIENT Mean	INEFFICIENT Mean	t	EFFICIENT Mean	INEFFICIENT Mean	t
Rorschach									
Klopfer (2-tail) W%	Inconsistent			50.7	33.5	2.24*	Difference small and inconsistent		
Holt (1-tail)									
% Level 2	Difference small, but consistent			Difference small, but consistent			32.2	39.8	1.75*
Mean DE	4.7	4.5	2.65†**	Difference small, and inconsistent			Difference small and inconsistent		
% DD × DE	47.4	40.0	2.61***	Inconsistent			Difference small, but consistent		
PT									
Anxiety (1-tail)									
Total	Consistent			Consistent			75.4	127.6	2.67†***
Threat	Consistent			Consistent			59.5	94.6	2.59†***
Nonthreat	No difference			Consistent			15.9	32.9	2.61†***
Schema Type (2-tail)									
Mother-son agg.	Difference small, but consistent			Consistent			7.8	13.4	2.47**
Heterosexual	Difference small and inconsistent			10.9	18.7	2.18*	11.3	17.7	2.12*
Receiving affect.	Difference small, but consistent			Consistent			7.3	14.0	2.83†**
Relaxation	Not relevant			Consistent			3.3	8.7	2.30†*

† *F* significant at least at .05 level; *df* halved in evaluating *t*.
1 Maturity sample: 9 men each group because of ties at median of TA-S distribution.

* p < .05
** p < .025
*** p < .01

TABLE B-4: PERSONALITY TRAITS OF TAJ JUDGMENTALLY EFFICIENT AND INEFFICIENT PERSONS

PERSONALITY TRAIT	ORGANIZED			STANDARD		
	EFFICIENT Mean	INEFFICIENT Mean	t	EFFICIENT Mean	INEFFICIENT Mean	t
Achievement (2-tail)						
Grade average	85.2	78.4	2.62**	Consistent		
Self-reports (1-tail)						
MMPI Total						
Hs	Inconsistent			Consistent		
D	44.7	54.5	2.58†**	48.8	44.4	2.14*1
Pd	50.9	58.9	1.97*	Difference small, but consistent		
Pt	49.6	58.5	1.86†*	46.2	51.9	1.75*
Sc	46.8	52.7	2.21**	Consistent		
Ma	Consistent			49.3	58.5	2.21†**
Si	41.8	47.8	1.95*	46.6	54.3	2.85***
Bern. Neurotic	23.4	45.8	1.92*	Inconsistent		
Introversion	27.3	50.3	2.39**	Inconsistent		
Lack self-conf.	37.4	58.7	1.91*	No difference		
Nonsocial	31.1	50.8	2.49**	Inconsistent		
SIQ Maturity2						
Judge	74.0	40.0	2.83***	Consistent		

358

PERSONALITY TRAIT	ORGANIZED			STANDARD		
	EFFICIENT Mean	INEFFICIENT Mean	t	EFFICIENT Mean	INEFFICIENT Mean	t
Social	61.9	41.3	2.10**	No difference		
Dimensions[2]						
Stability	37.3	46.5	1.75*	No difference		
Congruence	34.4	48.9	1.83*	Consistent		
Valuator SVIB (2-tail)						
Physicist	9.9	19.6	2.35*	Consistent		
Chemist	19.9	31.8	2.28*	Consistent		
CPA	30.3	39.6	2.08*	32.8	38.8	2.22*
Rorschach						
Klopfer (2-tail) #P	7.8	5.6	2.21†*	No difference		
Holt (1-tail)						
% Formal	Consistent			13.2	20.9	2.08**
Con DD/Form DD	16.3	11.3	1.74*	25.4	12.7	1.93†*

† F significant at least at .05 level; df halved in evaluating t.
* p $<$ .05
** p $<$ .025
*** p $<$ .01
1 Direction of mean difference opposite from prediction; two-tailed significance level.
2 Low Dimension scores mean greater maturity; high Maturity scores mean greater maturity.

359

TABLE B-5: Personality Traits of Persons Skillfully Efficient and Inefficient to Threatening Information

PERSONALITY TRAIT	ORGANIZED			STANDARD		
	EFFICIENT Mean	INEFFICIENT Mean	t	EFFICIENT Mean	INEFFICIENT Mean	t
Achievement (2-tail)						
CEEB English	Consistent			670	612	2.23*
Grade average	84.9	78.7	2.38*	Consistent		
Self-reports (1-tail)						
MMPI Hy	53.8	60.3	2.33**	Difference small, but consistent		
Sc	48.4	59.4	2.78***	Consistent		
Si	41.8	47.8	1.95*	No difference		
Ma	Consistent			47.9	53.0	1.76*
Bern. Nonsocial	29.8	52.2	2.94***	Consistent		
SIQ						
Maturity Judge	68.7	45.0	1.80*	No difference		
Dimensions						
Stability	20.1	27.3	2.80***	Consistent		
Accuracy	39.2	53.1	1.85*	Inconsistent		
Valuator						
Calif. F (1-tail)	24.81	42.2	1.83*	Not available		

PERSONALITY TRAIT	ORGANIZED			STANDARD		
	EFFICIENT Mean	INEFFICIENT Mean	t	EFFICIENT Mean	INEFFICIENT Mean	t
Rorschach						
Klopfer (2-tail) # R	60.3	39.5	2.85†**	Difference small, but consistent		
Holt (1-tail) % Form Acc.	Difference small and inconsistent			14.8	11.6	1.77†*
Con DD/Form DD	16.9	10.8	2.23**	Consistent		
PT						
Anxiety (1-tail) Total	Difference small, but consistent			82.4	120.5	1.87*
Threat	Difference small, but consistent			64.3	89.7	1.80*
Nonthreat	No difference			18.1	30.8	1.87*
Schema type (2-tail) Mother–desertion	Consistent			9.6	15.9	2.38*
Father–son agg.	No difference			8.8	15.5	2.48***
Homosexual	Consistent			7.7	13.6	2.44**

† F significant at least at .05 level; df halved in evaluating t.
* $p < .05$
** $p < .025$
*** $p < .01$
1 Constant added to scores. High score means greater authoritarianism.

361

APPENDIX C

TAJ Reliability Studies

Case Study and Maturity Reliability Study:

Several methodological studies investigating the type of procedure that would produce reliable measures of associative judgment led to the procedures eventually used with the TAJ. Having rejected a statistical (frequency) definition of judgmental appropriateness, the next step was to determine how reliable clinical judgments could be. Could clinicians trained in imaginative analysis reliably rank-order the anxiety thresholds of different schemata from imaginative material? If they could not, what hope was there that more reliable judgments could be made for assessing the more elusive quality of appropriate judgment?

Three clinicians,[1] following a systematic and regularized judging procedure, independently rated and ranked the anxiety threshold of the schemata used in the research. Imaginative stories, secured by means of the associative procedure (i.e., the students were asked to tell as many different stories as possible to each picture), to those TAT cards whose thematic meaning was close to that of the schemata types to be judged, (VIII, XII, and XIII), had been secured from the Case Study and Maturity samples. Additional stories, using the usual TAT procedure, had also been secured to TAT cards, I, II, III, VI, VII, and XVI. Individually administered Rorschach protocols were also available. All sets of data had been recorded, typed, coded, and randomly mixed. Each judge determined the anxiety threshold values of the different schemata for the associative TAT data, for the remaining TAT cards, and then for both types of TAT procedures combined. Appropriate precautions were taken to forestall contamination of ratings by changing code numbers. Two of the three judges then decided upon the anxiety thresholds of the schemata from the Rorschach data and then rejudged the thresholds of the schemata using all of the data available.

Table C-1 summarizes the medians of the *tau* correlation coefficients obtained for each pair of judges for each of the above judging procedures. Judges do show consistently positive but low agreement when clinically assessing the anxiety threshold of interpersonal schemata. The most reliable judging condition is when the judges have the maximal amount of information—a conclusion well in accord with general clinical knowledge. The judges agreed as well on the associative imaginative procedure as they did on the

[1] I am indebted to Kalman Benyamini and Marian Lahn who also served as judges.

other procedures. While not significant, the PT anxiety threshold and the judged anxiety threshold patterns matched reasonably well (the median *tau* for the PT-Associative Imagination pattern was .36 and the PT-Final Judging Ratings was .33).

We concluded that clinical ratings of degree of realistic judgment would probably be too unreliable. But before ruling out the use of clinical judgments, we investigated the hunch that increased interjudge agreement might result if judges judged the anxiety thresholds of schemata from stories to thematic material specifically designed to cue a person to the different schemata whose thresholds were to be assessed.

Michigan Reliability Study

The next study used the Michigan sample's stories to the TAJ pictures. The sixteen man sample of honor student volunteers took the PT and the TAJ on one day and the TA-S and the PT on a following day. The men's TAJ stories were typed, coded, and independently judged by two judges following similar procedures used in the first reliability study. The result was that global clinical judgments of the anxiety thresholds of different schemata to cued pictures were not very reliable (median interjudge *tau* = .51). The conclusion was now obvious. We had no choice but to pursue more objective ways to assess judgmental appropriateness, as reported in the text.

TABLE C–1: MEDIAN INTERJUDGE RELIABILITY
COEFFICIENTS (TAU)[1] ABOUT ANXIETY
THRESHOLDS OF SCHEMATA

JUDGE RELIABILITY PROCEDURE	PAIRED JUDGES		
	1–2	1–3	2–3
Assoc. Imagination	.39	.41	.25
Five Card TAT	.41	.35	.25
Combined judgment	.40	.37	.24
Rorschach	.41	—[2]	—
Final Judge Rate	.55[3]	—	—

[1] Kendall's rank-order *tau*, used because it does not require the ranked judgments meet certain assumptions, is usually lower than Spearman *rho*, although both use the same information and have the same power to reject the null hypothesis.

[2] This judge, the TAT expert, did not score the Rorschach.

[3] Tau .55, p ∠ .05, indicating judges agreed significantly better than expected by chance.

APPENDIX D

It was predicted the well organized men both initially *resist* disorganization of their schemata and subsequently *recover* from being disorganized more rapidly than the poorly organized men to the disturbing information. Figure one pictures the expected relationships and Table D-1 defines the sub-hypotheses, their statistical tests, and the summary results of the variance analyses of the raw scores of each of the three skill tests. The well and poorly organized men should not differ in their first encounter with the nonthreatening information. Both groups were expected to show some schemata disorganization to the threatening information, but the well organized men were supposed to be able to *resist* that potential disorganization more successfully than the poorly organized men. We expected the differences in efficiency to the threatening information, therefore, to be considerable, but, following Funkenstein's findings (1957), not significantly different. This complex of relationships is called the *resistance* hypothesis.

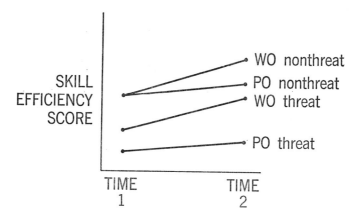

FIG. D-1. Theoretically predicted relations between well and poorly organized groups for threatening and nonthreatening information.

The *recovery* hypothesis was more complex and had to be analyzed in two ways. Judging just from the groups' skill efficiency at their second encounter with the disturbing information, we expected the well organized men to be still better, though not significantly so, in *mastering* the nonthreatening information, but to be significantly better than the poorly organized in mastering the threatening information. This *mastery* hypothesis was based on Funkenstein's results with successive stresses.

Comparing each group's efficiency in its first to its own second encounter with the disturbing information, we predicted the well organized men would significantly improve and the poorly organized would not significantly improve from time one to time two. This is called the *improvement* hypothesis.

TABLE D-1: RESISTANCE AND RECOVERY TO THE
CONCEPTUAL (TCT), ANALYTIC (TA-S),
AND JUDGMENT (TAJ) DISTURBING
INFORMATION

HYPOTHESES	STATISTICAL TEST
Resistance — Well organized men will not differ from the poorly organized men in skill efficiency at time one	
a. to disturbing information (threat + nonthreat scores), and	Nonsignificant Task (T) × Organization (O) interaction; if significant, difference between means at time one is nonsignificant
b. to nonthreatening information, but	Significant Task (T) × Information (I) × Organization (O) but at time one nonsignificant ts between Nonthreat (Nt) means and between Threat (Th) means but WO Th means \ than PO Th means
c. will tend to be, though not significantly, more efficient to the threatening information	
Recovery **1. Mastery** — Well organized men will be significantly better than poorly organized men in skill efficiency at time two	
a. to disturbing information (threat + nonthreat scores), and	Significant T × O and significant t for time two
b. to threatening information, but	Significant T × I × O and significant t for appropriate groups
c. will tend to be, but not significantly, better than the poorly organized in skill efficiency to nonthreatening information	Significant T × I × O with WO Nt mean at time two \ than PO Nt mean
2. Improvement — Well organized men will, and poorly organized men will not, significantly improve from time one to time two in skill efficiency to disturbing information	Significant T × O. WO mean difference time one-time two significant and PO's mean difference not significant

CONFIRMATION[1]

TCT	TA-S	TAJ
a. Confirmed	Confirmed	Confirmed
b. Confirmed	Confirmed by Organized sample	Confirmed
c. Confirmed	Confirmed by Organized sample	Trend in opposite direction for both samples
a. Supported but not confirmed by both samples	Confirmed by Organized and supported by Standard	Supported but not confirmed by both samples
b. Supported by standard but not supported by Organized	Supported but not confirmed by both samples	Supported but not confirmed by both samples
c. Supported by Standard but not supported by Organized	Supported by Organized but not supported by Standard	Supported but not confirmed by both samples
Supported by Standard but trend in opposite direction for Organized	Supported by Organized but not by Standard whose well and poorly organized men both improved significantly	Supported but not confirmed by both samples

[1] *Confirmed* means meets requirements of statistical test; *supported* means scores in predicted direction but do not meet statistical test.

APPENDIX E

TABLE E-1: PERSONALITY DIFFERENCES BETWEEN MATURE AND IMMATURE GROUPS DEFINED BY MMPI TOTAL SCORE

MEASURES OF MATURITY	MATURITY[1]			ORGANIZED[1]			STANDARD[1]		
	Mature Mean	Immature Mean	t	Mature Mean	Immature Mean	t	Mature Mean	Immature Mean	t
I. Dept. Chairman Judgments									
% Total Excell.	40	15		44	28		30	41	
% Determin.	38	13		60	36		33	54	
% Emo. Stab.	37	25		50	18		58	61	
% Personality	50	13		50	9		33	54	
II. Self-report (1-tail)									
Bern. Neurotic	18.8	45.6	2.22***	17.8	48.6	2.67***	Consistent		
Introversion	19.0	48.9	2.41†***	23.3	52.6	3.04***	Consistent		
Lack self-conf.	Consistent			30.7	62.1	2.98†***	Consistent		
Dominance	Consistent			73.5	51.9	1.88*	Consistent		
SIQ Maturity scores	Not available			In predicted direction			In predicted direction		
Dimensions	Not available			Inconsistent			No difference		
III. Rorschach									
Clin. Eval. (1-tail)	Not available			In predicted direction			In predicted direction		
Klopfer (2-tail)									
M%	Consistent			11.5	18.8	2.09*	Consistent		
m%	Inconsistent			Consistent			2.1	5.4	2.34†*
C' (C'F)%	Inconsistent			5.2	1.5	2.16†*	Inconsistent		
% R cds. VIII-X	31.0	41.1	2.19*	Inconsistent			Consistent		

368

Measures of Maturity	Maturity				Organized				Standard			
	Mature Mean	Immature Mean	t		Mature Mean	Immature Mean	t		Mature Mean	Immature Mean	t	
Holt (1-tail)												
Basic pripro scores	In predicted direction				In predicted direction				In predicted direction			
% Level 1	7.6	13.5	1.81*		Consistent				13.4	21.8	2.07**	
Mean DE	4.7	4.5	2.13†*		Inconsistent				Consistent			
% Form Acc.	20.3	15.3	2.90**		Inconsistent				Consistent			
IV. PT	In predicted direction				In predicted direction				In predicted direction			
V. Cognitive skills (1-tail)												
Total Time 1	Not available				213.4	190.5	2.24**		Consistent			
Threat Time 1	Not available				153.2	137.2	2.43**		Consistent			
Other scores	Not available				In predicted direction				In predicted direction			

† F significant at least at .05 level; df halved when Ns equal; Cochran and Cox formula used when Ns unequal.
* p < .05
** p < .025
*** p < .01
1 Maturity sample 8 men each group; Organized sample 11 men each group; Standard sample 14 men mature and 15 men immature group. Incomplete and overlapping scores at median resulted in reduced Ns.

TABLE E-2: Personality Differences between Mature and Immature Groups Defined by Rorschach Clinical Evaluation

Measures of Maturity	Organized			Standard		
	Mature Mean	Immature Mean	t	Mature Mean	Immature Mean	t
I. Dept. Chairman Judgments						
% Total Excell.	36	31		38	38	
% Determin.	45	55		50	50	
% Emo. Stab.	56	9		56	50	
% Personality	27	27		63	36	
II. Self-report (1-tail)						
MMPI D	Consistent			45.0	51.6	2.30**
Pa	Consistent			47.7	52.2	2.37**
Pt	Consistent			44.8	52.2	2.52***
Other scores	In predicted direction			In predicted direction		
Bern. Introversion	Consistent			24.5	37.8	1.94*
Dominance	Inconsistent			76.0	56.9	1.92†
SIQ Maturity						
Self	40.7	15.5	2.33**	44.2	33.6	1.75*
Social	Consistent			42.1	26.8	2.09**
Dimensions	In predicted direction			In predicted direction		

Measures of Maturity	Organized			Standard		
	Mature Mean	Immature Mean	t	Mature Mean	Immature Mean	t
III. Rorschach						
Klopfer (2-tail)						
W%	31.8	52.2	2.82***	35.7	53.8	2.19*
d%	7.1	2.2	2.63†**	Consistent		
Dd + S%	Consistent			15.2	8.7	2.49**
FK%	Inconsistent			2.1	.7	2.11†*
c(cF)%	1.4	3.4	2.45*	1.7	3.6	2.30†*
#R cds VIII–X	32.9	28.2	3.02***	Consistent		
Holt (1-tail)						
% PriPro	43.5	60.8	3.07†***	40.2	53.8	2.92***
% Content	33.8	49.2	2.89†***	33.3	43.1	2.24**
% Formal	19.3	33.7	2.24†**	Consistent		
% Level 1	9.7	22.4	2.47†**	7.7	13.9	2.75†***
Sum DD	Consistent			35.2	53.7	3.50***
Mean DE	4.6	4.2	2.18**	4.9	4.5	3.43***
% DD × DE	43.3	31.9	2.20**	27.8	20.6	3.03†***
% Form Acc.	18.7	13.3	2.59†***	16.4	9.9	4.10***
IV. PT	In predicted direction			In predicted direction		
V. Cognitive skills (1-tail)	Inconsistent			In predicted direction		

† F significant at least at .05 level; df halved in evaluating t.
* p ∠ .05
** p ∠ .025
*** p ∠ .01

TABLE E-3: PERSONALITY DIFFERENCES BETWEEN MATURE AND IMMATURE GROUPS DEFINED BY RORSCHACH % FORMAL SCORE

Measures of Maturity	Maturity			Organized			Standard		
	Mature Mean	Immature Mean	t	Mature Mean	Immature Mean	t	Mature Mean	Immature Mean	t
I. Dept. Chairman Judgments									
% Total Excell.	48	16		54	17		35	38	
% Determin.	50	0		70	33		46	50	
% Emo. Stab.	60	20		50	17		46	67	
% Personality	60	30		50	9		46	58	
II. Self-reports (1-tail)									
MMPI Total	Consistent			50.7	56.8	2.50**	Consistent		
Hs	Consistent			48.7	55.3	3.33***	Consistent		
D	Consistent			45.5	53.7	2.05*	Consistent		
Hy	Consistent			52.1	62.0	4.28***	Consistent		
Pd	Consistent			50.7	59.2	2.11**	45.0	52.3	2.13**
Pa	Consistent			50.7	55.8	1.72*	Consistent		
Ma	Inconsistent			Consistent			47.5	52.7	1.87*
Sc	Consistent			49.0	58.8	2.41**	Consistent		
Bern. Nonsocial	38.7	61.1	1.92*	30.3	51.6	2.74***	Inconsistent		
Other scores	In predicted direction			In predicted direction			Generally in predicted direction		
SIQ Maturity scores Dimensions	Not available			In predicted direction					
Stability	Not available			17.7	24.2	2.68***	Consistent		

MEASURES OF MATURITY	MATURITY Mature Mean	Immature Mean	t	ORGANIZED Mature Mean	Immature Mean	t	STANDARD Mature Mean	Immature Mean	t
Congruence	Not available			22.5	42.0	3.81***	Consistent		
Accuracy	Not available			Consistent			39.7	46.0	1.81†*
III. Rorschach									
Clin. Eval. (1-tail)	Not available			71.7	49.4	2.17**	Consistent		
Klopfer (2-tail)									
#R	60.2	38.7	2.63**	Consistent			Consistent		
d%	10.8	4.8	2.45*	Consistent			Consistent		
Dd + S%	23.8	9.2	3.05***	No difference			Consistent		
M%	Consistent			11.8	19.3	2.31*	14.5	26.0	3.65***
FM%	Consistent			Inconsistent			13.1	22.6	2.65**
FK + F + Fc%	55.9	34.5	4.20***	Consistent			48.1	31.5	2.62**
F%	47.9	27.5	3.89***	Consistent			39.9	22.5	2.91***
CF%	Inconsistent			10.3	5.2	2.46*	Consistent		
IV. PT Total (1-tail)	70.9	118.1	2.33*	Inconsistent			Inconsistent		
V. Cognitive skills (1-tail)	Not available			In predicted direction			In predicted direction		

†*F* significant at least at .05 level; *df* halved in evaluating *t*.
* p < .05
** p > .025
*** p < .01

TABLE E–4: PERSONALITY DIFFERENCES BETWEEN MATURE
AND IMMATURE GROUPS DEFINED BY
STABILITY OF THE SELF-IMAGE

MEASURES OF MATURITY	ORGANIZED			STANDARD[1]		
	MATURE	IMMATURE		MATURE	IMMATURE	
	Mean	Mean	t	Mean	Mean	t
I. Dept. Chairman Judgments						
% Total Excell.	40	20		27	53	
% Determin.	73	18		36	71	
% Emo. Stab.	45	18		50	64	
% Personality	27	18		36	64	
II. Self-reports (1-tail)						
MMPI K	59.3	52.0	2.20**	Difference small and inconsistent		
Bern. Nonsocial	29.0	52.9	3.23***	Consistent		
SIQ Maturity						
Social	64.6	38.6	2.81***	Consistent		
Judge	79.3	34.5	4.30***	Inconsistent		
III. Rorschach						
Clin. Eval. (1-tail)	In predicted direction			In predicted direction		
Klopfer (2-tail)						
D%	Inconsistent			46.2	31.6	2.21*
M%	Consistent			16.9	23.8	2.04*
FK%	3.7	1.3	2.26*	Consistent		
CF%	10.1	5.4	2.16*	Difference small, but consistent		
Holt (1-tail)						
% PriPro	Consistent			39.8	54.0	2.87***
% Content	Consistent			32.1	43.8	2.64***
% Level 2	Inconsistent			31.0	42.3	2.60***
ConDD/FormDD	18.3	9.3	3.77†***	Consistent		
IV. PT	No difference			In predicted direction		
V. Cognitive Skills (1-tail)						
Total	Consistent			436.6	405.7	2.21**
Threat	308.6	287.1	1.77*	311.1	289.7	1.83*
Nonthreat	Consistent			125.5	116.0	1.99*

† F significant at least at .05 level; df halved in evaluating t.
* p ∠ .05
** p ∠ .025
*** p ∠ .01
[1] N of mature group is 17 and immature group 16. Overlapping scores at median resulted in reduced Ns.

TABLE E–5: PERSONALITY DIFFERENCES BETWEEN MATURE
AND IMMATURE GROUPS DEFINED BY THE
CONGRUENCE OF THE SELF-IMAGE

MEASURES OF MATURITY	ORGANIZED			STANDARD		
	MATURE Mean	IMMATURE Mean	t	MATURE Mean	IMMATURE Mean	t
I. Dept. Chairman Judgments						
% Total Excell.	40	20		21	51	
% Determin.	64	27		21	75	
% Emo. Stab.	45	18		43	62	
% Personality	27	18		36	69	
II. Self-reports (1-tail)						
MMPI D	45.8	53.3	1.85*	Consistent		
Sc	Consistent			47.3	52.1	1.75*
Ma	No difference			47.9	53.0	1.76*
Bern. Neurotic	22.8	46.3	2.04*	Consistent		
Introversion	26.3	51.3	2.66***	24.4	37.9	1.98*
Nonsocial	28.0	53.9	3.65***	Consistent		
SIQ Maturity						
Self	71.1	53.5	2.01*	Difference small, but consistent		
Social	66.3	36.9	3.34***	Consistent		
Judge	74.3	39.4	2.91***	Inconsistent		
III. Rorschach						
Clin. Eval. (1-tail)	73.5	47.6	2.62***	Consistent		
Klopfer (2-tail) D%	No difference			46.8	31.4	2.43*
Holt (1-tail)						
% PriPro	44.7	59.7	2.53†**	40.6	53.4	2.69***
% Content	36.0	46.9	1.89†*	31.8	44.6	3.10***
% Formal	16.4	36.6	3.57†***	Consistent		
% Level 1	9.6	22.5	2.51†**	Difference small, but consistent		
% Level 2	Consistent			30.1	41.9	2.91***
Sum DD	Consistent			39.2	49.6	1.76*
Mean DE	4.6	4.3	2.06†*	No difference		
% DD × DE	43.3	32.0	2.16†*	Consistent		
ConDD/FormDD	17.9	9.8	3.24†***	Difference small, but consistent		
IV. PT	No difference			In predicted direction		
V. Cognitive skills (1-tail)	In predicted direction			In predicted direction		

* p ∠ .05
** p ∠ .025
*** p ∠ .01

† F significant at least at .05 level; df halved in evaluating t.

TABLE E–6: DIFFERENCES BETWEEN MATURE AND IMMATURE GROUPS DEFINED BY PT TOTAL SCORE

MEASURES OF MATURITY	MATURITY			ORGANIZED			STANDARD		
	MATURE Mean	IMMATURE Mean	t	MATURE Mean	IMMATURE Mean	t	MATURE Mean	IMMATURE Mean	t
I. Dept. Chairman Judgments									
% Total Excell.	36	28		28	40		45	30	
% Determin.	30	20		44	60		60	40	
% Emo. Stab.	50	30		42	20		67	40	
% Personality	60	30		23	30		67	40	
II. Self-report (1-tail)									
MMPI K	Inconsistent			59.4	51.9	2.27**	Consistent		
Block Under-control	Not available			7.5	12.7	3.18***	No difference		
Taylor	Not available			9.5	14.9	1.80†	Consistent		
Other scores	In predicted direction			Inconsistent			Inconsistent		
Bern. scores	In predicted direction			In predicted direction			In predicted direction		
SIQ Maturity scores	Not available			In predicted direction			Self, social predicted direction		
Dimensions	Not available			No difference			In opposite direction		

MEASURES OF MATURITY	MATURITY			ORGANIZED			STANDARD		
	MATURE	IMMATURE		MATURE	IMMATURE		MATURE	IMMATURE	
	Mean	Mean	t	Mean	Mean	t	Mean	Mean	t
III. Rorschach									
Clin. Eval. (1-tail)	Not available			In predicted direction			In predicted direction		
Klopfer (2-tail)									
Dd + S%	Consistent			8.1	14.6	2.45*	Inconsistent		
c(cF)%	1.0	3.8	2.53†*	Consistent			Consistent		
Holt (1-tail)									
Basic pripro scores	In predicted direction			In opposite direction			Inconsistent		
Control scores	In predicted direction			In predicted direction			Inconsistent		
IV. Cognitive skills (1-tail)									
Total Time 2	Not available			Consistent			229.5	218.2	1.81*
Nonthreat	Not available			127.7	106.8	2.91***	Consistent		
Other scores	Not available			In predicted direction			In predicted direction		

† F significant at least at .05 level; df halved in evaluating t.
* p ∠ .05
** p ∠ .025
*** p ∠ .01

377

APPENDIX F

TABLE F–1: EXPLORATORY ROTATED (ORTHOGONAL) FACTOR ANALYSIS OF SELECTED SCORES[1,2] OF ORGANIZED SAMPLE

FACTOR I.
ALLOCENTRICISM – AUTOCENTRICISM (12.4% OF THE VARIANCE)

Ror: % DD × DE	.74	Ror: % Formal	—.93
Ror: Mean DE	.68	Ror: % Level 1	—.87
Ror. Clin. eval. organization	.64	SIQ: Incongruence	—.73
PT: Adaptive improvement	.59	Ror: % Content	—.71
Ror: Con DD/Form DD	.57	MMPI: Sc	—.63
Ror: d%	.51	MMPI: D	—.60
Social judgment self-organization	.49	MMPI: Pd	—.58
Ror: # P	.47	Bern: Nonsocial	—.56
Ror: # R	.47	MMPI: Hs	—.52
SVIB: Interest maturity	.44	Ror: Sum DD	—.52
SIQ: Judged maturity	.42	AVL: Political	—.51
Ror: FC%	.42	Ror: M%	—.49
Cognitive skill: Time 2	.41	MMPI: Pt	—.48
		Ror: W%	—.46
		SIQ: Unstable	—.46
		CEEB: Verbal	—.41
		SIQ: Inaccurate	—.40

FACTOR II.
COMPETENCE – INCOMPETENCE (7.3% OF THE VARIANCE)

Grade average	.86	SIQ: Unstable	—.59
SIQ: Judged maturity	.76	Bern: Neuroticism	—.55
Social judgment self-organization	.75	MMPI: Si	—.48
Bern: Dominance	.64		
CEEB: Verbal	.52		
Terman Concept Mastery	.51		
TA–S: Threat	.50		
Ror: # P	.49		
Cognitive skill: Time 2	.44		
Ror: % Level 2	.43		
SVIB: Occupation level	.42		

FACTOR III.

SYMBOLIZATION OF EXPERIENCE – BEHAVIORAL SURGENCY

(6.1% OF THE VARIANCE)

Ror: Con DD/Form DD	.58	Bern: Dominance	—.55
MMPI: Pt	.54	Ror: Fc%	—.54
TAJ: # stories	.54	SVIB: Occupation level	—.51
Ror: #R	.53	Bern: Nonsocial	—.50
TAJ: Improvement	.52	Ror: D%	—.45
MMPI: D	.51	AVL: Political	—.43
TCT: Threat	.45		
Bern: Neuroticism	.42		
Cognitive skill: Time 2	.40		

FACTOR IV.

REFLECTIVE CONTROL – AFFECTIVE INSTABILITY (6.1% OF THE VARIANCE)

MMPI: K	.71	PT: Total	—.67
Ror: % DD × DE	.42	Ror: m%	—.57
TCT: Threat	.42	MMPI: Si	—.52
		AVL: Theoretical	—.43
		TAJ: # stories	—.42

FACTOR V.

EMOTIONAL RECEPTIVITY – INTELLECTUAL CONSTRICTION

(4.6% OF THE VARIANCE)

Ror: FC%	.57	Ror: F%	—.65
AVL: Aesthetic	.55		
Ror: FM%	.48		
CEEB: Verbal	.46		
PT: Adaptive improvement	.43		

[1] All scores loaded above .40 (p $\angle$ .05, two-tailed) are reported.

[2] Rotation was made through the test score that was most highly loaded on the unrotated factor, that was not highly loaded on other factors, that had the highest commonality, and that made some theoretical sense.

References

ABRAHAM, K., Character-formation on the genital level of the libido. (1925) In *Selected papers of Karl Abraham*. London: The Hogarth Press, 1949, ch. 25.

ADAMS, H. B., COOPER, G. D., & CARRERA, R. N., The Rorschach and the MMPI: a concurrent validity study. *J. proj. Tech.*, 1963, 27, 23–34.

ALLPORT, G. W., *Personality—A psychological interpretation*. New York: Henry Holt, 1937.

ALLPORT, G. W., The trend in motivational theory. *Amer. J. Orthopsychiat.*, 1953, 23, 107–119.

ALLPORT, G. W., *Becoming: basic considerations for a psychology of personality*. New Haven: Yale Univer. Press, 1955.

ALLPORT, G. W., VERNON, P. E., & LINDZEY, G., *Study of values*. (Manual 3rd ed.) Boston: Houghton Mifflin, 1960.

ALLPORT, G. W., *Pattern and growth in personality*. New York: Holt, Rinehart & Winston, 1961.

ALPER, T. G., Memory for completed and incompleted tasks as a function of personality: an analysis of group data. *J. abnorm. soc. Psychol.*, 1946, 41, 403–420.

ANDERSON, H. H., Creativity as personality development. In H. H. Anderson (Ed.), *Creativity and its cultivation*. New York: Harper & Row, 1959, ch. 9. (a)

ANDERSON, H. H., Creativity in perspective. In H. H. Anderson (Ed.), *Creativity and its cultivation*. New York: Harper & Row, 1959, ch. 15. (b)

ANGYAL, A., *Foundations for a science of personality.* New York: Commonwealth Fund, 1941.

ANGYAL, A., A theoretical model for personality studies. In C. E. Moustakas (Ed.), *The self: explorations in personal growth.* New York: Harper & Row, 1956.

ASHBY, W. R., *An introduction to cybernetics.* New York: John Wiley & Sons, 1956.

ATKINSON, J. W. (Ed.), *Motives in fantasy, action, and society.* Princeton, N.J.: D. Van Nostrand, 1958.

BARRON, F., An ego-strength scale which predicts response to psychotherapy. *J. consult. Psychol.,* 1953, 17, 327–333.

BARRON, F., Personal soundness in university graduate students: an experimental study of young men in the sciences and professions. *Univer. of California Publications Personality Assessment and Research,* 1954, No. 1.

BARRON, F., Towards a positive definition of psychological health. Symposium paper. *Amer. Psychol. Assn.,* 1955.

BARRON, F., *Creativity and psychological health.* Princeton, N.J.: D. Van Nostrand, 1963.

BARTLETT, F. C., *Remembering. A study in experimental and social psychology.* Cambridge at the Univer. Press, 1932.

BARTLETT, F. C., *Thinking. An experimental and social study.* New York: Basic Books, 1958.

BECK, S. J., BECK, A. G., LEVITT, E. E., & MOLISH, H. B., *Rorschach's Test I. Basic processes.* (3rd ed.) New York: Grune & Stratton, 1961.

BELL, C. R., Personality characteristics of volunteers for psychological studies. *Brit. J. soc. clin. Psychol.,* 1962, 1, 81–95.

BENEDICT, R., Anthropology and the abnormal. *J. gen. Psychol.,* 1934, 10, 59–82.

BERLYNE, D. E., *Conflict, arousal, and curiosity.* New York: McGraw-Hill, 1960.

BERNREUTER, R. G., *Manual for The Personality Inventory.* Stanford, Calif.: Stanford Univer. Press, 1935.

BETLHEIM, S. & HARTMANN, H., On parapraxes in the Korsakow psychosis. In D. Rapaport (Ed.), *Organization and pathology of thought.* New York: Columbia Univer. Press, 1951, ch. 13.

BIER, W. C., A comparative study of five Catholic college groups on the MMPI. (1948) In G. S. Welsh and W. G. Dahlstrom (Eds.), *Basic readings on the MMPI in psychology and medicine.* Minneapolis: Univer. Minn. Press, 1956, ch. 65.

BIRNEY, R. C., Thematic content and the cue characteristics of pictures. In J. W. Atkinson (Ed.), *Motives in fantasy, action, and society.* Princeton, N. J.: D. Van Nostrand, 1958, ch. 44.

BLACK, J. D., Adjectives associated with various MMPI codes. (1953) In G. S. Welsh & W. G. Dahlstrom (Eds.), *Basic readings on the MMPI in psychology and medicine.* Minneapolis: Univer. Minn. Press, 1956, ch. 17.

BLEULER, E., *Dementia praecox or the group of schizophrenias.* (1911) *Monogr. Series on Schiz.* New York: Int. Univer. Press, 1950, No. 1.

BLOCK, J. & THOMAS, H., Is satisfaction with self a measure of adjustment? *J. abnorm. soc. Psychol.,* 1955, 51, 254–259.

BLOOM, B. S., *Stability and change in human characteristics.* New York: John Wiley & Sons, 1964.

BOND, E. D., The student council study. A preliminary report. *Amer. J. Psychiat.,* 1950, 107, 271–273.

BOND, E. D., The student council study. An approach to the normal. *Amer. J. Psychiat.,* 1952, 109, 11–16.

BORING, E. G., Review of T. H. Pear, *The moulding of modern man: a psychologist's view of information, persuasion, and mental coercion today.* London: George Allen & Unwin., 1961. *In Contemp. Psychol.,* 1962, 7, 173–174.

BRONSON, G. W., Identity diffusion in late adolescents. *J. abnorm. soc. Psychol.,* 1959, 59, 414–417.

BROWN, D. R., Non-intellective qualities and the perception of the ideal student by college faculty. *J. educ. Soc.,* 1960, 33, 269–278.

BROWN, D. R., Personality, college environment, and academic productivity. In N. Sanford (Ed.), *The American College.* New York: John Wiley & Sons, 1961, ch. 16.

BROWNFAIN, J. J., Stability of the self-concept as a dimension of personality. *J. abnorm. soc. Psychol.,* 1952, 47, 597–606.

BRUCE, P., Relationship of self-acceptance to other variables with sixth grade children oriented in self-understanding. *J. educ. Psychol.,* 1958, 49, 229–238.

BRUNER, J. S., GOODNOW, J. J., & AUSTIN, G. A., *A study of thinking.* New York: John Wiley & Sons, 1956.

CAMERON, N., *Reasoning, regression and communication in schizophrenics. Psychol. Monogr.,* 1938, 50, No. 1.

CAMERON, N., Schizophrenic thinking in a problem-solving situation. *J. ment. sci.,* 1939, 85, 1012–1035.

CANNON, W. B., *The wisdom of the body.* (1932) New York: W. W. Norton, 1939, (Rev. ed.).

CARPENTER, B., WIENER, M., & CARPENTER, J. T., Predictability of perceptual defense behavior. *J. abnorm. soc. Psychol.*, 1956, 52, 380–383.

CATTELL, R. B., *Description and measurement of personality*. Yonkers-on-Hudson: World Book, 1946.

CATTELL, R. B., *Personality and motivation structure and measurement*. Yonkers-on-Hudson: World Book, 1957.

CHODORKOFF, B., Adjustment and the discrepancy between the perceived and ideal self. *J. Clin. Psychol.*, 1954, 10, 266–268.

CHURCH, J., *Language and the discovery of reality: a developmental psychology of cognition*. New York: Random House, 1961.

COMBS, A. W. & TAYLOR, C., The effect of the perception of mild degrees of threat on performance. *J. abnorm. soc. Psychol.*, 47, 1952, 420–424.

COOMBS, C., *A theory of data*. Lectures given Univer. Mich., 1957–1958.

COOPERSMITH, S., A method for determining types of self-esteem. *J. abnorm. soc. Psychol.*, 1959, 59, 87–94.

COUCH, A. & KENISTON, K., Yeasayers and naysayers: agreeing response set as a personality variable. *J. abnorm. soc. Psychol.*, 1960, 60, 151–174.

COWEN, E. L., HEILIZER, F., AXELROD, H. S., & ALEXANDER, S., The correlates of manifest anxiety in perceptual reactivity, rigidity, and self concept. *J. consult. Psychol.*, 1957, 21, 405–411.

COX, R. D., The normal personality: an analysis of Rorschach and Thematic Apperception Test responses of a group of college students. *J. proj. Tech.*, 1956, 20, 70–77.

CRONBACH, L. J., Statistical methods applied to Rorschach scores: A review. *Psychol. Bull.*, 1949, 46, 393–429.

CRONBACH, L. J., Processes affecting scores on 'understanding of others' and 'assumed similarity.' *Psychol. Bull.*, 1955, 52, 177–193.

CRONBACH, L. J., Proposals leading to analytic treatment of social perception scores. In R. Tagiuri & L. Petrullo (Eds.), *Person perception and interpersonal behavior*. Stanford, Calif.: Stanford Univer. Press, 1958, ch. 23.

CRONBACH, L. J., *Essentials of psychological testing*. (2nd ed.) New York: Harper & Row, 1960.

CROWNE, D. P., & STEPHENS, M. W., Self-acceptance and self-evaluative behavior: A critique of methodology. *Psychol. Bull.*, 1961, 58, 104–121.

DAHLSTROM, W. G., Commentary: The roles of social desirability and acquiescence in responses to the MMPI. In S. Messick & J. Ross

(Eds.), *Measurement in personality and cognition.* New York: John Wiley & Sons, 1962, ch. 9.

DAVIS, K., Mental hygiene and the class structure. *Psychiat.* 1938, 1, 55–65.

DEBBS, J. M., *Self-esteem, coping and influence.* Doctoral dissertation, Yale Univer., 1962.

DOLINKO, P., Set and conceptual defense. *Dissert., Abstr.,* 1957, 17, 1388.

DOLLARD, J. & MILLER, N. E., *Personality and psychotherapy.* New York: McGraw-Hill, 1950.

EBEL, R. L., Must all tests be valid? *Amer. Psychol.,* 1961, 16, 640–647.

EDWARDS, A. L., *Edwards Personal Preference Schedule.* New York: Psychol. Corp., 1954.

EDWARDS, A. L., Social desirability and probability of endorsement of items in the interpersonal check list. *J. abnorm. soc. Psychol.,* 1957, 55, 394–396.

EDWARDS, A. L., The social desirability hypothesis: theoretical implications for personality measurement. In S. Messick & J. Ross (Eds.), *Measurement in personality and cognition.* New York: John Wiley & Sons, 1962, ch. 6.

ENGEL, M., The stability of the self-concept in adolescence. *J. abnorm. soc. Psychol.,* 1959, 58, 211–215.

ERIKSON, E. H., *Childhood and society.* New York: W. W. Norton, 1950, ch. 2. (a)

ERIKSON, E. H., Growth and crises of the "healthy personality." In M. J. E. Senn (Ed.), *Symposium on the healthy personality.* Supplement II. New York: Josiah Macy, Jr. Foundation, 1950, 91–146. (b)

ERIKSON, E. H., Identity and the life cycle. *Psychol. Issues,* 1959, 1, No. 1.

EYSENCK, H. J., *Dimensions of personality.* London: Routledge & Kegan Paul, 1947.

EYSENCK, H. J., Classification and the problem of diagnosis. In H. J. Eysenck (Ed.), *Handbook of abnormal psychology. An experimental approach.* New York: Basic Books, 1961, ch. 1.

FARNSWORTH, D. L., *Mental health in college and university.* Cambridge, Mass.: Harvard Univer. Press, 1957.

FENICHEL, O., *The psychoanalytic theory of neurosis.* New York: W. W. Norton, 1945.

FESTINGER, L., *A theory of cognitive dissonance.* New York: Harper & Row, Peterson, 1957.

FISKE, D. W., Consistency of the factorial structures of personality ratings from different sources. *J. abnorm. soc. Psychol.,* 1949, 44, 329–344.

FLAVELL, J. H., *The developmental psychology of Jean Piaget.* Princeton, N.J.: D. Van Nostrand, 1963.

FOOTE, N. N. & COTTRELL, L. S. JR., *Identity and interpersonal competence: a new direction in family research.* Chicago: Univer. Chicago Press, 1955.

FREUD, S., *The interpretation of dreams.* (1900) New York: Basic Books, 1956.

FREUD, S., *The unconscious.* (1915) In *Collected Papers.* London: The Hogarth Press and The Institute of Psycho-Analysis, Vol. IV, 1925.

FREUD, S., *Beyond the pleasure principle.* (1920) New York: Liveright, 1950.

FREUD, S., *The ego and the id.* (1923) New York: W. W. Norton, 1960.

FREUD, S., *New introductory lectures on psycho-analysis.* New York: W. W. Norton, 1933.

FRIEDLINE, C. L. & BERMAN, A. B., A critical analysis of sub-tests in the Terman-Merrill revised Stanford-Binet intelligence scale, Forms L & M., *J. Psychol.,* 1941, 11, 279–284.

FROMM, E., *Man for himself: an inquiry into the psychology of ethics.* New York: Holt, Rinehart, & Winston, 1947.

FROMM, E., *The sane society.* New York: Holt, Rinehart, & Winston, 1955.

FRUCHTER, B., *Introduction to factor analysis.* Princeton, N.J.: D. Van Nostrand, 1954.

FUNKENSTEIN, D. H., KING, S. H., & DROLETTE, M. E., *Mastery of stress.* Cambridge, Mass.: Harvard Univer. Press, 1957.

GARDNER, R., HOLZMAN, P. S., KLEIN, G. S., LINTON, H. B., & SPENCE, D. P., Cognitive control: a study of individual consistencies in cognitive behavior. *Psychol. Issues,* 1959, 1, No. 4.

GARDNER, R. W., JACKSON, D. N., & MESSICK, S. J., Personality organization in cognitive controls and intellectual abilities. *Psychol. Issues,* 1960, 2, No. 4.

GETZELS, J. W. & JACKSON, P. W., *Creativity and intelligence. Explorations with gifted students.* New York: John Wiley & Sons, 1962.

GILL, M. M., Topography and systems in psychoanalytic theory. *Psychol. Issues,* 1963, 3, No. 2.

GOLDEN, J., MANDEL, N., GLUECK, B. C., JR., & FEDER, Z., A summary description of fifty "normal" white males. *Amer. J. Psychiat.,* 119, 1962, 48–56.

GOLDSTEIN, K., *Human nature in the light of psychopathology.* Cambridge, Mass.: Harvard Univer. Press, 1940.

GOLDSTEIN, K. & SCHEERER, M., Abstract and concrete behavior. An experimental study with special tests. *Psycho. Monogr., 53,* 1941, No. 2.

GOODSTEIN, L. D., Regional differences in MMPI responses among male college students. (1954) In G. S. Welsh & W. G. Dahlstrom, *Basic readings on the MMPI in psychology and medicine.* Minneapolis: Univer. Minn. Press, 1956.

GOUGH, H. G., McKEE, M. G., & YANDELL, R. J., Adjective check list analyses of a number of selected psychometric and assessment variables. *Technical Memorandum OERL TM-55-10.* Maxwell Air Force Base, Alabama: Officer Education Research Laboratory, May 1955.

GOUGH, H. G., The adjective check list as a personality assessment research technique. *Psychol. Report,* 1960, 6, 107–122.

GROESBECK, B. L., Toward description of personality in terms of configuration of motives. In J. W. Atkinson (Ed.), *Motives in fantasy, action, and society.* Princeton, N.J.: D. Van Nostrand, 1958, ch. 27.

GRUEN, W., Rejection of false information about oneself as an indication of ego identity. *J. consult. Psychol.,* 1960, 24, 231–233.

GUILFORD, J. P., The structure of intellect. *Psychol. Bull.,* 1956, 53, 267–293.

GUILFORD, J. P., *Personality.* New York: McGraw-Hill, 1959. (a)

GUILFORD, J. P., Three faces of intellect. *Amer. Psychol.,* 1959, 14, 469–479. (b)

GURIN, G., VEROFF, J., & FELD, S., *Americans view their mental health: a nationwide interview survey.* New York: Basic Books, 1960.

HACKER, F. J., The concept of normality and its practical significance. *Amer. J. Orthopsychiat.,* 1945, 15, 47–64.

HAMBURGER, V., The concept of 'development' in biology. In D. B. Harris (Ed.), *The concept of development.* Minneapolis: Univer. Minn. Press, 1957, 49–58.

HANFMANN, E. & KASSANIN, J., Conceptual thinking in schizophrenia. *Nerv. & ment. dis. Monogr.,* 1942, No. 67.

HANFMANN, E., Seminar on Personality Theory. Harvard Univer., 1950.

HARRIS, D. B., Problems in formulating a scientific concept of development. In D. B. Harris (Ed.), *The concept of development: an issue in the study of human behavior.* Minneapolis: Univer. Minn. Press. 1957, 3–14.

HARROWER, M. R. & STEINER, M. E., *Large scale Rorschach techniques; a manual for the group Rorschach and multiple choice tests.* (2nd ed.) Springfield, Ill.: Thomas, 1951.

HARTMANN, H., *Ego psychology and the problem of adaptation.* (1939) New York: Int. Univer. Press, 1958. (a)

HARTMANN, H., Psycho-analysis and the concept of health. *Int. J. Psycho-Anal.*, 1939, 20, 308–321. (b)

HARTMANN, H., Comments on the psychoanalytic theory of the ego. In *The psychoanalytic study of the child*, 1950, 5, 74–96.

HARTMANN, H., Notes on the theory of sublimation. In *The psychoanalytic study of the child*, 1955, 10, 9–29.

HARTMANN, H., Towards a concept of mental health. *Brit. J. Med. Psychol.*, 1960, 33, 243–248.

HARVEY, O. J., HUNT, D. E., & SCHRODER, H. M., *Conceptual systems and personality organization.* New York: John Wiley & Sons, 1961.

HEATH, C. W., *What people are; a study of normal young men.* Cambridge, Mass.: Harvard Univer. Press, 1945.

HEATH, D. H., The effect of severe emotional conflict on intellectual performance. Unpublished doctoral dissertation, Harvard Univer., 1954.

HEATH, D. H., Individual anxiety thresholds and their effect on intellectual performance. *J. abnorm. soc. Psychol.*, 1956, 52, 403–408.

HEATH, D. H., Projective tests as measures of defensive activity. *J. proj. Tech.*, 1958, 22, 284–292.

HEATH, D. H., The Phrase Association Test: A research measure of anxiety thresholds and defense type. *J. gen. Psychol.*, 1960, 62, 165–176.

HEATH, S. R., The reasonable adventurer. The nature and development of students in higher education. Pittsburgh: Univer. Pittsburgh Press, 1964.

HENRY, W. E., *The analysis of fantasy: the Thematic Apperception Technique in the study of personality.* New York: John Wiley & Sons, 1956.

HILLSON, J. S. & WORCHEL, P., Self concept and defensive behavior in the maladjusted. *J. consult. Psychol.*, 1957, 21, 83–88.

HINKLE, L. E., JR. & WOLFF, H. G., Health and the social environment: experimental investigations. In A. H. Leighton, J. A. Clausen, & R. N. Wilson (Eds.). *Explorations in social psychiatry.* New York: Basic Books, 1957, 105–137.

HINKLE, L. E., JR., Physical health, mental health, and the social environment: some characteristics of healthy and unhealthy people.

In R. H. Ojemann (Ed.), *Recent contributions of biological and psychosocial investigations to preventive psychiatry.* Iowa City, Iowa: State Univer. Iowa, 1959, 80–103.

HOBBS, N., A psychologist in the Peace Corps. *Amer. Psychol.,* 1963, 18, 47–55.

HOLT, R. R., Gauging primary and secondary processes in Rorschach responses. *J. proj. Tech.,* 1956, 20, 14–25.

HOLT, R. R., Formal aspects of the TAT—A neglected resource. *J proj. Tech.,* 1958, 22, 163–172.

HOLT, R. R., Manual for the scoring of primary process manifestations in Rorschach responses. Unpublished manuscript. New York: New York Univer., Research Center for Mental Health, 1959.

HOLT, R. R. & HAVEL, J., A method for assessing primary and secondary process in the Rorschach. In M. A. Rickers-Ovsiankina (Ed.), *Rorschach psychology.* New York: John Wiley & Sons, 1960, ch. 10. (a)

HOLT, R. R., Cognitive controls and primary processes. *J. Psychol. Res.,* 1960, 4, No. 3, 1–8. (b)

HOOTEN, E., *Young man, you are normal: findings from a study of students.* New York: G. P. Putnam's Sons, 1945.

HORNEY, K., *Our inner conflicts, a constructive theory of neurosis.* New York: W. W. Norton, 1945.

HUMPHREY, G., *Thinking. An introduction to its experimental psychology.* New York: John Wiley & Sons, 1951.

HUNT, E. L., *The revolt of the college intellectual.* New York: Human Relations Aids, 1963.

HUNT, J. McV., *Intelligence and experience.* New York: Ronald Press, 1961.

JACKSON, D. N. & MESSICK, S., Response styles and the assessment of psychopathology. In S. Messick & J. Ross (Eds.), *Measurement in personality and cognition.* New York: John Wiley & Sons, 1962, ch. 8.

JACOB, P. E., *Changing values in college: an exploratory study of the impact of college teaching.* New York: Harper & Row, 1957.

JACOBSON, E., The self and the object world: vicissitudes of their infantile cathexes and their influence on ideational and affective development. In *The psychoanalytic study of the child,* 1954, 9, 75–127.

JAHODA, M., Toward a social psychology of mental health. In M. J. E. Senn (Ed.), *Symposium on the healthy personality.* Supplement II, Josiah Macy, Jr. Foundation, 1950, 211–230.

JAHODA, M., *Current concepts of positive mental health; a report to the staff director, Jack R. Ewalt.* New York: Basic Books, 1958.

JAMES, W., *The principles of psychology.* Vol. I. New York: Henry Holt, 1890.

JANIS, I. L. & FRICK, F., The relationship between attitudes toward conclusions and errors in judging logical validity of syllogisms. *J. exp. Psychol.,* 1943, 33, 73–77.

JOHNSTON, R. A., A methodological analysis of several revised forms of the Iowa Picture Interpretation Test. *J. Pers.,* 1957, 25, 283–293.

JONES, E., The concept of a normal mind. *Int. J. Psycho-Anal.,* 1942, 23, 1–8.

JONES, R. M., The Negation TAT; a projective method for eliciting repressed thought content. *J. proj. Tech.,* 1956, 20, 297–303.

JOSSELYN, I. M., The ego in adolescence. *Amer. J. Orthopsychiat.,* 1954, 24, 223–237.

JOSSELYN, I. M., The psychoanalytic psychology of the adolescent. In M. Levitt (Ed.), *Readings in psychoanalytic psychology.* New York: Appleton-Century-Crofts, 1959, 70–83.

JUNG, C. G., *Two essays on analytical psychology.* London: Bailliere, 1928.

JUNG, C. G., The archetypes and the collective unconscious. (1934) In *Collected Works,* Vol. 9, Part I. New York: Bollingen Series XX, 1959.

JUNG, C. G., *The integration of the personality.* New York: Farrar & Rinehart, 1939.

KAGAN, J., The long term stability of selected Rorschach responses. *J. consult. Psychol.,* 1960, 24, 67–73.

KAGAN, J. & MOSS, H. A., *Birth to maturity.* New York: John Wiley & Sons, 1962.

KASANIN, J. & HANFMANN, E., An experimental study of concept formation in schizophrenia. I. Quantitative analysis of the results. *Amer. J. Psychiat.,* 95, 1938, 35–52.

KELLY, E. L. & FISKE, D. W., *The prediction of performance in clinical psychology.* Ann Arbor, Mich.: Univer. of Mich. Press, 1951.

KELLY, E. L., Consistency of the adult personality. *Amer. Psychol.,* 1955, 10, 659–681.

KELLY, E. L., Talk on the Peace Corps, Haverford College, 1963.

KING, F. W., Emotional maturity: its nature and measurement. Unpublished doctoral dissertation, Cambridge, Mass.: Harvard Univer., 1952.

KLEIN, G. S., Cognitive control and motivation. In G. Lindzey (Ed.), *Assessment of human motives.* New York: Holt, Rinehart & Winston, 1958, ch. 4.

KLEIN, M., On mental health. *Brit. J. Med. Psychol.,* 1960, 33, 237–241.

KLOPFER, B., AINSWORTH, M. D., KLOPFER, W. G., & HOLT, R. R., *Developments in the Rorschach technique.* Vol. 1: *Technique and theory.* Yonkers-on-the-Hudson: World Book, 1954.

KOGAN, W. S., QUINN, R., AX, A. F., & RIPLEY, H. S., Some methodological problems in the quantification of clinical assessment by Q array. *J. consult. Psychol.,* 1957, 21, 57–62.

KRIS, E., *Psychoanalytic explorations in art.* New York: Int. Univer. Press, 1952.

KUBIE, L. S., The fundamental nature of the distinction between normality and neurosis. *Psychoanal. Quart.,* 1954, 23, 167–204.

LAFFAL, J., The learning and retention of words with association disturbances. *J. abnorm. soc. Psychol.,* 1952, 47, 454–462.

LARSON, J. R., An analysis of the relationship between accuracy of and stability of self-concept and sociometric status. *Dissert. Abstr.,* 1959, 19, 1846–1847.

LECKY, P., *Self-consistency; a theory of personality.* New York: Island Press, 1945.

LEFFORD, A., The influence of emotional subject matter on logical reasoning. *J. gen. Psychol.,* 1946, 34, 127–151.

LEIGHTON, A. H., LAMBO, T. A., HUGHES, C. C., LEIGHTON, D. C., MURPHY, J. M., and MACKLIN, D. B., Psychiatric disorder among the Yoruba. Ithaca, New York: Cornell University Press, 1963.

LEVENTHAL, H. & PERLOE, S. I., A relationship between self-esteem and persuasibility. *J. abnorm. soc. Psychol.,* 1962, 64, 385–388.

LEVINE, J. M. & MURPHY, G., The learning and forgetting of controversial material. *J. abnorm. soc. Psychol.,* 1943, 38, 507–517.

LEVY, L. H., *Psychological interpretation.* New York: Holt, Rinehart & Winston, 1963.

LICHTENBERG, P., Emotional maturity as manifested in ideational interaction. *J. abnorm. soc. Psychol.,* 1955, 51, 298–301.

LICHTENBERG, P., CASSETTA, R. K., & SCANLON, J. C., One description of mental health and disorder. *Arch. gen. Psychiat.,* 1960, 3, 575–582.

LICHTENBERG, P., CASSETTA, R. K., & SCANLON, J. C., Mutual achievement strivings: a continuum for mental health. *J. abnorm. soc. Psychol.,* 1961, 63, 619–628.

LIPSITT, L. P., A self-concept scale for children and its relationship to the children's form of the Manifest Anxiety Scale. *Child. Develpm.,* 1958, 29, 463–472.

LUSTMAN, S. L., Psychic energy and mechanisms of defense. *The psychoanalytic study of the child,* 1957, 12, 151–165.

McCLELLAND, D. C., *Personality.* New York: The Dryden Press, 1951.

McCLELLAND, D. C., ATKINSON, J. W., CLARK, R. A., & LOWELL, E. L., *The achievement motive.* New York: Appleton-Century-Crofts, 1953.

McGEE, R. K., The relationship between response style and personality variables: I. The measurement of response acquiescence. *J. abnorm. soc. Psychol.,* 1962, 64, 229–233.

McGEHEE, T. P., The stability of the self-concept and self-esteem. *Dissert. Abstr.,* 1957, 17, 1403–1404.

MacKINNON, D. W., The highly effective individual. *Teachers College Record,* 1960, 61, 367–378.

McQUITTY, L. L., Theories and methods in some objective assessments of psychological well-being. *Psychol. Monogr.,* 1954, 68, No. 385.

MANDLER, G., MANDLER, J. M., KREMEN, I., & SHOLITON, R. D. The response to threat: relations among verbal and physiological indices. *Psychol. Monogr.,* 1961, 75, No. 9.

MARTIRE, J. G., Relationships between the self concept and differences in the strength and generality of achievement motivation. *J. Pers.,* 1956, 24, 364–375.

MARTIRE, J. G., & HORNBERGER, R. H., Self congruence, by sex and between the sexes, in a 'normal' population. *J. clin. Psychol.,* 1957, 13, 288–291.

MASLOW, A. H., Self-actualizing people: a study of psychological health. *Personality.* Symposium No. 1, 1950, 11–34.

MASLOW, A. H., *Motivation and personality.* New York: Harper & Row, 1954.

MASLOW, A. H., *Toward a psychology of being.* Princeton, N.J.: D. Van Nostrand, 1962.

MATHEWS, R., HARDYCK, C., & SARBIN, T. R., Self-organization as a factor in the performance of selected cognitive tasks. *J. abnorm. soc. Psychol.,* 1953, 48, 500–502.

MAY, R., The emergence of existential psychology. In R. May (Ed.), *Existential psychology.* New York: Random House, 1961, ch. 1.

MAYMAN, M., Rorschach form level manual. Unpublished manuscript, 1960.

MEAD, G. H., *Mind, self and society from the standpoint of a social behaviorist.* Chicago: Univer. Chicago Press, 1934.

MEADOW, A., A relation between dominance-feeling and a classroom test situation. *J. Psychol.*, 1940, 9, 269–274.

MEADOW, A., Anxiety, concrete thinking and blood pressure changes in schizophrenia. Unpublished Ph. D. thesis. Harvard Univer., 1950.

MEEHL, P. E., *Clinical vs. statistical prediction: a theoretical analysis and a review of the evidence.* Minneapolis: Univer. Minn. Press, 1954.

MESSICK, S. & Ross, J. (Eds.), *Measurement in personality and cognition.* New York: John Wiley & Sons, 1962.

MEYER, A., The meaning of maturity. In D. C. Fisher & S. M. Gruenberg (Eds.), *Our children.* New York: Viking Press, 1932, ch. 15.

MILAM, J. R., Examiner influences on Thematic Apperception Test stories. *J. proj. Tech.*, 1954, 18, 221–226.

MILLER, G. A., GALANTER, E., & PRIBRAM, K. H., *Plans and the structure of behavior.* New York: Henry Holt, 1960.

MONTAGU, M. F. A., Constitutional and prenatal factors in infant and child health. In M. J. E. Senn (Ed.), *Symposium on the healthy personality.* New York: Josiah Macy, Jr. Foundation, 1950, 148–175.

MORGAN, J. J. B. & MORTON, J. T., The distortion of syllogistic reasoning produced by personal convictions. *J. soc. Psychol.*, 1944, 20, 39–59.

MORGAN, J. J. B., Attitudes of students toward the Japanese. *J. soc. Psychol.*, 1945, 21, 219–227.

MOWRER, O. H., What is normal behavior? In L. A. Pennington & I. A. Berg (Eds.), *An introduction to clinical psychology.* New York: Ronald Press, 1948, ch. 2.

MURRAY, H. A., *Explorations in personality: a clinical and experimental study of fifty men of college age.* New York: Oxford Univer. Press, 1938.

MURRAY, H. A., *Thematic Apperception Test.* (Manual) Cambridge, Mass.: Harvard Univer. Press, 1943.

MURRY, H. A. & KLUCKHOLN, C., Outline of a conception of personality. In C. Kluckholn, H. A. Murray, & D. Schneider (Eds.), *Personality in nature, society, and culture.* (2nd ed.) New York: Alfred A. Knopf, 1953.

MUSSEN, P. H., CONGER, J. J., & KAGAN, J., *Child development and personality.* (2nd. ed.) New York: Harper & Row, 1963.

PESKIN, H., Unity of science begins at home: a study of regional factionalism in clinical psychology. *Amer. Psychol.*, 1963, 18, 96–100.

PETERSON, J., *Early conceptions and tests of intelligence.* Yonkers-on-the-Hudson, New York: World Book, 1925.

PIAGET, J., *The origins of intelligence in children.* (1936) New York: Int. Univer. Press, 1952.

PIAGET, J., *The construction of reality in the child.* (1937) New York: Basic Books, 1954.

PIAGET, J., *Play, dreams and imitation in childhood.* (1945) New York: W. W. Norton, 1951.

PIAGET, J., *The psychology of intelligence.* (1947) New York: Harcourt, Brace and World, 1950.

PINE, F. & HOLT, R. R., Creativity and primary process: A study of adaptive regression. *J. abnorm. soc. Psychol.,* 1960, 61, 370–379.

PRIBRAM, K. H., A review of theory in physiological psychology. In *Annual review of psychology.* Palo Alto, Calif.: Annual Reviews, 1960, 11, 1–40.

RAPAPORT, D., GILL, M., & SCHAFER, R., *Diagnostic psychological testing; the theory, statistical evaluation, and diagnostic application of a battery of tests.* Chicago: Yearbook Publishers, Vol. I, 1945; Vol. II, 1946.

RAPAPORT, D., *Emotions and Memory.* New York: Int. Univer. Press, 1950.

RAPAPORT, D., The structure of psychoanalytic theory. *Psychol. Issues,* 1960, 2, No. 2.

REICH, W., *Character analysis.* (3rd ed.) New York: Orgone Institute Press, 1949.

REIK, T., *Listening with the third ear; the inner experience of a psychoanalyst.* New York: Farrar, Straus & Co., 1948.

RICHMAN, J., The effect of the emotional tone of words upon the vocabulary responses of schizophrenics. *Amer. Psychol.,* 1953, 8, 420.

ROE, A., *The psychology of occupations.* New York: John Wiley & Sons, 1956.

ROGERS, C. R., The concept of the fully functioning person. Unpublished manuscript, 1955.

ROGERS, C. R., A theory of therapy, personality, and interpersonal relationships, as developed in the client-centered framework. In S. Koch (Ed.), *Psychology: A study of a science,* Vol. III. *Formulations of the person and the social context.* New York: McGraw-Hill, 1959, 184–256. (a)

ROGERS, C. R., Toward a theory of creativity. In H. H. Anderson (Ed.),

Creativity and its cultivation. New York: Harper & Row, 1959, ch. 6. (b)

ROGERS, C. R., *On becoming a person. A therapist's view of psychotherapy.* Boston, Mass.: Houghton Mifflin Co., 1961.

RORSCHACH, H., *Psychodiagnostics.* (1921) (4th ed.) New York: Grune & Stratton, 1949.

ROTTER, J. B., Word association and sentence completion methods. In H. Anderson & G. Anderson (Eds.), *An introduction to projective techniques.* New York: Prentice-Hall, 1951, ch. 9.

RUBINS, J. L., Notes on the organization of the self. *Amer. J. Psychoanal.,* 1958, 18, 171–193.

SANFORD, N. (Ed.), Personality development during the college years. *J. Social Issues,* 1956, 12, No. 4, 1–70.

SANFORD, N., The uncertain senior. *J. Nat. Assn. Women Deans & Counselors,* 1957, 21, 9–15.

SANFORD, N., What is a normal personality. In J. Katz, *et al., Writers on ethics: classical and contemporary.* Princeton, N.J.: D. Van Nostrand, 1962, 615–629.

SANFORD, N. (Ed.), *College and character.* New York: John Wiley & Sons, 1964.

SARBIN, T. R., A preface to a psychological analysis of the self. *Psychol. Rev.,* 1952, 59, 11–22.

SAUL, L. J., *Emotional maturity.* (1947) (2nd ed.) Philadelphia: J. B. Lippincott, 1960.

SCHACHTEL, E. G., *Metamorphosis.* New York: Basic Books, 1959.

SCHAFER, R., The expression of personality and maladjustment in intelligence test results. *Annals of the New York Academy of Sciences,* 1946, 46, 609–623.

SCHAFER, R., *Psychoanalytic interpretation in Rorschach testing: theory and application.* New York: Grune & Stratton, 1954.

SCHAFER, R., Regression in the service of the ego: The relevance of a psychoanalytic concept for personality assessment. In G. Lindzey (Ed.,), *Assessment of human motives.* New York: Holt, Rinehart & Winston, 1958, ch. 5.

SCHILDER, P., Comment. In J. KASANIN & E. HANFMANN, An experimental study of concept formation in schizophrenia. I. Quantitative analysis of the results. *Amer. J. Psychiat.,* 1938, 95, 35–52.

SCHNEIRLA, T. C., The concept of development in comparative psychology. In D. B. Harris (Ed.), *The concept of development.* Minneapolis: Univer. Minn. Press, 1957, 78–108.

Scott, J. P., The genetic and environmental differentiation of behavior. In D. B. Harris (Ed.), *The concept of development*. Minneapolis: Univ. Minn. Press, 1957, 59–77.

Scott, J. P., Critical periods in behavioral development. *Science*, 1962, 138, 949–958.

Scott, W. A., Research definitions of mental health and mental illness. *Psychol. Bull.*, 1958, 55, 29–45.

Shoben, E. J., Jr., Toward a concept of the normal personality. *Amer. Psychol.*, 1957, 12, 183–189.

Sinnott, E. W., The creativeness of life. In H. H. Anderson (Ed.), *Creativity and its cultivation*. New York: Harper & Row, 1959, ch. 2.

Smith, G. M., Six measures of self-concept discrepancy and instability: their interrelations, reliability, and relations to other personality measures. *J. consult. Psychol.*, 1958, 22, 101–112.

Smith, M. B., Optima of mental health: a general frame of reference. *Psychiat.*, 1950, 13, 503–510.

Smith, M. B., Bruner, J. S., & White, R. W., *Opinions and personality*. New York: John Wiley & Sons, 1956.

Smith, M. B., Research strategies toward a conception of positive mental health. *Amer. Psychol.*, 1959, 14, 673–681.

Smith, M. B., "Mental Health" reconsidered: a special case of the problem of values in psychology. *Amer. Psychol.*, 1961, 16, 299–306.

Smith, P. A., A factor analytic study of the self-concept. *J. consult. Psychol.*, 1960, 24, 191.

Smith, P. A., A comparison of three sets of rotated factor analytic solutions of self-concept data. *J. abnorm. soc. Psychol.*, 1962, 64, 326–333.

Snygg, D. & Combs, A. W., *Individual behavior; a new frame of reference for psychology*. New York: Harper & Row, 1949.

Soddy, K. (Ed.), *Cross-cultural studies in mental health: Mental health and value systems*. London: Tavistock Publications, 1961.

Solomon, P., Kubzansky, P. E., Leiderman, P. H., Mendelson, J. H., Trumbull, R., & Wexler, D., *Sensory deprivation*. Cambridge, Mass.: Harvard Univer. Press, 1961.

Stalnaker, J. M., Recognizing and encouraging talent. *Amer. Psychol.*, 1961, 16, 513–522.

Stein, M. I. & Heinze, S. J., *Creativity and the individual; summaries of selected literature in psychology and psychiatry*. Glencoe, Ill.: The Free Press, 1960.

Stern, G. G., Stein, M. I. & Bloom, B. S., *Methods in personality assessment*. Glencoe, Ill.: The Free Press, 1956.

STERN, G. G., The measurement of psychological characteristics of students and learning environments. In S. Messick and J. Ross (Eds.), *Measurement in personality and cognition.* New York: John Wiley & Sons, 1962, ch. 3.

STRONG, E. K., JR., Permanence of interest scores over 22 years. *J. appl. Psychol.,* 1951, 35, 89–91.

SULLIVAN, H. S., *The interpersonal theory of psychiatry.* New York: W. W. Norton, 1953.

SZASZ, T. S., The myth of mental illness. *Amer. Psychol.,* 1960, 15, 113–118.

SZASZ, T. S., The uses of naming and the origin of the myth of mental illness. *Amer. Psychol.,* 1961, 16, 59–65.

TAYLOR, D. M., Changes in the self concept without psychotherapy. *J. consult. Psychol.,* 1955, 19, 205–209.

TAYLOR, J. A., A personality scale of manifest anxiety. *J. abnorm. soc. Psychol.,* 1953, 48, 285–290.

TERMAN, L. M. & MERRILL, M. A., *Measuring intelligence.* New York: Houghton Mifflin Co., 1937.

TERMAN, L. M., The discovery and encouragement of exceptional talent. *Amer. Psychol.,* 1954, 9, 221–230.

THISTLETHWAITE, D., Attitude and structure as factors in the distortion of reasoning. *J. abnorm. soc. Psychol.,* 1950, 45, 442–458.

THORNDIKE, E. L., BREGMAN, E. O., COBB, M. V., & WOODYARD, E., *The measurement of intelligence.* New York: Teachers College, Columbia Univer., 1927.

TUDDENHAM, R. D., The nature and measurement of intelligence. In L. Postman (Ed.), *Psychology in the making.* New York: Alfred A. Knopf, 1962, ch. 8.

TURNER, R. H., & VANDERLIPPE, R. H., Self-ideal congruence as an index of adjustment. *J. abnorm. soc. Psychol.,* 1958, 57, 202–206.

VIGOTSKY, L. S., Thought in schizophrenia. *Arch. Neurol. Psychiat.,* 1934, 31, 1063–1077.

VINACKE, W. E., *The psychology of thinking.* New York: McGraw-Hill, 1952.

VON BERTALANFFY, L., *Problems of life; an evaluation of modern biological thought.* New York: John Wiley & Sons, 1952. (a)

VON BERTALANFFY, L., Theoretical models in biology and psychology. In D. Krech & G. S. Klein (Eds.), *Theoretical models and personality theory.* Durham, N.C.: Duke Univer. Press, 1952. (b)

WAELDER, R., The principle of multiple function. *Psychoanal. Quart.,* 1936, 5, 45–62.

WARREN, J. R. & HEIST, P. A., Personality attributes of gifted college students. *Science,* 1960, 132, 330–337.

WATSON, R. E., PRITZKER, L., & MADISON, P., Hostility in neurotics and normals. *J. abnorm. soc. Psychol.,* 1955, 50, 36–40.

WECHSLER, D., *The measurement and appraisal of adult intelligence.* (4th ed.) Baltimore: Williams & Wilkins, 1958.

WERNER, H., The concept of development from a comparative and organismic point of view. In D. B. Harris (Ed.), *The concept of development; an issue in the study of human behavior.* Minneapolis: Univer. Minn. Press, 1957, 125–148.

WHITE, R. W., *Lives in progress.* New York: The Dryden Press, 1952.

WHITE, R. W., *The abnormal personality.* (2nd ed.) New York: Ronald Press, 1956.

WHITE, R. W., Motivation reconsidered: The concept of competence. *Psychol. Rev.,* 1959, 66, 297–333.

WHITE, R. W., Ego and reality in psychoanalytic theory. *Psychol. Issues,* 1963, 3, No. 3.

WINDER, C. L., Some psychological studies of schizophrenics. In D. D. Jackson (Ed.), *The etiology of schizophrenia.* New York: Basic Books, 1960, ch. 8.

WINTERBOTTOM, M. R., The relation of need for achievement to learning experiences in independence and mastery. In J. W. Atkinson (Ed.), *Motives in fantasy, action, and society.* Princeton, N.J.: D. Van Nostrand, 1958, ch. 33.

WISHNER, J., A concept of efficiency in psychological health and in psychopathology. *Psychol. Rev.,* 1955, 62, 69–80.

WITKIN, H. A., LEWIS, H. B., HERTZMAN, M., MACHOVER, K., MEISSNER, P. B. & WAPNER, S., *Personality through perception: an experimental and clinical study.* New York: Harper & Row, 1954.

WOLFF, P. H., The developmental psychologies of Jean Piaget and psychoanalysis. *Psychol. Issues,* 1960, 2, No. 1.

WOODWORTH, R. S. & SCHLOSBERG, H., *Experimental psychology.* (Rev. ed.) New York: Holt, Rinehart & Winston, 1954.

WORCHEL, P., *Adaptability screening of flying personnel, development of a self-concept inventory for predicting maladjustment.* School of Aviation Medicine, U.S.A.F., Report No. 56–62, 1957. (Reported in Wylie, 1961).

WORLD FEDERATION OF MENTAL HEALTH, COMMISSION OF PUBLIC EDUCATION IN MENTAL HEALTH, Geneva, August 1949.

WYLIE, R. C., *The self-concept. A critical survey of pertinent research literature.* Lincoln, Neb.: Univer. Nebraska Press, 1961.

Name Index

When tests are referred to by the name of an author, they are indexed in the Subject Index.

Subject Index